NAPOLEON'S RUSSIAN CAMPAIGN
OF 1812

LECTOR HOUSE PUBLIC DOMAIN WORKS

This book is a result of an effort made by Lector House towards making a contribution to the preservation and repair of original classic literature. The original text is in the public domain in the United States of America, and possibly other countries depending upon their specific copyright laws.

In an attempt to preserve, improve and recreate the original content, certain conventional norms with regard to typographical mistakes, hyphenations, punctuations and/or other related subject matters, have been corrected upon our consideration. However, few such imperfections might not have been rectified as they were inherited and preserved from the original content to maintain the authenticity and construct, relevant to the work. We believe that this work holds historical, cultural and/or intellectual importance in the literary works community, therefore despite the oddities, we accounted the work for print as a part of our continuing effort towards preservation of literary work and our contribution towards the development of the society as a whole, driven by our beliefs.

We are grateful to our readers for putting their faith in us and accepting our imperfections with regard to preservation of the historical content. We shall strive hard to meet up to the expectations to improve further to provide an enriching reading experience.

Though, we conduct extensive research in ascertaining the status of copyright before redeveloping a version of the content, in rare cases, a classic work might be incorrectly marked as not-in-copyright. In such cases, if you are the copyright holder, then kindly contact us or write to us, and we shall get back to you with an immediate course of action.

HAPPY READING!

NAPOLEON'S RUSSIAN CAMPAIGN OF 1812

EDWARD FOORD

ISBN: 978-93-5336-102-0

First Published: 1914

© LECTOR HOUSE LLP

Lector House

LECTOR HOUSE LLP
E-MAIL: lectorpublishing@gmail.com

BAD NEWS FROM PARIS
Napoleon passing the night in a Russian château near Mikalevka, after receiving the news of General Malet's conspiracy in Paris
From the painting by Verestchagin

NAPOLEON'S RUSSIAN CAMPAIGN OF 1812

BY

EDWARD FOORD

AUTHOR OF "THE BYZANTINE EMPIRE"

ILLUSTRATED WITH THIRTY-TWO PORTRAITS
AND HISTORICAL PAINTINGS
AND SEVERAL MAPS AND PLANS

1914

PREFACE

During recent years the history of most of Napoleon's great campaigns has been given to the world, with the notable exception of that of the catastrophic Russian expedition of 1812. Apart from compilations, I have met only one original work on the subject, in the English language, during the ten years the present work has been in preparation.

The publication of thousands of documents dealing with the struggle from the French side by the Historical Section of the French War Office, has rendered easily accessible an immense mass of material for the earlier period of the campaign. A beginning in this respect has also been made by the War Office at St. Petersburg, and some interesting light is thereby thrown upon the preparations on the Russian side, as well as upon the personalities of the Russian leaders. There are also many documents from private sources which have been collected and published.

My aim has been simply to relate the history of the terrible campaign in straightforward fashion, without obscuring the narrative by too much digression. I believe that, as matters stand, a better service will thus have been rendered to the cause of history than by the composition of a huge essentially technical work—for which, indeed, there is no place in this country. At present, apart from the needs of soldiers—which they are better qualified to supply than myself—it is not so much scientific discussion of the campaign that is required as knowledge of its episodes. This I have conscientiously endeavoured to supply.

I have to express my obligations to Mr. F.J. Hudleston, of the Staff Library at the War Office, for permission to make researches among the works under his charge dealing with the campaign, as well as to his assistant, Mr. Baldry, for his kind help during my work there. I am indebted to Mr. Gordon Home for much invaluable assistance, which it is easier to name than to classify, since it extends to every part of the book.

E.F.

CONTENTS

Page

- PREFACE vi

CHAPTER I

- THE PRELIMINARIES. 1

CHAPTER II

- NAPOLEON'S ARMY AND ITS GENERALS. 13

CHAPTER III

- THE RUSSIAN ARMY AND ITS GENERALS 27

CHAPTER IV

- THE FIRST STAGE OF THE CAMPAIGN. OPERATIONS FROM KOVNO TO VITEBSK. 39

CHAPTER V

- THE OPERATIONS ABOUT SMOLENSK. 69

CHAPTER VI

- THE OPERATIONS IN VOLHYNIA AND ON THE DÜNA 101

CHAPTER VII

- SMOLENSK TO BORODINO. 118

CHAPTER VIII

- THE OCCUPATION AND DESTRUCTION OF MOSCOW. 143

CHAPTER IX

- THE FRENCH SOJOURN IN MOSCOW 157

CHAPTER X

- THE FIRST STAGES OF THE RETREAT. 171

CHAPTER XI

- THE OPERATIONS IN NAPOLEON'S REAR DURING SEPTEMBER AND OCTOBER 187

CHAPTER XII

- THE FRENCH RETREAT. MALOYAROSLAVETZ TO ORSHA 202

CHAPTER XIII

- ORSHA TO THE BEREZINA. 228

CHAPTER XIV

- CONCLUSION OF THE CAMPAIGN. LOSSES AND RESULTS 248

APPENDICES, BIBLIOGRAPHY & INDEX

- APPENDIX A 260
- APPENDIX B 262
- APPENDIX C 263
- APPENDIX D 267
- APPENDIX E 271
- BIBLIOGRAPHY 275
- INDEX 282

LIST OF ILLUSTRATIONS

		Page
1.	BAD NEWS FROM PARIS	iv
2.	PRINCE EUGÈNE	11
3.	SON OF THE EX-EMPRESS JOSEPHINE, VICEROY OF ITALY, AND COMMANDER OF THE 4TH FRENCH ARMY CORPS	12
4.	DETAILS OF THE UNIFORMS OF THE INFANTRY OF THE FRENCH ARMY IN 1812	17
5.	MARSHAL DAVOUT	22
6.	PRINCE JOSEPH ANTHONY PONIATOWSKI, NEPHEW OF STANISLAUS AUGUSTUS, THE LAST KING OF POLAND	24
7.	FIELD-MARSHAL PRINCE BARCLAY DE TOLLY	33
8.	FIELD-MARSHAL PRINCE GOLÉNISCHEV-KUTUZOV	35
9.	GENERAL PRINCE BAGRATION, COMMANDER OF THE SECOND RUSSIAN ARMY IN 1812	54
10.	THE BATTLE OF SALTANOVKA (July 23rd, 1812)	61
11.	JOACHIM MURAT, KING OF NAPLES	80
12.	BATTLE OF SMOLENSK	85
13.	THE OLD FORTIFICATIONS OF SMOLENSK	92
14.	BATTLE OF LUBINO,	96
15.	BATTLE OF GORODECZNA	106
16.	MARSHAL OUDINOT, DUKE OF REGGIO	110
17.	THE FIRST BATTLE OF POLOTSK	115
18.	GENERAL OF CAVALRY COUNT PLATOV	125

19. MARSHAL NEY.. 136
20. BATTLE OF BORODINO....................................... 141
21. MOSCOW FROM THE SPARROW HILLS................ 146
22. NAPOLEON'S FIRST VIEW OF MOSCOW............... 149
23. NAPOLEON WATCHING THE BURNING OF MOSCOW.... 154
24. THE KREMLIN, MOSCOW.................................... 158
25. MARSHAL VICTOR, DUKE OF BELLUNO............... 164
26. PLAN OF BATTLE OF VINKOVO,......................... 167
27. THE CHURCH OF VASILII BLAGORENNYI AT MOSCOW... 172
28. PLAN OF BATTLE OF MALOYAROSLAVETZ,.......... 181
29. THE COUNCIL OF WAR AFTER THE BATTLE OF MALO-YAROSLAVETZ.................................... 184
30. MARSHAL GOUVION ST. CYR............................. 188
31. COUNT WITTGENSTEIN..................................... 196
32. SECOND BATTLE OF POLOTSK........................... 198
33. ARMED RUSSIAN PEASANTS IN AMBUSH IN THE WOODS WAITING TO CUT OFF FRENCH STRAGGLERS.... 204
34. PLAN OF THE APPROXIMATE POSITIONS OF THE FRENCH AND RUSSIAN MAIN ARMIES ON OCTOBER 31ST, TO INDICATE THE DANGER INCURRED BY NAPOLEON'S EXTENDED ORDER OF MARCH................ 207
35. BATTLE OF VIASMA... 210
36. THE RETREAT OF THE FRENCH FROM MOSCOW... 214
37. RUSSIAN GRENADIERS PURSUING THE FRENCH ARMY.. 220
38. POSITIONS ABOUT 10 A.M. ON THE 17TH WHEN DAVOUT EFFECTED HIS JUNCTION WITH NAPOLEON... 225
39. NAPOLEON, BERTHIER, MURAT, AND RAPP (IN THE ORDER NAMED) ROUND CAMP FIRE.................. 234
40. GENERAL BARON EBLÉ...................................... 238
41. PASSAGE OF THE BEREZINA............................... 244
42. CROSSING THE BEREZINA.................................. 245

LIST OF ILLUSTRATIONS

43. MARSHAL NEY SUPPORTING THE REAR-GUARD DURING THE RETREAT FROM MOSCOW 249
44. NAPOLEON'S TRAVELLING KITCHEN 255
45. FIRST BATTLE OF POLOTSK 259
46. THE ADVANCE TO MOSCOW 278
47. THE RETREAT FROM MOSCOW. 280

NAPOLEON'S RUSSIAN CAMPAIGN OF 1812

CHAPTER I

THE PRELIMINARIES

The Russian Campaign of 1812 was the last and greatest of Napoleon's efforts to impose his dominion upon Continental Europe; and it resulted in perhaps the most tremendous overthrow that any world-conqueror has ever sustained. A review of the immediate causes of the mighty struggle is necessary and not without interest, but it is difficult, as one studies Napoleon's character, to resist the conclusion that it was inevitable. The career of the Corsican adventurer whom genius and good fortune had made Emperor of France, resembles the fateful development of a Greek tragedy. By 1812 his pride had reached its height. Whatever set itself in opposition to his will must be trodden under foot. Russia, impelled partly by a natural sense of independence, partly by economic causes, made up her mind to resist him, and the consequence was an attack upon her by the tyrant of south-western Europe.

The effects of the Continental system varied in different parts of Europe, but everywhere they were bad. France, wealthy in herself, and with the material advantage of being able to maintain her overgrown armies at free quarters in foreign countries, felt them least—a fact which probably accounts for Napoleon's long continuance in power. Elsewhere the pressure was cruel, especially in Sweden, which practically depended for economic existence upon her sea-borne commerce. Russia, though self-supporting as regards food supplies, also suffered materially from the cessation of her trade with Great Britain; and the classes which felt the pressure most were those of the nobles and merchants, which embodied and voiced such public opinion as existed in the country. There was also in Russia a healthy sense of independence, coupled with a feeling of possessing such strength as made destruction, at the hands even of Napoleon, impossible. Such opinions were certain to penetrate sooner or later to the Tzar and his advisers; and, in spite of much irresolution and diversity of views, they could not fail to exercise considerable influence. Besides, the commencement of a new independent Poland, in the shape of the Grand Duchy of Warsaw, established by Napoleon on the western frontier of Russia, was an ever-present source of anger and uneasiness. The Grand Duchy was, to all intents and purposes, a military camp, a sort of French advanced guard against Russia. Within its bounds everything was subordinated to military organisation, and its large army, organised and trained on French principles, and with French aid, was a very real menace.

Napoleon's political marriage with Maria Louisa of Austria, at a moment when he was ostensibly negotiating for the hand of Alexander's sister, added to the Tzar's sense of his people's sufferings and his empire's danger a feeling of personal injury. Next year this was aggravated by Napoleon's abrupt annexation of the coast-lands of north-west Germany, including Oldenburg, whose ruler was Alexander's brother-in-law. In the beginning of 1811 the Tzar issued a commercial decree which virtually prohibited various French imports into Russia, and also permitted the import of Colonial goods under a neutral flag. The measure must, of course, have been under consideration for some time, and Russia's financial straits amply account for it, but coming as it did on the heels of Alexander's protests against the seizure of Oldenburg, it enraged Napoleon. In a letter to the King of Württemberg he described it as a declaration of hostility, and, since any movement in the direction of independence inevitably called down his furious wrath, he was probably right.

At the same time these events were scarcely the cause of hostilities—they merely hastened them. Whatever diplomacy might do, neither Napoleon nor Alexander had any belief in the permanence of the truce which had been called in 1807. Soon after his second marriage Napoleon had observed to Metternich that war with Russia was in the nature of things. The retention of strong garrisons in the Prussian fortresses on the Oder, the steady increase in the forces of the Grand Duchy of Warsaw, and the continued occupation of Danzig, almost on the Russian frontier, were measures which can hardly be regarded as directed otherwise than against Russia. Moreover, besides the troops of Napoleon's German vassals, an army of 100,000 Frenchmen occupied Germany. It is absurd to suggest, in the face of all this, that war was forced upon Napoleon by Russia—except, of course, in so far as independent action of any kind always challenged his hostility.

Whatever Alexander's personal feelings might be—and there is no doubt that he was to some extent fascinated by the French Emperor's personality—he was gradually forced into the conviction that peace was impossible. In 1810 he appointed as War-Minister General Barclay de Tolly, an officer who had greatly distinguished himself in the French and Swedish wars; and the reorganisation of the Russian forces was energetically proceeded with. Count Arakcheiev, Alexander's harsh and brutal, but undoubtedly industrious and energetic, minister, had already done much, especially in the direction of improving the arsenals and reserves of arms. Barclay's measures were steadily directed to preparing for a war on the western frontier. The country was surveyed, roads examined and improved, magazines formed, fortifications planned and begun, and, above all, troops steadily concentrated. Progress was, however, slow. Apart from the backward state of the country as a whole, divided counsels in the Imperial Cabinet, the poverty of the exchequer, and the strain of the long and by no means successful Turkish war, it was necessary to proceed cautiously, for fear of provoking Napoleon too soon into offensive action.

CHAPTER I

The preparations were, in fact, entirely defensive in character, and appear very modest beside Napoleon's vast armaments and fortifications on territory which was not his own. The Russian ministers, indeed, appear to have been generally rather over-confident of their country's ability to resist a French invasion. Some of them, at any rate, wished to take up arms in 1811, counting on the support of Austria and Prussia. They pointed out that Napoleon would calculate upon Russia's steady weakening owing to loss of trade, and that therefore speedy action was desirable. The Grand Chancellor, Count Rumiantzev, was a strong partisan of the French alliance. Alexander himself, though determined to stand firm against aggression, was not anxious for war, and apparently hoped that it might be avoided—as indeed it might have been, but for the fact that peace with England, which was desired by, and necessary to, Russia, implied from Napoleon's standpoint war with France. The impression which the Russian Government generally conveyed in foreign countries was one of great irresolution.

This impression was indeed somewhat erroneous. The war-party in Russia was by far the larger of the two into which public opinion was naturally divided, since it included nearly everyone whose interests were adversely affected by the Continental system—in other words, the majority of the nobles and merchants. It was, however, divided, comprising a narrowly patriotic section which looked merely to the preservation of Russian territory, and another, naturally smaller, consisting of men who saw more or less clearly that to ensure European peace Napoleon must be not merely repelled, but crushed once and for all. The peace-party though small was very influential, including the Chancellor Rumiantzev, Alexander's own mother, and his brother Constantine.

Ultimately, of course, everything depended upon the character of the Tzar, and this was such as to give the friends of France great hopes of being able to influence him. Alexander was essentially a dreamer, much under the influence of vaguely exalted aspirations which were terribly contrasted with the mass of selfishness, luxury, and brutality which environed and repelled him. He was impulsive rather than calmly and steadily determined, and both at Tilsit and Erfurt Napoleon had dominated him. Probably he hoped to do so again. He was bitterly disappointed, and his vexation inspired the libellous remarks upon Alexander's character which occasionally pass for serious history. Alexander I was neither a great statesman, a great general, nor a hero. He was, as far as we can see him, a kindly and well-meaning man, somewhat dreamy and irresolute in general, called by an inscrutable providence to rule, from the midst of a luxurious Court and through a corrupt bureaucracy, a very backward and undeveloped realm. He was often shocked by the conditions about him, but lacked the moral courage to suppress them. But, like many other dreamers, he could at times rise to the occasion. He was intellectual enough to act both as general and statesman, by no means with discredit in either case, and morally elevated enough to play, in 1812, something at any rate of the part of a hero.

Nevertheless, Alexander was naturally slow in finally forming his resolution to fight to the death, and the causes here detailed made preparations for war also tardy. As it was, however, they were quickly detected by Napoleon, and used by him as the grounds for diplomatic protests and for pushing forward his own armaments.

Barclay's preparations, in brief, included the increase of the number of the regiments of the Russian army, the completion to war strength of two battalions per infantry, and four squadrons per cavalry, regiment; the organisation of depôts to complete the third battalions and fifth squadrons with all speed, and the concentration on the western frontier of all available forces—ultimately including 9 army corps, 2 independent divisions, 5 reserve cavalry "corps," and 3 corps of irregular horse. Information concerning the state of Napoleon's forces, especially in Germany and the Grand Duchy of Warsaw, was carefully collected, and the possible theatre of war studied and surveyed. The fortifications carried out had a purely defensive character, and cannot be for a moment compared with Napoleon's constant provocative preparations in Germany and Poland. Riga was fortified, and fortifications were projected at Dünaburg, where the St. Petersburg-Vilna road crossed the Düna. Other works were planned at Borisov on the Berezina, where the river is crossed by the Moscow-Warsaw high-road. Kiev, the famous old Russian city on the Dnieper, was also fortified, as was Bobruisk on the Berezina. A glance at the map will show how absolutely defensive these fortifications were. Riga is 150 miles from the frontier, and all the other places much farther back. As a fact some of them were not completed, hardly even begun, when war broke out.

These preparations were due in their inception to Barclay, but there were others which were inspired by the unpractical advisers immediately about the Tzar. Wellington's Torres Vedras campaign had made a great sensation in Europe, and General Phull, Alexander's Prussian instructor and adviser, had projected a great entrenched camp at Drissa, a town that was literally nowhere. It covered nothing; it was hardly even tactically well placed. It is a striking indication of the confusion in the Russian councils that, practically behind the back of the War-Minister who was nominally responsible for military preparations, a vast amount of time and labour was wasted on this pretentious and unprofitable camp of refuge. In a sentence, Drissa was absolutely useless. Yet the man who conceived this almost childish idea of drawing Napoleon against his will upon an arbitrarily placed entrenchment, and inducing him to waste time and lives before it, passed for a scientific soldier! The amount of time and labour expended on Drissa rendered all the other works slow in construction, and Dünaburg was hardly commenced when the war broke out.

Napoleon's preparations were naturally influenced by no chimerical ideas—except in so far as he appeared inclined to renew in 1811 his old plan of an invasion by sea of England! All through 1810 and 1811 the arming and strengthening of German and Polish fortresses was continued, and the bulk of the disposable French troops were collected in three so-called corps of observation in the northern provinces and in Germany. They numbered some 200,000 men. From Italy he could draw about 50,000 French and Italian troops. The contingents of his German vassals numbered nearly 130,000. The Grand Duchy of Warsaw could furnish some 50,000. Prussia was practically helpless, and Napoleon imposed upon her a treaty of alliance which required her to furnish 20,000 men, and subjected her to wholesale plunder by the Grande Armée on its passage through her territories. Napoleon was to make such requisitions as he pleased, and payment was to be arranged for them later! The misery caused, however, unfortunately for him, did not destroy Prussia, and only added to the heavy debt of vengeance soon to be paid. For the moment, however, Prussia had reached the depths of humiliation. Austria, though sorely humbled and distressed, was in a far more independent position; and Metternich's address succeeded in concluding a treaty by which Austria was to be indemnified for any territorial losses that she might sustain by a reconstitution of Poland, and should furnish an auxiliary corps of about 30,000 men. There was, of course, no guarantee that Napoleon would keep the first condition, and in all probability he would never have done so had the contemplated events come to pass; but that he consented to it, even nominally, indicates that he was anxious to conciliate Austria. Austria, on her side, furnished to the Grande Armée some 40,000 men in all.

Having completed these arrangements Austria and Prussia promptly communicated them to Russia! Despite the grim seriousness of the situation, and the terrible drama which was soon to be acted, it is difficult not to see that Napoleon's position was a somewhat ludicrous one. Austria gave Alexander full assurances that no attack should be made upon Russia by any but the auxiliary corps, and communicated to him the secret orders given to the troops in Galicia and Transylvania!

Poland—or the fraction of it represented by the Grand Duchy of Warsaw—was, naturally and necessarily, heart and soul with Napoleon. France had always been the model to which the Poles looked up; and since the Partition they regarded France as their natural helper. They had fought in the French ranks in large numbers during the Revolutionary and Napoleonic wars, and there was undoubtedly much sympathy of a kind felt for them in France. Farther than this feeling did not go. The chivalry with which the French national character is credited by its admirers certainly does not appear in history. French diplomatic annals are to the full as soiled as those of other countries, and French soldiers have usually been ruthless interpreters or breakers of the rules of war. And most certainly the natural instincts of the French people are essentially material. In so far as Poland was useful to France, France was very ready to sympathise with her. Otherwise the general opinion of the Poles, later expressed by the poet Gaszinski, is that they have obtained from France only tears!

Napoleon was, of course, fully alive to the advantages to be reaped from Polish enthusiasm and aspirations. Besides the army of Warsaw he brought up to the front all his own Polish regiments so as to give his operations as far as possible the appearance of a war for the restoration of Polish independence. Eventually in 1812 he sent De Pradt to Warsaw to organise the movement against Russia. He gave him detailed instructions as to how he was to carry out his orders, and it is hardly possible to read them without feelings of indignation against the man who ruthlessly traded upon the aspirations of a brave and patriotic people, and of pity for the people themselves. The ambassador himself was very conscious of the ignominious part which he was called upon to play. To all appearance he did his work well; certainly the poverty-stricken and requisition-wasted Grand Duchy raised a very large force for the campaign. Napoleon, however, chose later to be dissatisfied; and at St. Helena violently attacked De Pradt, as a chief cause of his defeat—a statement which may fairly be included in the mass of falsehoods which Napoleon emitted during his captivity.

On January 27th, 1812, Napoleon issued to his German vassals a declaration of his complaints against Russia, and required them to have their contingents ready by the 15th of February. The Army of Italy was ordered to march into Germany, and the King of Bavaria to clear the roads of snow and to supply it during its march through his territory. The troops were to live at free quarters; if they were not supplied with all that they required they were to take it! Anyone insulting a French soldier was to be court-martialled, and the sentences of prejudiced and often brutalised judges may be imagined. It is, of course, needless to add that both these orders were suppressed by the editors of Napoleon's correspondence. In order to extract additional supplies the Army of Italy was stated at 80,000 strong, its actual numbers being about 45,000. When Napoleon's allies were thus oppressed, one may imagine the misery in Prussia, which was treated as a conquered country.

All this time Napoleon and Alexander were negotiating, though with small chance of a peaceful result. Alexander desired peace, but would not surrender his independence: Napoleon required complete submission. Alexander sent his aide-de-camp, Colonel Chernishev, on a special mission to Paris, while at St. Petersburg the French Ambassador, Caulaincourt, was replaced by General Lauriston. Early in 1812 Napoleon induced the King of Prussia to send a special envoy to St. Petersburg, with the suggestion that Alexander might make fresh proposals. Alexander made a dignified reply: he had, he said, shown his strong desire for peace by keeping silent upon the subject of Napoleon's annexations: at the same time he was willing to hear what explanations France might have to offer. None were made, and French troops continued to flood across Germany. Napoleon believed that the Russian preparations were more advanced than they actually were—this is fairly apparent from his military correspondence—and was anxious to gain time. In April Alexander sent to Prince Kurakin, his ambassador at Paris, final instructions. He was to propose that Prussia be fully evacuated by the French, thus leaving a neutral space between the contending powers. Russia would then be ready to satisfy France—or Napoleon—on commercial questions. It can hardly be doubted that, come what might, Alexander did not intend entirely to return to the Continental system, and so far Napoleon was probably right in deeming the proposal a diplomatic move to gain time. He made no reply, but despatched Count Narbonne on a shadowy mission to Alexander at Vilna, and kept Kurakin, with studied insolence, waiting. The ambassador pressed repeatedly for a reply, but received none until nearly three weeks later. Then he was merely asked if he had full powers to treat! He rightly regarded such treatment as a gratuitous insult, and demanded his passports. Narbonne's mission naturally led to nothing, except that he obtained a better idea than Napoleon of the stern determination of the erstwhile soft and yielding Tzar.

Alexander, on his side, was endeavouring to free his hands for the approach-

CHAPTER I

ing struggle. The result of the Treaty of Tilsit had been the long and harassing war with Turkey; and Russia paid dearly for the blunder into which Napoleon's blandishments had led her. Negotiations for peace were very slow, and steadily opposed and hampered by the French ambassador at Constantinople. Peace was not signed at Bukharest until May, 1812, and even then French influence was still so powerful that there was fear that it would be broken by Turkey. It was not until August that the bulk of the Army of the Danube at last started from Bukharest under Admiral Chichagov, and by that time Napoleon was already on the line of the Düna and the Dnieper. As it happened the delay was fortunate for Russia, but it might easily have been fatal.

Yet more important to Russia than peace with the Osmanli Empire was peace with Great Britain, but in order to keep the gate of conciliation open for Napoleon until the last moment formal negotiations were not commenced until April, 1812. In point of fact, though the two powers were nominally at war, and the British fleet was blockading the Russian ports, there was a very good feeling between them. Through the Spanish envoy Zea Bermudez, Lord Wellesley had in 1811 assured Alexander that Britain was not really hostile, and Alexander in turn had promised Bermudez that he would keep his troops on the Polish frontier, so as to ensure that the suspicious French Emperor would not move more troops from Germany into Spain. Admiral de Saumarez, the fine seaman and excellent diplomatist who commanded the British Baltic fleet, handled the situation with unerring tact and skill, and effectively ensured the doing of nothing which might destroy the comparatively friendly relations which subsisted between the two nominally hostile states. All this is doubly interesting, as proving the hopelessly fragile basis upon which Napoleon's European domination rested.

Russia's first overtures were somewhat clumsy and exorbitant in their demands. They suggested that since Russia was obviously about to render vital services to the common cause Britain should take over a loan of nearly £4,000,000 just raised by her. The refusal of the British Government to accede to this demand, in itself not inexcusable, but failing to recognise Britain's own difficulties and the services which she was rendering, rather dashed the Russian Government, and the formal alliance was not concluded until July.

Finally, it may be noted that Napoleon, before entering upon hostilities, went through the time-honoured farce of making overtures of peace to Britain. It was purely a diplomatic move, and certainly not seriously intended, nor did the British Government regard it as being so. Britain was more confident than she had been for a long time. The French offensive in the Peninsula had very definitely reached its limit, and Wellington, by his capture of Ciudad Rodrigo and Badajoz, had taken the first steps in the great counter-attack which was eventually to roll the French back over the Pyrenees. Calm observers like Foy saw that the turn of the tide had come. It may be regarded as certain that terms of peace less unfavourable than those which Napoleon offered would hardly have been accepted.

Sweden, under the direction of Napoleon's old enemy and restive servant, Bernadotte, also allied herself with Russia in April—an act immediately brought about by Napoleon's arrogant seizure of Swedish Pomerania, but perhaps in the end inevitable. Sweden, however, partly owing to poverty, partly because of Britain's unwillingness to abet Bernadotte's designs on Norway, took no active share in the Continental war until 1813; but Russia was enabled to withdraw most of her troops from Finland for service against Napoleon.

Meanwhile the French and Russian preparations for war were actively pursued, though more rapidly and effectively by Napoleon than by his antagonist, who had to contend with far greater difficulties. On February 8th Napoleon ordered Prince Eugène with the Army of Italy and the Bavarians to advance upon Glogau, where they would arrive about April 1st. Davout's six divisions were advanced stage by stage from the Elbe to the Vistula, while the 2nd Corps (Oudinot) and the 3rd (Ney) followed in support. The Poles (5th Corps) were concentrated on the Vistula about Warsaw, Modlin and Plock; and the Saxons (7th Corps) and Westphalians (8th Corps) directed also upon Warsaw. Two corps of cavalry reserves—22,000 lances and sabres—and gunners of horse artillery were in the north; a third, 10,000 strong, with Eugène; and a fourth, not yet completely formed, was to accompany the 5th, 7th and 8th Corps. The Prussian contingent was assembling at Königsberg, the Austrian at Lemberg. Finally the Imperial Guard, horse and foot, was advancing from Paris to form the general reserve. Over and above all these formations, which composed the actual army of invasion, various reserve divisions, French, Polish and German, were being organised, some of which were later combined into a 9th Army Corps under Marshal Victor. The refractory conscripts, who were being trained in their island prison-camps, were formed into fresh regiments of infantry. The conscripts of the year, who were collecting at the depôts, were organised as soon as sufficiently trained into Regiments de Marche which were pushed forward into and through Germany to feed the fighting line. Out of these an 11th Corps was formed, the composition of which was constantly changing as the advanced troops were pushed across the Russian frontier, to be replaced by others at the rearward stages, while these were in their turn relieved by new conscripts from France. A division of King Joachim's Neapolitans was marching from Italy to form part of this great reserve corps. The King of Denmark also, at Napoleon's request, concentrated a division of 10,000 troops in Holstein. Napoleon did not believe that Britain could seriously molest his rear owing to her preoccupation with the Peninsular War, but he took no risks. In March, 1812, a Senatus-Consultum formed the entire male population of the empire into three bans, and of the first ban, comprising men from twenty to twenty-six years of age, a hundred battalions or "cohorts" were immediately called out for home defence. They actually produced a force of about 80,000 men, who by June had received a fair amount of training. Apart from them there were left for the defence of the empire 2 regiments of the Young Guard, 24 line battalions in 8 regiments of infantry, 8 foreign battalions, 8 squadrons of cavalry and 48 batteries of artillery. There were also 156 3rd, 4th and 5th battalions of regiments already on foreign service, the seamen, marines, coast-guards and veterans, and finally the depôts of the whole army.

At the beginning of 1812, when Napoleon was preparing to concentrate on the Oder, the Russian forces, exclusive of the isolated armies of Turkey and Finland, lay dispersed in cantonments from Courland to Podolia, over a line of some

CHAPTER I

six hundred miles. During March and April, as the French offensive on the Vistula became pronounced, Alexander drew in his scattered forces and organised them in two armies, calling up reinforcements from the Turkish frontier. The first army, under the War-Minister Barclay de Tolly, had its head-quarters at Vilna. The second, commanded by the fiery Georgian Prince Peter Bagration, was cantoned about Lutsk. Napoleon interpreted this to mean that Russia intended to invade the Grand Duchy of Warsaw with Bagration's army, while Barclay covered the road to St. Petersburg. It is indeed probable, if not certain, that had their preparations been more forward the Russians would have attempted something of the kind; Bagration was eager to advance on Warsaw. The plans discussed at the Russian head-quarters all appear to be based upon the the hypothesis of being able to meet the French near the frontier on fairly equal terms. Napoleon's overwhelming strength was not yet appreciated.

On April 17th Napoleon wrote to Davout, laying down the plan of action which he proposed in view of a Russian advance on Warsaw. The 60,000 men of the Saxon and Polish armies would, if possible, hold the line of the Vistula about Warsaw, but if overmatched must retreat on Glogau, where Davout would be able to come into line with them, while the main body of the Grand Army came up to the relief in two columns. He showed his confidence in his lieutenant by inviting him to examine and criticise the proposed plan.

At this date the French forces were approximately stationed as follows, left to right. The Prussians were about Königsberg, and Davout's six infantry divisions and a cavalry corps between Danzig and Thorn, all these forming what General Bonnal calls the Strategic Advanced Guard, under Davout. The 5th Corps was between Plock and Warsaw, the 7th Corps near Kalisch, 140 miles west of Warsaw, the 8th Corps between Glogau and Kalisch. The Bavarians (6th Corps) were marching from Glogau to Posen; the Army of Italy (4th Corps) was spread out over 100 miles of road in rear of Glogau; Ney was with the 3rd Corps about Frankfort on the Oder, eighty miles north-west of Glogau, and Oudinot with the 2nd about Berlin. As Bagration at Lutsk was some 250 miles from Warsaw, a study of the map will show that an offensive movement on his part could be opposed by at least equal numbers (the 5th, 7th and 8th Corps) in any case, apart from the 4th and 6th, which could be diverted on Warsaw, while a mass of over 200,000 men (Davout, Prussians, 2nd Corps, 3rd Corps and 2 cavalry corps) could oppose Barclay, besides the Guard.

Towards the end of April Napoleon obtained fairly accurate information of the Russian emplacements. Six Army Corps and 3 divisions of reserve cavalry were extended from near Shavli in Courland to Slonim in Lithuania—a distance of nearly 250 miles. At Lutsk, over 200 miles from Slonim, and separated from it by the huge barrier of the Pinsk Marshes, were 2 Corps under Bagration, while slowly converging upon Lutsk were 5 divisions of infantry and 2 of cavalry. He could therefore calculate with sufficient certainty that his strategic deployment along the Vistula would not be interrupted. By May 15th the bulk of his forces were on the Vistula from Danzig to Warsaw. The Prussians were at Königsberg, the Austrians at Lemberg, the 4th Corps in reserve at Kalisch, the Imperial Guards marching in detachments across Germany. The whole mass, exclusive of non-combatants, amounted to nearly 450,000 men, of whom 80,000 were cavalry. It had with it, including its reserve parks, 1146 guns and howitzers, nearly 200,000 horses and draft animals, and probably 25,000 vehicles.

The extent of the suffering entailed by the passage of this gigantic host through Germany may be imagined. The mere supplying it with food was enough to exhaust the country, but it was but a part of what had to be endured. The peasants were robbed of horses, vehicles and implements for the service of the troops, and forced themselves to accompany the columns to drive their carts laden with baggage or their own plundered crops. Honourable men in the French army saw such proceedings with shame and regret. De Fezensac tells with ill-suppressed indignation how he met German peasants fifty leagues from their homes acting as baggage drivers, and adds that they were fortunate if they reached their villages in a state of beggary. Testimony such as this is invaluable and damning. Organised plunder was rampant, and the French officers, brutalised and morally degraded by years of war maintaining war, were reckless of the misery inflicted. The Prussian official Schön tells how Davout, on entering Gumbinnen and finding supplies in his opinion not adequate, owing to the abject poverty to which Prussia had been reduced, coolly ordered his troops to pillage the town! The 1st Corps was the best administered in the army; and Davout is commonly held up to admiration by French writers as the pattern of honour and loyalty. But his execution of orders was commonly ruthless, and there were in Napoleon's army but too many officers who lacked even Davout's very limited sense of honour. Davout would sack a town remorselessly, as readily as Suchet massacred women and children at Lerida; but Suchet would hang a man who committed murder, and Davout, while subjecting people to every kind of officially ordered oppression, would sternly check private plunder or outrage. But other generals were less strict, and the bad characters who are found in every army had opportunities of committing all kinds of outrages. Napoleon himself at last complained of the misconduct of Ney's 3rd Corps. Ney was a worse disciplinarian than Davout, though a humane and kindly tempered man, but neither Ney nor Davout can really be blamed. The troops, by Napoleon's order, were to be supplied at the expense of the country, and the usual discipline of the French army was so shattered by years of organised brigandage that the rest naturally followed. The terrible misery inflicted upon Germany and other countries by Napoleonic warfare may be studied at length in reports and despatches, and furnishes a very grim commentary upon the moral value of military discipline.

Napoleon left Paris on the 9th of May, accompanied by the Empress, and reached Dresden on the 16th, where all his unwilling or willing allies and vassals were gathered to meet him. The details of his stay—how kings waited in his antechamber, how he made presents to them, how queens waited upon Maria Louisa—need not be repeated. The episode was a memorable example of pride preceding a fall.

Napoleon was not impatient. He had already told Davout that he should not commence operations until the grass had grown in order that he might therewith supplement his stores of forage; and he did not leave Dresden until the 30th of May. On that day the whole army was concentrated between Königsberg and Warsaw; the 2nd, 3rd, 4th and 6th Corps were all in line, and the Guard was collecting at Posen. Napoleon in his orders for the advance on the Niemen, on May 26th, contemplates the army as three masses: the right, consisting of the 5th, 7th and 8th Corps, under Jerome; the centre, of the 4th and 6th, under Eugène; and the left, of the Guard, the 1st, 2nd and 3rd, and the new 10th Corps (Davout's foreign division and the Prussians) which he would conduct in person. Two Reserve Cavalry Corps were allotted to the left, one to the centre, and one to the right.

Meanwhile, on the Russian side, the Emperor Alexander had arrived at Vilna on April 26th. As Emperor he nominally had the chief command, but unfortunately his motley following of German princes and relatives, military adventurers and theorists, had much more to suggest than the harassed sovereign, who must at times have been almost in despair at being called upon to decide between them. There were lengthy discussions and much drafting of strategic schemes, few of them at all applicable to the situation and resulting in little but waste of time. Barclay was practically superseded by the Emperor's following, and being naturally a man of diffident and retiring nature, and unused to supreme command, he did not sufficiently assert himself. Among the officers who appeared in Alexander's suite was old General Bennigsen, who had commanded not without credit against Napoleon in 1807, and probably hoped to induce the Tzar to give him an important command.

PRINCE EUGÈNE

SON OF THE EX-EMPRESS JOSEPHINE, VICEROY OF ITALY, AND COMMANDER OF THE 4TH FRENCH ARMY CORPS
From the picture by Scheffer at Versailles

By the beginning of June it was becoming clear that Napoleon's attack would be delivered across the Niemen. Bagration was thereupon ordered to leave a corps, under General Tormazov, to defend Volhynia against the Austrians about Lemberg, and to march with the 7th and 8th Corps through the Pinsk Marshes to Pruzhani. This movement appears to have escaped Napoleon until the last. As the French continued to advance, inclining more and more to the left, and pushing forward in dense masses into the north-east corner of Prussia, Bagration moved on to Volkovisk, about 100 miles south-southwest of Vilna, Napoleon believing him to be still at Lutsk and Brest-Litovsk.

Thus in the early days of June all was prepared for the opening of the grand drama. The hostile armies faced each other on a front of about 170 miles, with a distance of from 100 to 200 miles separating their main masses. Considerably to the southward, the Austrians, under Prince Schwarzenberg, and the army of General Tormazov confronted each other on the Galician frontier, and would evidently fight an independent contest. On May 30th Napoleon left Dresden for the front, and with his arrival at Gumbinnen on June 17th, after a detour by Thorn, Danzig and Königsberg in order to inspect the depôts at those places, the campaign may be said to have definitely commenced.

CHAPTER II
NAPOLEON'S ARMY AND ITS GENERALS

The army with which Napoleon invaded Russia in 1812 was the largest which he had yet commanded, and almost certainly the largest that had ever been gathered for the purposes of a campaign under the leadership of a single man. None the less it was too small for its task, and when, on August 23rd, Napoleon left Smolensk on the last stage of the advance on Moscow, his communications were already inadequately guarded. A greater defect was its lack of homogeneity. Even in the nominally French regiments which formed the core of the vast host there were great numbers of troops drawn from the German, Dutch, Flemish and Italian provinces of the Empire. Round this nucleus were ranged masses of allies from almost every country in southern and western Europe.

The French Imperial Army in 1812 contained 107 regiments of infantry of the line and 31 of light infantry—138 in all. According to numeration there should have been 164, but 26 had disappeared from the roll for various reasons. During 1812 several new regiments were formed, chiefly from the *conscrits réfractaires*—men who had endeavoured to escape the remorseless conscription, and were confined and trained in special remote camps.

An infantry regiment comprised 1 depôt battalion and from 2 to 5 field battalions, each of 6 companies of 140 officers and men. One company consisted of Grenadiers and 1 of Voltigeurs; the former were chosen for height and strength, the latter, whose duties were those of skirmishers, for activity. All were, however, armed with the flintlock musket, though that of the Voltigeurs was of a lighter and improved pattern. Voltigeur sergeants carried a special *carabine*. Sappers were armed with a *mousqueton* or carbine. All these weapons were fitted with a triangular bayonet. Fire training was frequently of a very elementary character. The number of cartridges carried on the person was from 50 to 60.

Non-commissioned officers, Grenadiers and Sappers, were provided with a short sabre (*sabre-bricquet*) in addition to their fire-arms. Musicians also were armed with swords.

The total weight carried on the march, including weapons, ammunition, rations, kit, and share of camping essentials, was about 50 English pounds.

The line cavalry comprised 16 regiments of Cuirassiers and *Carabiniers*, 24 of Dragoons, 28 of *Chasseurs-à-cheval*, 11 of Hussars, and 9 of *Chevau-légers*. The last were special regiments designed to accompany the heavy Cuirassiers, who were ill adapted for performing scouting and outpost duty. Each cavalry regiment had, as a rule, 1 depôt squadron and 4 field squadrons, each of 2 companies of 125 officers and men, or a total of 1000 sabres. *Chevau-léger* regiments appear to have had only 3 field squadrons.

Cuirassiers were protected by steel helmets and cuirasses. The cuirass covered both back and breast, and weighed about 15 pounds. The breastplate was theoretically bullet-proof at a range of 40 metres, and really seems to have afforded fairly adequate protection, judging from the small proportion of killed and wounded among the cuirassier officers disabled at Borodino. Cuirassiers were armed with a long, straight sword and a pair of pistols. Dragoons carried in addition a carbine. *Chasseurs-à-cheval* and Hussars had carbine, pistol and a curved sabre. In the *Chevau-léger* regiments two-thirds of the troopers were armed with lance, sabre and one pistol; the remainder had, in place of the lance, a carbine in order to perform skirmishing and outpost duties.

The cavalry was largely mounted upon horses of German breed; but even so the supply was hardly adequate. Besides, many of the horses were too young, and the hardships of the war destroyed them at a rate which was steadily on the increase. The pace of the charges was never the wild gallop familiar to us from many a spirited but inaccurate painting. A trot was the best that Cuirassiers could usually do, and light cavalry was often little faster.

It has become a kind of legend that Napoleon's artillery was always his strongest arm, but this was by no means the case. In his earlier campaigns he was weak in artillery; in 1805 and 1806 he had but 5 guns to 3000 men. It is true that his gunners were generally better trained than their opponents; but at Eylau at any rate this hardly compensated for numerical inferiority, the French having only some 250 guns to oppose to 460 Russian pieces. At Aspern, again, Napoleon put only some 200 guns into the field against more than 300 admirably served Austrian cannon. His infantry also was evidently deteriorating in quality, and needed the moral as well as the physical support of powerful batteries. In and after 1809, therefore, Napoleon greatly augmented his field artillery. He also revived a practice of very doubtful utility in attaching to each regiment of infantry 2 or 4 light guns, served by a detachment of regimental gunners. The experiment had very qualified success; corps commanders were inclined to regard the regimental artillery as a mere nuisance. It would surely have been better to attach batteries of regular artillery to the regiments.

There were 9 22-company regiments of foot artillery, 43 companies of horse artillery in 6 regiments, and 27 6-company battalions of artillery train. The company of foot artillery consisted of 120 officers and men, that of horse artillery of 100. A battery consisted of a company of artillery and a company or half-company of train.

The field and horse artillery was armed with 12- and 6-pounder guns and 32- and 24-pounder howitzers. There were also some 4-pounders. A battery usually contained 4 or 6 guns and 2 howitzers. The regimental guns were light 3-pounders.

The quality of the artillery was high. Many of its officers had made a scientific study of their profession; and the force as a whole was highly trained. The material was good, but British officers considered it much inferior to that of their own army. Manœuvring was for the foot artillery a slow process, and for the rapid formation of his great preparatory batteries Napoleon was generally obliged to rely upon the horse artillery.

The technical troops were sufficient in number, admirable in quality, and directed by scientific officers. All through the Napoleonic wars the engineers did splendid service, and never was their skill and devotion more evident than in Russia. The construction and maintenance of the bridges of the Berezina, amid every kind of misery and disadvantage, is perhaps the fairest leaf on the crown of the French engineers.

Napoleon, realising that in thinly peopled Russia he could not wage war as in Germany, had made great exertions to organise a transport service, especially for the conveyance of food supplies. There were 26 battalions. Most of these had each 252 four-horsed waggons, each waggon with a load of 1500 kilogrammes. Four of them had 600 light carts, each with a load of 600 kilogrammes; and 4 were supplied each with 600 ox-waggons with a capacity of 1000 kilogrammes. The oxen were later to be killed and eaten—a foolish idea, which it is needless to say could not be carried out. Overworked draft cattle cannot be used for food. In practice the transport broke down hopelessly. Despite ruthless plundering in Prussia it was short of draft beasts from the outset. So, too, was the artillery, and it may be imagined that when horses were found the latter appropriated them as a matter of course. Forage was scarce. Finally there were hardly any roads which would bear the weight of the trains. They soon fell far to the rear, and from the first there was a shortage of supplies at the front.

Distinct from the army as a whole was the Imperial Guard. The inception of this force dated from 1800, when Napoleon formed a "Consular Guard" of 2 infantry and 2 cavalry regiments, selected from men who had served four campaigns. In 1806 and 1807 fresh regiments were raised on the same principle, and then numerous battalions of picked recruits. When Holland was incorporated in the Empire the Dutch Guards were also included.

The Old Guard comprised 3 regiments of Grenadiers (1 Dutch) and 2 of Chasseurs. The infantry of the New or Young Guard included 1 regiment of "Fusilier-Grenadiers" and 1 of "Fusilier-Chasseurs," formed in 1806, 6 regiments of Tirailleurs (Sharpshooters), 7 of Voltigeurs, and 1 of "Flanqueurs-Chasseurs." The last was a new regiment. The Voltigeurs and Tirailleurs had for the most part served two campaigns in Spain, and were seasoned troops. The 2nd and 3rd regiments of each arm remained in Spain, and the 7th Voltigeurs in France. All the other regiments went to Russia. They formed one division of the Old Guard and two of the Young Guard. The "Legion of the Vistula"—3 regiments of veteran Polish troops—was attached to the Guard on entering Russia. All Guard infantry regiments consisted of 2 field battalions, generally weaker than line units.

The cavalry included the two original regiments of the old Consular Guard, the Chasseurs-à-cheval and the Grenadiers-à-cheval, and a Dragoon regiment. These were French. There were also 2 Lancer regiments, 1 Dutch, 1 Polish. Guard cavalry regiments had 5 field squadrons. There were 2 squadrons of Gendarmerie d'Élite, and the celebrated Mameluke company—a troop of Oriental cavaliers.

The artillery of the Guard consisted of 10 foot and 4 horse artillery companies with their train. In August, 1812, the foot batteries were armed (apparently) with 32 4-pounder guns, 18 6-pounders, 24 12-pounders, and 14 32- and 24-pounder howitzers; the horse batteries with 16 6-pounder guns and 8 24-pounder howitzers. The Guard also possessed its own service of engineers, and eight companies of seaman for work on coasts or inland waters.

The pay of the Guards was higher than that of the troops of the line, and non-commissioned officers ranked with line subalterns. The Guards were envied and disliked by the line troops, who regarded them as a pampered corps. Napoleon certainly nursed them as far as possible, and in 1812 they were only in action, as a body, on a single occasion. The idea that they were the deciding factor in all Napoleon's great victories is without foundation.

Marshal Berthier, as Prince of Neufchâtel, was attended at head-quarters by a battalion of Guards raised in his own principality; and a troop of specially selected horsemen formed Napoleon's personal escort. During the campaign a battalion of Hesse-Darmstadt Guards, under Prince Emil, and a regiment of Portuguese light cavalry were also attached to head-quarters.

The higher organisation of the army was by brigades, divisions, and army corps of infantry or cavalry as the case might be. The strength of these units varied greatly. A brigade of infantry often consisted of a single large regiment; and divisions varied in the number of their battalions from 6 to 22. Compans' division of Davout's corps was equal in strength to the two Westphalian divisions taken together. The army corps also varied much in strength, owing to Napoleon's reasonable practice of entrusting specially talented generals with greater numbers than less able officers. The 1st Corps of the Grand Army in 1812 consisted of five large divisions, and totalled some 72,000 men; while the entire Westphalian Corps counted only 18,000.

The science of clothing soldiers simply and sensibly is so little understood even to-day that it can hardly be sought in 1812. There was less of polish and pipeclay in the French army than in that of Great Britain; but the uniforms were frequently as comfortless and awkward as they well could be. One wonders how the men could march and fight in them. The headgear was often especially clumsy and absurd. To deal with the many types of uniform would need a separate work. The infantry were generally attired in the blue uniform coat which had replaced the Bourbon white at the Revolution. Cuirassiers wore blue; Dragoons green; Chasseurs and Hussars green, with facings of every colour. In general it seems that there was a good deal of rather tawdry display about the uniforms of Napoleon's soldiers. Love of ostentation appears to be so deeply emplanted in the French character that at this day the abolition of the old glaring uniforms has been much delayed.

The soldier's daily rations consisted of, roughly, 28 ounces of bread, 4 ounces of vegetables or 2 of rice, 10 ounces of meat, and beer or wine according to the country. French soldiers, with their national genius for cookery, were adepts at making themselves comfortable; and when rations were regularly distributed they fared well enough. But Napoleon's system of subsisting his armies on the country would not work in Russia. Even in Germany in 1806, and still more in 1813, the troops were often in dire distress for food. In 1812 almost from the first it was impossible to keep up any regular distribution of rations. The soldiers were reduced to marauding for supplies, but in a poor country they were often not procurable, and the unfortunate men early began to feel the pinch of want. Napoleon did his best. He ordered the construction of bakeries at every halting-place; but orders can effect little without materials, and the latter were frequently lacking. The rye of Russia, also, did not suit the stomachs of men accustomed to flour ground from other grains; and the quality both of flour and bread was generally bad. Herds of beef-cattle were driven with the army, but their flesh rapidly deteriorated under the effects of bad fodder and fatigue. Generally speaking, the periods when the Grand Army was not living from hand to mouth were few, even on the advance. During the retreat it was half-starved at best.

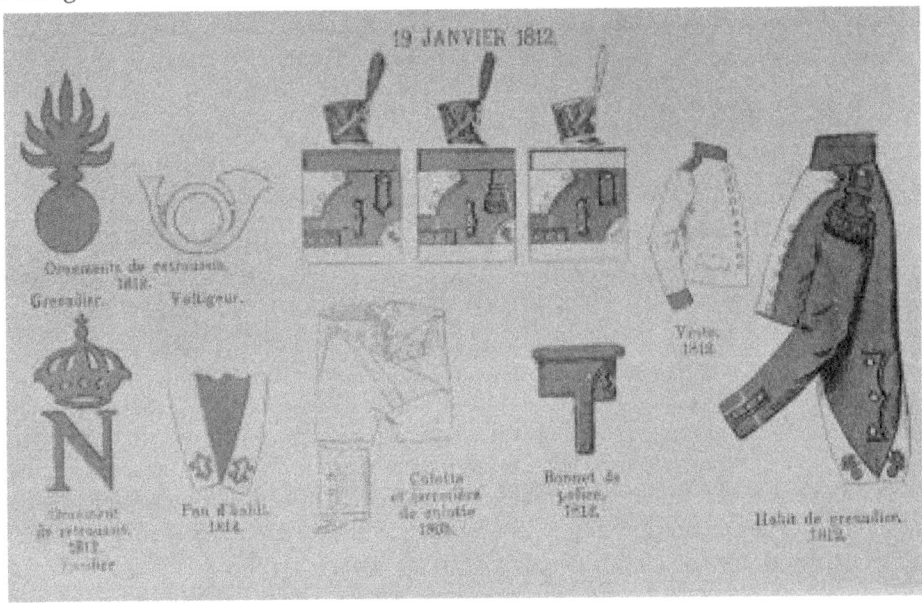

DETAILS OF THE UNIFORMS OF THE INFANTRY OF THE FRENCH ARMY IN 1812
From *"Uniformes de l'Armée française."* By Lienhart and Humbert

In the disorganisation of the transport the hospital service fared badly. There was a fairly adequate staff of surgeons and medical officers; but their efforts—often devoted and persevering in the highest degree—could effect little when supplies of every kind were lacking. On the outward route, no less than the return, men died in thousands by the roadsides, uncared for and unnoticed. Nearly half the Bavarian Corps died or was invalided without seeing an enemy. The hospitals were inadequate and badly equipped from the outset; later on their condition became too frightful for words. All whom ill-fortune or duty brought into contact with them describe them in terms of horror. They eventually became mere charnel-houses, in which men were left to perish in thousands of every kind of misery.

The French army in 1812 was undoubtedly, from the military standpoint, the best organised in Europe; but its officers, as a whole, left much to be desired. The rapid increase of the numbers of the rank and file since 1806 had involved the improvisation of thousands of officers, often from doubtful material. The best of the regimental officers were those who united education to practical experience, but they were relatively few in number. The cadets of the military school were admirable material, but naturally lacked experience and, as De Fezensac adds, the physical strength which was so necessary. But besides those classes of educated officers there was a third composed of promoted sergeants, whose education was, as a rule, elementary. One of them, the worthy Staff-Captain Coignet, tells us in his delightful autobiography that he did not learn to write until he was thirty-three years of age! He was, indeed, a man of much natural sagacity, and keenly regretted his deficiencies; but it is obvious that these illiterate men can scarcely have made good company officers. The officers of the artillery and engineers were indeed generally excellent; but many of those of the cavalry, though dashing leaders on the field, possessed little solid knowledge of the duties of their arm, and the work of keeping in touch with the enemy was often very badly performed.

As regards their ideas of personal ease the French officers were no better than their opponents. Their private vehicles and baggage swelled the trains to gigantic dimensions—a fact which contributed much to the disasters of the retreat.

The quality of the rank and file was by no means what it had been in the great years of Austerlitz and Jena. The bloody campaign of 1807 had created gaps not easily to be filled at the time, and the Austrian and Peninsular wars deprived the army of the leisure necessary for it to repair its losses. The French divisions of the 1st, 2nd, 3rd and 4th Army Corps contained many old regiments, but even in them there was a large proportion of recruits; and there were a number of regiments, belonging to newly annexed provinces, which were not altogether trustworthy. Their material—the sturdy peasantry of the Low Countries and North Germany—was excellent, and their conduct on the field usually irreproachable; but their administration and discipline left much to be desired. Their bad condition was continually exercising the soul of the order-loving Davout. In one despatch he describes the Dutch 33rd Léger as *canaille*, and declares in disgust that he can do nothing with it. Ney likewise complained of the 129th, and pointed out that it would have been better to draft the recruits of which it was composed into older regiments. It is probable that Napoleon's object in forming new units was to train as many officers as possible.

The deterioration of the troops rendered it necessary to employ deep tactical formations, with consequent risk of heavy losses. The usual formations for attacking infantry were (1) the "column of companies," in which each battalion advanced with its companies in three-deep line, one behind another, and (2) the "column of divisions," with a front of two companies instead of one. At best the front was narrow and the volume of fire proportionately weak, even when, as was usual, each battalion was preceded by a skirmishing line of Voltigeurs. Napoleon was fully aware of the fire weakness of these attack formations, and recommended as the ideal the *ordre mixte* in which battalions in column alternated with others in line. This order, like the others, failed hopelessly against the British two-deep line which brought every musket into action; and it is remarkable that able French generals continued to employ it when its inefficiency had been so clearly demonstrated. It is at least probable that the excitable and imaginative French soldiery could not advance steadily in line. At any rate, French tacticians trusted, to the end, in the thick skirmishing line which preceded the advance being able to clear a way for the masses behind. As the Russians, with less intelligent and (on the whole) worse trained troops, adopted similar tactics, the problems which troubled the French in Spain did not arise in Russia.

The French cavalry was excellent on the field, but otherwise often unsatisfactory. In scouting and outpost work it was inefficient; more than once during the campaign touch with the Russians was entirely lost. No doubt much of this inefficiency was due to the exhaustion of the horses. Forage was generally scarce, and to losses from fatigue and lack of food were soon added those in action. The men were frequently poor horse-masters. Murat took no care for the mounts, and over-worked his force from the first. When the central army began its retreat only 15,000 horsemen remained mounted, and none but the Guard regiments were really fit for service.

Concerning the internal condition of the French army something must be said. With the old soldiers devotion to their leader was still the watchword; but it would be a grave mistake to imagine that this sentiment was universal, especially among the better educated elements of the army. Yet the loyalty of the troops, as a whole, admits of no doubt. Sir Robert Wilson and De Fezensac are at one in bearing witness to this. The desire for plunder no doubt counted for something, but it was hunger rather than greed that made the French soldier a marauder. The spirit of brigandage was indeed rife in the army, and infected everyone from the commanders downward. On the whole, it may fairly be said that in the ranks the sense of loyalty was strong and the general spirit good, but that discipline was often badly maintained and naturally tended to become more and more relaxed as hardships increased. Further, it may be observed that while there were numbers of irreproachable men among the officers, there were also many greedy adventurers, besides those who were demoralised, like their men, by years of predatory warfare. Finally, there was, of course, in the army the ruffianly element, which is never absent. To this element must be attributed the commission of most of the atrocities which undoubtedly took place, and for which the whole army had later to suffer. One further point must be touched upon. The evidence as to the presence of women and children with the army, especially during the retreat, is abundant and overwhelming. This unhappy element consisted, in the first place, of female camp-followers—*vivandières, cantinières* and the like—mostly the wives of soldiers. Some of the officers, at any rate, were ill-advised enough to take their wives with them. The foreign population of Moscow mostly awaited the invaders, and fled with them in fear of Russian vengeance. Finally, the morals of the French army in sexual matters can only be described as low, at any rate from the

British standpoint. Napoleon himself was not so much immoral as unmoral—not that there is any absolute proof that he gave way to his passions during the Russian campaign—and many of his officers followed his example. On the whole, it seems clear that for one reason or another the invading army was burdened with thousands of women and children, whose sufferings during the retreat constituted probably its most harrowing feature.

The troops of the allied states who accompanied and outnumbered the French were, generally speaking, the fair equals on the field of their comrades-in-arms. The Bavarians, Westphalians and Württembergers all behaved splendidly; and some of the finest fighting in the war was accomplished by the Berg and Baden regiments at the passage of the Berezina. The Italians fought admirably at the one general action at which they had the fortune to be present. The great Polish contingent performed splendid service for the man to whom Poland looked for its restoration to the roll of independent nations. Nor can any fault be found with the conduct in battle of the Spanish and Portuguese troops, though they were no better than prisoners, serving by compulsion. The Austrians and Prussians generally took no very prominent part in the campaign; but what they did was by no means to their discredit.

It was in administration rather than fighting quality that the allied troops fell below the French standard. They were also generally so badly supplied that the best administration could have effected little to improve their lot. The fine Bavarian and Württemberg troops wasted away by half before they had seen an enemy, and the Poles, to judge from Poniatowski's despatches, were often little better off. That the Spaniards and Portuguese supplied more than their proportion of deserters and pillagers is merely what might have been expected, and the same may be said of the Croats and Illyrians, whose interest in the war in which they were sacrificed was absolutely *nil*. Yet, on the whole, it cannot well be said that the foreign troops showed conspicuously worse discipline than their French comrades, though doubtless the general mixture of races and languages tended to lower the general standard.

As to the absolute quality of the allied troops it is very difficult to speak. The German and Swiss infantry were very solid and good, though of course the quality of the different contingents varied, and perhaps the Bavarians, Württembergers and Badeners rose above the general level. The Saxon cavalry were admirable, and probably the best in the entire *Grande Armée*. The German artillery also, especially that of Württemberg, was good.

The best of the Polish troops were very good indeed; but the regiments were largely composed of raw recruits, hastily raised for the great effort which, as the Poles of Warsaw fondly hoped, was to re-establish their national existence. The cavalry was good; the infantry less so. Discipline does not appear to have been very satisfactory; the officers included too many *Pans*, owing their commissions to their noble birth.

The Prussians were probably the best disciplined and best officered of all the allied troops. The general quality of the Austrians, also, was good.

Upon the whole, it cannot be doubted that the *Grande Armée* of 1812 was too heterogeneous, and that its quality was not of the best. Much of it had been hastily raised; and its enormous numbers merely added to the difficulty of provisioning it and, in consequence, to its misery and losses. General Bonnal thinks that Napoleon, when he collected the gigantic force, was more or less suffering from megalomania; and that he would have achieved more had he depended upon a Franco-Polish first line of about 250,000 troops, perfectly organised, disciplined and supplied. The point is certainly worthy of consideration.

Something must be said of the commanders who, under the direction of Napoleon, conducted the greatest of his armies during the most ambitious and disastrous of his campaigns.

For Napoleon himself a very few words must suffice. More has probably been written about him than of any other single figure in history. No good purpose can here be served by anything more than some brief animadversions upon the share which he himself had in the catastrophe of 1812.

Napoleon's position as the greatest military leader of modern times is as yet unchallenged; and it is needless therefore to discuss it. In 1812 he was, as far as years go, a comparatively young man. He was barely forty-three; his bodily energy and capacity of endurance were yet enormous. Nevertheless, he was not the Napoleon of 1800 and 1805. He had grown stout and somewhat unwieldy; and his gross habit of body must at times have affected his mind. Nor is it possible to ignore the first-hand evidence as to his indifferent health on more than one important occasion.

Napoleon's fierce and impetuous nature always made light of obstacles, and lack of patience was certainly a very pronounced feature in his character. Wellington is said to have remarked that it incapacitated the Emperor from defensive action in 1814, when circumstances imperatively demanded it.

Finally, Napoleon in 1812 was ruler as well as general; and political considerations probably had something to do with his adoption of courses of action indefensible from the military standpoint.

Napoleon's natural impatience, and his rage at being unable to strike a crushing blow, will probably explain the fatal rush in August past Smolensk on to Moscow. Bodily suffering appears to the author to account satisfactorily for his undoubted lack of energy at Borodino. The fatal delay at Moscow may fairly be attributed to a combination of political circumstances and not entirely unfounded optimism as regards the future.

For some of Napoleon's amazing blunders on the retreat reasons such as these will hardly account. The fatal dispersion of the marching columns along 60 miles of road, even after passing Smolensk, when the army was already worn down to a mere remnant; the unnecessarily slow pace of the march, the burning of the pontoon train previous to the passage of the Berezina, are cases in point; and can hardly be attributed to anything save declining intellectual powers.

On the whole, it seems difficult to deny that Napoleon, in 1812, had definitely entered upon his decline; that his perception was less clear than of old; that his bodily energy had decayed; that his genius, though still capable of burning brightly, now only blazed forth fitfully. Certainly there were times during the Moscow campaign when it appeared to be almost extinct.

Marshal Berthier, Prince of Neufchâtel, served in 1812, as in every campaign of Napoleon since 1796, as chief-of-staff. His methodical habits and untiring industry, coupled with his complete familiarity with Napoleon's character, rendered him indispensable to the latter. His military talents were not remarkable, and his general position was rather that of a confidential secretary than that of a modern chief-of-staff—for whom, indeed, there was no place near a man of Napoleon's essentially despotic temperament.

MARSHAL DAVOUT
Commander of the 1st French Army Corps
From the painting by Gautherdt at Versailles

Marshal Louis Nicolas Davout, Prince of Eckmuhl and Duke of Auërstadt,

CHAPTER II

commander of the huge 1st *Corps d'Armée*, was probably the best of all Napoleon's generals, though he never had such opportunities of distinguishing himself in independent command as were granted to Masséna and Soult. He was a fine example of the modern scientific soldier, a stern disciplinarian and an admirable administrator, with a passion for order and method; and very careful of his men. The charges of cruelty brought against him do not appear to the author to have been satisfactorily made out—certainly not according to the standards of humanity generally accepted in Continental warfare. At the same time, there was undoubtedly a harsh and rough side to his character, and he seems to have lacked self-control and tact. Davout had excellent strategic insight, and his tactical ability and tenacity in action had been frequently and brilliantly demonstrated. He took a distinguished part in the first half of the campaign of 1812, but rather failed in the unaccustomed post of rear-guard commander. Men of his methodical habit of mind are probably ill-fitted to shine in such a turmoil of misery and disorder as the retreat from Moscow.

Marshal Oudinot, Duke of Reggio, was a hard-fighting veteran of the Revolution, who had received his bâton for services rendered in supporting Davout at Wagram. He was an excellent subordinate, but failed in separate command like so many of Napoleon's generals, though his action previous to the passage of the Berezina was highly meritorious.

Michel Ney, Duke of Elchingen, Marshal of France, reaped most of the credit gained by Napoleon's generals in 1812. Ney is commonly regarded as a mere hard fighter, but he was fairly well educated, and to all appearance a careful administrator. Among the papers of the French War Office relating to 1812 is an order in which he carefully instructs his suffering troops how to cook the unground grain which was their only food. As a strategist Ney did not excel, and he failed in independent command, but he was a fine tactician, and as a corps commander probably unsurpassed. His famous title "Le Brave des Braves" fairly sums up his character. His courage was indeed of that nobler type which rises to its height at the moment when that of meaner men declines.

Prince Eugène, Viceroy of Italy, son of the ex-Empress Josephine, was by virtue of his Imperial rank the commander of the army of Italy. He was brave, disinterested and devoted to his stepfather, but his military talents were not great, and he lacked experience. In 1809 he had been opposed to a commander even less capable than himself, and his officers and soldiers had helped him successfully out of his difficulties.

Prince Joseph Anthony Poniatowski, nephew of the last King of Poland, could hardly have been passed over in appointing a commander for the 5th (Polish) Army Corps; especially as he was Minister of War of the Grand Duchy of Warsaw. He was brave and popular with his men, but possessed of no great capacity, and was indolent and pleasure loving.

General Gouvion St. Cyr, who was promoted Marshal for his victory over Wittgenstein at Polotsk in August, was a very capable though disaffected officer, who had, as far as good service counted for anything, won his bâton long before.

General Reynier, the commander of the Saxon 7th Corps, was a hard-fighting, experienced soldier of no special ability, and extremely unfortunate in war. Junot, who took over the Westphalian Corps from King Jerome, owed his position chiefly to Napoleon's friendship for him.

PRINCE JOSEPH ANTHONY PONIATOWSKI, NEPHEW OF STANISLAUS AUGUSTUS, THE LAST KING OF POLAND
Commander of the 5th (Polish) Corps of the Grand Army
From the painting by T.A. Vauchelet at Versailles

King Jerome Napoleon of Westphalia would probably have done well enough at the head of the troops of his own kingdom; his courage, as he showed at Waterloo, was beyond question. But to place him in command of three army corps, operating in a difficult country, and charged with a vitally important mission, was a gigantic blunder on the part of Napoleon. It is no especial discredit to Jerome that he failed so completely. General Bonnal observes that he cannot be blamed for transgressing military principles with which he had never been acquainted.

Marshal Victor, the commander of the 9th Corps, was an experienced officer, but had been very unfortunate in the Peninsula against the British.

Marshal Macdonald, commanding the 10th Corps, took a very small part in the campaign; and, unless he had special orders, cannot be said to have displayed much activity. He was a man of high personal character and a good hard-fighting corps commander, but of no eminence as a general.

Napoleon, during the latter part of his career, was repeatedly accused of placing his relations in positions for which they were not fitted. The case of King Jerome is one in point; so also perhaps, to a certain extent, is that of Napoleon's celebrated brother-in-law, Joachim Murat, King of Naples, commander of the Cavalry Reserves. Audacity and tactical ability on the field Murat certainly possessed, but he was hardly a great cavalry leader. His outpost and reconnaissance work was often very badly performed, and his impetuosity caused him to overwork and harass his men and horses. He lacked stability of character and steadiness in adversity, as he was soon to show. Yet as King of Naples he possesses more than one title to esteem, and in his character, amidst vanity and absurdity, there was much that was elevated and noble.

The commanders of the four corps under Murat's orders were all men of experience as cavalry leaders. The best of them, perhaps, was Nansouty, at any rate in his own estimation, but the name of Grouchy is better known in Great Britain. Montbrun and Latour-Maubourg had seen much service in Spain.

Marshal Lefebvre, Duke of Dantzic, commander of the Old Guard, was much attached to Napoleon, but otherwise merely a rough, honest old soldier of little strategic or tactical ability. His title was much better deserved by the brilliant engineer, General Chasseloup, who accompanied the army in 1812 as chief of his branch of the service.

Marshal Mortier, Duke of Treviso, commander of the Young Guard, was an excellent corps commander, as had been demonstrated in Spain.

Marshal Bessières, Duke of Istria, had been associated with the cavalry of the Guard since its formation. He was a fine cavalry leader, and a man of integrity and devotion to his chief, otherwise deserving of no special mention.

Generally speaking, Napoleon's commanding officers had one great defect. With few exceptions they had become so habituated to submission to the dominating personality of the Emperor that they had lost all power of initiative.

In an army so huge and of such experience there were naturally many officers who in a less warlike age would have been acclaimed as great generals. The majority of the divisional and brigade leaders were excellent, though some were already wearing out. Several of them—men such as Verdier—had had considerable experience in independent command, and some had acquired therein a by no means savoury reputation. Gudin, the leader of Davout's 3rd Division, was perhaps the most distinguished as a soldier, but his colleagues Friant, Morand, Desaix and Compans were all fine officers. Legrand, Merle, Verdier, Ledru, Marchand, Broussier, Pino, Bruyère, Sebastiani, St. Germain, Claparède, Tharreau, and others were men of considerable merit and experience.

Of the General Staff it may be said that it had scarcely any affinity with the board of specially trained officers which accompanies and assists a modern commander-in-chief. Napoleon's absorption, in his single person, of all military and administrative functions had reduced it to a position of complete insignificance. For all practical purposes it was nothing but a mass of orderlies, and though it contained many talented and meritorious officers they had small opportunity of distinguishing themselves so long as they remained members of it. Napoleon in one moment of exasperation declared that "the General Staff is organised in such a manner that nothing is foreseen." The remark was more or less true; but that such a state of affairs could exist is a very severe comment upon his methods. The invading host was, in short, the army of a despot who endeavoured to supervise everything himself and discouraged initiative in others, with the natural result that much that might have been done to minimise the catastrophe was not attempted.

The numbers of the invading army and its composition, according to the states and peoples who contributed contingents, are given in detail in Appendices A and B. Roughly it may be said that during the campaign Napoleon disposed of the following numbers:—

First Line

Head-quarters; Imperial Guard; 1st, 2nd, 3rd, 4th, 5th, 6th, 7th, 8th, 10th, Corps; Austrian Corps; Cavalry Reserve	449,000

Second Line

9th Corps; Polish and Lithuanian levies; 2 French Divisions; German Troops, Drafts, Parks, etc.	165,000

Third Line

Drafts and organised troops in touch with Russians at close of campaign, including garrisons of Danzig and on Vistula	60,000

                                                                                                     674,000

The composition by nations of the first two lines may be stated as follows:—

French and New French	302,000
Germans and Swiss	190,000
Poles and Lithuanians	90,000
Italians, Illyrians, Spaniards, Portuguese	32,000
	614,000

CHAPTER III

THE RUSSIAN ARMY AND ITS GENERALS

The circumstance which most impresses the reader who for the first time, and without knowledge of the conditions, peruses the story of the Franco-Russian campaign of 1812 is that the forces of Russia were, as compared with those of Napoleon, very weak. This weakness in war is familiar enough to all students of Russian history, nor are the reasons far to seek. Since, however, it must appear peculiar to all who regard Russia as a power essentially huge and powerful—the "Colossus of the North"—its causes must be briefly reviewed.

It is true that Russia is a country of vast extent; but her huge territory, to-day very imperfectly developed, was in 1812 largely in an almost primeval condition, while the population was even more sparsely distributed. The country was and is covered in many places by wide expanses of almost impenetrable forest, and by vast tracts of morass. In the western provinces the marshes of Pinsk cover an area of more than 20,000 square miles; and in 1812 they were pierced by only three indifferent roads. The majority of the numerous rivers do not in themselves present grave obstacles to intercommunication or military operations, being in summer shallow and easily fordable, and in winter usually frozen over, but they are often wide, and frequently have soft or sandy beds. The larger of them must be negotiated by means of bridges, and in 1812 bridges were few. Moreover, in Central Russia the soil is generally yielding and sandy, and every small stream has hollowed for itself in the course of ages a gully more or less deep. These gullies, repeatedly recurring, presented considerable obstacles, especially since they were rarely bridged.

The distances to be traversed were and are enormous. Readers of Herodotus will remember how the prospect of the three months' march from Miletus to Susa frightened Kleomenes and the elders of Sparta. To transfer troops from the Caucasus to St. Petersburg in 1812 involved a journey of even greater magnitude—without the aid of the Royal Road of Persia. Even to-day the Russian roads are comparatively few and bad. In 1812 it was infinitely worse. The few high-roads were frequently very badly maintained; cross-roads of use for military purposes were almost non-existent.

Finally, Russia was as undeveloped politically as economically. The bulk of the peasantry were serfs chained to the soil. The accepted method of enrolling them for the national defence was to call upon the nobles, who owned the greater part of the land, for a levy of so many per hundred or thousand souls. Their interests naturally induced them to endeavour to retain the best and most industrious of their serfs, and to furnish for the army the ill-conditioned or idle, as far as possible. In a country in which corruption has always been rampant the recruiting officials were doubtless amenable to the influence of judicious bribery, and the actual result of a military levy was often far less than it should have been. The slowness of communication, the general poverty of the Government, the lack of factories of clothing, arms and ammunition, added to the difficulty of rapidly and efficiently increasing the armed strength. In 1812 Russia was suffering also from an almost complete cessation of commerce, the result of the British blockade of her coasts brought on by the alliance with Napoleon in 1807, and the financial difficulties were in consequence even greater than usual.

The Russian army, since its organisation on European methods by Peter the Great, has usually tended to be a rather crude and imperfect copy of the most modern force of the time. In 1812 French ideas naturally predominated, and their influence was apparent in many respects, especially in the direction of the higher organisations.

Early in 1810, as already noted, General Barclay de Tolly became Minister of War in Russia, and set himself earnestly, with the support of the Emperor, to reorganise the army. Divided counsels near the Tzar, and the adverse influence of the conditions above detailed, rendered the execution of his plans slow and difficult. Nevertheless, a great deal was effected, and whatever opinions may be held as to Barclay's military ability there can be no doubt of his talent for organising.

In 1812 the Russian infantry comprised 6 regiments of Imperial Guards, 14 of Grenadiers, 50 of light infantry (Chasseurs), and 96 of the line. Each regiment consisted of 3 4-company battalions with an establishment of 764 officers and men per battalion in the Guards, and 738 in the line. As a fact, only the Guard regiments were able to complete 3 field battalions. The strengths of the line regiments were so low that Barclay could only complete 2 battalions of each regiment at the expense of the third. One company of the third battalion was also completed by drafts from the other three, and these companies combined in threes or fours to form battalions of "combined grenadiers." There then remained to each regiment a weak battalion of three depleted companies. These were collected at various strategic centres as "Reserve Divisions," and Barclay hoped to complete them with recruits. He designed the formation of thirty-six depôts at suitable points, at which new levies were to be trained into additional battalions and squadrons for the infantry and cavalry regiments. In this respect, however, there was not enough time for his judicious arrangements to have much effect. In practice Russia was able to do little more than maintain her field army at something like war strength. The third battalions, reserves and new levies were chiefly absorbed in feeding the fighting line.

A large proportion of the troops were by 1812 armed with a musket of new model, about equal to that with which the French and British infantry were furnished, but many still carried the older and clumsier weapon which had been employed in 1807. The bullet was rather heavier than that of the French infantry musket; but, judging from the fact that the Russians usually appear to have had a higher proportion of killed to wounded than their adversaries, it is probable that the powder was often inferior.

The Russian cavalry included 6 Guard regiments—2 of Cuirassiers, 1 of Dragoons, 1 of Hussars, 1 of Uhlans (Lancers) and 1 of Cossacks—each of 4 field squadrons and 1 depôt squadron. The Cossack regiment included a detachment of Orenburg Cossacks, and apparently had 5 or 6 field squadrons. The line cavalry comprised 8 regiments of Cuirassiers, 36 of Dragoons, each of 4 field squadrons and the depôt; 11 of Hussars and 5 of Uhlans, each with 8 field and 2 depôt squadrons. The establishment of a Guard squadron was 159 officers and men, that of a line squadron 151. The cavalry was well and adequately mounted, much better so than that of Napoleon. The men were less well trained than their opponents, but, belonging to a country in which there is a horse to every five or six human beings, were probably good horse masters. Hay was the usual forage, and, to the surprise of Clausewitz, the horses throve upon it. Accurate details of armament I have been unable to procure, except that the line Cuirassiers were only protected on the breast. Helmets and cuirasses were painted black, not polished—a very sensible and labour-saving device.

The gradual inclusion in Russia of nomadic peoples and of the old border moss-trooping or Cossack (really *Kazak*=freebooter) settlements enabled the Government to supplement its forces by swarms of irregular horsemen. Besides the Cossacks these were Crimean Tartars, Kalmuks and Bashkirs—the latter still clothed in chain mail and armed with the bow! In June there were perhaps 15,000 of them on the western frontier. Their numbers later increased to 30,000 or more. Their reputation rests largely upon the dread with which they inspired the demoralised Napoleonic army during its retreat. In the field they could not contend with regulars, and even during the retreat could never achieve anything against such of the French infantry as kept its ranks. For guerilla operations and for harassing the retreat they were invaluable.

In artillery Russian armies have usually been very strong. The inefficiency of the mediæval Muscovite levies of horse and foot led early to a remarkable and precocious development of the artillery arm. Peter the Great in his reorganisation paid special attention to it, and his crowning victory at Poltava was very largely due to his excellent artillery. After Peter's reign his policy was continued, and Russia owed many victories to the masses of well-served guns which accompanied her armies.

In 1812 the Russian artillery of the line comprised 44 heavy, 58 light and 22 horse-artillery batteries organised in 27 foot and 10 reserve brigades, besides single horse artillery batteries attached to the cavalry. There were also 29 depôt companies. The numbers of gunners and drivers varied from an average of 240 for the heavy batteries to 160 for light artillery companies. They were each armed with 12 guns and howitzers. Cossacks had their own horse batteries.

The artillery of the Guard comprised 2 heavy and 2 light batteries, each of 16 guns and howitzers, and 2 horse artillery batteries of 8, with establishments in proportion.

The armament consisted of 18-pounder (½-*púd*) howitzers and 12-pounder guns for the heavy batteries, 9-pounder howitzers and 6-pounder guns for the light artillery, and 6-pounders for the horse batteries. The heavy ammunition waggons customary in other European armies were not employed in Russia, their place being taken by a larger number of light vehicles. The quality of the material appears generally to have been excellent, though Sir R. Wilson and General Kutaïsov recommended various improvements; and the draft horses were very numerous and good. The Russian artillery continually performed feats of transport that speak volumes for its high quality, and the number of pieces abandoned or captured was extraordinarily small.

The technical troops were few in number and lacking both in scientific officers and training. The medical department, though far better than in 1807, when it was practically non-existent, was still terribly inadequate and ill equipped, and trained physicians and surgeons were very few.

There were 32 garrison regiments, 1 Guard garrison battalion, garrison artillery, and pensioners.

A detailed statement of the Russian forces is given in Appendix C, but of course all of these were not available. Immediately disposable to meet the invasion there were:—

FIRST LINE

	About	
First Army of the West	126,000	
Second " "	40,000	
Third " "	45,000	
	— — — —	211,000

SECOND LINE

	About	
27th Infantry Division	7,500	
Reserve Troops and Riga Garrison	37,500	
	— — — —	45,000

Total	256,000

To reinforce the fighting line there were brought up during the campaign—

	About	
From Finland	14,000	
" the Turkish frontier	44,000	
" the Crimea	5,000	
Militia, Recruits, Cossacks, etc.	90,000	
	— — —	153,000

Total actually employed	409,000

The last item can only be a very rough estimate. It is, however, certain that the large figures given in some authorities bear no proportion to the numbers of reinforcements which actually reached the front. It is of course obvious that the entire armed strength of Russia cannot be reckoned as opposed to Napoleon. The Asiatic, Caucasian and Crimea troops could at best only furnish small detachments.

The First and Second Armies had received at the hands of Barclay a fairly complete army-corps organisation, each corps containing two infantry divisions, a brigade or division of cavalry, and two brigades of artillery, with a battery of horse artillery attached to the cavalry. The Third Army and the Army of the Danube were still organised in the main on the old system of mixed divisions.

The characteristics of the Russian soldier have never varied. He was and is endowed with remarkable endurance and courage, but is comparatively unintelligent. In 1812 illiteracy was practically universal.

The conditions of service were bad. The period was twenty-five years, and brutal methods were often necessary to compel the recruits to leave the homes which they would probably never see again. Life in the ranks was hard, and only the fact that it was probably no harder than the existence of the average peasant could have rendered it endurable. The men were well clothed, for obvious reasons; but they were in general ill-fed, ill- lodged, ill-cared-for, and practically unpaid. The methods of maintaining discipline were brutal, and if in theory military service meant emancipation from serfdom, in practice the men were treated as slaves. It is all to their honour that they made and make such good soldiers.

The great characteristic of Russian troops is their extraordinary solidity and imperturbability under the most terrible punishment. A Russian army hardly ever dissolves under the influence of defeat; it must literally be battered to pieces. A good example of this was afforded at Zorndorf in 1758, when Frederick the Great gained a Cadmean success over a largely raw, badly trained and equipped, and ill-led Russian army not greatly superior in number to his own. He nearly destroyed both wings of the Russian host, but the centre stood firm, rallied the survivors, fought doggedly until nightfall, and lumbered defiantly away with some show of equality. The campaign of 1812 was to afford further proof of these characteristics.

There is a tendency to regard the Russian soldiers as generally large men, but there is abundant evidence that this was not the case. An English observer, writing about 1854, describes them as usually undersized, but they were doubtless hardy enough. The Guards were picked men. The cavalry, artillery, light infantry and grenadiers absorbed the best of the remaining recruits; the ordinary line regiments, with very inadequate means, had to assimilate and train the poorest of the available material.

The officers, as a class, were not capable of adequately training the fine material at their disposal. There were honourable exceptions, but at his best the Russian regimental officer was hardly the equal of his opponent of corresponding rank, though often, perhaps, a better linguist and a finer social figure. The Guards, as a whole, obtained the best officers, and after them the pick went to the cavalry and artillery, while the line infantry regiments were often very badly off. The ordinary battalion and company leaders frequently lacked all but the most elementary military instruction. Appointment and promotion were too often due to Court favour, female influence or corruption. The officers were, as a class, indolent. Too often they were not at the head of their men; their private carriages or sledges swelled the trains to enormous proportions, while the fighting line was weakened by the numbers of men detailed for their service. Gambling and drunkenness were very prevalent, and personal cowardice by no means uncommon, as Duke Eugen of Württemberg and Löwenstern testify. It is fair to add that defects such as these existed more or less in all armies of the period, but the Russian army has always been badly or inadequately officered.

In the higher ranks the conditions were not more satisfactory. There was a superabundance of general officers, but their quality often left much to be desired, and appointments were frequently due to other causes than military efficiency. This was, it is true, not especially the case in 1812. Alexander, presumably with the assistance of Barclay de Tolly, seems to have made a very fair choice of corps commanders, and several of the divisional leaders later acquired a well-deserved renown.

The foreign officers were a most important element. Germany furnished the largest contingent, but there were many French *émigrés*, as the Duc de Richelieu, Langeron, and St. Priest, and at least one Italian, the Marquis Paulucci. It may fairly be said of them that their general intellectual and scientific level was higher than that of the native officers. The latter were naturally bitterly jealous; and the foreigners rarely receive justice at the hands of popular Russian writers. It is humiliating to find even Tolstoï stooping to perpetuate these jealousies and employing the term "German" in an obviously contemptuous sense. Many of these foreigners did excellent work for Russia in 1812—though it is true that Phull, perhaps the most prominent of them, was an unpractical dreamer.

Mikhail Bogdanovich, Baron Barclay de Tolly, Minister of War and Commander-in-Chief of the First Army of the West at the outbreak of hostilities, was himself in some sense a foreigner, and seems to have been regarded as one, much to his misfortune, by the ultra-Russian officers. He was a Livonian by birth, and ultimately of Scottish extraction, being descended from a member of the family of Barclay of Towie, who had settled in Livonia in the seventeenth century. In 1812 General Barclay de Tolly was fifty-one years of age. His rise in the army had at first been very slow, owing to his unassuming character and to lack of influence; but his skill and courage as a divisional leader in 1807 and 1809, especially displayed in his march across the frozen Baltic in the latter year, had brought him to the front rank in the Russian councils. His reorganisation of the Russian army in 1810-12 will probably constitute his best title to fame. The published Russian documents bear emphatic witness to his industry, energy, and scientific spirit. His deficiencies in high command are to be attributed partly to inexperience in handling large masses of troops—an inexperience which he shared with all but a very few contemporary leaders. He was overburdened with work, being War Minister as well as general, and was constantly harassed by the insubordination, sometimes verging upon mutiny, of his assistants. His personal character stands very high. Patriotism and devotion to duty were to him a religion; and he was one of the few men in Russia who rose above narrowly patriotic views. His scorn of personal

CHAPTER III

profit and ease do him the highest honour, since they were shared by few indeed of the men about him. Alexander's trust in him never seems really to have faltered. The dreamy, romantic, crowned knight-errant and the simple, devoted soldier of his country had indeed much in common. Russia has had few sons to compare with Barclay de Tolly; and it is not to her credit that his worth has been so little appreciated.

FIELD-MARSHAL PRINCE BARCLAY DE TOLLY
General, War Minister, and Commander of the First Army of the West in 1812

General Prince Peter Ivanovich Bagration, commander of the Second Army of the West, was a man of different stamp. He was descended from the Armenian royal line of the Bagratidae; and to his exalted rank his rapid rise in the service was largely due. Though only born in 1765, he was a major-general in 1795. At the same time Bagration's abilities were considerable enough to have ensured his rise under any circumstances. Suvórov had a high opinion of him; and the great leader's judgment cannot be lightly set aside. Bagration was essentially a fighter: his tactics were usually influenced by his combative instincts; and his excitable temperament rendered him reckless of his person. His impatient temper rendered him an intractable colleague for the calm and methodical Barclay; and the latter's courtesy and deference to the senior who had come under his orders did not always relieve their strained relations. On the whole, it would seem that Bagration possessed better strategic insight than his comrade; but his tactical ideas were not always happy. Having regard to his impetuosity, it was, perhaps, fortunate for Russia that he was not, as his admirers wished, placed in supreme command. But in pressing the French retreat his fiery energy would have been invaluable; and from this point of view his death was a national disaster. It is but due to his memory to say that he really appears to have been a man of too high and noble a character to condescend to wilful insubordination or intrigue; his intractability was the outcome of temporary ill-temper, as were his occasional unjust remarks concerning Barclay. Towards the end of their association relations between the two chiefs improved; and, on one occasion at least Bagration openly testified to his regard for Barclay.

General Count Alexander Petrovich Tormazov, the commander of the Third Army of the West, does not appear to have been a man of any exceptional ability. His early successes were due to numerical superiority; but he then unduly dispersed his forces, and was in his turn overwhelmed. At Gorodeczna he would probably have been destroyed but for the methodical slowness of his opponents.

General Prince Mikhail Hilarionovich Golénischev-Kutuzov, who in August became Commander-in-Chief of all the Russian armies in the field, was a veteran of sixty-seven years, of which fifty-two had been spent in arms. He was certainly a man of ability, both political and military; and his practical experience of war was great, though largely acquired in service against Polish *guerrillas* and Turkish irregulars. Though he had been nominal Commander-in-Chief at Austerlitz, his reputation had scarcely suffered; for it was well known that he had exercised practically no authority, which had been usurped by the young Tzar and his confidants. That he could take advantage of his opponents' blunders had been demonstrated at Dürrenstein in 1805, and on the Danube in 1811. But in 1812 Kutuzov was too old for the emergency; and wounds and infirmity had diminished his bodily activity. Even in the Turkish war this had been noticeable. As an ultra-Russian he was able to command more loyal support than Barclay. His conduct of the battle of Borodino was at least energetic, and his subsequent strategy sound; but during the French retreat his lack of enterprise was evident. His last campaign made him Field-Marshal and Prince of Smolensk, but can hardly be said to have enhanced his reputation.

CHAPTER III

FIELD-MARSHAL PRINCE GOLÉNISCHEV-KUTUZOV
Commander-in-chief of the Russian Armies in 1812

General Baron Levin Bennigsen, the stout antagonist of Napoleon in 1806-1807, was for a time Kutuzov's principal assistant; but the two did not work well together, and eventually Bennigsen was retired. Bennig sen, a Hanoverian soldier of fortune, was as old as Kutuzov, but much more energetic. He appears to have been a selfish and jealous, but able, man, and in the following year once more did Russia good service. Barclay, according to Löwenstern, said of him, that despite his ability, he was a "veritable pest" to the army, owing to his egoism and envy; and this view is certainly borne out by a perusal of Bennigsen's unreliable and self-laudatory memoirs.

General Matvei Ivanovich Platov, Ataman of the Cossacks of the Don, is probably better known to British readers than any of his colleagues. He was a burly, genial officer, uniting to considerable military talents the daring and good-humour which were even more important in the eyes of his wild followers. He was an ideal leader of irregulars; his ceaseless activity and energy will presently be more apparent.

Admiral Pavel Vasilievich Chichagov, Commander-in-Chief of the Army of the Danube, is a somewhat remarkable figure in Russian history. He perhaps owed some of his characteristics to his frequent association with Englishmen. He seems to have been somewhat impetuous and excitable; and certainly possessed a very independent temper, not hesitating to speak his mind to his despotic master. A seaman and diplomatist, placed in command of a land army at a great crisis, it would not have been strange had he failed badly, but this was far from being the case. Once clear of the Turkish embroglio he brought his army to the front with all speed; and though, as a general, too slow, he carried out his operations with a steady pertinacity, refusing to be diverted by contradictory orders. For Napoleon's escape at the Berezina he was only very partially responsible; but the entire blame was laid upon him by the hasty injustice of his countrymen, and his career ended in voluntary exile many years later. It is not pleasant to find his name still rancorously assailed. The Tzar Alexander II was of a different opinion; one of the first ships of the Russian ironclad navy was named *Chichagov*.

Of the advisers who surrounded and influenced—not always for his good—the Tzar, the most prominent was the Prussian Phull. He had occupied an important position on the Prussian staff in the fatal year 1806, a fact which should surely have warned Alexander against his counsels. Certainly none but the Tzar had any confidence in him, and his utter lack of real military capacity was shown in the famous project of the camp at Drissa.

Of the staff-officers the most notable were Major-General Alexei Petrovich Yermólov and Colonel Baron Charles Toll. The former was an extraordinary personality, who seems to have retained more barbarian characteristics than any European military leader of modern times. He was a man of great courage, considerable ability, and remarkable will-power; but of a savage and unstable disposition. He could be guilty of gross cruelty to prisoners of war, and later, as Viceroy of the Caucasus, relied, as he admitted with cynical frankness, upon a policy of indiscriminate massacre. Yet he was a kind and considerate commander, beloved by his troops, and not ungenerous in his treatment of subordinates. This treacherous side of his character would induce him to intrigue against a rival, with whom he would then suddenly become reconciled on some impulse of generosity. He intrigued against Barclay, but wept bitterly when that ill-used chief left the army. It may have been hypocrisy, as Löwenstern says; but it really has more resemblance to one of those impulses which civilised men can hardly understand, but which are characteristic of barbaric natures, such as Yermólov's. Yermólov's policy of massacre failed to pacify Caucasia, and his successor Paskievich declared it to have been a gross blunder. Nevertheless, Yermólov has continued to this day to be the subject of somewhat indiscriminate eulogy. It is perhaps better to take the opinion of men who knew him. Barclay's was terse and to the point: "An able man, but false and intriguing." Alexander's was pithy: "His heart is as black as his boot." Clausewitz, who was little associated with him, admitted his ability.

Toll was a scientific soldier of considerable attainments, and played a distinguished part during the years 1812-1815.

Of the officers who, during the campaign, commanded detachments or army corps several were men of real distinction.

General Mikhail Andreïevich Miloradovich—»the Russian Murat»—was in charge of the advance-guard which pressed the French retreat. The Russian documents show that he was hardly so much the mere swordsman as Tolstoï would make him. Both in 1812 and 1813 Miloradovich distinguished himself greatly, showing himself to be as admirable in rear-guard command as he was in the leading of the pursuit.

Lieutenant-General Count Peter Wittgenstein, the German commander of the 1st Army Corps, gained considerable renown by his independent operations against Napoleon's left wing. In high command he always failed; but as a corps commander he was equal to most of the French marshals, and, though frequently rash and inconsiderate, was never lacking in stubbornness and energy.

General Dmitri Sergeievich Dokhturov, commanding the 6th Corps, had served with distinction as a divisional leader in 1805, 1806 and 1807; and reaped fresh laurels in 1812. His conduct before and during the battle of Maloyaroslavetz reflected the highest credit upon him, and may be said in effect to have sealed the fate of the retreating Napoleonic host.

Lieutenant-General Nikolai Nikolaievich Raievski, the commander of the 7th Corps, gained a reputation little inferior to that earned by Dokhturov. During the critical days of August 14-16, when Napoleon was executing his famous flank march on Smolensk, Raievski's ready acceptance of responsibility and fine resolution ensured the defence of the city, and gave Barclay and Bagration time to concentrate. His action undoubtedly saved the Russians from severe defeat, if not, indeed, from crushing and irretrievable disaster.

Lieutenant-General von der Osten-Sacken, commanding the reserves of the Third Army, was detailed by Admiral Chichagov to guard his rear against Schwarzenberg in November, while he himself marched to hold the crossings of the Berezina. He executed his task with unfailing courage and energy, though opposed to greatly superior numbers. Though an elderly man, his fighting energy was great. In the two following years he added to his reputation as a dauntless and hard-fighting commander.

None of the other Russian corps commanders was accorded the opportunity of rendering such eminent service as these three; but none, whatever his other defects, showed himself deficient at need in that stubbornness which was probably the most necessary of all qualities when opposed to Napoleon.

Nor can any serious fault be found with the majority of the divisional commanders. Conspicuous among them were Konovnitzin, Neverovski, and the young Prince Eugen of Württemberg, who next year gained a great reputation as chief of the 2nd Corps. Among those who later rose to the highest rank may be mentioned Voronzov, a brave, capable, and altogether estimable man, the hero of the terrific struggle on the plateau of Craonne in 1814, and thirty years later Viceroy of the Caucasus. Also, in command of one of Raievski's divisions was a difficult-tempered, vain, and jealous young major-general, who in after years was to achieve a European renown—Paskievich, presently to be Field- Marshal Paskievich of Erivan and Prince of Warsaw. Another prominent figure was that of the youthful Major-General Count Kutaïsov, who commanded the artillery of Barclay's army. Though only twenty-eight years of age, he does not appear to have been unfitted for his post; all who came in contact with him bear witness to his tireless energy. Certainly the Russian losses in artillery were very slight, and to Kutaïsov must part at least of the credit be given. He ended his brief and brilliant career on the field of Borodino while leading a successful counter-attack.

Of the Russian army as a whole it is to be said that there were too many generals entitled by their rank to high command, and whom it was deemed necessary to placate by giving them commands. At Borodino, besides the general officers on the staffs of Barclay and Bagration, Bennigsen was present as Chief-of-Staff of all the Russian armies; Konovnitzin was "general of service," and there were others. Miloradovich commanded two army corps under Barclay, and General Gorchakov was also on the field in a somewhat undefined capacity—all these in addition to the Commander-in-Chief and the leaders of the two armies. Most of them were useless on the field, for Barclay, Bagration, and Kutuzov naturally sent orders direct to the corps and divisional commanders. In 1813 matters were even worse. In order to employ as many as possible of the ambitious general officers a practice was adopted of combining corps in pairs. In this fashion a force of about 35,000 men was burdened with more than thirty generals and three distinct staffs! In 1812 the confusion at head-quarters, owing to the presence of unattached generals or relatives of the Tzar, was often great, and that disaster did not ensue was more than once due to something like sheer good fortune. Alexander also committed what might have been a fatal error in not giving one general precedence over another when acting together. Barclay and Bagration often found it hard to agree; and though Chichagov and Tormazov, and, apparently, Wittgenstein and Steingell, succeeded in working together, it was fortunate that trouble did not arise.

CHAPTER IV

THE FIRST STAGE OF THE CAMPAIGN. OPERATIONS FROM KOVNO TO VITEBSK

The Russian frontier in 1812, from the Black Sea to where the River Bug issues from Galicia, was practically as it is to-day. The ten Polish Governments, however, then formed the greater part of the Grand Duchy of Warsaw: the border therefore stopped short at the Bug and the lower Niemen below Grodno. The Niemen, rising near the city of Minsk, flows roughly westward for about 150 miles to Grodno, thence about 80 miles northward to Kovno, and then some 110 miles westward into the Kurisches Haff. From Grodno to Kovno the channel is deeply sunk and difficult to cross. There were in 1812 bridges at Grodno and Tilsit; but at Kovno the Königsberg-Vilna high-road was served only by a ferry. For the last 60 miles of its course the Niemen is in Prussian territory. It thus became extremely important for Napoleon as soon as he had occupied its right bank. He had already collected a large flotilla of gunboats and barges, under Rear-Admiral Baste, in the ports of the Frisches and Kurisches Haffs, and was able therefore to bring immense quantities of supplies from his advanced depôts to Kovno and thence to Vilna.

For about 100 miles south-westward from Grodno there was no natural frontier; thence to the Austrian border it was formed by the Bug, which, issuing from Galicia below the town of Sokal, flows northward for some 110 miles to Brest-Litovsk, and then north-westward for 70 miles more to what was in 1812 the Polish border. For nearly 100 miles near Brest-Litovsk the Pinsk Marshes close in upon the river. The Austro-Russian border need not be considered, for it was neutralised; Schwarzenberg operated only as an auxiliary, in Poland. Trade continued as usual, and when Admiral Chichagov's army passed close along the frontier on its way to attack Schwarzenberg it was not molested by Russia's nominal enemies.

The first provinces on the right bank of the Niemen entered by the *Grand Armée* were Courland to the north and the various districts which had once formed the Grand Duchy of Lithuania to the southward. Lithuania was and is a region of woods and marshy plain land, broken in places, and intersected in every direction by streams flowing in deeply sunken channels. In the south there stretched inland from the Bug the famous marshes of Pinsk, one of the largest tracts of fenland in the world, extending as it does for some 300 miles east and west, by over 100 north and south. The soil, even when not actually swampy, was generally soft, and there were hardly any good roads. Towns were few; the population was sparse and wretchedly poor.

At distances varying from about 120 to over 300 miles eastward of the Bug and Niemen a second natural line is formed by the Düna and the Dnieper. The Düna rises near the Volga, flows roughly south-west to Vitebsk, there turns west-northwest and runs for nearly 300 miles to the Baltic at Riga. Above Vitebsk it is fairly often fordable during the summer heats. In 1812 it was bridged at Vitebsk and Dünaburg, half-way to Riga, but, since the left bank is generally higher than the right between these places, the river does not afford a good line of defence.

From the Düna at Vitebsk southward to the Dnieper at Orsha is a gap of about 45 miles. At Orsha the Dnieper, one of the great rivers of Europe, turns to the southward, to flow for 800 miles into the Black Sea. Seventy miles above Orsha is Smolensk, where in 1812 there was a bridge. At Mohilev, 50 miles below Orsha, there was another. The river is rarely fordable even during the summer. Its tributary the Berezina, which was a most important strategic feature in the campaign, flows towards it on the east at an acute angle for 200 miles, joining at a point nearly due east of Warsaw and west of Orel. In 1812 there were bridges at Borisov and Bobruisk, but in general the river is fordable in summer. The right bank is usually higher than the left.

Napoleon's advanced bases were the places on the Vistula, especially Danzig and Warsaw—though Danzig was infinitely the most important. The road from Danzig to the frontier divided at Wehlau; the left branch going by Tilsit through Courland to Mitau and Riga, and thence to St. Petersburg; the right by Insterburg and Gumbinnen to the Niemen at Kovno, thence by Vilna, Ochmiana, Minsk, Borisov and Orsha, to Smolensk. From Mitau and Riga two roads converged on Jakobstädt, and then passed along the right bank of the Düna, by Dünaburg, Drissa, Desna and Polotsk, to Vitebsk, whence two or three roads led to Smolensk. From Polotsk and Smolensk ran roads north-westward to St. Petersburg.

From Vilna a road led by Sventsiani and Glubokoie to Desna and Polotsk. From near Sventsiani a branch went to Dünaburg, and from Glubokoie another fork led by Lepel and Bechenkowiczi to Vitebsk. Cross-roads connected Vitebsk with Orsha, and Lepel with the Smolensk-Minsk road, half-way from Orsha to Bobr. From Orsha the main road to Kiev ran down the right bank of the Dnieper through Mohilev and Staroi Bykhov. From Bobr another road led to Bobruisk and thence into the Orsha-Mohilev-Kiev highway. A third road went from Bobruisk to Minsk by way of Igumen.

The road eastward from Warsaw forked some 30 miles out, separating into two branches, which united again at Novi Svergen, 250 miles farther on. The southern branch proceeded by Brest-Litovsk, Slonim and Nesvizh; the northern one passed by Bielsk, Bielostok, Grodno and Novogrodek. From Novi Svergen the road ran nearly north-eastward to Minsk, about 60 miles farther on. From Brest-Litovsk a road branched off to Lutsk, through the Pinsk Marshes. At Kobrin, some 30 miles farther on, a road pierced the marshes eastward, turning to the right about 30 miles short of Pinsk, and eventually coming out in the direction of Lutsk and Ostrog. A branch connected Pinsk with this road, and from Pinsk another highway led through the fens northward to Nesvizh. From Slonim a road led northward to Vilna, intersecting the Grodno road about a third of the way out, and another

CHAPTER IV 41

cross-road connected the two Warsaw roads, east of Grodno, by way of Volkovisk. Finally a road led from Nesvizh by Slutsk to Bobruisk, and from the latter place another passed through the eastern end of the Pinsk fens by Mozyr-on-Pripet to Kiev. There were, of course, many minor roads or tracks, but these were practically all that could be used for military purposes, and most of them were inferior. From Smolensk eastward the road system became, so far as the campaign was concerned, very simple, consisting merely of a single trunk leading to Moscow.

Russian high-roads are commonly of considerable breadth, so that it was possible for vehicles to move upon them several abreast. Both armies, however, were so encumbered by immense trains that their columns covered enormous lengths of road.

With the exception of Moscow, Warsaw and Riga, there were no large towns, in the modern sense of the word, within the theatre of war, and even Riga can scarcely be regarded as one. Moscow had somewhat over 200,000 inhabitants, Warsaw about half as many. Vilna, Grodno, Minsk, Vitebsk and Smolensk had each from 20,000 to 30,000 inhabitants; Kovno, Dünaburg, Mitau, Brest-Litovsk, Bielostok, Mohilev and Bobruisk perhaps from 15,000 to 20,000; Polotsk possibly 15,000. Borisov, Orsha, Bobr, Smorgoni and many other places described as towns were merely villages—not often large villages, according to modern ideas. From Moscow to Smolensk, a distance of over 250 English miles, there were only three small towns,—Viasma, Gzhatsk and Dorogobuzh—and the largest of these had but about 5000 inhabitants.

While Napoleon was inspecting his depôts, completing the organisation of his water transport, and setting in train the formation and pushing to the front of his numerous reserve forces, the Grand Army, now practically secure from Russian attack, was moving up to the Niemen. By the 12th of June the advance-guard of the 10th Corps was at Tilsit, and the Imperial Guard and five army corps, besides three corps of the cavalry reserves, were steadily advancing behind towards the line of the Niemen between Tilsit and Kovno. The 5th and 8th Corps were in advance of Warsaw, and the 7th a little way in rear of it. The Emperor still expected that Bagration would invade the Grand Duchy, for on June 10th he wrote to Eugène on that hypothesis. He also appears to have anticipated that Bagration's advance would be supported by at least a part of Barclay's army. At all events he speaks of a possible attack upon Eugène, which indicates that he looked for something like a general encounter along his whole front.

He explained to Eugène that his echelon formation, with the left in advance, would enable him to take in flank the attack of the Russians directed against his right or centre. If Jerome were attacked, Eugène with the 4th and 6th Corps would be able to fall on the flank of the hostile columns, while if Eugène himself were assailed he could be supported at need by the whole left wing. All this certainly appears to point to the idea of a general Russian advance. Whether the somewhat complicated manœuvres anticipated by the Emperor took sufficiently into account the inexperience of Eugène and Jerome, and the frightful Polish tracks by which they would be obliged to move, may be doubted. Moreover, it is clear that their successful execution depended upon the Russian generals being so obliging as to play into Napoleon's hands. The armies, it must be remembered, were not yet in touch, and the Russians had perfect freedom to manœuvre at will.

By June 18th Napoleon had about 320,000 men (Imperial Guard, 1st, 2nd, 3rd, 4th, 6th and 10th *Corps d'Armée*, and 1st, 2nd and 3rd Reserve Cavalry Corps) concentrated on a front of about 130 miles from Tilsit south-westward to the Prusso-Polish frontier. Thence to Warsaw stood the 5th, 7th and 8th Corps and the 4th Cavalry Corps—80,000 men on a line of 80 miles. Finally, the Austrians, 34,000 strong, constituted the detached right flank-guard, marching from Zamosc Lublin on Warsaw.

Total 434,000 combatants, 1076 guns.

The Russians were cantoned as follows: The First Army was strategically disposed in a main body, a reserve, and two semi-independent wings. The 1st Corps (Wittgenstein) constituted the right wing, about Rossieni, some 100 miles northwest of Vilna, and nearly opposite to Napoleon's detached left flank-guard, under Macdonald, at Tilsit. About Lida, 60 miles south of Vilna, on the road to Slonim, stood the 6th Corps (Dokhturov) and the 3rd Cavalry Corps (Pahlen II), forming the left wing, under Dokhturov. The 2nd Corps (Baggohufwudt), the 3rd (Tuchkov I) and the 4th (Shuvalov) were guarding the line of the Niemen above and below Kovno, on a front of about 60 miles. The 1st Cavalry Corps (Uvarov) was at Vilkomirz, 40 miles north-north-west of Vilna, and the 2nd (Korff) at Smorgoni, nearly 50 miles on the road to Minsk. The 5th Corps (H.I.H. the Grand Duke Constantine) formed the general reserve at Sventsiani, about 45 miles north-east of Vilna. The "Flying Corps" of Cossacks under the Ataman Platov was pushed forward to the frontier about Grodno, 60 miles west of Lida. The First Army, including Platov, numbered some 126,000 men, including 19,000 regular cavalry and 584 guns.

Of the two army corps which composed the Second Army the 8th (Borozdin I) was at Volkovisk, 60 miles south-south-west of Lida, and the 7th (Raievski) at Novi Dvor, 20 miles farther south. The 4th Cavalry Corps (Sievers), and about 4000 Cossacks, under General Ilovaïski, connected the two. The newly formed 27th Division (Neverovski) which was marching from Moscow to join Bagration, had not yet passed Minsk. Including it the Second Army comprised about 47,000 men, including 7000 regular cavalry, and 168 guns.

The Third Army was widely dispersed and could not take the field for some weeks. It numbered in all perhaps 45,000 men.

Thus, owing to various causes—divided counsels, imperfect organisation, bad roads and especially the lack of any real command-in-chief—the Russian forces were, almost up to the very moment of hostile contact, in a state of dangerous dispersion. The secret history of the months during which Alexander had been at Vilna will probably never be accurately known. Dissension and intrigue were rampant in the Tzar's personal *entourage*. Much valuable time was wasted in drafting and discussing plans of action, all impracticable, because based upon hypotheses which proved untenable. They all considerably underestimated Napoleon's fighting strength, and appear to have assumed a concentration of the Russian forces about Vilna. There was great disorder in the higher commands. Barclay was nominally commander-in-chief, but Alexander frequently issued orders, through his adjutant, Prince Volkonski, over the head of the harassed War-Minister, while to make confusion worse confounded Phull, as Clausewitz expresses it, "sometimes put in *his* oar." Contrary to the usually accepted belief, it appears that Barclay would have preferred to stand to fight, granted a favourable opportunity. The deciding factor in the situation seems to have been that almost at the last moment the Russian staff obtained better information as to the strength which Napoleon had with him in Prussia.

At all events the party of prudence finally obtained the upper hand in the Tzar's councils. The policy of retreating before the invader had been so often discussed that there was nothing unexpected in the resolution which was adopted. It was determined to draw back the whole First Army at least as far as Sventsiani. All the corps commanders were warned to be ready to retreat thither immediately upon receiving orders, except Wittgenstein, who was given permission to anticipate them if pressed by a rapid advance of Napoleon's extreme left wing over the Niemen. Platov, it was vaguely supposed, would be able to threaten Napoleon's communications, and would be supported by Bagration from Volkovisk. Tormazov, with the Third Army, was to retreat on Kiev if hard pressed; but, if not, was to leave General Sacken with his incomplete division to observe the Austrian frontier, and with the rest of his army to fall upon the right of the forces which were opposed to Bagration. General Okunev, in his commentaries upon the war, suggests that Bagration and Tormazov should have effected a junction and advanced in force against Napoleon's communications while he was engaged in front with Barclay. As, however, Napoleon could detach 80,000 men, under Eugène, to support the 114,000 whom he already had in the Grand Duchy, Bagration, Tormazov and Platov would eventually be outnumbered by at least two to one; while Napoleon would still have possessed a double superiority of numbers over Barclay. In fact the Russians were so enormously outmatched at every point that retreat was the only sensible strategy. Napoleon, it is true, assumed that the Russians would stand to fight. This was partly, no doubt, due to mistaken but not unreasonable calculations as to their state of preparation, but also largely, it is to be feared, to the obstinate optimism which during his latter years became something like an acute mental disease with him. He had developed a fatal habit of believing that his enemies would always play into his hands.

Accordingly, still proceeding on the assumption that Bagration would invade the Grand Duchy of Warsaw, while Barclay stood fast to oppose his own advance upon Vilna, the French Emperor decided to operate the passage of the Niemen close to Kovno. Kovno lies at the confluence of the Vilia, the river of Vilna, with the Niemen, and was therefore admirably adapted for the collection of stores by water from Danzig and Königsberg, and forwarding them to Vilna as soon as that place and the surrounding country were in Napoleon's power. In point of fact the Vilia proved too sinuous and difficult to be of much utility, but this could hardly be known at the time, and in any case did not greatly affect the value of Kovno as a base. The forest of Pilwiski or Wilkowiski, extending over a considerable area on the bank of the river opposite Kovno, furnished an excellent screen for Napoleon's operations. Finally, by bridging the river and debouching rapidly in the direction of Vilna, Barclay might be separated from his detached right wing under Wittgenstein. All this obviously assumed that the Russians would remain stationary.

On June 22nd Jerome was directed to be at Augustowo on the 25th. On that day his three corps were extended along the Warsaw-Augustowo road, and the head of the 5th Corps, which was leading, was nearly 50 miles away. The 8th was still farther behind, and the 7th as yet in the neighbourhood of Warsaw, awaiting the Austrians, who were slowly advancing from Lublin. Napoleon was probably misinformed as to distances, and certainly had not taken into full consideration the wretched Polish roads. He apparently calculated upon being able to throw his main body suddenly across the Niemen at Kovno, deal a smashing blow at Barclay and then wheel round to crush Bagration.

Fortunately for the Russians they had now decided to do the right thing, and had no intention of awaiting their enemies' pleasure. The three corps on the Niemen were drawn back to Vilna, leaving only a light cavalry screen along the right bank. Wittgenstein retired from Rossieni to Keidani, 40 miles nearer Vilna. On June 23rd, therefore, Barclay had four corps echeloned on a line of 70 miles, nearly two marches from the Niemen at its nearest point; and, as all were ready to retreat on Sventsiani at the shortest notice, Napoleon's plans were already half disconcerted. Irresolution, however, clung to the Russian counsels, and Dokhturov was still left in a dangerously isolated position at Lida.

On the 22nd Napoleon, being himself at Wilkowiski, about 40 miles from Kovno, drafted a proclamation to the army which may be regarded as the official declaration of war. It was of the usual Napoleonic type, chiefly compounded of false statements and prophecies which were never fulfilled. Mr. Hereford George is probably correct in pronouncing that "a more unfortunate document was perhaps never penned."

On the afternoon of the 23rd Napoleon had under his hand opposite Kovno in the Pilwiski Forest some 214,000 men, comprising the Imperial Guard, the reserve parks and engineers, the 1st, 2nd and 3rd *Corps d'Armée*, and the 1st, 2nd and 3rd Corps of Reserve Cavalry. At Tilsit, in line with the main body, was the 10th Corps, under Macdonald. Eugène, with the 4th and 6th Corps, was still some 60 miles to the right rear, and could hardly reach the Niemen near Kovno before the 28th. General Bonnal appears to consider that his absence materially contributed to the failure of the Emperor's strategy, but it is a little difficult entirely to agree with him. Even had the situation been as Napoleon imagined it, with the Russians extended in a long, thin line upon the frontier, Eugène's absence could not have fatally influenced results. The invaders, with their overwhelming numerical superiority, could not fail of success. Without Eugène Napoleon had 247,000 men in all opposed to Barclay's 120,000. Bagration could hardly under any circumstances have gained more than a temporary success over the head of the long column of divisions marching from Lublin to Augustowo, and as yet not disquieted by Tormazov on its rear. Given that Reynier and Schwarzenberg were forced to turn back to face Tormazov—as did ultimately happen—Jerome would still have over 60,000 regulars against Bagration's 36,000; and Eugène's retardation would place

CHAPTER IV 45

him in a favourable position for supporting him. It is even permissible to argue that Eugène's absence was rather a favourable circumstance than otherwise, since the knowledge that Napoleon was short of over 70,000 men might have induced Barclay to stand to give battle, which was precisely what Napoleon desired.

As a fact the situation was quite other than Napoleon envisaged it. Had all his corps been in position to time, the manœuvre of Vilna would still have failed. Had Jerome, with his whole force, reached Augustowo on the 25th June, as contemplated, he could not have reached Grodno before the 27th. Volkovisk is nearly 50 miles farther on, and Bagration evacuated it on the 28th to retreat on Minsk. It was absolutely impossible for Jerome to reach him. Of Barclay's corps, the 1st was nearly two days' march from the Niemen, and Wittgenstein had permission to retreat as soon as he had information of the French passage of the river. Baggohufwudt, Tuchkov and Shuvalov were still farther back, out of touch with the French, who could not reach them in less than two forced marches, even if they stood fast. Dokhturov alone was somewhat isolated, and ran considerable risk of being cut off from the main body. Still even had Dokhturov been cut from Barclay it is highly probable that the course of events would have been little different. A junction of the two Armies of the West would have eventually been effected, and it is possible that Barclay, short of 20,000 men, would not have made, as he did, at least one very perilous halt on his march to Smolensk.

To conclude, when once the Russian commanders had determined to adopt a policy of steady retreat, and to adhere to it with more or less resolution, the campaign may almost be said to have decided itself. Napoleon was ever striving to obtain contact with his elusive foes and to fight the great battle which should crush the heart out of their resistance. But only thrice all through the advance was he able to establish this contact, and in each case the Russians drew away without having sustained decisive defeat. The first operations on the Niemen were typical of most of those which were to follow.

On June 23rd all the troops under Napoleon's immediate command were nearly opposite Kovno. Napoleon gave the strictest orders that only light cavalry were to approach the river; infantry, artillery and heavy cavalry were to be kept under cover in the forest, so as to conceal from the enemy until the last moment the exact direction in which the blow was to be dealt. Meanwhile the river was reconnoitred for a point of passage, and a bend between Kovno and the village of Poniemon, a little higher up, was selected by General Haxo, Davout's chief of engineers.

At daybreak on the 23rd Napoleon in person arrived in his travelling carriage at the bivouacs of the 1st Cavalry Corps. He descended at that of the 6th Polish Lancers, and, still anxious to conceal everything from the Russians until the last moment, removed his famous Guard uniform and cocked hat, and donned the coat of a Polish officer—an example followed by the staff-officers with him. Count Soltyk, an officer of the Lancers, has minutely described the episode. Napoleon's strong common sense appears in his refusal of the heavy Polish cavalry shako, and acceptance of a cap instead. He then rode forward to a village directly opposite Kovno, and carefully reconnoitred the place from the windows of the house of the village doctor. Returning to the Lancers' bivouac, he made a hasty meal, chatting meanwhile with the Polish officers, and especially asking if their uniform suited him. He then resumed his own garments and rode off to reconnoitre the course of the river elsewhere. He approved Haxo's selection of Poniemon, and issued elaborate orders for the passage. They obviously imply that vigorous resistance was anticipated; nothing was yet known of the Russian retirement on Vilna. They also contain much minute regulation of detail, which might well have been left to Haxo or Davout.

During the afternoon and evening the 1st Corps was brought up to Poniemon, whither the pontoon trains, under General Eblé, were also despatched. Three bridges, about 300 yards apart, were to be thrown across. As soon as it was completely dark—that is to say, about 10 p.m.—General Morand, the commander of the 1st Division, crossed in person with three companies of Voltigeurs and one of Sappers, who were ferried over in boats. As they were disembarking they were detected by the nearest Russian picket—a detachment of the Hussars of Yelisabetgrad. They rode up to the mustering Voltigeurs, and their leader challenged in French: "Qui vive?"

"France!" came the reply.

"What do you do here?" asked the Russian officer.

"You'll soon see!" was the answer; and the bold officer turned rein, to report to his superiors that the long-expected invasion had begun at last. His troopers emptied their carbines in the direction of the French party as they rode away, but apparently without effect; and the Voltigeurs did not reply, Napoleon having issued orders that there was to be no firing except in case of extreme necessity. The bridges were completed by about 1 a.m. on the 24th, and Davout's corps began to defile across. There was no resistance; the only approach to fighting consisted in the interchange of a few shots between the advanced French troops and the rearguards of the retreating Russian cavalry regiments. The day broke as the passage was in progress: it continued practically without intermission all through the 24th and 25th. As a military spectacle it has, perhaps, never been surpassed; but the ease with which it had been effected was probably by no means entirely pleasing to Napoleon. He must have been unpleasantly conscious that the Russians had no intention of delivering themselves into his hands, though he probably hoped that they would stand to fight in advance of Vilna.

In the morning of the 24th Davout's 1st Light Cavalry Brigade, under Pajol, occupied Kovno, expelling the Cossack squadron which was the only garrison; and in the afternoon Napoleon himself transferred his head-quarters thither. He ordered a permanent pile bridge to be constructed at the ferry, and threw another bridge over the Vilia, just above its confluence with the Niemen.

The news of the invasion reached Alexander the same evening while he was at a garden party at General Bennigsen's mansion near Vilna. Next day he announced it to his army in a proclamation, and to the nation at large in another, addressed to Marshal Saltikov, Military Governor of St. Petersburg. The tone of both was worthy of the occasion, and contrasted strongly with the arrogant and theatrical ring of that of Napoleon.

CHAPTER IV

Orders were issued to all the corps commanders to retreat on Sventsiani. It was recognised that Platov alone could hardly achieve any serious damage to Napoleon's communications, and he also was directed to retire on Sventsiani by way of Lida and Smorgoni. Bagration was warned not to allow himself to be cut from Minsk. All the orders reached their destination safely, except those to Major-General Dorokhov who, with the advance-guard of the 4th Corps, was at Orani, southwest of Vilna. The 3rd and 4th Corps retired leisurely to the suburbs of Vilna, which Barclay did not intend to evacuate until it became absolutely necessary.

By the evening of the 25th the whole French army was over the Niemen and pushing forward to Vilna. Murat opened the march with the 1st and 2nd Cavalry Corps. Behind were the 1st and 3rd Corps, the 3rd Cavalry Corps, and the Imperial Guard, while the 2nd Corps had crossed the Vilia at Kovno and was marching along its right bank, thus forming the flank-guard of the advance on Vilna, and threatening to cut off Wittgenstein towards Keidani. Davout and Ney had each detailed a foreign regiment to guard Kovno and the bridges. The 10th Corps was ordered to advance from Tilsit upon Rossieni, sweeping the right bank of the Niemen, and thus clearing the course of the river for Baste's supply flotillas, which were now collecting at Tilsit, whence they were pushed forward to Kovno.

There was practically no fighting on the march to Vilna. The thin chain of Russian cavalry posts steadily retired as the French pressed forward: only a few shots were fired from time to time. Napoleon hoped for a battle at Vilna and the troops made forced marches day after day to attain the desired end, at great cost to themselves, for the weather was sultry, the roads were bad, and the provision trains were already falling to the rear. The men began to leave the ranks in order to forage for supplies, and the horses, ill-fed and over-worked, broke down and died in great numbers. Even the artillery was ill-horsed from the first, and the officers were forced to scour the country for draft animals, often with very little success. Barclay was in position before Vilna with the 3rd Corps and most of the 4th, and Baggohufwudt was in touch to the north; but Alexander and his suite had already left for Sventsiani, and Barclay was merely waiting until the French began to close. The stores which could not be carried off were destroyed, and at 4 a.m. on the 28th the 3rd and 4th Corps began to defile through the town. Barclay and his staff left about 1 p.m.; and the rear-guard followed, burning the bridge over the Vilia. Bruyère's cavalry division, which was heading the French advance, came through the town before Barclay's cavalry rear-guard was quite clear of the suburbs; and its leading regiment, the 8th Hussars, was charged and driven back, with the loss of several prisoners, by the Cossacks of the Imperial Guard. The Russian columns were well on their way to Sventsiani, and after three days of forced marching in tropical weather the French impulse had expended its force.

On the same day a more serious skirmish took place near Vilkomirz. Wittgenstein, falling back from Keidani, heard that Oudinot was marching up the right bank of the Vilia and, fearing that he might be anticipated at Vilkomirz, stationed his rear-guard, under Major-General Kulnev (4 battalions, 4 squadrons, 1 Cossack regiment and 6 guns), on the 27th at Develtova, requesting General Uvarov to support him with a regiment of Dragoons. Meanwhile the 1st Corps defiled through

Vilkomirz on the Sventsiani road. As Kulnev, in his turn, was retiring through the place from Develtova, he was attacked by Castex with Oudinot's advanced guard. The French cavalry charged the Russian Hussars and Cossacks and drove them into the town with considerable loss, but Kulnev succeeded in withdrawing his force across the Vilia, and burnt the bridge, and Castex could only cannonade the Russians until the arrival of infantry. Uvarov's cavalry regiment, marching rather carelessly to join Kulnev along the river-bank, came under artillery fire and lost several men and horses. When Oudinot's infantry began to arrive Kulnev followed his chief. He had lost about 300 men, including 240 prisoners. Oudinot reported a loss of 50 killed and wounded. The 2nd Corps occupied Vilkomirz, and bivouacked for the night some 2 miles on the Sventsiani road.

Napoleon himself entered Vilna in the afternoon of the 28th. Alexander had sent his aide-de-camp, General Balashov, with a final message to his opponent, offering to reopen negotiations if the French troops withdrew across the Niemen. Napoleon, with his usual dramatic instinct, received Balashov in the quarters which Alexander had lately quitted. Needless to say, nothing came of the interview. Napoleon regarded the message as an insult, or at best as an attempt to gain time. He merely wrote a long letter to Alexander repeating all his real or imagined grounds for the war. Danilevski says that Balashov was directed to tell Napoleon that if he declined to listen to Alexander's last overtures he must expect war to the death. It is also said that Napoleon asked questions concerning the roads to Moscow. Balashov replied that there were several, and His Majesty might do as other monarchs had done, and choose. Charles XII, for example, had taken the road that led by way of Poltava!

Napoleon had, in fact, little reason for satisfaction. He had, as he hoped, debouched suddenly into the midst of his opponent's line of defence; he had collected enormous forces upon his chosen point of attack, and had carefully concealed it until the last moment. His troops had made tremendous exertions to carry out his strategy. And yet hardly anything had in reality been achieved. He was in possession of his enemy's empty head-quarters, and that was all. His army had suffered severely in the impetuous rush upon Vilna, while that of Russia had quietly withdrawn out of his reach. The carefully planned blow, which was to have been crushing, had been wasted upon the empty air.

On the 29th there was a violent thunderstorm, followed by five days of continuous rain. The results were most disastrous. Movements of troops, though much impeded, were not absolutely checked; but the vast trains on the Vilna-Kovno road were entirely disorganised. The bad roads and tracks became little better than quagmires. The horses broke down completely under the additional strain, especially since the country could supply very little fodder to replace that left behind in abandoned vehicles. The defects of the transport became evident. The waggons were too heavy for the bad Polish roads, and in order to forward any supplies at all they had to be replaced by country carts, which were only capable of carrying much smaller loads. The natural consequences were a shortage of food supplies, and much marauding in quest of them. The Lithuanians, whom the French were supposed to be freeing from the Russian yoke, were maltreated

CHAPTER IV 49

and plundered everywhere by their so-called deliverers. Requisitions, however unsparing, entirely failed to re-establish the wrecked transport. The army was so huge, its encumbrances so enormous, that the poverty-stricken country could not supply the number of draft animals needed. The artillery alone left 120 guns or more and hundreds of waggons at Vilna owing to lack of horses. The number of the latter lost may be conservatively estimated at 10,000; and some 30,000 soldiers were straggling about the country, marauding for food and committing every kind of outrage.

Napoleon himself remained in Vilna for over a fortnight. The 4th and 6th Corps had only just reached the Niemen, and it was absolutely necessary to bring up to the front the magazines from Königsberg. He also wished to organise Lithuania, or rather to exploit it. A provisional government of French partisans was set up at Vilna; garrisons were distributed; and officials placed over the various towns and districts. The first act of the Government was to order levies of horse and foot for Napoleon's service; one cavalry regiment was to consist entirely of Lithuanian squires, and to be attached to the Imperial Guard. Otherwise the Government could exercise practically no civil functions; its duties were simply such as arose from the military occupation of the country. The peasants were reduced to abject misery by endless requisitions, and by the lawless violence of the stragglers who swarmed everywhere. The French *sous-préfet* of Novi Troki, a place less than 20 miles from Vilna, was plundered and stripped by marauding soldiers on his way thither, and if such an event could take place within a day's march of Napoleon's head-quarters, the state of affairs farther afield may be imagined. Napoleon's stringent orders against pillage and disorder were little better than useless. The pillage arose simply from lack of food, and the latter was the natural outcome of the fact that the expedition was too large to work in the existing conditions. Napoleon had taken immense pains to organise it, and up to a point he had foreseen and provided for everything. But he had not taken into full account physical difficulties: he had, amongst other blunders, organised a wheeled transport for which roads hardly existed, and he had failed to perceive that the vast magnitude of his enterprise automatically created fresh obstacles to success, or at any rate enormously increased those which already existed.

Though on reaching Vilna Napoleon must have realised that his strategy had already in part miscarried, he at once entered upon the execution of the second part of the plan—the crushing of Bagration's army which, as he hoped, was already closely pressed by Jerome. As a fact Bagration left Volkovisk that very day for Minsk, while Jerome did not reach Grodno until the 30th. So far as Jerome was concerned, therefore, Bagration was in no danger, and it was only the vacillation at the Russian Imperial head-quarters which later brought him within measurable distance of destruction. There were other forces within Bagration's sphere of operations which the French Emperor might hope to sweep also into his net. Platov, from Grodno, could hardly hope to reach the First Army with the French in force at Vilna; while the advance-guard of the 4th Corps, after waiting at Orani for orders until the 27th, was also isolated. A more important quarry than either of these, however, was Barclay's detached left wing under Dokhturov, which had only just started from the neighbourhood of Lida, having of course received its orders last.

Napoleon therefore ordered the following movements: Oudinot, supported by Doumerc's Cuirassier Division from Grouchy's Corps, was to follow Wittgenstein from Vilkomirz towards Sventsiani. Murat, with Montbrun's Cavalry Corps and Friant's and Gudin's Infantry Divisions, was directed to pursue Barclay's central columns. Nansouty, with two of his three divisions and Morand's Infantry Division, was directed upon Svir, nearly due east of Vilna, with the object of falling on the flank of Dokhturov's column. Davout with his 4th and 5th Divisions, Pajol's Cavalry Brigade, the Lancers of the Guard, Grouchy's two remaining cavalry divisions, Valence's Cuirassier Division from Nansouty's Corps, and the Legion of the Vistula, about 45,000 men in all, was to advance upon Minsk and intercept the retreat of Bagration. Davout's other light cavalry brigade (Bordesoulle) was sent south-westward from Vilna to scout in that direction, and on the 30th encountered Dorokhov's detachment, which he took for the rear-guard of Baggohufwudt's Corps. Dorokhov, seeing that French troops were now at Vilna, retreated southward in the hope of joining Platov and, ultimately, Bagration.

Meanwhile Davout and Dokhturov, advancing on converging lines, were rapidly approaching. Dokhturov was marching from Lida in two columns, and on the 30th his left flank-guard, consisting of a brigade of Pahlen's cavalry, under General Kreutz, reached Ochmiana on the Vilna-Minsk road just as Pajol's brigade was approaching from Vilna. The danger must, to the Russian generals, have appeared very great, and had they not shown extraordinary energy it would have been so, for although Davout's infantry was considerably in rear of Pajol it could easily arrive next day and assail the left flank of Dokhturov's column as it crossed the road. Dokhturov however, as on another and greater emergency, rose to the occasion. He called upon his men for a great effort; and on the 1st of July the 6th Corps and Pahlen's cavalry crossed the Vilna-Minsk road just ahead of Davout's advancing columns, and pressed on towards Sventsiani. There was some brisk skirmishing at Ochmiana between Kreutz and Pajol; but at night the bulk of Dokhturov's force had reached Svir, after a splendid forced march of 28 miles on an execrable road, with a loss of only some scores of men and a few retarded baggage-waggons. During the march of the 2nd the trains were harassed by Nansouty's advanced guard and a portion of them captured, but that evening Dokhturov was in line with the rest of the First Army about Sventsiani. His prompt decision, admirably seconded by the steadiness and fine marching of his troops, had extricated him safely from a very dangerous position.

Meanwhile Barclay and Wittgenstein had operated their retreat from Vilna and Vilkomirz with little difficulty, and with hardly any fighting. On the 2nd of July the First Army about Sventsiani numbered about 114,000 men; but the Tzar's advisers had now definitely decided not to fight before reaching the Düna. The magazines which could not be carried away were burned; and on the 3rd the retreat was continued, the 2nd, 3rd, 4th and 5th Corps retiring directly on Drissa, covered by a rear-guard under Korff, while Wittgenstein and Dokhturov fell back on the wings.

CHAPTER IV

The retreat was conducted steadily and with no great haste. Alexander and Phull were impatient for the arrival of the army at Drissa, and the latter sent Clausewitz, afterwards the historian of the war, to hasten the march. Barclay, who knew better than Phull the demoralising effects of a hasty retreat, was very angry, and declined to hurry. On the 5th there was a slight action at Davigelishki between Sebastiani's leading brigade under Subervie and Korff's cavalry rear-guard. The French were repulsed, and Prince von Hohenlohe, the Colonel of the 3rd Württemberg Chasseurs, was captured. On the 6th and 8th, however, the Russians made night marches and distanced their pursuers; and on the 11th the whole of the Russian centre and left were at Drissa, while Wittgenstein was at Druia, a little lower down the Düna. There were at Drissa and Dünaburg 19 reserve battalions, all very weak, and 20 fairly strong depôt squadrons. Most of them were assigned to Wittgenstein, who formed them into provisional regiments.

Eugène and St. Cyr reached the Niemen on the 29th of June, and crossed at Prenn on the 30th, one of the pontoon bridges from Kovno being used for the purpose. Thence they marched for Vilna, the 4th Corps leading. The roads were frightfully bad; the rain poured in torrents without intermission, and, to add to their other miseries, the men were half-starved, the trains being even less able to keep up with the march than they had been a few days before. Eugène reached Novi Troki on the 4th, and there rested for two days. St. Cyr had halted about halfway from the Niemen. On the 30th Poniatowski and Latour-Maubourg reached Grodno. King Jerome, with the 8th Corps, was near Augustowo. Reynier, with the 7th, was at Bielsk on the Warsaw-Bielostok road; and Schwarzenberg, advancing with characteristic slowness and caution, some way east of Warsaw. Reynier's special duty was to cover Warsaw, and Jerome could not therefore count upon him until he had been relieved by the Austrians. On the 30th Jerome received orders to march on Ochmiana—this was under the impression that Dokhturov's corps, which had just reached that place, was the army of Bagration. Next day, however, he received fresh directions. Napoleon had ascertained the real identity of the troops at Ochmiana and now ordered his brother to direct the 5th and 8th Corps upon Minsk, and the 7th upon Nesvizh. It is obvious that these contradictory directions must have harassed and confused the inexperienced general whom his brother's will had placed in command of three army corps; and his chief-of-staff Marchand, a good enough divisional leader, was hardly the man to make good his chief's deficiencies. Jerome's troops were so exhausted by the march from Warsaw, over bad roads and in pouring rain, that he felt himself obliged to give them a brief rest at Grodno. Reynier was delayed at the passage of the Narew, Platov having carefully destroyed all the boats. Minsk, Jerome's indicated objective, is nearly 180 miles from Grodno by Novogrodek and Mir, and Nesvizh 140 from Bielostok.

Bagration left Volkovisk for Minsk late on June 28th. He expected to reach it on July 7th, but on the same day Davout was approaching Ochmiana, and could easily arrive before him. On the 30th, however, Colonel Benkendorff, one of Alexander's aides-de-camp, arrived with fresh orders, by which Bagration was to march upon Drissa to join Barclay. Bagration, unaware that Davout was already advancing on Minsk from Vilna, and probably believing that the order would not have been sent had not Napoleon been following Barclay with the bulk of his forces, decided to join his colleague by the shortest possible route. He reached Slonim on July 1st, and on the 3rd arrived at Novogrodek, 40 miles on the Ochmiana road, where the 27th Division, marching from Minsk, joined him. Early on the 4th the head of the column was at Nikolaev-on-Niemen, and, although there were by no means too many pontoons, two bridges were thrown over the flooded river. The passage was begun as early as possible, and the 8th Corps was already across when reports arrived from Platov. He announced that he was at Vologin, some 20 miles from Nikolaev, that he was skirmishing with French cavalry, and that they belonged to Davout's Corps, which was marching on Minsk. Platov had reached Vologin on his way to join Barclay; and there he was met by Dorokhov returning to effect a junction with Bagration at Minsk.

On the 3rd Jerome's advance-guard had started eastward from Grodno, and on the 4th his main body was at last under way. Contradictory orders and lack of information had led Bagration into a situation of grave danger.

The Second Army, with Platov and Dorokhov, counted now about 45,000 regulars, 9000 irregulars and 192 guns. Davout had about 42,000 men, but only 30,000 actually in hand. Jerome was advancing from Grodno with nearly 55,000 more; his advance-guard was some 60 miles from Novogrodek in Bagration's rear.

Bagration, of course, estimated Davout's force as about 70,000 men — the original strength of the 1st Corps; and probably reckoned Jerome's army at about equal numbers. After considering his position, he decided to make a dash for Minsk by way of the left bank of the Niemen and the Slonim-Minsk high-road, hoping that Platov and Dorokhov would be able to impose on Davout and hinder his march until the 8th, by which date Bagration hoped to reach Minsk. The 8th Corps was hastily crossed back over the Niemen; the pontoons were taken up; and the Second Army pushed for the Minsk road beyond Mir, which it reached on the 6th, having covered nearly 40 miles in two days.

As might have been expected, Platov's mass of irregulars and Dorokhov's small detachment could not for a moment withstand the march of Davout's column. When the French infantry pushed steadily forward the Cossacks could only withdraw, and Dorokhov was not strong enough to defend an open town against 30,000 sabres and bayonets. Platov therefore retreated southward to join Bagration, and on the 7th Davout's advanced guard entered Minsk unopposed, Compans, Desaix and Valence arriving next day. He captured in the town over 300,000 pounds of flour, and a vast quantity of forage, as well as much barrack and hospital equipment. On the same day Colbert's Lancer Brigade, which was covering Davout's left flank and rear, entered Vileika, where he found 180,000 pounds of flour, 200,000 of biscuit, 4500 bottles of spirits, and over 200 tons of forage, besides clothing and hospital stores. These captures were the first of any importance that had yet been made. The loss to the Russians was of far less importance than the gain to the French, upon whom inadequate supplies, hard marches, and trying climatic conditions had already had the worst effect. Even in the regiments of Davout's Corps, notoriously the best disciplined and administered of the army, disorder was rife. The Dutch 33rd Léger was a prime offender. During the march to Minsk it left nearly half its numbers behind as marauders; and eventually Napoleon was obliged to issue a special order against them. Davout's anger at its misconduct vented itself for days in his despatches and conversation; and, as was but too often the case with him, he allowed it to exceed the bounds of consideration and decency. The result was a permanent breach between himself and Desaix.

Bagration at Mir learned that Davout, greatly his superior in numbers as he believed, was across his path at Minsk, while Jerome's advance-guard was approaching Novogrodek, and Reynier was on the march from Bielostok to Slonim. He decided, rightly under the circumstances as they presented themselves to him, to march for the Berezina at Bobruisk, which, as we have seen, was fortified, and thence make for the Düna by way of Mohilev and Orsha on the Dnieper. A more perilous march can hardly be imagined, for it would take him right across the front of the French columns moving eastward from Vilna and Minsk. Bagration, however, expected that Davout's objective was Bobruisk, as appears by his action a few days later, and evidently hoped to get round his left flank. On July 7th the 8th Corps marched to Nesvizh on the Brest-Litovsk-Bobruisk high-road, and the 7th to Novi-Svergen on that to Minsk, in order to rally Dorokhov, while Platov, with some Cossacks and one of Raievski's infantry regiments, took post at Mir to guard the road from Novogrodek against Jerome. On the 8th Raievski joined Borozdin, and both corps remained at Nesvizh until the 10th. A halt was imperative to rest the weary troops, who had marched over 150 miles in nine days, on wretched roads and in generally terrible weather; and it was also necessary to enable the jaded trains to get well forward on the road to Bobruisk. Bagration was fuming at the necessity for continual retreat, and on the 8th wrote an excited letter on the subject to Count Arakcheiev.

On the same day Jerome's advance-guard, Rosniecki's Polish Cavalry Division, reached Novogrodek. On the 9th the bulk of the 5th and 8th Corps arrived, Reynier reached Slonim from Bielostok, and Rosniecki started for Mir. On that day his leading brigade under General Turno came in contact with Platov, and a brisk action ensued, as the result of which the Poles were driven back with a loss of over 100 prisoners, besides killed and wounded.

GENERAL PRINCE BAGRATION, COMMANDER OF THE SECOND RUSSIAN ARMY IN 1812

Next day Bagration started Borozdin with the divisions of Neverovski and Prince Karl of Mecklenburg on the road to Bobruisk. He kept the 7th Corps still at Nesvizh to give the men another day's rest, and held back Voronzov's division to support Platov if necessary, reinforcing the latter with one regiment of infantry and three of cavalry, under Major-General Vassilchikov.

Platov had already evacuated Mir and drawn back towards Nesvizh. On the 10th he was attacked by Rosniecki, and a cavalry action on a large scale ensued. Rosniecki had with him six regiments—some 3300 lances and sabres, while Tyskiewicz's brigade, about 1200 more, was at Mir. Platov and Vassilchikov had at

CHAPTER IV

their immediate disposal at least 2000 regular cavalry and 3000 Cossacks. Rosniecki's first two brigades, including that of Turno, and Vassilchikov's regulars crashed together in a furious hand-to-hand combat, with fairly equal fortune; but the third brigade coming up in support was enveloped by a cloud of Cossacks and broken. Thereupon the whole division was forced to give ground, hotly pressed by the Russian Hussars, Dragoons and Cossacks. A complete rout was only averted by the gallant advance of Tyskiewicz's brigade, which covered the retreat and enabled the broken regiments to rally near Mir. The Russians thereupon drew off. They had suffered considerably, and two Cossack colonels had been killed. But the Poles had lost over 700 men, and it may be imagined that the morale of the Polish army was considerably shaken.

On the 11th Raievski and Voronzov evacuated Nesvizh and marched some 20 miles to Romanovo, while Platov fell back on Nesvizh. On the 12th Bagration made another long march to Slutsk, while Platov followed to Romanovo.

At Slutsk Bagration learned that French troops had been located at Svisloc on the Berezina, about 27 miles north of Bobruisk. The inference was that Davout was marching to anticipate him at the latter place. He sent forward Raievski at once to the threatened fortress with the 7th Corps and some cavalry and Cossacks, while the 8th waited at Slutsk for the arrival of Platov.

Romanovo lay on the small river Morvez, which was there spanned by a bridge. The advance-guard of Jerome's army was formed on the 14th, as before, by Rosniecki's division and Tyskiewicz's brigade; Latour-Maubourg, with the German and Polish Cuirassiers forming the rest of his cavalry corps, was following some distance to the rear. Platov had part of his force in advance of the bridge, and as Tyskiewicz's brigade came on it was suddenly charged, cut up and driven back. The Russians then retired across the bridge, and Rosniecki, following, plunged into a heavy cross-fire from Platov's infantry regiment and horse artillery, and only extricated himself with severe loss. The whole division was thrust back in disorder until it reached Latour-Maubourg and his cuirassier division. The Polish losses had been very heavy; the 1st Chasseurs had been practically destroyed. Platov took 300 prisoners. He knew better than to expose his irregulars and light horsemen to the charge of the Saxon and Westphalian Cuirassiers and retired in the night to Slutsk. This released Borozdin, who followed in the track of Raievski; and in this way the Second Army, Raievski leading and Platov bringing up the rear, arrived at Bobruisk, where it was completely concentrated on the 18th. It had suffered much from fatigue and sickness during its long and painful marches, and Bagration felt it necessary to use six of the weak reserve battalions in the fortress to recruit his depleted regiments. But the Second Army was at least safe. A glance at the map will show that all the way from Nesvizh it had the Pinsk morasses on its right; and had Jerome and Davout been able to combine their attacks, the result to it might well have been fatal.

In following Bagration on his march to Bobruisk the course of events elsewhere has been somewhat anticipated. On July 14th King Jerome had thrown up his command. A little previously he had quarrelled with Vandamme, who commanded the 8th Corps under him. Vandamme was a man whose general character is entitled to no kind of respect. His conduct in Germany had been abominable. He was, however, a thorough soldier, and could not endure Jerome's easy-going ideas of military discipline. The consequence was an open quarrel and the supersession of Vandamme. Napoleon, who knew his insubordinate disposition, did not traverse Jerome's action. But the delay at Grodno and the failure to close with Bagration kindled his wrath, all the more so since his own immediate operations had miscarried. He vented his rage and disappointment in two violently abusive letters, and Jerome left the army.

As regards the degree of blame which attaches to Jerome, it is obvious that, but for the ill-advised order to march upon Drissa, Bagration would have been in no danger. He left Volkovisk on June 28th; Jerome did not even reach Grodno until the 30th. The vile Polish roads, rendered worse by the rain, made marching extremely difficult. A rest may well have been necessary for the over-worked and ill-fed troops; and Jerome was obliged to wait until Reynier had been relieved by the slowly advancing Austrians. Owing to the orders which he had received from head-quarters, Bagration all but marched into the midst of the forces manœuvring to intercept him. It is clear that, had Jerome moved eastward from Grodno at once, he would have pressed his antagonist hard. On the other hand, he had to take into account the harassed state of his troops, their lack of adequate supplies, the miserable roads, the absence of Reynier, the slowness of Schwarzenberg, and last, not least, the hidden Russian army of Tormazov, which might prove very formidable. Napoleon in his place would probably have taken the risk of an advance of Tormazov on Warsaw. Jerome did not, and, indeed, seeing his position as a subordinate, could not, do so. It is possible that he did not act with all the vigour which circumstances demanded; but in that case the blame must be laid at the door of Napoleon for appointing to a vitally important command a man who lacked the necessary qualifications for it. Napoleon also was directing manœuvres on the basis of hypotheses which might, and in fact did, prove unfounded. He appears rather to have ignored geographical and climatic conditions; he was certainly ill-informed as to distances. Finally he was committing the same error which had already cost him dear in Spain, in endeavouring to direct complicated strategic manœuvres from a distance; and the optimism which was becoming a mental disease with him badly affected his calculations.

The Emperor, apparently believing that Bagration was stronger than was actually the case, and that he might break northward, directed Eugène with the 4th Corps on July 7th in the track of Davout; but soon becoming aware that his intelligence was false, recalled him to Smorgoni, where he arrived on the 12th. On the 14th Eugène left to support the advance on Drissa, marching by way of Vileika, where the magazines captured by Colbert afforded supplies. Nevertheless food was invariably scanty. The wretched roads wore out the men, who fell sick or straggled in numbers. The horses fared still worse, and many died. St. Cyr, meanwhile, had marched by Novi Troki to Vilna, whence he was directed by Glubokoïe also on Drissa. The march of the unhappy Bavarians will later be alluded to. On July 11th Napoleon ordered Mortier with part of the Guard also upon Glubokoïe, and next day the first detachment of the Head-quarters Staff was directed thither.

De Fezensac, who was with this detachment, notes that the Young Guard were already suffering from the effects of the tropical heat, scanty rations and fatigue—especially the newly formed "Flanqueurs- Chasseurs." Yet Napoleon in a letter of the 11th suggests that Mortier can live on the country!

The 10th Corps, after clearing the right bank of the Niemen, had been directed north-eastward towards Mitau and Riga, which latter place it was destined to besiege. The operations of the 10th Corps were so isolated and otherwise of so languid a nature that they may for the moment be ignored. Here it is only necessary to observe that the 10th Corps was moving north-eastward on a broad front, the Prussians advancing on Mitau, the 10th Division, Poles and Germans under Grandjean, on Dünaburg. At the latter place there was a bridge-head garrisoned by some reserve battalions.

Davout, having occupied Minsk, remained there for some days. The halt was necessary in order to rally the stragglers and re-establish discipline. It was also utilised in commencing the organisation of Minsk as one of the main depôts of the army, for which its situation at the intersection of the Warsaw-Moscow and Vilna-Kiev high-roads admirably fitted it.

Davout had rightly inferred that his occupation of Minsk would oblige Bagration to retire upon Bobruisk. He might then endeavour to march up the left bank of the Berezina to the Minsk-Smolensk road at Borisov or Bobr, and thence press on to join Barclay. The Marshal accordingly sent forward his advance-guard, under Bordesoulle, to reconnoitre Borisov and occupy it if possible. He estimated Bagration's strength, from the reports of spies and peasants, at 16 to 18 regiments of infantry and 120 guns, besides cavalry. The evaluation was much below the truth, and gives the impression that his informants had only seen and counted the regiments of one of Bagration's two corps and the 27th Division.

Borisov was undefended. Working parties were busy almost until the last on the entrenchments of the bridge-head; but the only troops available to defend it were two skeleton battalions, which retired on the approach of the French to Mohilev. The place was occupied by Bordesoulle on the 11th, and there and in the vicinity were taken a large amount of flour and forage, about 80,000 pounds of salt, 16 spiked guns, 4000 cannon-balls and shells, some thousands of entrenching tools, and a quantity of hospital equipment and supplies.

Davout's other cavalry brigade, under Pajol, was directed on Igumen, 35 miles south-east of Minsk, and thence also upon the Berezina. On the 13th it captured a Russian convoy of 180 waggons, which, however, being left slenderly guarded, was retaken next day by Cossacks. Pajol, meanwhile, occupied the crossings of the Berezina at Berezino and elsewhere, and awaited the arrival of Davout. He reconnoitred towards Bobruisk, and it was the presence of one of his detachments at Svisloсz which alarmed Bagration and induced him to precipitate his march.

Davout decided that to advance on Bobruisk would probably be waste of time, since Bagration could almost certainly reach the place before him. He therefore rightly determined to march for Mohilev, 110 miles east of Minsk, and only some 60 from Berezino. Bagration was on the 14th still two days' march west of Bobruisk with his advance-guard, while Borozdin and Platov were yet farther off, and could not reach the fortress until the 18th. Thence to Mohilev was four long days' march on bad roads, while Davout had a much shorter distance to traverse. Even if he reached Bobruisk before the Russians, they could cross the Berezina under cover of the fortifications.

While Davout remained about Minsk, Grouchy, with his two cavalry divisions and Colbert's Lancers, supported by Claparède's Polish Legion, was making a sweep northward and westward to the great bend of the Dnieper near Orsha. On the 14th he entered Lepel, 48 miles north of Borisov, capturing large magazines of food-stuffs and forage, besides about 160 Russian prisoners. He then turned south-eastward to Orsha, which was occupied on the 18th without resistance. The magazines of provisions were even more important than those at Lepel, and a number of boats and pontoons were also taken.

The withdrawal of King Jerome left Davout in command of the whole Napoleonic right wing. Napoleon had intended that the Marshal should assume chief command only when the junction of the two forces should be complete, and later he reprimanded him for doing so before it had been effected. It is difficult to perceive what other course lay open to Davout. He made various efforts to induce the offended King to retain his command, but in vain: Jerome was thoroughly disgusted.

Davout's advanced guard left Minsk on July 12th, and by the 15th his main body was concentrated near Igumen. Bagration's whole force could not reach Bobruisk until the 18th, the French thus had a long start in the race to Mohilev. The untrustworthy 33rd Léger was left to garrison Minsk. The 5th Corps and Latour-Maubourg were directed by Igumen on Mohilev, and the 8th, temporarily commanded by General Tharreau, by Minsk and Borisov on Orsha.

The 7th Corps was ordered back to Slonim by Napoleon. The Emperor, deceived by Tormazov's long inactivity, had made up his mind that he need fear nothing from him. As a fact it was lack of preparation and the necessity for completing it which was keeping Tormazov inactive; his army was very far from a sham. Napoleon, however, deciding that the 34,000 Austrians were unnecessary in that region, determined to call them up to the centre. Schwarzenberg had crossed the Bug at Mogilnitza on July 3rd, and a week later reached Pruzhani, 60 miles on the Brest-Litovsk-Minsk road. Detachments occupied Pinsk and other places, and captured large supplies and immense quantities of salt. Otherwise the Austrians had been inactive. The spirit both of officers and men was decidedly hostile to the enterprise in which they were engaged, and though Schwarzenberg himself was a Francophile he was naturally very cautious, and probably under orders to do as little as possible. Such considerations would naturally incline Napoleon to wish to have the Austrians under his own eye. Reynier, with the 7th Corps, was to take Schwarzenberg's place and cover the frontier of the Grand Duchy of Warsaw. These plans, however, could not be executed, for on July 23rd the Russian Third Army appeared on the scene with momentous results, and both Schwarzenberg and Reynier had to be diverted to check it.

CHAPTER IV

Davout crossed the Berezina at Berezino on July 15th and advanced on Mohilev, leaving Pajol with three regiments of cavalry and one of infantry to guard communications. On the 19th he was near Mohilev with Compans, Desaix and Valence. The place was defended only by four skeleton battalions, and was easily carried by Desaix on the 20th. Eighteen officers and 200 men were taken; with 120,000 rations of biscuit and flour, some thousands of muskets, and several thousand pounds of gunpowder.

Pajol on the 19th reported that Bobruisk was full of Russian troops. Davout therefore inferred that he would soon be attacked, and made preparations accordingly. He called up Claparède from the northward, where he was supporting Grouchy, and sent for his reserve artillery, which was still in rear. He had already sent to Poniatowski and Tharreau to hasten their march. He was by no means at his ease, since he had, as he says, only 16,000 men (an underestimate) and expected to be attacked by 50,000. He looked about for a position in which he could receive battle against superior numbers, and found one at Saltanovka, about 8 miles on the Bobruisk road.

Bagration had received orders to advance on the Düna by way of Orsha, and on the 19th he started Raievski with the 7th Corps, Platov, Dorokhov and the bulk of Sievers' cavalry, for Mohilev. Borozdin, with the divisions of Karl of Mecklenburg and Neverovski, followed on the 20th, while Voronzov brought up the rear with his division of combined grenadier companies, the 5th Chasseurs from Paskievich's division and the Kharkov Dragoons. The garrison of Bobruisk, under General Ignatiev, consisted now of about 6000 men. The artillery armament was fairly powerful, but the fortifications were by no means very formidable. General Zapolski, commanding the reserve troops at Mozyr, was ordered to hold firm there so as to cover Tormazov's line of communications with Kiev.

Bagration himself was furious at the necessity for retreating, and his letters are couched in terms of angry disgust at the inaction of the main army. "You have 100,000 men," he says in one place. "Well, fight!" And elsewhere, "Why don't we fight? We are worse than the Prussians and Austrians." His troops were weakened by nineteen days of marching in rain, heat and over vile tracks. Had there only been a little fighting Bagration would have been less exasperated. He says in one letter that he had galloped forty versts on the chance of seeing an engagement—an admission which throws a somewhat amusing light upon his impetuous character.

On the 21st Bagration's leading troops reached Staroi Bykhov, some 25 miles south of Mohilev, and on the same day the advanced Cossacks, under Sissoiev, met the remains of the Mohilev garrison pursued by the 3rd Chasseurs-à-cheval, the only light cavalry regiment which Davout had retained. Unexpectedly assailed, the Chasseurs were broken and pursued to within a few miles of Mohilev, losing over 200 prisoners alone, and only rallying under cover of the 85th Regiment, which moved out to their relief.

Davout, having ascertained that behind the Cossacks were at least two Russian infantry divisions, collected on the 22nd his whole disposable force in his chosen position at Saltanovka. His left rested on the marshy bank of the Dnieper and was unassailable. His front was covered by a stream flowing in a difficult ravine, spanned at Saltanovka, some 1200 yards from the Dnieper, by a wooden bridge. About a mile farther up stood the hamlet and water-mill of Fatova, where a second rivulet, flowing parallel to the Dnieper, joins the first. On this, a mile from Fatova, lay the village of Selets. About Saltanovka there were thick woods, especially on the north bank of the stream; farther west the ground was more open, but broken and difficult. Generally speaking, the position was extremely strong; only on the right was it at all assailable. Desaix's division guarded it, the 85th Regiment, under General Friederichs, on the left, the 108th on the right. The bridge was barricaded; the villages were prepared for defence. One of Compans' regiments supported Desaix near Selets; the other two were held back to meet a turning movement, and only brought up later. Valence's Cuirassiers and the remains of the 3rd Chasseurs were in reserve near Selets. The whole force counted some 20,000 men with 56 guns. Claparède and the artillery reserve could not arrive before the 23rd.

On the 22nd the head of Bagration's army was at Dashkova, 5 miles south of Saltanovka. Bagration ordered Raievski with the 7th Corps and Sievers' cavalry to attack next day. His reason seems to be expressed in his letter to Raievski on the 22nd. He tells him that he has only 6000 men in his front, according to his own intelligence; he is therefore to attack with God's help and enter Mohilev on the heels of the enemy. Bagration's reasoning clearly is that, Mohilev being only held by a detachment, Raievski may easily clear the way, and the army get through towards Orsha before the arrival of the French main body. There is no indication that he intended to turn Davout's right with Borozdin and Neverovski while Raievski was attacking in front: they could not reach Dashkova until late on the 23rd.

CHAPTER IV

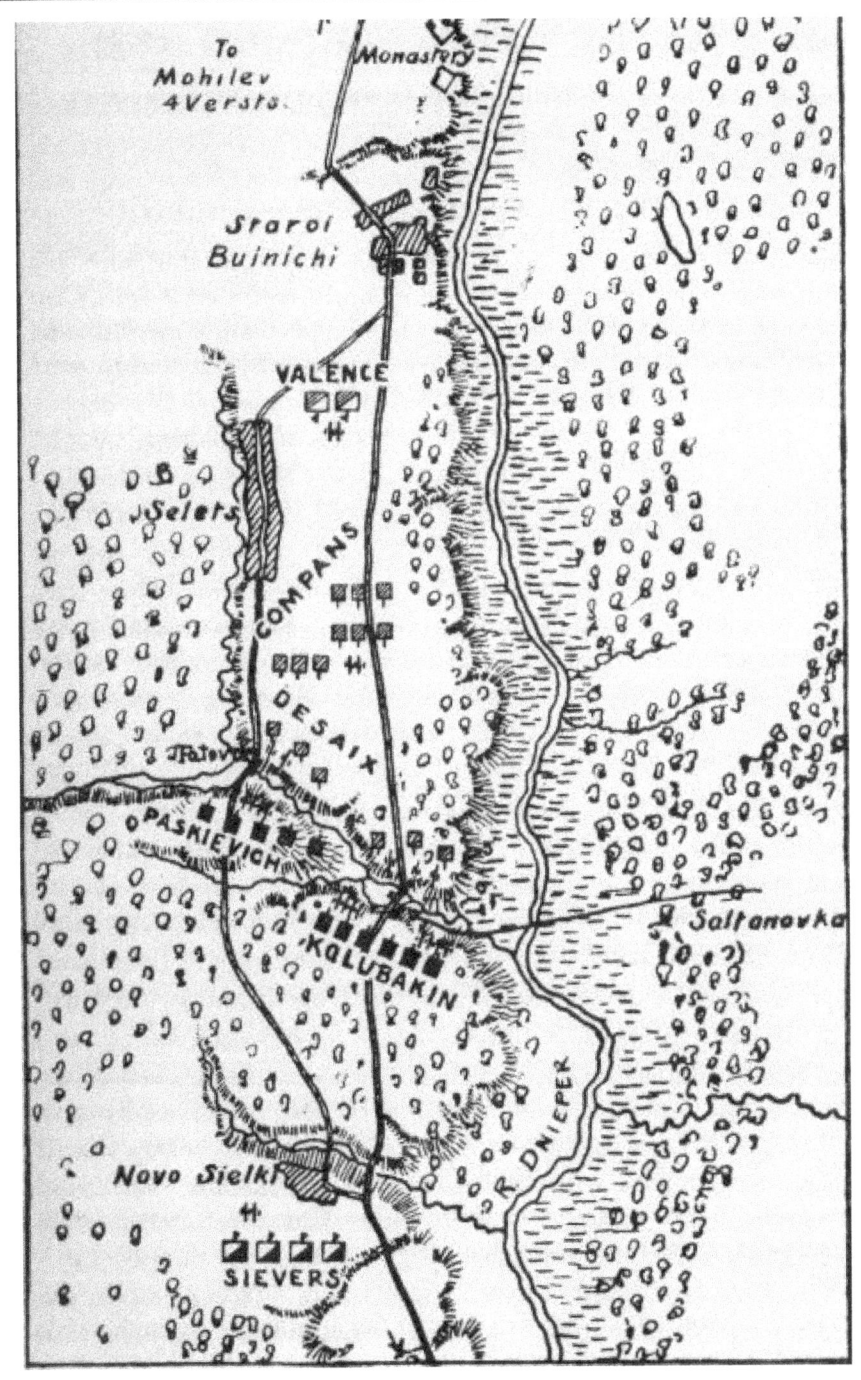

1 verst = 2/3 mile. Russian Troops shown black, French shaded.
THE BATTLE OF SALTANOVKA (July 23rd, 1812)
Fought by Marshal Davout to check Bagration's advance on Mohilev.

Raievski advanced from Dashkova at 6 a.m. on the 23rd. He had with him about 17,000 men with 84 or 96 guns. His cavalry he left in reserve at Novo Sielki, 3 miles from Dashkova. He ordered Paskievich's division to endeavour to turn the French right, promising that as soon as the attack made headway he would hurl Kolubakin's division at Saltanovka.

Paskievich, driving in the French skirmishers, fought his way across the rivulet, and, bringing up a battery to cover his advance, pushed on against the 108th Regiment beyond it. Raievski, marking the advancing roll of Paskievich's fire, believed that the time had come, and sent forward Kolubakin's division. The Russians flung themselves at the bridge, drove off a battalion of the 85th which endeavoured to take them in flank, and pressed doggedly on under a murderous fire which swept them away by platoons. Unable to advance, with the stolid courage of their race they refused to fall back, and stood facing the French volleys until Raievski withdrew them.

Paskievich's leading troops, attacking Fatova, were charged and repulsed across the stream by two battalions of the 108th under Colonel Achard. Achard, in his turn, hotly pursuing, was driven back to his own side; and Paskievich, again advancing, carried Fatova, and penetrated almost to the outskirts of Selets; but his offensive power had exhausted itself, and before the heavy fire of his well-posted and well-protected opponents he could advance no farther. Meanwhile Raievski, determined not to abandon his lieutenant, called up Kolubakin's reserves, and made another desperate attempt upon the bridge, himself and General Vassilchikov leading on foot, with reckless bravery. All was in vain; the splendid infantry went forward only to die, and as the last attack reeled back from Friederichs' front, an aide-de-camp arrived to report Paskievich's failure. It was now past four o'clock, and Davout, feeling safe on his right, ordered forward Compans with the 61st and 111th Regiments and began a general advance. Prisoners told Raievski that Davout had about Mohilev 3 infantry and 2 cavalry divisions, and, believing that he was opposed by overwhelming forces, he gave orders to retreat. Compans followed as far as Novo Sielki, but as the road was practically a defile between woods he could do nothing to seriously harass the Russian retreat, and Davout's handful of light cavalry was of course useless. Claparède and the heavy artillery reached Mohilev during the closing stages of the battle. Raievski at Dashkova was met by Bagration, and the latter, judging that the way was barred by the bulk of Davout's corps, decided to pass the Dnieper and retreat on Smolensk.

Raievski gave his loss as 2504 killed, wounded and missing. That of the French was naturally, under the conditions of the fighting, much less. Davout stated it at less than 900. General Desaix was slightly wounded. Davout was on worse terms with him than ever, and pointedly ignored him in his reports.

Bagration wrote to Barclay that he had failed to break through at Mohilev, and so would make for Smolensk. On the 24th Platov and Dorokhov—except one fatigued infantry regiment—forded the Dnieper at Verkalobovo, and pushed on to join Barclay. Raievski, supported by Voronzov, held firm at Dashkova. Borozdin went back to Staroi Bykhov, while the pontooneers were sent on to bridge the Dnieper at Novi Bykhov, 14 miles farther south. On the 25th Borozdin marched for the selected place of passage, and Raievski followed to Staroi Bykhov, unpursued by Davout, who could not meddle with Sievers' and Vassilchikov's squadrons. The Second Army crossed the Dnieper on the 26th and 27th, and marched rapidly upon Mstislavl. On the same day Platov was in touch with Barclay, having passed the Dnieper at Dubrovna on the 27th. Davout had remained practically inactive. He has been blamed for his inertness; but it must be remembered that he was inferior in numbers to Bagration. He had in hand only some 25,000 men, and his nearest reinforcement was the 5th Corps, which, harassed by fatigue, disease and lack of supplies, only reached the Berezina on the 24th. On the 25th Bordesoulle reported that Bagration was bridging the Dnieper, and on the same day Latour-Maubourg sent a detailed and fairly accurate statement of Bagration's strength, which probably made Davout more than ever inclined to caution. On the 27th Poniatowski's leading brigade was at last within reach, but on the same day Bordesoulle reported that Bagration was across the Dnieper. Whatever Davout might have wished to attempt it was now too late. On the 29th Napoleon sent orders for him to canton his three corps along the Dnieper.

As has been seen, the First Russian Army had concentrated at the camp of Drissa, but it had scarcely arrived when proposals for its abandonment were made.

The Russian army can scarcely be said to have had a commander at this moment. Clausewitz gives a graphic account of the disorder that prevailed. The Emperor was of course nominally the supreme head, and he was more or less at the mercy of his personal entourage. He himself believed in Phull, but everyone else distrusted the Prussian theorist—certainly not without good reason. The Tzar's relations often exercised undue influence over him, and were distrusted and disliked by the courtiers and soldiers; the courtiers were at odds with the military men; finally, the native Russian officers were jealous of the foreigners. Barclay himself was included among the objects of their dislike, and Colonel von Wollzogen, one of his German aides, was regarded with poisonous hatred, merely because his manners were unpleasing! Projects of strategy were almost as numerous as advisers. Count Lieven, late ambassador at Berlin, had there seen much of Scharnhörst, who considered that no attempt should be made to fight before reaching Smolensk. Barclay protested repeatedly against remaining at Drissa, and he was supported by the Tzar's relative, Alexander of Württemberg. Paulucci, the chief-of-staff, declared furiously that the man who had selected such a position could only be either a fool or a traitor, and resigned.

The camp of Drissa lay in a bend of the Düna between Drissa and Bridzievo. Its land front was about 6500 yards in length, that on the river about 8000. The land front had ten redoubts, connected by batteries. In front of redoubts 6, 7, 8 and 9 was an abattis 2000 yards long and 120 broad; but before the left wing a marshy wood gave excellent cover to an attacking enemy. Two more redoubts strengthened the first line of defence. The second was formed of five closed works, and another formed a kind of citadel behind it. Communication was maintained with the right bank by four bridges, which had only just been constructed and were incompletely protected with outworks. The subsidiary means of defence—pitfalls, palisades, entanglements and abattis—were also very incomplete. The stores were largely accumulated in wooden sheds in the village of Drissa, opposite the left wing and exposed to hostile fire.

These tactical defects were, however, slight as compared with the strategic disadvantages. Lying far away from the Moscow road it could afford no defence against an enemy who chose to advance by that line, and it did not even cover that to St. Petersburg. The roads which led to it were mere country tracks, which ruined the convoys which had to use them. Moreover, by retiring on Drissa the First Army had actually retreated away from, instead of towards, Bagration, and if the two separated forces wished to effect a junction they could do so only by retiring far to the rear, or by perilous marches across the front of Napoleon's advancing columns.

Alexander, perhaps at Phull's instigation, reprimanded Bagration for retreating, as if he could have done anything else. Finally, however, Phull was induced to give way, and it was decided, just in time, to evacuate Drissa. The 1st Corps was ordered to cover the St. Petersburg road, and on July 14th the rest of the army began its march for Vitebsk.

The French advanced troops were already almost on the Düna. On the 13th Oudinot with Legrand's division made a somewhat unnecessary demonstration against the bridge-head of Dünaburg. On the night of the 14-15th Wittgenstein bridged the Düna and sent across a detachment under Kulnev, which surprised St. Genies' cavalry brigade, and captured the brigadier and over 100 men. Meanwhile the First Army pursued its march, covered by the river, and reached Polotsk on the 18th.

On July 16th Napoleon left Vilna and on the 18th arrived at Glubokoïe. Next day, learning that Drissa was abandoned, he turned Eugène towards Vitebsk, placed the cavalry of the 6th Corps under his orders, and called Grouchy also to join him. The 6th Corps was marching for Glubokoïe, already in a sad condition owing to heat, bad roads and deficiency of bread. It should have received 70,000 bread rations at Vilna, but so completely had the commissariat broken down that only 27,000 could be furnished. Diarrhœa and dysentery had broken out; and the unhappy Bavarians fell out in thousands, mostly to die untended by the wayside.

Murat's three infantry divisions, under the general command of Comte Lobau, were extended from Perebrod, 20 miles west of Drissa, towards the southeast. Oudinot was approaching on the left. Ney and Nansouty were near Desna, some 20 miles below Drissa.

The conditions among the leading troops were less pitiable than with the 6th Corps, but still very bad. Supplies were scanty. Bread was scarce; the troops were lucky if they received even flour. Owing to the breakdown of the transport clothing and equipment—especially footgear—were becoming deficient. The roads were bad, the heat was great and there was much sickness. Lack of supplies led to a general slackening of the bonds of discipline. The country was ravaged by marauding stragglers, who committed every kind of outrage. All efforts to check the evil failed completely.

On the 18th Barclay was at Polotsk. He rightly inferred that Napoleon would direct his attacks against the Russian left, and informed Alexander that he must continue his retreat on Vitebsk. Fresh orders were given to Wittgenstein; and the reserve troops at Dünaburg and elsewhere were placed under his command.

At Polotsk the Tzar left the army. It was a wise step, for he was useless at the front, while at the seat of government his presence would be invaluable. Paulucci accompanied him, and was replaced by Major-General Yermólov, while Colonel Toll became Quartermaster-General. On bidding farewell Alexander bade Barclay not to endanger his army, for it was the only one that Russia possessed. This injunction undoubtedly made a strong impression upon Barclay, and is the best explanation of his irresolution some weeks later.

On July 20th Napoleon's plan was definitely formed. He would turn Barclay's left by throwing forward the Guard and the 4th and 6th Corps to Bechenkoviczi on the road to Vitebsk, while Murat and Ney contained the Russians in front, and Oudinot occupied Drissa and threatened their right.

Barclay, however, was already moving. On the 19th Uvarov's cavalry corps started from Polotsk, and by the 23rd the entire army was collected round Vitebsk. There Barclay heard that Bagration had reached Mohilev, and wrote begging him to hasten his march on Orsha. He sent Major-General Tuchkov IV with his infantry brigade, 3 cavalry regiments and 1 of Cossacks, towards Babinovichi on the Orsha road, and Lieutenant-General Count Ostermann-Tolstoï, who had succeeded Shuvalov (retired through illness) with the 4th Corps, a brigade of Dragoons, and the Hussars of the Guard and of Sumi, towards Ostrovno on the way to Bechenkoviczi. The rest of the Russian army remained at Vitebsk to rest and reorganise.

The advance-guard of the French 4th Corps was already at Bechenkoviczi. Oudinot had two divisions at Polotsk and the third at Drissa. Lobau was to Eugène's left rear, with Ney some 20 miles farther back: Murat, with Nansouty's corps, was near Bechenkoviczi; Montbrun was moving up the right bank of the Düna towards Vitebsk; Napoleon with the Guard was at Kamen, about 21 miles from Bechenkoviczi. The unhappy 6th Corps was toiling along the Glubokoïe-Polotsk road.

At 6 a.m. on the 25th Murat's and Ostermann's outposts collided near Ostrovno. Here the road, coming from Vitebsk between woods, made a sharp turn to the right, and another equally abrupt to the left some way farther on. The leading Russian regiment, the Guard Hussars, charged headlong and, sabring the French pickets, blundered up against Piré's brigade in the rear. It was driven back with heavy loss upon a horse battery which was following, and in the confusion the French captured six guns. Ostermann, who was some way behind, sent forward the Sumi Hussars to check the French advance. He then formed for battle, with Choglokov's division deployed across the road and Bakhmetiev's in columns behind, and in this order the 4th Corps marched forward to Ostrovno, and took position between the woods.

Ostermann had in all 18 battalions and 20 squadrons—some 13,000 men and perhaps 60 guns. The French troops which could take part in the action included Bruyère's and St. Germain's cavalry divisions and Delzons' infantry division—10,000 bayonets, 6000 lances and sabres, with about 40 guns.

Ostermann proved a very poor tactician. Against infantry and artillery in position the French cavalry could do nothing, and until the head of Delzons' division, the two battalions of the 8th Léger, arrived the action was confined to some spectacular but useless cavalry skirmishing. When the 8th Léger came up it was attacked by three Russian battalions, which moved forward against it, but they were charged in flank by two cavalry regiments and driven back. They should not have been exposed alone in front of the position. Ostermann then attacked both flanks of the French at once, but with only four battalions, which were charged by the cavalry and broken. Delzons' division was now coming into action, and Ostermann withdrew to a position two miles farther back. The action was certainly not to his credit.

Barclay on this day had sent Lieutenant-General Konovnitzin with his division of the 3rd Corps (less Tuchkov IV's brigade) and the 1st Cavalry Corps to support his advanced guard. Early on the 26th Ostermann retired behind Konovnitzin, who took up a defensive position behind a ravine, with a wood on his left. At 10 a.m. Murat arrived in his front with Delzons and Nansouty. Huard's brigade (two regiments) was directed against the Russian right, Roussel's upon the left; the 106th Regiment and Nansouty's cavalry, except one brigade which covered the left, remained in reserve.

Roussel's troops found much difficulty in penetrating the wood on the Russian left and, assailed by Konovnitzin's reserve, were driven out and over the ravine. The Russians, however, pursuing heedlessly, were repulsed by a charge of one of Nansouty's brigades; and Roussel, rallying his troops, penetrated into the wood. Huard, meanwhile, was steadily pushing forward on the Russian right, and, being presently supported by the 106th, gained ground rapidly. Konovnitzin drew off in good order and retreated on Vitebsk, little harassed by the way, the broken and wooded nature of the country greatly impeding the pursuit. Napoleon, wishing to deliver a general action at Vitebsk, directed Eugène not to press too closely, lest Barclay should take alarm and retreat without fighting.

On the 27th Napoleon had near Ostrovno the Guard (less Claparède and Colbert), Lobau's three divisions, the 3rd and 4th Corps, and Nansouty's and Montbrun's cavalry, about 120,000 men in all. The 2nd Corps was at Drissa and Polotsk, in contact with Wittgenstein, and the 6th at Uchach, 60 miles in rear of Ostrovno. During the night Konovnitzin had been joined by the corps commander, Tuchkov I, with Strogonov's division; and the united force now retired on Vitebsk.

Barclay had made up his mind to fight at Vitebsk. His reasons, as detailed to the Tzar, were that Napoleon had in hand only the Guard, the 3rd and 4th Corps, and Murat's cavalry, while the steadiness of the Russian troops in the recent fighting gave good hopes of victory; and that he felt it his duty to draw Napoleon's attention upon him and give Bagration time wherein to come up. As regards the first reason he did not know that Napoleon had with him three divisions of Davout's corps, and was therefore 30,000 stronger than his estimate. Respecting the second, if Bagration really were making the terribly dangerous march from Mohilev

CHAPTER IV

by Orsha and Babinovichi, Barclay was indeed bound to fight for the sake of his comrade. That the plan of attempting a junction by way of Orsha was hazardous is clear, but it scarcely affects Barclay's reasoning. On the assumption that Bagration was coming by the Orsha road, and that Napoleon was only 90,000 strong, his determination was not unwise.

The Russian army was drawn up on the 27th behind the Luchizza, a stream flowing into the Düna just below Vitebsk. Clausewitz criticises the position severely; but he seems rather prone to ignore the fact that good tactical positions are not plentiful in Russia—as he himself elsewhere admits. Strategically it had the grave defect of lying almost parallel to the Orsha road by which communications with Bagration were expected to be established. But it is at any rate certain that it would, like the faulty position of Eylau, have been defended with desperate courage. An advance-guard of 8 battalions, 2 Cossack regiments and all the regular light cavalry was stationed on the left bank of the Luchizza, under General Pahlen, the commander of the 3rd Cavalry Corps.

Though the Russian army had suffered less than its opponents during the long marches from the Niemen to Vitebsk it had not escaped considerable losses by disease and fatigue. The reinforcements along the Düna had mostly been assigned to Wittgenstein. Platov and Dorokhov were also absent. Barclay's strength at Vitebsk appears to have been about 82,000 men, of whom 14,000 were cavalry—mostly regulars—and over 400 excellently horsed guns.

On the 27th the French advance-guard moved upon Vitebsk, and there was some brisk fighting between Pahlen's detachment and Broussier's and Bruyère's divisions. The Cossacks of the Russian Guard overthrew the 16th Chasseurs-à-cheval, who endeavoured to stop them with carbine fire, and made a mad dash right among Broussier's infantry squares, while some Voltigeurs of the 9th French Regiment, pushed across the Luchizza, defended themselves brilliantly against a cloud of Russian horsemen. Pahlen steadily retired as the French advanced, and Napoleon did not wish to press, since his concentration would not be complete until the evening. Ney was still on the march from Ostrovno, and Montbrun on the other bank of the Düna opposite Vitebsk. In the afternoon Barclay received Bagration's despatch announcing that he was marching for Smolensk. Barclay at once issued orders for a retreat. In the night the whole army, leaving its camp-fires burning, evacuated its position and moved silently away in three columns, General Dokhturov, with the 5th and 6th Corps, marching directly on Smolensk by way of Rudnia, the rest of the army taking the more circuitous routes by Surazh and Poriechie. Dokhturov's march was covered by a rear-guard, under Major-General Shevich, that of the other two columns by Pahlen with 14 battalions and 32 squadrons. The withdrawal from the position was a triumph of good management and discipline. Scarce a single straggler was left behind, and the retiring columns were well on their way before the fact of their departure was ascertained. The diverging lines of retreat confused the French cavalry, and not until the 30th was Murat definitely able to report that Barclay had retreated on Smolensk. Except for some not very serious skirmishing between the advanced guards of the French and the rear-guards of the Russians there was no fighting. The Russians moved at a pace which set pursuit at defiance. On July 31st Dokhturov was outside Smolensk, having marched 80 miles in four days. On August 1st Barclay arrived from Poriechie. Bagration, hurrying from Novi Bykhov by Propoïsk and Mstistavl, came up two days later. His troops had covered 150 miles through sands, bogs and forests in eight days. The pedestrian feats of the Russians are remarkable. Since June 28 the Second Army had marched over 540 miles, giving an average of 15 miles a day. As there were some days of rest or battle the actual pace was much more rapid.

The Russian losses in the fighting round Vitebsk may be estimated at about 4000, with 6 (or 8) guns. Those of the French may have been a little less.

Napoleon entered Vitebsk on the 28th. He must have been bitterly disappointed at the negative result of his operations. Once more the Russians had quietly with drawn out of reach at the very moment of contact. The French losses through fatigue and disease had been relatively enormous, and the manœuvre of Vitebsk had failed as completely as the manœuvre at Vilna. In a sense the failure was even worse, for the Russians had emerged from the situation with a great strategic success to their credit. In spite of blunders and miscalculation, despite contradictory orders and lack of any unity of command, Barclay and Bagration had achieved what had been the primary object of their weary marches and manœuvres to the rear, and had effected their union.

CHAPTER V
THE OPERATIONS ABOUT SMOLENSK

With the arrival of Napoleon's main army on the Düna and Dnieper the first stage of the campaign came to an end. To all appearance the invaders had gained immense advantages. Nearly the whole of the ancient Duchy of Lithuania, together with most of Kurland, had passed into Napoleon's hands almost without a blow having been struck in their defence. A number of considerable towns had been occupied, and a great quantity of Russian stores captured. The Russian armies, which six weeks earlier had been ranged along the line of the Bug and the Niemen, had now retreated behind that formed by the Düna and the Dnieper, and the passage of both these rivers could be effected by the French at their convenience. The Russian troops, apart from the discouragement caused by constant retreating, had suffered considerable material loss.

When the withdrawal from the frontier began the armies of Barclay and Bagration had numbered together some 174,000 men. On the Düna the First Army had been joined by about 9000 reserves, and at Smolensk by 17 depôt battalions and 4 batteries of artillery—probably 6000 more. Bagration had incorporated in his army the garrison of Mohilev and six reserve battalions from Bobruisk—say 3000. These figures, added together, give a total of 192,000.

On August 6th the Russian forces were as follows:—

The First and Second Armies presented a total of 121,000 men; besides a detachment of 1 Dragoon and 3 Cossack regiments detached towards Poriechie. Three regiments of Cossacks had been detached to Riga and elsewhere. Two of Raievski's infantry regiments, which had been the worst sufferers at Saltanovka, had been sent into the interior to recruit. The deduction under these headings may be fairly estimated at 4500 men. Wittgenstein's corps and the reserves from Drissa and Dünaburg were on July 12th over 28,500 strong. The total effective of the Russian First and Second Armies early in August was therefore 154,000, showing a deficiency since June of 38,000 men. The fighting round Mohilev and Vitebsk had scarcely cost more than 6000 or 7000 men, and 5000 is a high estimate for losses in the rear-guard actions. The diminution from other causes was therefore 27,000. It is to be accounted for by sickness, by straggling and fatigue due to the long and painful marches, but also in large measure to desertion among the Lithuanian troops. These half-hearted men were probably no great loss, nor can it be said that the diminution was, on the whole, excessive; still it was serious. Over and above the abandoned magazines a portion of the material had been lost. Only eight guns had been captured in action, but some thirty more had been abandoned during the long marches through sands, swamps and forests; it says volumes for the Russian artillery that the number was not greater.

If, however, the Russian losses had been serious, those of the French had been more so. The causes which diminished the strength of the Russians operated also against the invaders, and apparently the latter, for the most part used to a higher standard of living, were less able to endure hardships. Fatigue and heat might have been endured without any very serious results, but owing to the breakdown of the transport, the supplies of bread and biscuit could never keep up with the troops; even flour was rarely to be had. Meat was, as a rule, not lacking, but it was often of bad quality, the cattle being overdriven and frequently themselves ill-fed. A diet of poor meat, unseasoned, and unaccompanied by bread or vegetables, is not suitable for men who have to endure hard labour and fatigue under the rays of a Russian midsummer sun. Such bread and biscuit as were procurable were bad, and the ill-ground rye had serious effects upon the stomachs of men accustomed to well-prepared wheaten flour. Every effort was made to bring up adequate supplies, but the ill-fed and over-worked draft beasts were utterly unable to cope with the transport, and died in great numbers. The men, foraging for themselves, were rarely able to obtain more than small quantities of grain, and as there were no portable mills in the equipment of the troops it had to be consumed boiled. The water available in Lithuania was scanty in quantity and often bad; and in the general disorganisation of the commissariat brandy, which formed part of the usual ration, and might, at any rate, have done something towards rendering the water less unwholesome, was rarely served out. The result was a frightful amount of sickness—diarrhœa, dysentery and typhus—and in a wretchedly poor and sparsely populated region little could be done to reduce it. The sick were left behind in temporary hospital camps; where they died by thousands in the midst of filth, starvation and general destitution. Of those who went into these dens of misery it was calculated that not one in ten ever emerged alive.

The fighting line was seriously weakened by the immense number of sick. It was also reduced by the necessity of making large detachments to bring up the belated supply trains and to forage for bread, and yet further depleted by straggling, partly for purposes of foraging, partly owing to fatigue, and in some measure to indiscipline. This straggling had always been one of the bad features of the Napoleonic army, and the marches always appear, except when in face of the enemy, to have been conducted with great irregularity. A German eyewitness was amazed to see the regiments of Davout's corps, the best disciplined of the army, making a short march in the most disorderly array.

There is, of course, something to be said for this permission to the men to take their ease when there was no necessity for precise formation and watchfulness; and certainly nothing is ever gained by harassing and overworking soldiers distinguished for cheerful readiness—as Frenchmen have always been. But it is difficult to avoid the conclusion that the irregularity went beneath the surface. With the gaiety and readiness of the French nature is intermixed a decided strain of impatience under restraint which easily degenerates into lawlessness. The straggling

CHAPTER V

which, in earlier days, had perhaps been necessary for the ill-compacted Revolutionary armies, had now become a habit, and soon developed into a monstrous abuse, which ultimately, as much as anything, proved the ruin of the army. The writer is far from wishing to defend a hard and inelastic discipline which crushes personal initiative. But he is strongly of opinion that had the French march discipline been better at the outset, the army would not have broken up as it did during the retreat. Upon this subject more will be said in its proper place.

Finally, it must be observed that the proper means of checking the evils which afflicted the contending armies were very little understood. Not only was there a deficiency of trained *personnel*, but the medical art was, as compared with what it is to-day, in a very undeveloped condition. It cannot be said that Napoleon did not endeavour to provide his troops with medical and surgical assistance, but it was never adequate, either in quantity or quality. The officers were rarely qualified to make good the deficiencies of the sanitary services. Among the corps commanders there were certainly some who thoroughly understood the details of administration. Davout was undoubtedly the best of them; but Ney was also a careful and conscientious administrator. As early as August he is found issuing orders for the preparation of winter clothing. Among the divisional leaders, also, there were some who thoroughly understood how to look after their men—De Fezensac instances Ledru des Essarts as one of them. Still, the careful administrators were certainly in a minority, and their excellent intentions were often hampered by lack of scientific knowledge.

Turning from the general examination of these evils to consideration of the intrinsic damage which they caused, it is to be noted that the 1st, 2nd, 3rd, 4th, 5th, 6th and 8th Army Corps and the 4 corps of Reserve Cavalry totalled on June 24th about 315,000 men. The returns of August 3rd and 4th give an aggregate of less than 213,000. There were, therefore, even on the showing of the official returns, 102,000 men in rear. Detachments account for about 20,000. There remain 82,000; and, since allowance must be made for drafts and absentees rejoined, it will probably be fair to estimate that the losses amounted to 100,000. The loss in battle cannot be estimated higher than 15,000; it follows that 85,000 men had disappeared from the muster-rolls by reason of straggling and sickness—that is, nearly 30 per cent. Of course, they were not all permanently lost to the army, but a very large proportion were, owing to the terrible lack of provision for the temporarily disabled soldiers.

The mortality among the horses had been very large, mainly owing to lack of forage. The number dwindled day by day, and this circumstance was, in a sense, more fatal than loss of men. Every disabled horse meant further lessening of the means of transport. The cavalry regiments were unable to mount even their diminished effectives except by sweeping up horses from the countryside; and these were rarely of much service. The guns of the reserve parks had to be left at Vilna, and even part of the artillery of several army corps.

When Napoleon reached Vitebsk the number of men missing among the 450,000 who had crossed the frontier in June and July, may be conservatively calculated at 120,000, and a very large proportion of them were either already dead or disabled from further service. Straggling and desertion were especially prevalent among the foreign regiments. Their administration was generally less efficient; less care was taken of them by the French officials. They had naturally little affection for the cause in which they had been enlisted by their sovereigns, and their officers must have been exasperated at the disgraceful fashion in which Napoleon invariably endeavoured to saddle their troops with the sole blame for disorders. It is more than probable that disgust at this, no less than the way in which they had been sacrificed, was one of the motives which impelled so many German officers to turn against Napoleon in the following year.

For every reason a halt was imperatively necessary, and Napoleon called it as soon as the escape of the First Russian Army was an accomplished fact. On the 29th he wrote to Davout, ordering him to canton his troops. The various corps took up quarters on a line extending from Surazh to beyond Mohilev, with the cavalry pushed out in front and on the flanks. Latour-Maubourg was about Rogachev-on-Dnieper, some 60 miles south of Mohilev, with a Polish infantry division in support.

There was a little skirmishing between the advanced French cavalry and belated Russian detachments. On July 30th Murat's horsemen picked up about 100 prisoners and 40 abandoned vehicles, and captured a welcome supply of flour and forage. On the 31st Villata's Italian cavalry brigade surprised a Russian convoy at Velizh, escorted by 4 depôt battalions. The 2nd Chasseurs under Colonel Banco charged, and captured 60 waggons and 250 prisoners. The total Russian loss was estimated by Eugène at 700, and 600 sacks of flour and a herd of bullocks fell into the hands of the Italian troopers. But for these captures the French cavalry could hardly have advanced another step. The regiments were, with few exceptions, very weak, and the horses exhausted by fatigue and privation. Sebastiani—perhaps with some exaggeration, for he was ill and discouraged—declared that his division had only 2300 mounted men remaining, out of over 4000. Hardly one of the corps was really fit for service except perhaps the 1st. Ney had not yet received his reserve of artillery, which was toiling up from the rear. Not even in the 1st Corps were things altogether satisfactory. Davout was growling at the disorder in the regiments, threatening Desaix, whom he accused of abetting it, with arrest, and re-establishing discipline by stern methods, including the shooting of marauders caught in the act.

During the last days of July Oudinot had fought several very bloody and inconclusive actions with Wittgenstein. The 2nd Corps had been forced back upon the Düna; and on August 4th Napoleon ordered St. Cyr, who was near Bechenkoviczi, to march to its support, though the unhappy Bavarians had scarcely begun to refit and were still smitten with disease. St. Cyr complained bitterly, but he had to obey.

By August 4th the Grand Army had settled down in cantonments. Head-quarters were at Vitebsk, where ovens were being built, and hospitals and magazines established. The 4th Corps was at Surazh, Velizh and Poriechie, the 1st, 2nd and 3rd Cavalry Corps about Rudnia, the 3rd Corps around Liozna, north-west of Rudnia, with the 24th Light Infantry supporting Sebastiani. The 1st Corps, not yet reunited, was spread from Vitebsk to Orsha, with the 8th Corps at the latter place, and the 5th between Sklov and Mohilev, whither Latour-Maubourg was also moving.

The general results of the halt were very beneficial. The establishments of the regiments began to rise. It is true that the muster rolls for August 4th only show about 197,000 men present out of a nominal 270,000, but stragglers were rallying each day; and men and horses were at least reposing from fatigue. The supply department was not entirely satisfactory. Davout's troops were able to draw breadstuffs from the country along the Dnieper, and had, as has been seen, captured several Russian depôts. The corps north of the Dnieper, however, depended for bread mainly on what could be brought up by the over-worked transport from Vilna and Minsk. Here, however, there was an improvement, since the halt allowed the trains to close up. If bread were not regularly served out the men at any rate obtained something, and the corps commanders were able to begin to accumulate a small reserve.

Besides the increase caused by stragglers and convalescents rejoining, reinforcements were arriving. The rear detachments of the Imperial Guard were beginning to come up, also the Hesse-Darmstadt Guards, under Prince Emil, of which one battalion joined at Vitebsk, while the other was marching from Vilna. Three newly formed battalions for the Vistula Legion were also on the way, and various *régiments de marche* (i.e. drafts, convalescents, etc.). A Portuguese cavalry regiment had joined Davout, and the Grand Quarter-General, 4690 strong, reached Vitebsk on the 7th. When hostilities recommenced the Grand Army was considerably the better for its rest. Davout's troops especially were in excellent order, and carried on the person bread, biscuit and flour for fifteen days. The Westphalians also were well supplied. North of the Dnieper matters were less satisfactory. Friant on rejoining Davout stated that he had always had to forage for breadstuffs, though he had plenty of meat.

The administration of the hospitals was still very bad, even at Vitebsk; and elsewhere no doubt it was much worse. Matters were not improved by the fact that Surgeon-General Larrey and General Mathieu Dumas, the chief of the military administration, were on bad terms with each other.

Some changes were at this time made in the commands. Napoleon's old, but not very capable or energetic, friend, Junot, was appointed to the command of the 8th Corps. Marchand was given the Württemberg division of Ney's corps. It had been commanded at the outset by the Crown Prince Wilhelm, but, partly owing to disgust at the disorder, and the fashion in which he and his men were slandered to save the faces of the French, partly owing to illness, he had returned to Vilna, leaving the command to Lieutenant-General Scheler. Marchand declined to take the direct control out of the hands of the latter, and the two worked well together. Otherwise, being an old comrade and subordinate, Marchand was probably welcome to Ney.

The Marquis d'Alorna, one of the few Portuguese officers who had preferred to serve Napoleon willingly, was appointed Military Governor of Mohilev. General Charpentier was placed in charge of Vitebsk, and Gomès Freyre, another Portuguese, of Glubokoïe. The two brigades of Bavarian light cavalry belonging to the 6th Corps were combined into a division, under General Graf von Preising, and transferred to the 4th Corps, which now had 36 squadrons.

Napoleon, of course, did not intend the halt to be more than temporary. At the outset of the campaign he had told Metternich that he did not intend to go farther than Smolensk in 1812, but, having established himself there, purposed to organise Lithuania and consolidate his rule in the former Polish provinces before attempting to conquer Russia Proper. This statement he repeated to others—notably to Jomini—and it can hardly be considered as a mere blind. Up to the present he had failed to strike a heavy blow at the opposing Russian army The extent of country which he occupied was by no means an advantage, since it was too poor to support his huge forces, and merely lengthened his already long line of communications. But now, at last, a battle might reasonably be expected. Barclay and Bagration had united their forces, and it was scarcely within the bounds of probability that Smolensk, a home of the ancient Rurikovich line, long contended for with hated Poland, one of the sacred cities of Russia, would be abandoned without fighting. The halt had for its primary object the putting of the army into good condition preparatory to a fresh and energetic advance.

As early as August 6th Napoleon told Eugène that an early renewal of hostilities was to be anticipated, and that he should probably advance on Smolensk by the left bank of the Dnieper. On the same day he was asking Davout for information as to which bank of the river was in his opinion the better for the advance. Davout's reply was that upon the whole he thought the left bank the more suitable, and apparently this decided the Emperor. The merits and demerits of the plan will be discussed later. Here it is only necessary to observe that it was preconceived, and not due to the influence of Russian operations.

The two Russian armies were concentrated at Smolensk by August 4th. The city had practically no fortifications of value. Its massive brick walls were capable of resisting the attack of field guns, but there were several ill-closed breaches; and the only guns in the place were antique pieces without carriages, kept mainly as relics. Smolensk was garrisoned by a column of 17 depôt battalions, 8 squadrons and 4 batteries of artillery—about 6000 or 7000 men—which had been brought from Kaluga by General Winzingerode. The infantry was drafted into the two armies, ten battalions going to the 1st, seven to the 2nd, which had dwindled during its forced marches, and needed more strengthening in proportion. The artillery was also divided, but the squadrons were sent back to Kaluga to serve as a nucleus for fresh formations. Winzingerode was sent with the Kazan Dragoons from Uvarov's division and 3 regiments of Cossacks to observe the French left wing towards Surazh and Poriechie. There then remained a held army of 121,000 men, of whom over 18,000 were regular cavalry, with some 650 pieces of artillery.

Unhappily there was no unity of command. Barclay, as minister of war, was the hierarchical chief, but both Bagration and himself were Generals of Infantry, and the former was the senior in rank. Though a Georgian by birth he posed as an ultra Russian and received accordingly the willing, not to say eager and unscrupulous, support of the many officers who chose to regard Barclay as a half-hearted and even treacherous foreigner. His fighting record was a good one, and he might, with some justice, consider that he had the better title to the command-in-chief. Barclay also, with all his fine qualities, appears to have been deficient in tact. He does not appear to have fully realised the difficulties with which Bagration had had to contend, nor the very creditable attempts which he had made to effect a junction. After crossing the Dnieper Bagration appears to have considered that his best service would be performed in operating upon Napoleon's flank. Von Wollzogen, sent to urge him to hasten the union of the two armies, found him, according to his own account, by no means willing to do so, and informed Barclay. The latter thereupon wrote pressing him to hasten, in phrases which, though hardly beyond what the urgency of the case required, were perhaps unjust in their implications, and were certainly fiercely resented by Bagration. He reached Smolensk in a frame of mind which would find cause of offence in every trifle. Barclay, however, displayed unusual tact, for which his aide-de-camp Löwenstern gives himself the credit. When Bagration came to report himself the War-Minister met him in his antechamber in full uniform, and expressed his regret that he had been anticipated in calling upon him. The two chiefs then had a conversation, as the result of which Barclay apologised by letter for any injustice which he might have done his colleague. For the moment good relations were established, and Barclay wrote to the Tzar expressing his admiration of Bagration's character. But it is to be feared that Bagration's friendly feelings were of no very long continuance, and a sense of injury still rankled in his mind. What was worse, many of the general officers were almost openly intriguing for the definite appointment of Bagration to the supreme command. Yermólov actually wrote to the Tzar urging him to make it. The chief of the malcontents was the Grand Duke Constantine, who, as the Tzar's brother and heir apparent, was the most important commander in the army. Constantine was a violent and irrational person, bearing, both in disposition and in the exceeding ugliness of his features, a strong resemblance to his ill-fated father. Barclay's position rapidly became almost an intolerable one.

 For the moment all went well. A council was called for the 6th of August, and to it came the two commanders-in-chief, the Grand Duke Constantine, whom Barclay dared not omit, Yermólov, Toll and St. Priest, Bagration›s French chief-of-staff. The decision as to an offensive had been taken before the meeting, and only the details were to be settled. There was naturally considerable divergence of opinion. The extension of the French cantonments appeared to afford an excellent opportunity. It was determined to throw strong forces against Napoleon's extreme left, under Eugène, which might perhaps be completely destroyed. Bagration, however, wished to drive the attack home with the full force of both armies, and to this Barclay would not agree. He was very naturally uneasy as to what the mighty conqueror opposed to him might do to turn the tables. Smolensk, weak as it was, was the pivot of the Russian operations, and its loss would shatter the entire strategic plan. Barclay therefore proposed that Bagration should hold it while the First Army pushed forward against Vitebsk. To this Bagration demurred, and eventually it was decided to leave only a detachment to cover the city and to march upon Vitebsk with the combined armies, the Second holding rather back on the left to guard against a turning movement.

Barclay, however, was very uneasy. The Tzar had bidden him preserve his army at all hazards, and, though he underestimated Napoleon's strength, it was no light thing to advance to the attack of so terrible an adversary. Sir Robert Wilson, the British military commissioner, who reached head-quarters a few days later, says that Barclay was terrorised by his opponent's renown, but, seeing the situation and the tremendous consequences which would ensue on the destruction of Russia's single formidable army, it can hardly be wondered that he was resolute to take no risks. He informed the Council of Alexander's words, and expressed his firm determination not to move more than three marches from Smolensk.

It is, of course, possible to argue that the plan, thus confined, was but a half-measure; but it is equally possible that Barclay's caution saved the Russian army from destruction. He was certainly so far dominated by Napoleon that he expected to be turned, and prepared to throw back his right wing at the first alarm. On the other hand, it was certain that if Napoleon pursued his usual strategy he would endeavour to turn one or the other of the Russian flanks, and probability pointed to the right.

General Neverovski was left to guard Smolensk. His division was improved in quality by making over two regiments to Paskievich, and receiving in return those of Poltava and Ladoga. The Kharkov Dragoon regiment and three regiments of Cossacks were also attached to him, and he was directed to move out along the left bank of the Dnieper.

Having thus, as he hoped, provided for speedy intelligence, and for the security of Smolensk, if it were threatened, Barclay, on August 7th, set his forces in motion. Bagration moved along the right bank of the Dnieper to Katan, some 16 miles from Smolensk. The 5th and 6th Corps and the 3rd Cavalry Corps advanced on Rudnia, and the 2nd, 3rd and 4th Corps and the rest of the cavalry in the direction of Poriechie. A detachment of light infantry under Baron Rosen connected the First and Second Armies. Each column was preceded by an advance guard of infantry and cavalry, and in front of all were the Cossacks under the general command of Platov. The advancing army totalled about 113,000 men.

At the end of the first day's march, Barclay received intelligence from Winzingerode that Eugène and Nansouty were at or near Poriechie. This naturally suggested that Napoleon had obtained information, and was moving to turn the Russian right. Barclay accordingly halted, and faced to the north-east, requesting Bagration to advance to Prikaz Vidra, 16 miles north of Katan, to guard the left flank. Platov was still moving north-westward, and on the 8th he encountered Sebastiani's division near Inkovo, east of Rudnia. Sebastiani was supported by the 24th Léger and Beurmann's light cavalry brigade from Ney's corps. Beurmann, however, hardly showed the vigour which the occasion required, and only his Württemberg horse artillery battery took a decided share in the action, the brunt of which fell upon Sebastiani. The French division, which was less than 3000 strong, fought well, but was forced to fall back before superior numbers. A company of the 24th was captured by the Cossacks, and the loss probably totalled 600 men, of whom 300 were prisoners. Murat was at head-quarters during the action, and by some the reverse is attributed to his absence. Undoubtedly he would have been better able to combine the operations of Sebastiani and Beurmann than was his chief-of-staff, Belliard, and would also have brought pressure to bear upon Ney. The latter, who was cantoned about Liozna, concentrated his troops, but made no move to Sebastiani's support, for which he was next day severely reprimanded by Napoleon.

On the same day Nansouty's outposts near Velizh were attacked by those of Winzingerode. The intelligence all went to show that the Russians were advancing against the French left wing. On the 8th Napoleon received Davout's report upon the roads along the Dnieper; and at 2 a.m. on the 9th he replied to say that he had decided to march upon Smolensk by the left bank, and ordered the Marshal to trace the itinerary. Murat hurried to the front to resume his command. Ney drew towards him the three divisions of the 1st Corps to meet a Russian advance. On the 8th the Guard had been paid, and had received brandy for ten days. Friant, who was to fall at the head of the Old Guard on the field of Waterloo, was nominated Colonel-General of the Foot Grenadiers in place of General Dorsenne, recently deceased. He was welcomed at a parade on the 9th by Napoleon himself—much to his pleasure.

On the 10th General Eblé was sent to Rasasna, 22 miles above Orsha, with orders to throw four bridges over the Dnieper. The weather was very bad, with heavy rain, which broke up the roads and impeded the march of the troops. Nansouty's and Montbrun's cavalry (except Sebastiani's division), Ney's corps, and the divisions of Morand, Friant and Gudin, were directed on Rasasna. Eugène would follow, forming the rear-guard of the movement, which was covered on its left by extensive forests. Davout's army was also ordered on Rasasna, except Dombrowski's division, which was to remain near Mohilev to observe Bobruisk. It is characteristic of Napoleon's methods that Ney knew nothing of the proposed movement until late on the 10th. On the 11th the Guard left Vitebsk. The weather was still bad, and it was probably owing to this that Ney was unable to evacuate all his sick, earning thereby another reprimand from Napoleon.

General Charpentier was left to garrison Vitebsk with the new Guard regiment of "Flanqueurs-Chasseurs," Guyon's cavalry brigade of the 4th Corps, the 3rd battalion of the 1st Vistula Regiment, and a Hesse-Darmstadt battalion on the way from Vilna—3800 men in all, a number which would be increased by the 16th to over 7000 by various *bataillons de marche*. Sebastiani's division, temporarily commanded by General Pajol, was to remain in observation near Rudnia. Dombrowski's division was between Rogachev and Mohilev. A battalion of Westphalians garrisoned Orsha. Deducting these detachments, Napoleon had available for the advance on Smolensk over 200,000 men, exclusive of the head-quarter troops. By the 13th the whole huge mass was either at or within easy reach of Rasasna, and Nansouty, Montbrun and Ney crossed the river and took the lead.

It is somewhat remarkable that there is no indication during this period of any attempt to ascertain the whereabouts of the Russians. Napoleon knew that they had not pushed their advance on Vitebsk, but he was apparently so confident that his move would meet all emergencies that he does not seem to have troubled himself about the 120,000 enemies who were somewhere to his left.

Barclay, as has been seen, was facing towards Poriechie. About this time he received a direct order from Alexander to take the offensive. Bagration moved to Prikaz Vidra on the 9th; and Barclay reported that the two armies could concentrate in a day if necessary, that in their position they covered Smolensk and the country between the Düna and Dnieper, and could easily be supplied from the magazines which had been prepared beforehand at Toropetz and other places.

Bagration, however, was not satisfied. He was in a mood which would probably have induced him to quarrel with anything that Barclay did. He told Arakcheiev that the War-Minister's head-quarters were so choked with Germans that a Russian could not live there, and that constant marching and counter-marching would drive him mad. To Yermólov he wrote that he had neither hay, straw, bread nor a position, and that Barclay must either do something or else supersede him (Bagration). He expected that Napoleon would amuse them by demonstrations about Rudnia, and move on Smolensk by their left. It is not clear whether this anticipation of the French Emperor's intentions was the result of careful reflection, or simply due to the natural tendency of every commander to imagine himself the especial object of the enemy's attentions.

The result was that Barclay, in despair, gave Bagration a free hand. He empowered him to withdraw upon Smolensk if he judged it necessary, and in general to take his own measures for the protection of the Russian left flank. The unfortunate War-Minister was beset by open and secret foes, and this, added to the responsibility which weighed upon him, probably explains this extraordinary step, which practically amounted to an abdication of the supreme command.

On the 12th, accordingly, Bagration withdrew towards Smolensk. On the same day, however, Barclay received fresh information that the French were in force near Poriechie. It was absolutely baseless, but he could scarcely discredit it, more especially as he was obsessed by the idea of an attack from that quarter. He wrote to Bagration that he expected an attack on the 15th, and took up a position between the Kasplia lake and the village of Volokovaia, about 22 miles north-west of Smolensk. He called up Bagration to Katan and Nadva, about 8 miles farther north-west, in order to guard his own left. On the 13th the Second Army was retiring on Smolensk, and the 7th Corps had actually reached the place when Barclay's order of recall arrived.

This seems almost to have disturbed Bagration's mental balance. He complained bitterly of the constant counter-marching, which was steadily exhausting and depleting the Second Army. For this there was good excuse, but little for the violent letters which he wrote to Yermólov, in which he describes Barclay as a traitor worthy of death. The latter had certainly carried his cautious policy too far, since another march in advance on the 9th or 10th would have shown that there were no large forces in his front, and he was certainly in a state of great irresolution. Still, seeing the character of his adversary, this was, at any rate, excusable, and one may fairly ask why the masses of Russian light cavalry had not better

CHAPTER V

enlightened the situation.

It must be said in defence of Bagration that however much he allowed his fiery temperament to master him, and though his letters to a dangerous intriguer like Yermólov were subversive of all military subordination, he did not himself set the example of disobedience. On the 14th he counter-marched the 8th Corps on Katan, pushing Sievers' and Vassilchikov's cavalry, with a supporting brigade of the 7th Corps, on towards Volokovaia. The bulk of the 7th Corps was at Smolensk, and the men needed rest, so that Raievski did not commence his march until 7 p.m. As he moved off, cannonading was heard in the direction of Krasnoï. Towards 10 o'clock an aide-de-camp arrived from Neverovski with the news that French troops were advancing by the south bank of the Dnieper. Bagration had also, by some means, received intelligence, for soon after came orders from him to halt. In the night, Raievski received a fresh order to return to support Neverovski. At daybreak on the 15th the 7th Corps re-entered Smolensk.

On the morning of the 14th the Grand Army began to advance from Rasasna. Murat led the way with Nansouty's, Montbrun's and Grouchy's corps and the light cavalry of the 1st and 3rd Corps; and behind him came Ney's three infantry divisions. In rear of Ney came Davout's corps, and then the Guard. Eugène was crossing at Rasasna; the 8th Corps was marching from Orsha on Davout's right, and the 5th farther out, covered towards the south by Latour-Maubourg. Between two and three in the afternoon the advance-guard reached Krasnoï, occupied by Neverovski's division.

Various French writers have expressed astonishment at this small force having been left exposed, and apparently by accident on the south side of the Dnieper. All this is, of course, little better than nonsense, or, at best, adulation of Napoleon's genius, which was so great that it robbed his opponents of common sense! The sending of the 27th Division along the left bank of the river was a perfectly rational measure of precaution. It was in observation, and not intended to abide the attack of a greatly superior force, though it was quite capable of dealing with a division or flying detachment. By whichever bank the Russian leaders chose to operate they could not leave the other unobserved, especially since the French held the crossings at Orsha and elsewhere. The mistake—presumably Bagration's—appears to have been in not stationing the infantry closer to Smolensk and sending only the cavalry to observe the Orsha road.

Krasnoï is a small town about 30 miles from Smolensk. Neverovski's cavalry outposts were about Liady, a few miles west. They were driven out by Grouchy's corps, which formed Murat's left wing; and Neverovski learned that overwhelming forces were marching upon him.

JOACHIM MURAT, KING OF NAPLES
Commander of the French Cavalry
From the painting by Gérard at Versailles

He at once made his dispositions for retreat. A little east of Krasnoï the Lossmina river flows to the Dnieper through a gully over which the high-road passed by the usual wooden bridge. Neverovski ordered the 50th Chasseurs with 2 guns to march with all speed to Korythnia, nearly half-way to Smolensk, to form a sustaining force in case of a grave defeat, and began to withdraw. When Murat and Ney arrived they found him with 9 battalions, his cavalry and 8 guns, behind the ravine, with 1 battalion and 2 guns in Krasnoï.

The general order of the French advance is a little uncertain, but Grouchy,

CHAPTER V 81

with Chastel's light horse and De la Houssaye's dragoons, appears to have been on the left, the light cavalry of the 1st and 3rd Corps with the 24th Léger, personally led by Ney, in the centre; Montbrun's two Cuirassier divisions on the right, with Nansouty in support. The 24th Léger attacked and carried Krasnoï about 3 p.m., capturing the two guns and driving the remains of the garrison over the ravine. The 9th Polish Cavalry followed them over the bridge, but, throwing themselves rashly upon the supporting infantry, were repulsed. The Kharkov dragoons pursued, but declined to charge in face of the masses behind, and Neverovski, seeing the French numbers, sent his cavalry off to the rear, and began to withdraw, with his ten battalions ranged in two dense columns.

The hostile horsemen were now crowding over the Lossmina ravine. Murat, having got some squadrons together, flung himself at the Russian rear-guard, threw it into disorder and captured five or six guns more. Neverovski rallied the broken troops, and then, apparently doubting the steadiness of his young recruits, supported now by the fire of only two guns, united his force into a single great square. As the battalions were formed, in Continental fashion, six deep, and as the number of men was about 5000, each face was probably 130 yards long.

As the French and allied cavalry crossed the ravine each regiment hurried up to the front and singly and apparently haphazard charged the retiring square. To all appearance Murat exercised no general control, but acted like a mere regimental commander, riding furiously about, leading isolated charges which were futile against steady infantry. The artillery was mostly blocked at the Lossmina, and only three Württemberg guns succeeded in coming into action; while Ney's infantry, which might have held the Russians until the guns could do their work, could not force its way up through the impeding hosts of cavalry. The country was much broken and cut up by small hollows and gullies; while the road was generally bordered by trees. Over this country, eastward of Krasnoï, on the way to Korythnia, was moving the host of French, Polish and German horsemen, while in its midst the great square of the 27th Division lumbered solemnly along, with the attacks of the cavalry breaking upon it like waves upon a rock, firing and stabbing doggedly at everything that troubled it, and making its way steadily to Korythnia in spite of what its assailants could do. The firing of the Russian recruits appears to have often been wild, but their steadiness was exemplary. Even when the three Württemberg guns at last worked their way up and opened fire there was no shattering them. A Württemberg regiment did succeed, at one moment, in breaking into the square, but was forced out again, and the 27th Division steadied its ranks and went on its dogged way. The charges grew more and more ineffective owing to the fatigue of men and horses; and about 8 p.m. Neverovski arrived in safety at Korythnia. There he rallied his cavalry and rear-guard, and next day retreated on Smolensk. He had lost about 1500 men in all, of whom half were prisoners, with 8 guns. The French losses do not appear to have exceeded 800.

The action was extremely creditable to the young Russian troops, though it is only fair to say that they owed much to Murat's mismanagement. Ney, in the midst of the action, went to the King and endeavoured to induce him to allow the infantry to pass to the front, but without avail. He was furious, and wrote a memorandum to Napoleon begging him to have a regular advance-guard of infantry. Cavalry, as he pointed out, were powerless to prevent the retreat of infantry.

Raievski reached Smolensk at dawn on the 15th. In the town was General Bennigsen, who was accompanying the army apparently in the hope of succeeding to the chief command. To him the anxious commander of the 7th Corps went for advice, but Bennigsen was not the man to assist juniors in difficulties, much less to allow himself to become associated with what might be a great disaster. He put Raievski off with a few meaningless words, merely counselling him to save his artillery. Raievski, as he says, felt that when the fate of Russia hung in the balance it was no time to think of a few guns. He took up a position about 2 miles in advance of the town, and awaited Neverovski, who arrived at 2 p.m. From him Raievski learned that probably the whole French army was advancing upon Smolensk, and hurried off a despatch to Barclay. At 5 p.m. he heard artillery fire at his outposts, and, hurrying to the front, saw the masses of Murat's cavalry coming up from Korythnia.

Raievski did not falter. As he saw it his duty was plain. He and his men must die, if necessary, in defence of the city, for if it fell Napoleon could take Barclay and Bagration in rear, cutting their line of communication with Moscow and the south. He was supported by Paskievich, to whom, according to his biographer, the main credit of the resolution was due. This assertion may be taken for what it is worth, though there is no reason to doubt that Paskievich cordially supported his chief's resolution.

Smolensk, in 1812, lay chiefly upon the southern bank of the river. It had formerly been a great frontier fortress, but since the advent of artillery its importance had dwindled, owing to the fact that it was more or less commanded by low heights. Its nucleus consisted of the ancient fortified city, whose massive brick walls formed an irregular pentagon of nearly four miles in circumference. These walls were generally about 30 feet high and from 15 to 20 in thickness. At the top were galleries open to the sky, too narrow to admit of guns being placed in position. At intervals were 32 towers, in which staircases gave access to the walls. It was only on the platforms of these towers that artillery could be placed, and they were in general less solidly constructed than the walls. Inside the walls were backed by ancient earthen ramparts. At the south-west angle was a small regular fort of earth, in so neglected a condition that its ramparts could easily be scaled by infantry. This so-called "Royal Citadel," dating from the days of the Polish occupation, constituted in reality perhaps the weakest point in the line of defence. Close to the southern or Malakova Gate a breach, made during the siege by Sigismund III of Poland in 1611, was covered by an earthen redan. The walls were encircled by a ditch and covered way, also in a neglected condition. Along the east side a considerable gully gave further protection, and at the west side was another but shallower depression. All round the city were extensive suburbs, mostly consisting of wooden buildings. Among them were many dismantled earthworks. These suburbs extended almost up to the walls of the inner city, and, since they afforded cover to assailants, the defenders were practically forced to take up position either in or in advance of them. They were generally called after the town the

CHAPTER V

road to which passed through them.

On the south side four chief roads ran into Smolensk, that from Warsaw entering the city from the south-west by Krasnoï. The road from Mohilev by Mstislavl led nearly directly southward; that to Roslavl and Orel branched off from it near the Malakova Gate; the Ielnia-Kaluga road led south-eastward for some distance, finally turning eastward.

From the north gate, over a long wooden bridge, led three roads, that to Vitebsk on the left, that to Velizh and St. Petersburg in the middle, and that to Moscow on the right. The latter ran for some 5 miles along the bank of the Dnieper, and then crossed the chord of a great bend of the river to Soloviévo, about 27 miles east of Smolensk, where it passed again to the south side. A cross-road passed by the village of Gorbunovo in a shallow curve to the high-road at Lubino, 14 miles distant. From the south side of Smolensk another track crossed the Dnieper by a ford at Prudichevo, about 6 miles out, and also joined the high-road about 2 miles west of Lubino. These tracks must be noted, since a few days later they became of immense importance.

Raievski had with him only 8 regiments and 6 batteries of his own corps, and Neverovski's weakened force. According to himself his strength (probably infantry and artillery only) was scarcely 13,000 men. He had 72 guns. Realising that his duty was to contest the city inch by inch, he ranged his force in advance of the suburbs. Paskievich's division occupied the Krasnoï suburb and the ditch before the citadel, with the Vilna Regiment from the 27th Division and a makeshift battalion of convalescents stationed in reserve behind the wall. Kolubakin's division defended the Mstislavl suburb, and Stavidzki's brigade of the 27th that of Roslavl. These 23 battalions could only guard about half of the south front of the suburbs. Four more were in reserve in the town, and only two could be spared to watch the line of nearly 2 miles from the Roslavl suburb to the river. To make the best possible show Raievski stationed his cavalry there. Eighteen guns were placed on the Royal Citadel; the rest along the earth ramparts behind the walls. Thus placed, the Russians awaited attack. Raievski says that though he had had little rest the night before he could not sleep.

In the night the Lancers of Lithuania and the New Russian Dragoons reached Smolensk, thus giving Raievski 12 more squadrons, with which he strengthened his screen on the left.

By 10 p.m. on the 15th the bulk of Murat's cavalry was about 3 miles from Smolensk, with its outposts in touch with Raievski. Ney's corps was immediately behind. Davout had reached Korythnia. The Guard was in rear of Davout; the head of the 4th Corps at Liadi. The 8th Corps had lost its way, but the 5th was nearly in line with Davout, and could come up in the afternoon. Without reckoning Eugène and the Guard, 120,000 men could be in front of Smolensk before evening.

What, meanwhile, were Barclay and Bagration doing? Barclay was still anxious about an attack from the direction of Poriechie and sent pressing orders to his cavalry commanders to endeavour to clear up the situation. He doubted whether the advance on Smolensk was being made by more than a part of the French army.

Bagration was directed to cross the Dnieper at Katan, and join Raievski and Neverovski in defending the Smolensk road. Dokhturov's corps would take his place at Nadva. Bagration moved to Katan and threw a bridge, but he soon became aware that to cross would simply mean his annihilation. He sent word to Barclay that an army which he estimated at 115,000 men, without Eugène and the Guard, was marching on Smolensk, and that he himself must now go thither by the right bank. The reports of Bagration and Raievski removed Barclay's doubts, and he issued orders for all his corps to march upon Smolensk next day. To Raievski Bagration sent a characteristic message:

"Dear Friend,

"I shall not march to rejoin you—I shall run. I only wish I had wings. Courage! God will help you!"

At midnight on the 15th-16th Napoleon wrote to Eugène saying that Smolensk was evacuated. A little later Ney was ordered to occupy it. It does not appear that the Emperor had any definite information upon which to base his over-confident opinion. He seems indeed to have been impressed by Bagration's bridge-building at Katan, which had been observed on the 15th by a reconnaissance from head-quarters. A flank attack upon his army as it lay stretched along the Rasasna-Smolensk road might have serious consequences. He consequently halted the whole of the 1st Corps about Korythnia, except Gudin's division, which continued its advance on Smolensk.

CHAPTER V

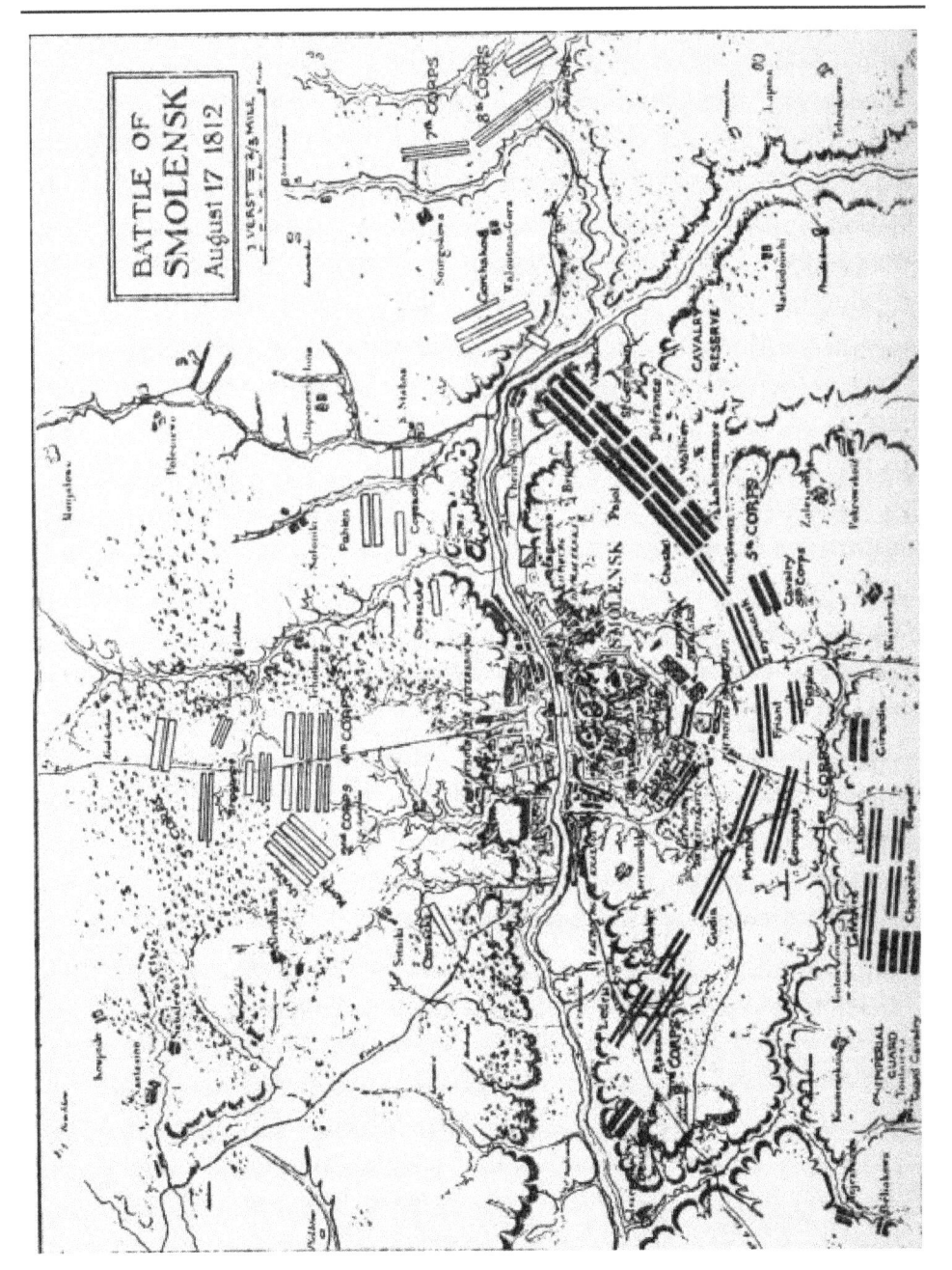

BATTLE OF SMOLENSK
August 17 1812

Very early on the 16th the French and Russian outposts before Smolensk were bickering with each other. Between 8 and 9 a.m. the bulk of Ney's and Murat's force reached the front. The King and the Marshal brought some batteries into action against Raievski's artillery, and Ney deployed his corps opposite the Krasnoï suburb and the Royal Citadel, Ledru's division on the right, Scheler's Württembergers on the left rear, Razout in reserve. Murat's divisions extended to the right. The advance posts were skirmishing hotly, and on both sides a number of guns were engaged, but, to the astonishment of Raievski, no attack was made. He spoke afterwards of his success having been due to the feeble measures of the French. Ney and Murat were, of course, awaiting orders. Ney also had less than 19,000 infantry, scarcely enough to attempt to carry the city by main force, especially since he did not know Raievski's strength. Napoleon was keeping the bulk of his army ready to face towards Katan and endeavouring to clear up the situation by reconnaissances. Towards noon he heard that the bridge had been removed, and started for Smolensk. He arrived about 1 p.m. and, going at once to the front, closely reconnoitred the Russian position.

It was perhaps in consequence of inferences made from what he had seen, that Napoleon directed Murat and Ney to press their advance. The indications as to time are very vague, but in all probability nothing like an attack was made until the afternoon. Apparently about 1.30 p.m. the Russian cavalry were forced to retire under the walls of the town, and the Württembergers began to press home the attack on the Krasnoï suburb. Raievski's line was so thin that an advance in force at any point would shatter it. In strengthening the defence in the Krasnoï suburb troops had to be moved in that direction. All along the opposing fronts extended a line of fire, and, though the attack was nowhere being energetically pressed, the Russian troops were almost all engaged. There remained in reserve only the two regiments in the town, when Raievski was informed that the French had penetrated his skeleton left and were approaching the bridge. He rushed off to repel them with his feeble reserve, and at this moment a battalion of the French 46th, seeing the Royal Citadel almost denuded of defenders, dashed forward, easily mounted the crumbling earth rampart, and penetrated into the interior. The garrison, however, resisted desperately. Raievski, finding the report of the advance upon the bridge baseless, hurried back to the threatened point, supports were brought up, and the gallant assailants thrown back over the rampart just as a second battalion was mounting to their assistance, carrying it away in their retreat. As they went to the rear they were heavily fired upon, and suffered great loss. Elsewhere the only successes gained had been the driving in of stubbornly resisting outposts, and the French opportunity was fleeting. At 3.20 p.m. General Sokolnicki, a Polish officer attached to the General Staff, reported Russian troops on the road to Rudnia. Gudin's division did not reach the front until 4 p.m., Poniatowski not until 5 p.m., and time was needed for the men to rest and to take up position. The critical period for the Russians was, in fact, over. Firing continued until dusk, but no attempt was made to press home an attack. The Russian main army was pouring down towards the city, and any success could hardly be more than a temporary one. Raievski's fine resolution had robbed Napoleon of his chance; and it is no discredit to him that his own immediate peril had been less great than he had imagined.

Bagration, despite his encouraging words, was not able to arrive to Raievski's assistance until the evening, and as the distance from Katan to Smolensk is not

CHAPTER V

more than 17 miles, it must be supposed that he felt himself obliged to halt in order to become satisfied that Napoleon's reconnaissances did not prelude a serious attack. He himself hastened on to Smolensk, and having ascertained that Raievski was not as yet pressed and also, apparently, that no attack was intended at Katan, hurried back to the latter place and directed Borozdin on Smolensk. The Second Cuirassier Division had already been sent on. Raievski, feeling that cavalry was useless in the town, kept them on the north side of the Dnieper.[1]

Barclay, having convinced himself of his error as to the direction of Napoleon's attack, turned the heads of all his corps towards Smolensk, and the march was pressed with desperate energy. All through the hot summer's day, over roads so bad as not to deserve the name, the Russian soldiers pressed forward. Tuchkov I with the 3rd and 4th Corps and Uvarov's cavalry came from Kasplia by the Poriechie road; the Grand Duke Constantine, with the 2nd and 3rd, and Korf's and Pahlen's cavalry, from Volokovaia by Prikaz Vidra; Dokhturov from Nadva by the Rudnia road; while Borozdin and Vassilchikov marched along the bank of the Dnieper. Tuchkov's and Dokhturov's troops had to march over 24 miles in a direct line without allowing for sinuosities in the roads and additions occasioned by moving into position, Constantine's over 22. Nevertheless, by five in the afternoon the whole army was within easy reach of the threatened town, and an hour later Borozdin's leading brigade reached the bridge to the support of Raievski.

Smolensk being saved, the problem before the Russian generals was what next to do. Barclay anticipated that, having failed to capture Smolensk, Napoleon's next move would be on Solovievo. Its seizure would force the Russian armies either to reopen their chief line of communications at the sword's point, with all the chances against them, or to retreat northward. The abandonment of Smolensk would then become practically inevitable. It would, of course, have been perfectly feasible to leave a garrison in the place which might have held out for a week or two, but it may reasonably be asked what end could be gained by sacrificing it. At any rate, it was obvious that a possible French move upon Solovievo must be guarded against, and it was arranged that the Second Army should move eastward ready to anticipate the enemy at the threatened point, while the First remained about Smolensk to defend the line of the Dnieper.

To this end Dokhturov, with the 6th Corps, Konovnitzin's division of the 3rd and the Chasseurs of the Guard, was ordered to relieve Raievski, and about midnight his troops arrived to take up the positions in the suburbs vacated by those of the former. Raievski left the 6th Chasseurs at the disposal of Dokhturov; and

[1] This is my own explanation of what happened. Bagration says that he reached Smolensk at 10 a.m.; but Raievski declares that the leading brigade of the 8th Corps did not arrive until past 6 p.m., and speaks of Bagration coming later. Either the march of the 8th Corps was much delayed, or it moved with amazing slowness under the circumstances. Seeing what Bagration had written to Raievski, it is difficult to suppose that he would not make all speed to his rescue. It is only possible to reconcile the conflicting statements as to the hour of Bagration's arrival at Smolensk by such an assumption as is made in the text. For the rest it must be admitted that Bagration's despatches are often unreliable, and he naturally endeavoured to present himself in the best light. When there is a conflict of testimony between him and Raievski, I prefer to believe the latter.

the Dragoons of Siberia, Irkutsk and Orenburg replaced the cavalry of the Second Army. Paskievich assisted Dokhturov's divisional leaders in posting their troops; while the 7th Corps and 27th Division crossed the Dnieper and rejoined the 8th Corps. Next day Bagration started eastward, leaving a rear-guard at Sheïn Ostrog, 3 miles east of Smolensk, to guard a ford on the Dnieper.

In Smolensk Likhachev's division held the Krasnoï suburb and the Royal Citadel, and that of Kapsevich those of Mstislavl and Roslavl. Konovnitzin's division was held in reserve. For the present the left was only watched by the 6th Chasseurs and the cavalry. The Guard Chasseurs were at the bridge. Dokhturov had at his disposal about 120 guns, some of which were hoisted on to the platforms of the towers.

The rest of the First Army was stationed on the St. Petersburg road, about a mile and a half from the city, on a low plateau overlooking it. The corps of Baggohufwudt and Ostermann-Tolstoï were in front line, the former on the right of the road, the latter on the left. On Baggohufwudt's right were the 1st and 2nd Cavalry Corps, while behind him stood Strogonov's division of the 3rd Corps. The 3rd Cavalry Corps (less the regiments in Smolensk) was stationed to the left and in advance of the 4th Corps. The general reserve was formed by the 5th Corps, stationed 1 verst in rear of Strogonov. Finally, Platov's and Karpov's Cossacks watched the course of the river as far as Katan.

While Dokhturov's troops were taking up their positions they came into collision with the French outposts, which were driven back some short distance, Likhachev and Kapsevich making a general move forward at daybreak on the 17th in order to clear their front. This has been usually regarded as a general sortie on the part of Dokhturov to regain the suburbs, but neither in the French documents nor in Raievski's account is there any indication that they had been evacuated. Meanwhile, Davout's corps and the bulk of the Guard had arrived; and Napoleon had before Smolensk on the morning of the 17th the 1st, 3rd and 5th Corps, the Guard, and Murat's eight cavalry divisions—in all over 120,000 men. Junot's corps, owing to a series of mischances and misdirections, for which Napoleon blamed Junot, and the latter his senior divisional commander Tharreau, was still in rear. Latour-Maubourg was observing the country some distance to the south, while the 4th Corps was extended from Korythnia back to Rasasna.

Napoleon was still uneasy concerning the Russian troops at Katan, so much so that on the 17th, by his orders, Ney sent thither Mourier's cavalry brigade, supported by 6 battalions of Würtembergers and 6 guns, to guard against a possible flank attack. The force had a sharp action with the Cossacks and supporting infantry, which cost them 11 officers and probably 200 men killed and wounded.

During the morning there was continual skirmishing in the suburbs, but it was not until past midday that Napoleon ordered the advance. His reasons for assaulting the city at all are obscure, but it is possible that he expected to be able to carry the suburbs without excessive difficulty, and that the old walls of the city would easily yield to a steady cannonade. He may have counted upon the disadvantage of Dokhturov's position on a down slope, and on the fact that he himself could

CHAPTER V

overlook both the city and the opposite bank of the river. Bogdanovich says that he wished to cross the Dnieper and cut off Bagration's army, and only when no ford could be found did he make a direct assault—but there is no trace of this in the French documents. De Chambray thinks that Napoleon expected the Russians to deliver battle before the city. But from his higher ground he could see every movement of troops from Barclay's position. He therefore had no grounds for making such an assumption, and there is no reason for supposing that he did so. It is, of course, possible that he hoped by developing an assault, to induce Barclay to support Dokhturov with the bulk of his forces and fight with his back to the river, but there appears to be no evidence in favour of the supposition.

At about 12.30 the French advanced to the attack. Ney moved against the Royal Citadel and the Krasnoï suburb, with Ledru's division on the right, the remainder of the Württembergers on the left, and Razout in reserve. Davout assailed the Mstislavl suburb, Morand's division in the centre, Friant's on the right, and Gudin's, accompanied by the Marshal in person, on the left. Compans and Desaix were in reserve. Still farther to the right advanced Poniatowski's corps, with Zayonczek's division marching on the left against the Malakova Gate, and Kniaziewicz's on the right against the Nikolska suburb. The whole east front of the city was merely observed by Murat's cavalry.

On the whole the attack was, up to a certain point, successful—as might have been expected, when some 55,000 infantry were advancing downhill against about 19,000, whose position among a straggling maze of timber buildings was swept by the fire of over 300 guns. Progress was, however, very slow. Ledru and the Württembergers eventually carried the riverine suburbs, but could get no farther; the Royal Citadel, now formidably armed and garrisoned, defied attack. Davout's three splendid divisions went forward with admirable determination, drove Kapsevich's troops into the suburbs, and gained ground steadily, though at the price of very severe losses. On the right the Poles, after fierce fighting, captured the suburbs opposite to them, but, coming under the fire from the ramparts, were brought to a stand. The result was that by five o'clock the French and Poles had carried all the suburbs. Kapsevich's division was being pressed back towards the walls by Davout's advance. Konovnitzin's troops had all been used up in supporting the fighting line.

On the French right the Russian dragoons were charged and driven back into the city by the Polish cavalry. A battery of heavy artillery opened from the north bank of the Dnieper and checked the pursuers, but as it was isolated the Poles, with great gallantry, forded the river and rode forward to charge. They were attacked and repulsed by the escort of Barclay, who had just come thither to reconnoitre. A Lancer regiment was then detailed to escort the battery. Murat and Poniatowski now established a mass of artillery on the bank which fired over the city upon the permanent bridge and the temporary ones which had been thrown near it. Barclay thereupon placed several batteries in position on the north bank opposite the French and Polish guns, and after a hot cannonade succeeded in silencing them or forcing them to withdraw. Sir Robert Wilson says that he chose the position for the Russian artillery.

As he saw himself driven from the suburbs Dokhturov sent to Barclay for reinforcements. The latter sent an encouraging message; and ordered forward the division of the young Prince Eugen of Württemberg, who had never yet commanded in action, and was burning to distinguish himself. Eugen reached the front at the most critical moment of the action. Dokhturov's reserves were all engaged; Ney was furiously assailing the Royal Citadel; Davout and Poniatowski had driven Kapsevich and Konovnitzin upon and into the city, and were massing for an assault on the Malakova Gate. Kapsevich's division was broken and crowding back in complete disorder; Generals Skalon and Balla had fallen; and Dokhturov, having no fresh troops to put in, was greatly depressed. The appearance of Eugen's division relieved him. Pushnitzki's brigade was sent off to the right to help Likhachev against Ney, Rossi's to the left to strengthen the defence against Poniatowski; and the Chasseur brigade, led by Eugen himself, marched straight forward to the Malakova Gate and, charging furiously out through the midst of the fugitives, re occupied the covered way and checked the farther advance of Davout.

The driving of the Russians out of the suburbs marked the end of the French success. Rossi's brigade reached the Royal Citadel just in time to help Likhachev to resist Ney's final attack, which was repelled with heavy loss, though Ledru and Scheler were now supported by the 4th Regiment from Razout's division. Dokhturov rallied Kapsevich's division, and posted his force along the walls, Prince Eugen taking command on the left. The French halted within musket-shot, sheltering as best they could behind the houses and the old earthworks among them, but losing heavily by the fire from the battlements, and especially from the light guns on the towers. It was clearly hopeless to attempt an assault until a breach had been effected, and Napoleon sent forward 24 12-pounder guns of the Imperial Guard, which joined Davout's reserve and opened a furious fire. The Russians retorted vigorously, and as the infantry attacks slackened, the battle became a tremendous cannonade. The Russian artillery strove its hardest to silence the 12-pounder batteries, but in vain; they pounded steadily at the ancient walls, the gunners encouraged by the example set by Davout and Comte Sorbier, who personally directed their fire; but they could make little impression. Accounts are conflicting as to the fate of the covered way, the Russians insisting that they occupied it; while the French equally declared that they carried it. Captain François of the 30^e de Ligne says that the enfilading fire of the French artillery finally obliged the Russians to abandon it; and that Davout's sappers began to undermine the wall. Probably fortune varied at different points. It is only certain that the French and Poles were definitely checked at the wall, and the battle died out when darkness came on.

By this time the city and suburbs were everywhere on fire. The French later declared that the city had been deliberately destroyed; but this is entirely improbable. Being very largely constructed of wood, it was certain to take fire, and both time and means were lacking to extinguish a conflagration which spread with the fall of every shell.

The losses on both sides had been heavy. The Russians had engaged only 55 battalions, and Dokhturov's entire force, including cavalry, Cossacks and artillery, probably hardly exceeded 30,000 men. Barclay probably understates his loss at

CHAPTER V

4000, but no Russian authority admits more than 6000. Prince Eugen gives his own loss at 1300. Though his division came into action late it must be remembered that one brigade had to execute a desperate sortie in the face of enormous odds and a concentrated fire of cannon and musketry. Konovnitzin's division can hardly have suffered more; that of Likhachev and the detachments on the left probably lost less in proportion. On the other hand, Kapsevich's troops must have lost heavily. Probably the Russian figure of 6000 casualties is near the mark. In other words, Dokhturov had lost one-fifth of his effective strength. Raievski estimated his losses on the 16th at about 1000, giving a Russian total for the two days of 7000.

The French losses were naturally much greater, since they had brought far larger numbers into action, but were apparently not heavier in proportion. Davout gave the losses of the 1st Corps at from 5000 to 6000 men. Gudin returned a loss in his single division of 294 killed and 1436 wounded, and his list was by no means complete. The 7th Léger, for example, figures in it for 655 casualties, while, according to its Colonel, it had 707. Ney, according to Martinien's lists, had 129 officers killed and wounded in his infantry and cavalry, and his total loss must have been in the neighbourhood of 3500. Poniatowski reported a loss of 518 killed and 812 wounded; we must suppose that only the seriously hurt were registered. Reckoning the Polish losses at 2000, Ney's at 3500, Davout's at 5500, and adding a possible 1000 for losses among the artillery, reserve cavalry and Guard, we have a total of 12,000. Prisoners there were few on either side.

At 11 p.m. Barclay issued orders to evacuate Smolensk. He stated in his memoir to the Tzar that he had only intended to hold it to give Bagration time to get well forward on the Moscow road. This end was now attained, but the result of the order was what practically amounted to an open mutiny. A number of general officers, headed by the Grand Duke Constantine and by Bennigsen, who had no command and was not entitled to be present, went to Barclay's quarters and furiously protested against the abandonment of the city. Sir Robert Wilson received urgent letters from many generals on the same subject. Bagration, though he was not personally concerned in the mutinous demonstration, was bitterly indignant at Barclay's determination. He persisted that the First Army could easily hold its ground on the high ground behind Smolensk, while the Second Army could pass the Dnieper and attack Napoleon in flank. Barclay was of opinion that for the Second Army to adventure itself over the Dnieper would mean its destruction, and that, as regarded holding the line of the Dnieper, Napoleon had merely to extend his right to cut the Russian communications. Furthermore, he points out bitterly, operations of this kind, to be successful, require harmony between commanders. Towards the mutinous deputation he acted with firmness and dignity. He declined to withdraw his orders, and bade them leave his presence. Foiled in the attempt to bring pressure to bear upon him, the malcontents enlisted Wilson on their side, and induced him, as a personal friend of Alexander, to carry a letter to St. Petersburg demanding a new general. They also entrusted him with a declaration on their part that if orders came from the capital to suspend hostilities the army would regard them as not truly expressive of the Tzar's real determination, and would continue the struggle. All this was not altogether discreditable to the hearts of the generals, if it did no special honour to their heads. Wilson, who had rather hastily concluded that Barclay was not a fit person for the post of commander-in-chief and was also, it is to be feared, unduly influenced by his personal feelings towards Bennigsen and Bagration, accepted the mission. The result of wasting time in this mutinous delegation was that the retirement from Smolensk was not properly carried out.

THE OLD FORTIFICATIONS OF SMOLENSK
The north-east front abutting on the river. The illustration gives a good impression of the deeply-sunken course of a Russian river

Dokhturov withdrew his four divisions from the city without great difficulty, carrying off all his guns and all but the most severely injured of his wounded, took up the temporary bridges, broke the permanent structure, and was safe. But in the confusion at head-quarters no measures had been taken for properly occupying the *tête du pont* on the right bank. At 2 a.m. Ney ascertained that the wall in his front was deserted and entered the city, while a little later Davout also marched in by the Malakova Gate. The bridge was broken, but the river was only four feet deep, and at 9 a.m. a detachment of 600 Württembergers and Portuguese dashed through it and surprised the *tête du pont*. The Chasseurs holding it were driven out pell-mell. Hügel's Württemberg brigade at once followed; Ney brought up his artillery to the river's edge and the work was maintained. Barclay could only mask it with his rear-guard, under Baron Korff, consisting of 7 regiments of Chasseurs and 3 of Lancers and Hussars, which occupied the northern suburb. Davout promptly set to work to restore the bridge.

Barclay did not at once commence his retreat. For this Clausewitz blames him severely, but it must be remembered that on the 16th his whole army had made a forced march, and that on the 17th part of it had been heavily engaged. Then also

CHAPTER V

he was probably still harassed and distracted by the mutinous state of his subordinates. For the moment his firmness appears to have crushed insubordination. The Grand Duke was sent off to St. Petersburg under the pretext that his presence was needed there. Otherwise Barclay's delay was perhaps due to a desire to mislead Napoleon as to his line of retreat. In this he certainly succeeded; but it was scarcely necessary to retain the whole of his army in position; a well-handled rear-guard could have masked the direction of the march.

Early on the 18th Napoleon was at the river-bank opposite Korff's position, but then he appears to have retired to rest, after sending a brief letter to Maret at Vilna to announce the capture of Smolensk. He certainly may have needed sleep, and it may also be imagined that the bulk of the army, which had fought all day and been astir all night, was reposing. At any rate the day was one of inaction for both sides, except at the bridge, where desultory fighting went on until nightfall. Ney slowly reinforced the *tête du pont* by means of boats and rafts, but the bridge could not be completed until Korff withdrew. It does not seem to have been ready until late at night. During the day Junot's corps and the head of the 4th reached Smolensk.

There is some reason to believe that on this day Bagration's ugly temper led him into the commission of what was practically an act of treason. He took off his entire army to Solovievo, leaving only four regiments of Cossacks at the important road junction at Lubino. As the high-road by the river was commanded by French artillery on the south bank, Barclay would be forced to use for his retreat the cross-road by Gorbunovo, which reached the highway at Lubino, and certainly a handful of light horsemen was a most inadequate guard for this vital last point. Barclay says that he only learnt at the last moment that it was practically uncovered. Bagration's retreat was natural, now that Smolensk was abandoned, but in leaving no infantry at Lubino, and not apparently informing his colleague, he committed, to say the least of it, a very dubious action. Otherwise the incident throws light on the bad staff-work of the Russians, and one may fairly ask why Yermólov and St. Priest were not in close and frequent communication with each other.

Between 7 and 8 p.m. Dokhturov, with the 5th and 6th Corps, and Korff's and Pahlen's cavalry (less detachments to rear-guard), was ordered to march by cross-roads to Solovievo. An hour or so later the 2nd, 3rd and 4th Corps, with Uvarov's cavalry corps, started by the Gorbunovo track for Lubino. At this moment apparently, Barclay heard that there were no troops at that vital point except Karpov's Cossacks. He at once directed Major-General Tuchkov III with the Yelisabetgrad Hussars, the Revel Regiment, the 20th and 21st Chasseurs and a horse artillery battery to hasten thither. At 2 a.m. Korff withdrew from before Smolensk.

From the first everything went wrong. The retreating columns encountered all kinds of difficulties. The roads were, of course, unspeakable. Gullies were frequent, and often had to be bridged for the artillery to pass, nothing having been done in advance by the inefficient staff. The darkness and the troubles incidental to filing some 40,000 men along a single bad track caused endless delays. To crown all, the column missed its way and wandered into a side track, with the result that at daybreak its rear was only 2 or 3 miles north-east of the St. Petersburg suburb!

On the withdrawal of Korff, Davout had completed his bridge-restoring, and at 4 a.m. Ney's main body began to pass.

Barclay, whose great military virtue was perfect self-possession in the face of danger, ordered Prince Eugen, with as much of his division as remained with him, to take up a position at the hamlet of Gedeonovo, bidding him recollect that the fate of the army might depend upon his firmness. Ney's advance-guard was soon in contact with Eugen, who held his ground obstinately, in order to give Korff time to file past. After a good deal of fighting Eugen was forced back, but by that time Korff had got his 14 battalions on to the Gorbunovo-Lubino track. Eugen then fell back to another position towards Gorbunovo, and Ney was preparing to follow, when orders arrived directing him to incline to his right to the Moscow road. This appears to have been about 11 a.m.

Early on the 19th Napoleon sent Eblé to Prudichevo to bridge the Dnieper, and ordered Junot's corps to cross the river there, a movement which would bring him to Lubino. Grouchy was sent along the St. Petersburg road, Montbrun along that to Moscow, while Bruyère's division of Nansouty's corps was ordered to support Ney. Evidently Napoleon had no certainty as to the precise direction of Barclay's retreat, and so far the Russian general's delay on the 18th had justified itself. About 11 a.m. Davout's corps began to cross the bridge. The Guard, now rejoined by Claparède, was in Smolensk. Eugène and Poniatowski were in the ruins of the suburbs. The Emperor apparently spent the morning in his cabinet, but in the afternoon mounted and proceeded to the high ground east of the city, opposite Sheïn Ostrog.

General Tuchkov III in his march had to contend with the same difficulties and obstacles which impeded the main column, so that he did not reach the Moscow road, some 4 miles west of Lubino, until 8 a.m. Toll accompanied him, and they went forward to confer with Karpov. It soon became evident that a force of cavalry, presumably the advance-guard of Napoleon's main body, was moving eastward from Smolensk, and also that a strong column was passing the Dnieper at Prudichevo. Tuchkov pushed Karpov out to observe Junot, and with his own column took up a position across the road, where it passed over a low swell, with his flanks covered by some small woods and his twelve guns on the crest of the rise, and awaited events.

Soon after 10 o'clock skirmishing began on the high-road, probably with the advanced guard of Bruyère's division, supported perhaps by some battalions of light infantry; but it cannot have been until about 1 p.m. that the head of Ney's main column appeared, and the battle of Lubino definitely began.[2] By this time the 3rd Corps, which was at the head of Barclay's column, had reached Lubino. As it tramped through, Tuchkov I detached Tornov's brigade of Grenadiers to support his brother.

---

[2] Only thus is it possible to reconcile the statements of the Russian historians that the action began at 10 a.m. with that of Eugen of Württemberg, that he did not withdraw from Gedeonovo until about that hour. Ney seems to have followed him to his second defensive position before he was recalled, which brings us to 11 a.m. at least; and then time must be allowed for the march of nearly 6 miles to Tuchkov's front.

CHAPTER V

At 1 p.m. the head of Ney's infantry column began to attack. The Russians offered a steady resistance, and it was not until three that, seeing the heavy masses coming into line, and knowing that Junot was threatening his left, Tuchkov decided to withdraw behind the Stragan rivulet, some 2 miles to his rear, and about the same distance from Lubino. Ney inferred from the obstinate resistance that Tuchkov covered some important movement, and asked Napoleon for support. It was probably while he was awaiting a reply that Tuchkov drew off, covered by his cavalry, towards Lubino. Napoleon ordered Gudin's division to reinforce Ney, sent Morand's towards the left with a view to a turning movement, but gave Junot no directions; clearly he had no conception of the real importance of the action.

Meanwhile the Russians had safely retired behind the Stragan, where they were joined by Barclay, bringing with him 8 heavy guns, 7 battalions, and a mass of cavalry. The 3rd and 4th Corps had now reached Lubino, but Baggohufwudt and Korff were far to the rear, and the cross-road was packed with baggage and hundreds of guns, which would be the prey of the French could they break through. But Barclay on the field, calm, brave and resourceful, was a very different man from the anxious and harassed Barclay of the cabinet. Without hesitation he ranged his scanty force in order of battle, and ordered Yermólov to bring up the 3rd and 4th Corps with all speed.

The high-road, after crossing the Stragan, passed over the southern end of a low wooded plateau which extended northward for some 2 miles. South of the road a stretch of marsh, in most places passable owing to the dry weather, extended to the Dnieper. Out of it arose several low swells of firm ground, studded with hamlets and patches of wood. One of these lay near the road, and needed to be occupied.

On the northern plateau Barclay posted 5 infantry regiments, and to the south of the road 2 more, with 3 battalions in reserve. Twenty guns were posted to sweep the road. On the swell in the marsh he stationed 26 squadrons of Hussars under General Orlov-Denisov. Of infantry and guns there were no more available, and, to make a show of support for Orlov-Denisov, Barclay ordered Uvarov's cavalry to dismount, and occupy a village behind the marsh on his left. At 5 o'clock, just as the action was renewed, Konovnitzin and, a little later, Choglokov arrived, bringing with them 7 regiments of their divisions and a horse-battery. Choglokov's troops were ordered to support the cavalry, and Konovnitzin's 4 regiments brought up to the centre.

At 5 p.m. Gudin's division reached the front, and Ney at once sent it forward, Razout's advancing level with it on the left. Some Württemberg artillery was carried forward with the advance to silence Barclay's battery. Ledru and Scheler remained in reserve.

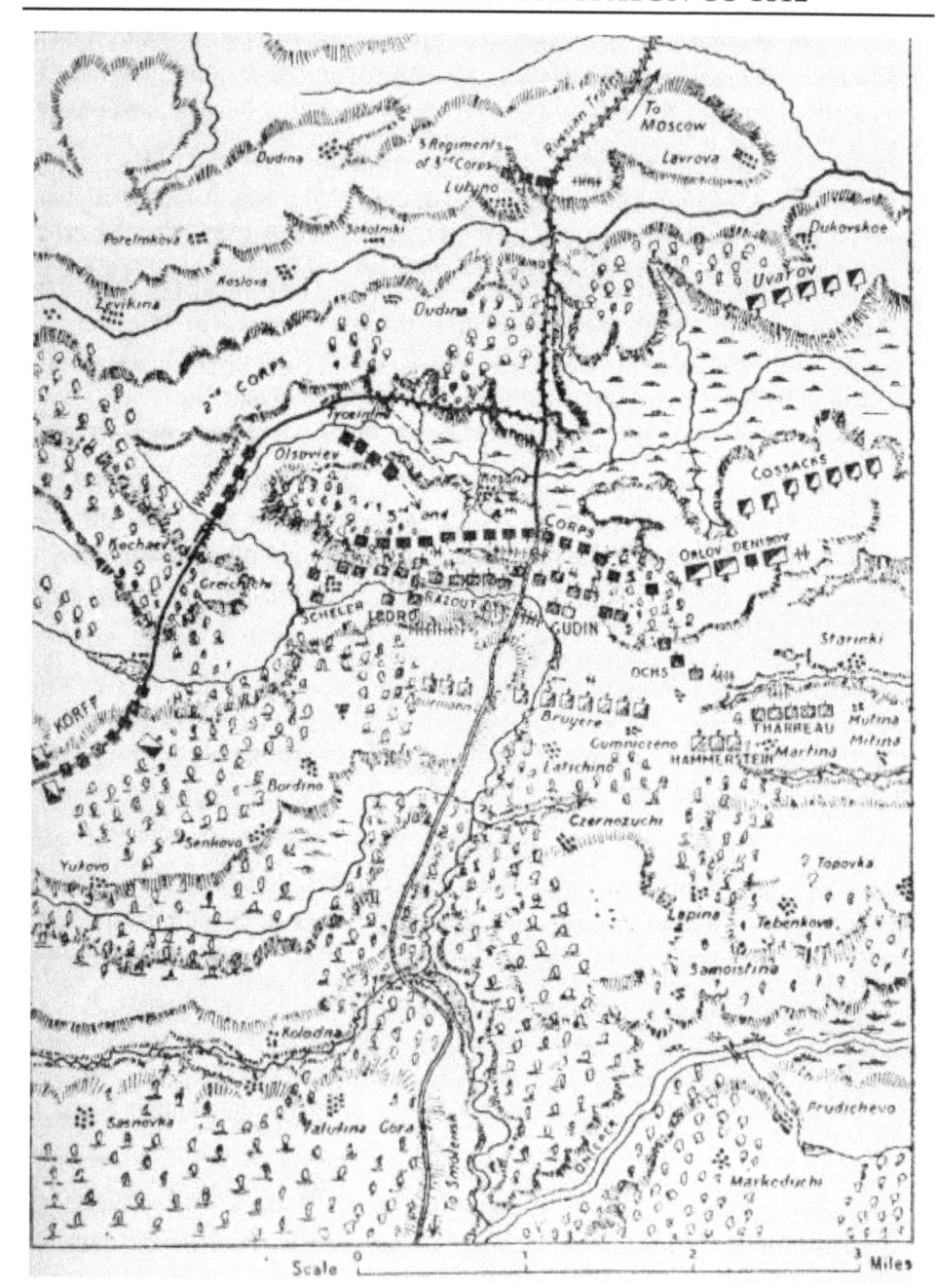

BATTLE OF LUBINO,
AUGUST 19th, 1812

Fought to cover the passage of the 2nd, 3rd and 4th Russian Army Corps from the north of Smolensk to the Moscow road at Lubino

Comte Gudin, one of the finest officers in the French service, conducted the

CHAPTER V

attack with splendid vigour. The 7th Léger, supported by 2 battalions of the 21st and 127th Regiments, crossed the Stragan, and, maddened by the fall of the General, who was struck down as he led the charge, broke the Russian infantry to the south of the road and drove them back, threatening to pierce Barclay's thin defensive line. Barclay at once sent forward Konovnitzin's division which, charging resolutely, checked the advance and enabled the broken troops to rally. General Gérard, who succeeded to Gudin's command, sent forward the 12th Regiment, and restored the battle on the right. Meanwhile, a fierce struggle was raging north of the road where Razout was making desperate but fruitless attempts to carry the plateau. Attack after attack was steadily met and repulsed.

Beyond Gudin's right, Murat was coming up from Smolensk with Nansouty's and Montbrun's cavalry, but only his single light division (Bruyère) could be of much service. Still farther to the right Junot was advancing from Prudichevo, but showed great irresolution. He at first declined to move at all, and what actually took place is very obscure. He seems, about five o'clock, to have reconnoitred the Russian left with his cavalry brigade and two battalions of light infantry; and some desultory fighting ensued. His cavalry do not appear to have gained any success, and a company of light infantry which established itself across the marsh was destroyed by the Russian Hussars. Then, when Choglokov's infantry was seen coming into action, Junot formed his corps in squares opposite the Russian left. At last General Ochs obtained permission to advance with 2 battalions of light infantry, presently supported by Junot with 4 companies of Voltigeurs. He was successful in driving back the Russian outposts, and with this Junot's attack came to an end. Murat had obliged Karpov's Cossacks to retire behind the main Russian line, and his light horsemen executed one or two more or less successful charges on Orlov-Denisov's troopers, but without Junot's co-operation he could do no more.

At 6 p.m. Tuchkov I had brought forward all his corps, and was himself at Lubino with his 3 rear-guard regiments, and 3 horse batteries which he had drawn out of the stream of retreating artillery. The position was still critical. Baggohufwudt had not yet arrived. Korff was still farther back; the trains were still pouring along the road from Gedeonovo. But everyone on the Russian side was at last thoroughly awake to the emergency. Every attempt was made to hasten the march; and the incompetent gilded youth of the General Staff, at whom Eugen of Württemberg sneers bitterly, were doing useful work in saving the trains and the precious artillery. At Lubino the bridge was utterly inadequate for the vast throng of vehicles. Prince Alexander of Württemberg suggested that another should be made. Löwenstern dismounted a squadron of Hussars and set them to tear down the houses, while Alexander and Baron Salza went with a company of pioneers to the stream; and so, by desperate exertions, a bridge was constructed, to which a part of the mass was diverted. The tracks were all but impassable in many places, and had to be corduroyed and made up with fascines and boughs before the trains could be got forward. The gunners and drivers, admirably directed and encouraged by Count Kutaïsov, made superhuman exertions to drag the artillery along, and, to their glory, not a gun or caisson was abandoned.

On the Stragan the battle raged with unabated fury. Barclay de Tolly was doing his uttermost, and though the line was often shaken it was always reformed and steadied. Some of Ledru's and Scheler's troops endeavoured to get round the Russian right, but their attempts had no result; the Revel Regiment and the Bodyguard Grenadiers, fighting doggedly with the bayonet, held them off; while Konovnitzin and Tuchkov III still successfully defended the road. About seven Ney made a general advance, calling up his reserves and sending forward every available man. Gérard joined in on the right, throwing in his last three battalions. The Russian position was critical, for Barclay had sent forward all his reserves; but at this moment Baggohufwudt's corps at last made its appearance. Olsuviev's division, which was marching at its head, was at once put in; and again the opposing forces closed in deadly strife. At first it seemed as if the French would carry all before them in their impetuous onslaught, and matters looked so dark that Tuchkov III went himself to ask Barclay for aid—as did Windham in 1855 in the Great Redan of Sevastopol. Barclay was furious. "Go back to your post," he stormed, "and get yourself killed! If you come back I'll shoot you!"

Colonel Voïkov came up the road with his heavy battery just in time to check Gérard's onslaught. Still the French held their own and, believing themselves victorious, were slowly gaining ground; when Eugen's division at length marched upon the field, and Tuchkov, burning to redeem himself, led on a counter-attack. He himself was wounded and taken at the head of the Ekaterinoslav Regiment, but Eugen at once supported, and after a bitter struggle, in which the bayonet was freely employed, the French were finally repulsed. It was 9 o'clock when the roar of conflict died away in the darkness. Korff had reached the field; the artillery and trains were on the way to Solovievo; and the Russians had gained a great strategic victory.

Morand's division had been unable to come into action, having been entangled in a piece of virgin forest, and was eventually recalled by Napoleon. It has been suggested that had he been allowed to continue his advance it would have ensured the destruction of the Russian army. Lacking definite information as to time and topography, it is difficult to express an opinion, but, judging from such descriptions as are available, it seems very doubtful whether Morand could have debouched with a force strong enough to be effective.

Barclay, having attained the object for which he had stood to fight, had no intention of waiting to be overwhelmed by Napoleon's main army about Smolensk. At 4 a.m. on the 20th his much-tried troops evacuated the field, and marched 20 miles to Solovievo, where Dokhturov arrived the same day. Bagration, having thrown three bridges over the Dnieper, was already across. On the 21st the First Army followed, took up the bridges, and marched for Dorogobuzh.

French writers for the most part consider Lubino, or Valutina-Gora as they call it, a victory, but to regard it thus is merely to make a mock of the word. A battle is not necessarily fought for the possession of a few yards of ground. Barclay had fought at Lubino in order to secure the safe passage of his right column into the Moscow road. This had been successfully achieved, and very heavy loss inflicted on the pursuers, who had failed to capture a single gun or any appreciable amount of baggage. Napoleon regarded the battle as a mere advance-guard engagement.

Had he realised its real importance he would not have failed to send forward everything available. Barclay must have been disastrously defeated, and probably driven northward with the remains of his army.

The French had on the field at Lubino about 50,000 men, of whom perhaps 37,000 were seriously engaged. The number of Russian troops successively brought into action was probably about 30,000. The losses were naturally heavy. Gérard alone reported 2297 killed and wounded, and Ney can hardly have lost less than 4000. Junot probably overestimated his losses at 700, but, including casualties among Murat's cavalry, the French total must have been over 7000. The losses of the Russians were probably rather less, as they were standing on the defensive, and for the most part succeeded in repelling attack, nevertheless, they were very heavy—probably in the neighbourhood of 5000. Few prisoners were taken—not more than some hundreds on both sides.

It is impossible to conclude this chapter without some remarks upon the strategy which led up to the battles about Smolensk. It is tolerably certain, judging from the evidence of documents, that Napoleon's plan of marching upon Smolensk by the left bank of the Dnieper was a preconceived one. Considered by itself, there is little to say of the manœuvre. It was in no way hazardous, since the left flank of the columns moving from Vitebsk was covered by forests, and once across the Dnieper the march was protected by the river against a Russian flank attack. Moreover, having two lines of supply, Napoleon risked nothing by moving his army across from one to the other.

The manœuvre was certainly unexpected by the Russian leaders—except perhaps by Bagration—and it is clear that it was only the firmness of Raievski and the prompt return of the main army that saved Smolensk from falling into Napoleon's hands.

Nevertheless, when we turn from the manœuvre to its purpose it seems doubtful whether it was by any means the best under the circumstances.

Napoleon's object was the bringing to bay of the Russian main army and the crushing of it in a decisive battle. As the Russians had chosen to take the offensive, the opportunity was apparently in his hands. Barclay might march fast enough to force an engagement before Davout could arrive from Orsha, but even so Napoleon could meet him with equal or superior numbers. If Barclay returned to the defensive, Napoleon's best manœuvre was to advance to Poriechie, threatening the Russian communications with Moscow. To reopen them Barclay and Bagration must either give battle or retreat eastward in all haste, in which case Smolensk would fall of itself. The utmost that could be expected of the march south of the Dnieper was that the Russians might be forestalled at Smolensk.

The modern French opinion appears to be that this forestalling was the essence of the plan, and that Napoleon, having occupied the city, intended to debouch from it and attack Barclay and Bagration in the rear.

To the writer it appears that all criticism must necessarily base itself upon the fact that Napoleon's strategy was preconceived. Before he knew anything of the Russian plans he had practically made up his mind to advance on Smolensk by the left bank of the Dnieper. The offensive movement of the Russians produced no change in his resolution.

It is highly probable that his determination was taken on grounds not purely military. He must by now have recognised that warfare in Russia was subject to conditions which did not obtain in Germany or Austria. His opponents were elusive; but there were certain places regarded by soldiers and people as holy, which the popular voice would probably force the generals to make a show of defending. He therefore resolved to threaten Smolensk directly, believing that thereby the Russian army would be constrained to give battle.

Even so it appears somewhat doubtful whether this end could not have been as well attained by manœuvring on the right bank. The advance by the left appears to have assumed that Smolensk would be uncovered and undefended, and that the Russian field army would be too far away to return to its rescue. Napoleon, on this hypothesis, would have been able to occupy it and give battle to his outmanœuvred opponents with all the prestige of the capture of the sacred city behind his onset. As a fact Barclay had provided for speedy information by his flank-guard under Neverovski, and his resolution not to move far from Smolensk afforded the means of frustrating Napoleon's strategy. That he only arrived in the nick of time hardly affects the discussion, since his obsession about an attack from the direction of Poriechie delayed him for a day. On the other hand, Napoleon's hesitation, owing to the appearance of Bagration's army at Katan, also caused him to lose a day, during which Barclay was able to arrive.

According to Barclay's memoir to the Tzar he had no intention of wasting his army in the defence of Smolensk, a place of no military value, and merely held it in order to allow Bagration time to occupy Solovievo. Bagration and the majority of the Russian generals appear to have expected that he would have made it the centre of the Russian operations. It is, of course, possible that Barclay, harassed and perplexed, did make some conditional promise as to defending Smolensk should a favourable opportunity offer. General Okunev—who may perhaps voice the views of Paskievich—apparently thinks that it could have been held. But it must be said that as the Russians' line of retreat was in extension of their left flank such a policy would have been hazardous at best. There seems every reason to believe that Barclay's ideas were sound; what he lacked was commanding strength of character to enforce them on his unruly officers.

Napoleon's assault upon Smolensk is very difficult to account for: and led to little but waste of human life.

CHAPTER VI
THE OPERATIONS IN VOLHYNIA AND ON THE DÜNA

It has been seen that when King Jerome resigned his command, the 5th and 8th Corps went to reinforce Davout, Latour-Maubourg to observe Bobruisk, while the 7th Corps returned to Slonim. Reynier was instructed to take the place of Schwarzenberg in guarding the frontier of the Grand Duchy of Warsaw, while the latter marched on Minsk. Reynier himself was convinced that his corps was far too weak for the prescribed duty, while he had better information than his master of Tormazov's real strength. Nevertheless he endeavoured to carry out Napoleon's orders. On the 19th he ordered Klengel's infantry brigade and a regiment of cavalry to take the place of an Austrian detachment at Kobrin. On the same day Schwarzenberg informed Napoleon that Tormazov had some 30,000 men at Lutsk. The Emperor, however, was sceptical. On the 22nd he ordered Reynier to enter Volhynia, saying that Tormazov's "army" was merely a collection of reserve battalions. On the same day he told Davout that Tormazov had only 8000 men of 3rd battalions. The movements which he had ordered continued, and by the 24th the Austrians were about Slonim, on the way to Minsk, while the 7th Corps, moving in the opposite direction, was approaching Kobrin, some 30 miles east of Brest-Litovsk.

Napoleon's information was hopelessly inaccurate. So far he could not be accountable for the unforeseen situation which was now to disclose itself. But his refusal to believe Schwarzenberg and Reynier is distinctly blameworthy, and can only be attributed to the fatal optimism which had now become fixed in him.

General Tormazov, when hostilities broke out, commanded an army which was neither concentrated nor complete in its organisation. Three infantry divisions, a brigade of combined Grenadier companies, 3 regiments of Hussars, and a cavalry corps 36 squadrons strong, were scattered over western Volhynia. General Sacken's reserve troops—12 depleted battalions and 24 squadrons—were at Zaslavl and Staroï Konstantinov near the frontier of Podolia, and the irregulars were scattered along the Austrian and Polish borders. It was not until the middle of July that a respectable force was at last concentrated near Lutsk.

Tormazov's original task was the defence of Volhynia, but Napoleon showed no intention of making any eccentric movements in that direction. On hearing of Bagration's retreat on Bobruisk, he thought that he himself might be obliged to fall back towards Kiev, in order not entirely to lose touch with the Second Army. By the middle of July, however, the situation became clearer. The allied troops were pouring along the Warsaw-Smolensk road, and there were only few and small detachments guarding the Polish frontier. He therefore determined to invade the Grand Duchy of Warsaw by way of Lublin; and General Lambert, his cavalry commander, had already crossed the Bug, when he was recalled.

On July 17th instructions reached Tormazov from Alexander to advance northward against the flanks and rear of the forces that were opposed to Bagration. It is probable that this manœuvre promised more immediate results than the contemplated advance on Warsaw. At the same time it is by no means certain that Tormazov was wrong in his original decision. The capture of Warsaw would have been a terrific shock to Napoleon's prestige. The Russians could not have held it long, but they would have been able to destroy the depôts there collected, and might have cut up Reynier's corps had Napoleon, as was probable, urged it in overhasty pursuit of an enemy whose strength he underestimated. In that case Napoleon would have been obliged to divert against him not merely Schwarzenberg's Austrians, but perhaps also the 8th Corps. In any case he would have been forced to employ some of his new formations in the rear to meet the irruption.

The plan now imposed upon Tormazov had the advantage that it must, in the nature of things, call back Schwarzenberg from his march to reinforce Davout. On the other hand, it involved passing the Pinsk Marshes, which would oppose a dangerous barrier to retreat in case of a reverse; and the chances of crushing the 7th Corps were minimised, since a few concentric marches would unite Reynier and Schwarzenberg.

General Sacken with his reserves had been left in eastern Volhynia; some of his troops were detached to strengthen the force at Mozyr. On July 22 Tormazov ordered Lambert to leave General Kruchov, with a brigade of dragoons and 2 regiments of Cossacks, to observe the Polish frontier, and with 4 battalions, 16 squadrons, 5 Cossack regiments and 6 guns, to march by both banks of the Bug upon Brest-Litovsk. Four battalions and 7 squadrons, under Major-General Melissino, were to make a demonstration towards Pinsk, while the corps of Kamenski and Markov advanced upon Brest-Litovsk and Kobrin. Tormazov's strength, exclusive of Kruchov, was probably about 36,000 men, with 144 guns. He was consequently nearly three times as strong as Reynier's corps; but the latter could be sustained within a few days by 30,000 Austrians.

On the 24th Reynier's main body was about Bezdizh on the Brest-Litovsk-Pinsk high-road. Klengel's brigade occupied Kobrin. Two squadrons of cavalry were at Brest, and another detachment was on the road to Pinsk. Reynier's small corps was thus spread out over a line of 80 miles. Reynier appears to have realised his danger, and provided against it to the best of his ability by keeping his main body together. He was perhaps to blame in detaching Klengel, but in justice it must be said that his duties were out of all proportion to his strength.

On the 24th Lambert expelled the Saxon cavalry from Brest-Litovsk. Melissino drove in the outposts on Reynier's left, and occupied Pinsk, expelling its Austrian garrison and capturing a gun. Reynier was thus alarmed on both flanks, and

CHAPTER VI

doubted in which direction to turn. Early on the 27th Tormazov's advanced guard, under Major-General Chaplitz, approached Kobrin from the south, while at the same time Lambert's cavalry came up from the west. His infantry, who were fatigued by hard marching, he had left in the rear.

Klengel's brigade consisted of only about 2600 men with 8 guns. Obviously he could make no effective resistance to the Russian army; but he considered himself bound by Reynier's orders to defend Kobrin to the last extremity. Reynier's comment was that, being the advanced guard of the corps, the brigade should have retired when it became obvious that it ran the risk of being surrounded. It appears to be a somewhat uncertain point among military men as to how far detachment commanders are justified in departing from the letter of their orders. On the morning of the 27th Klengel's line of retreat on Pruzhani was certainly open. On the other hand, his corps commander would probably come by the Pinsk road; and he appears to have made at least one attempt to break through in that direction, which gives some index to what was passing in his mind. By midday Lambert had cut the road to Pruzhani, and the brigade was surrounded. The Saxons were driven by overwhelming numbers from their hasty entrenchments into the town, and after a gallant resistance, and having expended all their ammunition, were forced, about 2 p.m., to surrender. They had lost 76 killed and 182 wounded, including 13 officers. Seventy-six officers and 2382 rank and file were captured, with 8 guns and 4 standards.[3] Reynier's advance-guard had only reached Horodetz, about 11 miles east of Kobrin, when it was met by fugitives who bore tidings of the disaster.

Tormazov, with diplomatic courtesy, complimented the Saxon officers on their really creditable defence, and returned them their swords. He could not, however, push his advance. His commissariat was defective and supplies were running short. He had also his prisoners to dispose of. His infantry were fatigued with hard marching on execrable roads. He therefore was obliged to halt for two days, which Reynier utilised to effect his retreat. He appealed for help to Schwarzenberg, who informed Napoleon that Reynier was too weak to resist Tormazov, who was estimated to be 40,000 strong, and that he must perforce turn back to his rescue from Nesvizh. On August 2nd he reached Polonka, 18 miles from Slonim, now occupied by Reynier. Tormazov, leaving Kobrin on the 30th, occupied Pruzhani and Antopol and pushed out detachments; while Kruchov's force crossed the Bug and made reconnaissances towards Warsaw. The Poles were panic-stricken; and Loison, the Governor of Königsberg, thought it necessary to advance towards Bielostok with nearly the whole of his force—some 10,000 men. More than this Tormazov could not do. He was still very short of supplies; every march in advance took him farther from his base, and he had the Pinsk Marshes in his rear.

Napoleon, probably with some misgivings, informed Schwarzenberg on July 31st that he was to support Reynier according to his information, which, as he was on the spot, must necessarily be better than that of the Emperor. On August 2nd he placed the 7th Corps under his orders, and instructed him to march against Tor-

---

[3] Klengel gives his whole strength as only 1985; but he had obvious motives for minimising the disaster. The figures given in the text are confirmed by the muster-rolls of the 7th Corps.

mazov and drive him into Volhynia. The Government at Warsaw meanwhile was making desperate efforts to form a field force at Zamosc, under General Kosinski.

On August 3rd the Austrians and Saxons were in close communication, and on the 4th the united force began to advance. Tormazov's advanced guards were attacked on August 8th and driven back, except at Pruzhani, from which Lambert was only expelled on the 10th after a well-contested rear-guard action. Tormazov, finding his outposts everywhere assailed by superior forces, ordered Markov and Kamenski to Gorodeczna, about half-way from Pruzhani to Kobrin. Lambert and Markov united there in the night of the 10th-11th, and next day Kamenski also arrived. Melissino's detachment and the other advanced guards, under Generals Chaplitz and Prince Khovanski, could not rejoin under some days. Tormazov therefore had only 24 battalions, 36 squadrons, and 3 regiments of Cossacks, amounting with artillery to about 21,000 men. In artillery, however, he was strong, having 84 pieces, a large proportion of which were heavy.

The Russian position was a fairly strong one, if defended by adequate numbers. The Pruzhani-Kobrin road passes over a low plateau, at the foot of which flows a marshy stream. This plateau is some three miles long and a little less in breadth. It extends roughly east and west, its eastern extremity being opposite Gorodeczna. West of it is a valley about a mile in breadth, beyond which rises a second plateau, thickly wooded, through which another road leads from the village of Cherechev to join that to Kobrin some miles south-west of Gorodeczna. The eastern end of the plateau was also shut in by woods. Besides the causeway across the marsh at Gorodeczna, there was a second at Poddubno about three miles above, and a third a mile farther on at the Cherechev road. Obviously all should have been guarded; but only that at Gorodeczna was actually held. The reasons for this extraordinary oversight are not clear. It is possible that Tormazov expected a turning movement on the right rather than the left. It is also possible that he did not intend to fight a general action, but only a rear-guard engagement, in order to gain time for Chaplitz, Khovanski and Melissino to close up. Apparently also he considered that Schwarzenberg and Reynier were following him in one column on the Kobrin road. In any case he merely kept the bulk of his force opposite Gorodeczna. His opponents were moving in two columns, the Austrians upon Gorodeczna, Reynier with the Saxons on the right towards Poddubno. Schwarzenberg had made considerable detachments to guard his communications, but his entire force can hardly have numbered less than 36,000 men, including 12,000 Saxons, with 96 guns.

Reynier pointed out to Schwarzenberg that Tormazov's negligence afforded opportunities for a flanking movement. Schwarzenberg assented and supported him with Siegenthal's division, Hesse-Homburg's brigade of Bianchi's division, and a brigade of light cavalry, while with the rest of his forces he observed the main Russian force. Tormazov was drawn up in three lines on the Kobrin road, facing Gorodeczna, Markov's 12 battalions in front line, Kamenski's 12 (temporarily commanded by Prince Cherbatov, Kamenski being ill) a verst to the rear, Lambert with the cavalry behind Cherbatov.

In the night of the 11th-12th a Saxon detachment seized the Poddubno dyke.

CHAPTER VI

Tormazov apparently heard of this about 9 a.m. on the 12th and promptly sent Cherbatov with 10 battalions, 2 dragoon regiments and 24 guns to Poddubno. This appeared temporarily to secure the left, but about noon Siegenthal arrived and threatened a direct attack, while Reynier, who had moved the bulk of his corps along the Cherechev road, debouched from the woods and menaced the Russian rear. Tormazov at first simply fronted Cherbatov to the left, leaving the guns and a single infantry regiment at Poddubno, and covered the new front with the fire of 24 more guns brought up from the reserve. It soon, however, became evident that the turning movement was being executed by considerable forces, and that Cherbatov could not withstand it unaided. Tormazov thereupon called up Markov with 8 battalions to prolong Cherbatov's line, and Lambert with 4 battalions and 24 squadrons to cover the left flank. Lambert deployed across the Cherechev road, barring it against the farther advance of General Zechmeister with his Austrian cavalry and Saxon infantry. Schwarzenberg on his side, instead of attacking the weak detachment now before him at Gorodeczna, sent another infantry brigade and one of cavalry to the right, and himself proceeded thither.

At 3 a.m. Frimont's Austrian cavalry and Trautenberg's infantry at Gorodeczna were demonstrating against weak detachments, while nearly the whole Russian army had faced to the left and rear. Tormazov, considering that the extension of the hostile line afforded an opportunity for piercing it, developed a fierce attack by Cherbatov's infantry upon Sahr's Saxon brigade, which was driven back, barely saving its artillery from capture by the Russian dragoons. To extricate it General Bianchi led forward Lilienberg's brigade, while Schwarzenberg, now at Poddubno, ordered Hesse-Homburg's across the stream, and Siegenthal sent forward part of his division. By these combined efforts the advance of the Russians was brought to a stand and finally converted into a retreat. The brigades of Lilienberg and Sahr moved forward together, Hesse-Homburg joining in on the left, Lecoq's Saxon division prolonging the line to the right, while Zechmeister, reinforced by Froelich's Austrian and Gablenz's Saxon cavalry, renewed his attacks on Lambert. The latter had hitherto held his own with considerable success, but was now driven back and forced to seek shelter behind Markov's line. Night ended the conflict, and under cover of darkness Tormazov rallied his detachments and retreated on Kobrin, covered by a rear-guard, under Lambert. At Teveli, 7 miles from the battle-field, Chaplitz rejoined and took over rear-guard duty from Lambert.

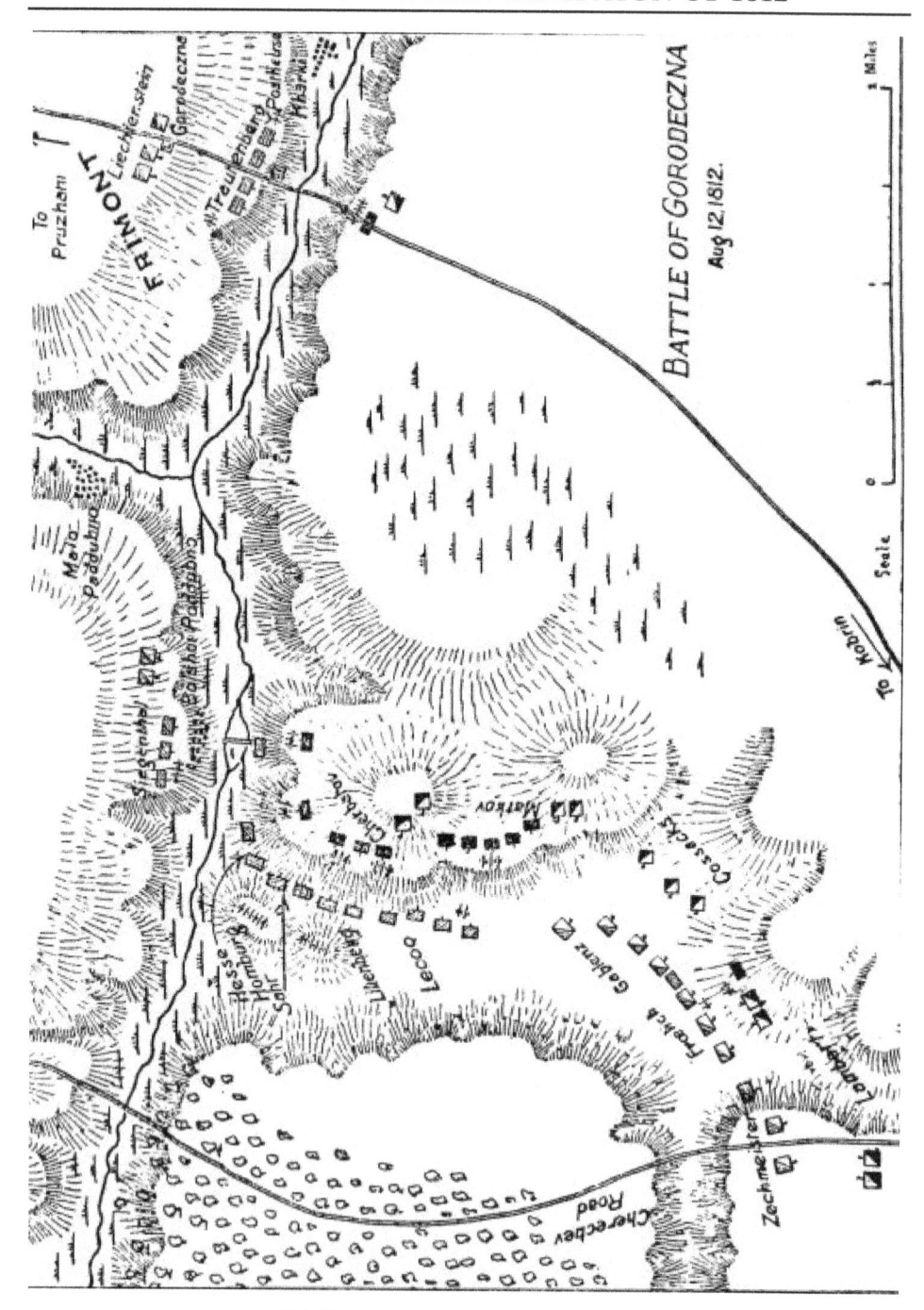

BATTLE OF GORODECZNA
August 12, 1812
Fought between Napoleon's detached right wing (Austrians and Saxons) under Prince Schwarzenberg against the Russian Army of Volhynia

CHAPTER VI

The Russian loss appears to have been about 3000 men out of a total of about 18,000 actively engaged: of these perhaps 500 were prisoners. That of the allies was probably a little less. Schwarzenberg estimated the loss of the Austrians at about 1300, of whom 865 were in Bianchi's division. Reynier only admitted 931 casualties.

Tormazov did not stay his retreat at Kobrin, but continued on his way southward, intending to make for the Styr and stand on the defensive behind it. His resolution was undoubtedly wise. With Chaplitz's and Khovanski's troops he had in hand 30,000 men, and might abide the chances of another battle. But his force was too small to rout Schwarzenberg's, and a heavy defeat might leave Admiral Chichagov, who was at last on the way from Bukharest, too weak to face Napoleon's right wing. On the other hand, by retreating on Lutsk he would lessen the distance between himself and the Admiral, would be in closer communication with his base at Kiev and Sacken's reserves, and his position behind the marshy Styr might well induce the cautious Austrian general and his half-hearted or openly disaffected lieutenants to call a halt.

On the 13th there was some rear-guard fighting on the Kobrin road, but it was not serious, and Tormazov continued his retreat to Kovel, which he reached on the 24th. There he apparently would have stood firm, but Schwarzenberg threatening to turn his left he abandoned his position and marched towards Lutsk, where he arrived on the 29th. Schwarzenberg's pursuit was not very energetic, owing to scarcity of supplies and the difficulty of the Pinsk fenlands.

Tormazov therefore found himself at the beginning of September in the same position which he had occupied five weeks before. His strategy had been far from faultless: in particular his detachments previous to the battle of Gorodeczna seem to have been unnecessarily large. His tactics at Gorodeczna had been bad at the outset, however much his boldness and energy may have compensated for his earlier carelessness. Still, whatever his faults, he had inflicted a heavier loss than he had sustained, and had drawn upon himself, away from the main theatre of war, the whole of the Austrian auxiliary army and the 7th Corps, as well as Kosinski's Polish column from Zamosc. Moreover, Admiral Chichagov's advanced guard was only fourteen or fifteen marches away, and might be relied upon to join him by the middle of September.

It has already been seen that when Barclay evacuated Drissa he had left Count Wittgenstein to cover the road to St. Petersburg. Wittgenstein had for his principal bases of operations the ancient towns of Pskov and Velikii Novgorod; his advanced depôt was Sebezh, some 60 miles from Polotsk, on the road to Pskov. In addition to his own 1st Corps he was given the bulk of the depôt troops at Drissa and Dünaburg, and his artillery was strengthened by a heavy battery. The 18 reserve battalions hardly mustered 5700 bayonets, but the 15 depôt squadrons could furnish 1900 sabres and lances, and included those of the Imperial Guard, some of the finest in Europe. Wittgenstein's fighting strength, after the departure of Barclay, totalled some 29,000 men, of whom 4500 were cavalry and Cossacks, with 108 guns. Of this total 10 reserve battalions and 4 squadrons, about 3700 strong, were at Dünaburg; the rest were united under Wittgenstein's immediate command.

The 1st Corps contained in its staff a considerable foreign element. Wittgenstein, his chief-of-staff, Major-General D'Auvray, and the Quartermaster-General Diebich, were all Germans. Wittgenstein himself was a man of no special talent, but active and energetic, and in the prime of life. D'Auvray was an older man, but possessed plenty of vigour, and was a good theoretical officer, though somewhat deficient in practical experience of warfare. Colonel Diebich, a Prussian, only twenty-seven years of age, was probably the most intellectually distinguished of the three. His enduring fame as "Zabalkanski"—the Balkan-Passer—dates from the year 1829, when he commanded in chief against the Turks. For the present all that need be observed is that the command of the Russian army of the Düna was in vigorous hands. Clausewitz notes that D'Auvray, especially, could "lay about him" at need; and doubtless the process was often necessary in dealing with the gallant but amateurish and frequently indolent Russian officers.

From Dünaburg to Riga, a distance of some 130 miles, there were practically no Russian troops. In the great Baltic port and its neighbourhood there were 30 depôt battalions, 8 squadrons, and some Cossacks and field artillery, which, with garrison troops, totalled perhaps 14,000 men, sufficient to defend the fortifications and outlying places, but not to furnish any considerable detachment for the field. Riga was furthermore defended by Russian and English gunboats and bomb-brigs; and naval assistance to almost any amount was available from the British Baltic fleet, should it be necessary. Riga was practically secure against any but a very large army. Its commander, Lieutenant-General Essen I, was an officer of no great ability, and in poor health.

The Russian forces therefore available for the defence of Kurland and the line of the Düna amounted in all to perhaps 43,000 men, but could be reinforced to nearly double that number by militia and regulars, the latter partly depôt troops, but chiefly belonging to Count Steingell's army of Finland, soon rendered disposable by the conclusion of peace with Sweden.

Towards Riga Napoleon had directed the so-called 10th Corps, under Marshal Macdonald. It had, in fact, as Macdonald complained, no proper corps organisation or administration; and consisted of two distinct bodies—Grandjean's Polish and German division, formerly attached to the 1st Corps, and the bulk of the Prussian contingent under General Grawert. The operations of the corps were languid; it certainly was not strong enough to besiege Riga; and Napoleon paid curiously little attention to it. It would almost seem as if his real object in constituting it at the last moment was to have the notoriously disaffected Prussian contingent accompanied and watched by a competent force of troops drawn from states which he regarded as devoted to him.

The 10th Corps, having swept the right bank of the Niemen, concentrated on Rossieni, whence it set out on July 8th for Riga, Grawert advancing directly on the port by way of Mitau, while Grandjean's division, accompanied by Macdonald, moved on the right. Before the 30,000 or 32,000 men of the 10th Corps the Russian detachments in Kurland were helpless, and fell back at all points into Riga. By the

18th the invading forces were ranged along the Aa river, which passes by Mitau, the capital of Kurland, and, flowing nearly parallel to the Düna, enters the Baltic some 20 miles west of Dünamunde. Mitau, Bausk, and the other towns along the Aa were occupied, and the Prussians reached out with their left to the sea. Essen could form for field operations only a force of 8 depôt battalions, 8 squadrons, a battery and some Cossacks—4500 men at most, with 10 guns—which he sent under Lieutenant-General Lewis towards Bausk. Lewis was too late to defend Mitau or Bausk, and took up a defensive position at Eckau between the latter place and Riga. Against him Grawert advanced on July 19th with 7 battalions, 4 squadrons and 4 batteries—5000 men and 32 guns. Lewis was beaten with a loss of over 600 prisoners besides killed and wounded, and driven back upon Riga. The Prussians moved up nearer to the city, and Essen, on July 22nd, losing his head, ordered the suburbs to be fired. There was absolutely no need for this reckless step. Macdonald had not a siege gun within reach. The misery and destitution occasioned were, of course, terrible; the mere immediate material loss is said to have been valued at 15,000,000 paper rúbles (about £600,000).

Macdonald, after Eckau, moved with Grandjean's division towards Jakobstädt, and established his head-quarters there on the 22nd. His advance-guard of 4 Polish battalions, under Prince Radziwil, moved down the left bank of the Düna on Dünaburg. Radziwil occupied the place on the 30th and 31st, the garrison having been withdrawn by Wittgenstein, and on August 8th Macdonald arrived with the rest of Grandjean's division. He blew up the half-finished fortifications, and destroyed all the artillery, ammunition and tools which he could not carry away. De Chambray blames him for this, saying that he should have retained them for the siege of Riga; he also criticises him for not crossing the Düna and striking at Wittgenstein's communications. It seems, however, clear that Macdonald's appointed task was the siege of Riga; and he obviously could not undertake independent operations without Napoleon's order. His position, as he told Oudinot, was very difficult. His force was scattered over a wide extent of country, and in the absence of any proper staff he was burdened with petty details.

MARSHAL OUDINOT, DUKE OF REGGIO
Commander of the 2nd French Army Corps
From the painting by Robert Lefèvre at Versailles

On August 7th Essen made an attack on Schlock, the port at the mouth of the Aa, with 6 British and 13 Russian sloops and gunboats, and about 1000 troops, all under General Lewis. Schlock was taken, but the light craft could not pass the Prussian batteries on the Aa, and Lewis abandoned Schlock and withdrew.

Oudinot, after his fruitless attack on the bridge-head of Dünaburg on July 13th, moved up the left bank of the Düna to join in the general advance on Vitebsk. He also endeavoured to render the works at Drissa indefensible. Wittgenstein, realising that Macdonald and Oudinot could not easily combine their operations, at first resolved to attack the 2nd Corps as it passed up the Düna; but on receiving a report that Macdonald was bridging the river at Jakobstädt he took up a position near Razitzi (? Pazitzi), about 16 miles from Druia on the road to Sebezh, and awaited events.

Oudinot, moving up the left bank of the Düna, left Merle's division, chiefly Swiss, and Corbineau's brigade of light cavalry to watch the river about Drissa, and with the rest of the 2nd Corps and Doumerc's Cuirassier division, occupied Polotsk on the 26th. On the 28th, leaving a battalion at Polotsk, he advanced on Sebezh to cut Wittgenstein's communications with St. Petersburg. He crossed the Drissa at Sivokhino and, early on the 30th, reached the hamlet of Kliastitzi, some 34 miles from Sebezh. As he was very badly informed as to Wittgenstein's movements he decided to halt and send out reconnaissances.

Meanwhile Wittgenstein, informed of Oudinot's advance, had determined to attack without delay. On the 30th he was within easy reach of Oudinot's left flank; and about four in the afternoon his advance-guard came into contact with Legrand's division at Jakubovo, about 2 miles west of Kliastitzi, posted on a narrow front between two woods.

Wittgenstein had with him the whole 1st Corps and 6 depôt battalions, in all about 21,000 men and 96 guns, organised into a vanguard, under Kulnev, 2 infantry divisions under Major-Generals Berg and Sazonov, and a mixed division commanded by Major-General Kakhovski.

Kulnev, a fiery cavalry officer, at once attacked Legrand, sending to Wittgenstein for reinforcements. Legrand was posted between the woods on a front of apparently only 800 yards, half of which was occupied by the mansion and hamlet of Jakubovo. Verdier and Doumerc were on the main road, there being no room wherein to deploy. An obstinate action ensued as reinforcements were thrown in on both sides and without any special success for either. Legrand's narrow front, though it enabled him to concentrate his infantry, only permitted him to bring into action twelve guns as against 36 Russian pieces. On the 31st Wittgenstein, having collected his whole force, ordered a general attack. The fighting was very fierce. Jakubovo, defended by the 26th Léger, was taken and retaken; but on the whole the French held their own, and there was no sound reason for the retreat which Oudinot ordered. He says that he feared for the security of his left flank, threatened by an enemy twice as strong as himself! This latter idea is scarcely in accordance with his confident advance upon Sebezh. At any rate, he evacuated Jakubovo and retreated across the Nitcha, southward to Sivokhino, pursued and harassed by the Russians who, not unnaturally, claimed the affair as a complete victory. Wittgenstein had actually engaged 18 battalions. He claimed to have taken 900 prisoners and much baggage, but the estimates of the French losses in the Journal of the 1st Corps are greatly exaggerated. The Russians, also, must have lost severely in the fierce fighting about the mansion of Jakubovo; and Oudinot claimed 500 prisoners.

At Sivokhino Oudinot was rejoined by Merle's division, coming from Drissa. He deliberately left the ford unguarded; and took up a position a little to the southward at the hamlet of Oboiarzina, with his flanks thrown forward and his whole force skilfully concealed in the woods and gullies with which the country abounded.

At daybreak on the 1st of August the impetuous Kulnev was leading the pursuit. He had with him some companies of sharpshooters, 7 infantry battalions, 6 squadrons and a horse battery, with which he crossed the ford and pushed forward into the sort of *cul-de-sac* formed by Oudinot's position to the southward. The Marshal had more than 40 guns ranged in a deep curve round the advancing Russian columns. As they opened fire Kulnev realised that something more serious than a mere rear-guard action was toward, and requested Sazonov, whose division was following, to support him. Sazonov sent forward the Tula Regiment and a heavy battery at once, but it was too late. The vanguard was overwhelmed by a furious cross cannonade, and broke before the charge of Verdier's and Legrand's infantry. The reinforcements were swept away in the rout; and the Russians poured back through the ford in a wild crowd of struggling men and horses, amid which the French fire made terrible havoc. Kulnev strove desperately to repair the consequences of his fatal impetuosity, but in vain. He was following the retreat when a cannon-ball shattered both his legs, ending at once his despair and his life. He bade his aides carry away his orders and insignia—"lest these French triumph over a Russian general"; and so passed a fiery and enthusiastic spirit who might have rendered his country good service.

Verdier's division, driving before it the broken Russians, pressed through the ford in hot pursuit. Wittgenstein, who was advancing with his whole force, sent on Major-Generals Prince Iachvil and Helfreich to rally the vanguard, and took up a position at the hamlet of Golovitzi to sustain it, with 48 guns ranged before his line. Berg's division was on the right and Kosakovki's on the left. As soon as the remains of the vanguard had passed behind the batteries they opened a heavy cannonade, and Berg and Kozakovski moved forward to the attack. Wittgenstein's second line, under Sazonov, also moved forward, and as the leading divisions diverged somewhat in their advance some of its battalions filled up the gap thus opened. Verdier, assailed by a greatly superior force, was unable to bear up against it; and was driven back, fighting hard but losing heavily, to Sivokhino, where he repassed the Drissa, covered by Legrand's division.

The losses of the 2nd Corps from July 30th to August 1st amounted according to Oudinot's returns (which appear trustworthy) to 464 officers and men killed, 2925 wounded, and 1596 prisoners and missing. This was certainly a gaping chasm in an effective strength of about 28,000 men; but the Russians admitted 4300 casualties, and again there was no solid reason for the French retreat upon Polotsk next day. Napoleon was greatly annoyed, and expressed his angry astonishment at the movement, which appeared to him entirely unnecessary. He ordered Oudinot to resume the offensive and, on August 4th, directed St. Cyr, with the 6th Corps, to reinforce him.

Wittgenstein on August 1st had been wounded, and had handed over the command to D'Auvray. The really indecisive nature of the fighting is shown by the fact that no attempt was made to pursue the French. On the contrary, D'Auvray

CHAPTER VI

withdrew by his right towards Dünaburg, in order to rally Hamen's detachment, which was now to join the 1st Corps. On August 7th he once more took position at Razitzi. He decided to cross the Düna and to destroy Macdonald's small force at Dünaburg; and to this end was already bridging the river, when he was recalled by a fresh advance of Oudinot from Polotsk.

St. Cyr, with the suffering remains of the Bavarian infantry and artillery—about 12,000 bayonets—reached Polotsk on August 7. Apart from his feeling that his troops were being sacrificed, he was angry at his subordination to Oudinot. St. Cyr had, in truth, a far better right to the Marshal's bâton, and nothing but Napoleon's dislike for him had hitherto deprived him of it. Oudinot, leaving the 6th Corps to follow, started westward from Polotsk with the 2nd on the 7th, and on the 9th reached Valéinzi, 8 miles from Drissa. Next day D'Auvray marched from Razitzi; and on the 10th the Russian advance-guard, now under Helfreich, collided with Oudinot's advance, consisting of his light cavalry, supported by the 11th Léger, at Svolna, a few miles north of Valéinzi. D'Auvray arrived with his main body on the 11th. Expecting that Oudinot would advance in full force, he at first stood on the defensive, but, finding that the bulk of the 2nd Corps remained inactive at Valéinzi, attacked the advance-guard and drove it back. Thereupon, with curious timidity, Oudinot once more, on the 13th, retrograded to Polotsk, where he arrived on the morning of the 16th. On the 13th Hamen joined the Russian 1st Corps, and next day Wittgenstein resumed the command.

Polotsk, a place of much importance in the struggles between Poland and Russia during the 15th and 16th centuries, lies on the right bank of the Düna, at the point where it is joined by the little river Polota. The country around was in 1812 wooded to within a few miles of the town. Polotsk was traversed from north-west to south-east by the Riga-Vitebsk high-road, to which that from St. Petersburg united itself some miles out. From the south-west the Vilna road reached the town across the Düna. A fourth road left the Riga highway on the right a little way from Polotsk, and ran north-eastwards to Nevel.

The advance-guard of the Russians came in contact with the French outposts during the afternoon of the 16th, and the sound of the firing broke up a council-of-war which Oudinot had called to consider the situation.

During the evening the French troops took up position. Oudinot's plan of action is difficult to understand. He left nearly the whole of Verdier's and Merle's divisions and the bulk of his cavalry on the left bank of the Düna. On the right bank, along the Polota, stood St. Cyr's weak corps, with its right at the village of Spas, about a mile from Polotsk. Wrede's division was in front line and Deroy in reserve. To the left of the Bavarians were Legrand's division, 1 regiment of Verdier's, and Corbineau's cavalry brigade. Oudinot's whole force was over 35,000 strong, with about 130 guns.

The Russian 1st Corps and the reserve troops attached to it—the latter now combined into regiments—totalled about 23,000 or 24,000 men and 99 guns. It was distributed in three mixed divisions, under Major-Generals Berg, Sazonov and Kakhovski, and two mixed brigades commanded respectively by Major-General

Helfreich and Colonel Vlastov.[4]

Wittgenstein and his staff considered that Oudinot's position about Polotsk was too strong, defended as it was by superior forces, to be attacked, and decided to confine themselves to a vigorous demonstration upon Spas to cover the bridging of the Düna and a raid on Oudinot's communications. Early on the 17th, covered by Helfreich and Vlastov, the Russian main body debouched from the woods and deployed. The divisions as usual were broken up in the line of battle. In general, however, it may be said that Vlastov's detachment formed the extreme left opposite Spas, and thence Berg's division and Helfreich's vanguard continued the line towards the Düna. Sazonov and Kakhovski were in reserve.

Vlastov, and part of Berg's division, under the general direction of Prince Iachvil, attacked Spas, which was gallantly defended by the Bavarians. To sustain the attack Wittgenstein was obliged to direct to the left the rest of Berg's division, replacing it by only two battalions of his second line. Oudinot thereupon ordered Legrand to attack the weakened Russian centre, but after some sharp fighting this was repelled by the advance of fresh battalions from Sazonov's division. Legrand renewed his attacks, but was again forced to retire, but to repulse him nearly the whole of Sazonov's division had to be employed. Around Spas a furious conflict raged all day, the Russian attacks being repelled time after time by a much smaller force of Bavarians. The outlook for Oudinot was entirely promising; by night almost all Wittgenstein's army had been engaged and had been held at bay by the division of Legrand, about half of Wrede's and one regiment of Verdier's. All this time two strong divisions were inactive south of the Düna. It was probably fortunate that in the evening Oudinot was severely wounded and forced to transfer the command to the stronger hands of St. Cyr.

The latter general made up his mind that the badly shaken morale of his army, no less than the Emperor's interests, imperatively demanded a victory, and determined to give battle. But he was too wary to deprive himself of the advantage of allowing the Russians to waste their strength against his defensive position before himself taking the offensive. He therefore waited during the morning of the 18th for Wittgenstein to come on. The latter, on his side, having driven Oudinot again into Polotsk, decided to withdraw, his mission being to defend the St. Petersburg road, and greatly overestimating the strength of the force opposed to him. His troops were to commence their march at 9 p.m.

St. Cyr during the morning made a parade of retiring his trains and reserve parks through the town towards Vitebsk, while Merle and Verdier were brought nearer to it as though to cover an evacuation. Some of the cavalry also defiled along the southern bank of the Düna with their horses laden with forage. These devices do not appear to have tricked the Russian staff into the belief that Polotsk was about to be abandoned; but they did give it the impression that there was no fear of an attack. The Russian army lay bivouacked in the order in which it had fought on the 17th, and head-quarters were at the hamlet of Prizmenitza, only half a mile from Spas.

---

[4] For Plan see Appendix.

St. Cyr, finding that Wittgenstein did not show any sign of attacking, and doubtless marking the obvious unpreparedness of the Russians, decided to take the offensive. About 2 p.m. Verdier's division began to cross the Düna, screened from the sight of the Russians by the houses of Polotsk and the high banks of the Polota. Merle, Doumerc, and Castex's light cavalry followed. Meanwhile at Spas Deroy's division relieved Wrede's, and a battery of 31 guns was massed at the village.

St. Cyr's plan, as he defines it, was to smash Wittgenstein's line by a heavy and concentrated attack of four infantry divisions advancing at the double, Wrede's Bavarians leading on the right, Deroy to their left rear, Legrand and Verdier in echelon on the left of Deroy, while the cavalry followed in support, and Merle's division stood in reserve at Polotsk. St. Cyr in his report to Berthier says that he had intended to commence the attack at 4 p.m., but the bringing up of the troops from the left bank of the Düna proved a tedious operation; and it was not until nearly 5 that St. Cyr was able to give the signal to commence the battle.

The French and Bavarian artillery opened a tremendous cannonade against the unsuspecting Russians, with great effect, especially among two batteries in advance of Prizmenitza, which lost nearly all their horses, and had a number of guns and waggons disabled or blown up against the Bavarian artillery. Diebich skilfully placed some guns in a battery on the extreme Russian left, which, being masked, caused considerable loss, but could not silence the far stronger array of pieces ranged before Spas.

THE FIRST BATTLE OF POLOTSK
Gained by General St. Cyr (in succession to Marshal Oudinot wounded) on 18th August, 1812

For some reason which is not very apparent the infantry attack did not take place immediately. Possibly St. Cyr hoped that the fire of his 130 guns or thereabouts would soon demoralise the Russians, but he was deceived. Wittgenstein's troops fell quickly into their places in the line, and their artillery stoutly responded to the greatly superior mass of Franco-Bavarian batteries.

After a cannonade of about an hour's duration, Wrede moved forward, threatening to turn the Russian left, while Deroy marched straight against Prizmenitza. Legrand's division, however, moved forward rather slowly, and Verdier's division (temporarily commanded by General of Brigade Valentin) was still farther to the rear. The result was that the Russian resistance was by no means crushed by the impetus of a combined charge. As the Bavarians advanced they screened the fire of their guns, and the Russian artillery was able to play heavily upon the infantry. Deroy, a venerable officer respected by all, was mortally wounded as he directed his division, and the Bavarians, shaken by their losses, began to give way. Legrand, now in line on their left, carried Prizmenitza, but was driven out again by Hamen with seven battalions of Sazonov's division. St. Cyr himself hastened to the front and directed a fresh advance of Legrand against Prizmenitza, supported by Sieben's brigade of Deroy's division. Wrede was directed to assume the command of the whole 6th Corps, and himself rallied and led on Deroy's shaken troops. The four French and Bavarian infantry divisions, now supported by Merle on the left rear, moved forward together, breaking down the obstinate resistance of the Russians and forcing them back into the woods. The Russian cavalry charged repeatedly and brilliantly to cover the retreat of their infantry, and the combined Guard regiment created a panic in Corbineau's brigade, and rode almost up to the walls of Polotsk. St. Cyr himself, who had been slightly wounded on the 17th and was obliged to use a carriage, was nearly captured, and the daring horsemen were only checked by the fire of the reserve artillery. They were fired into from all sides, and charged by one of Doumerc's Cuirassier regiments, but the survivors regained the Russian line, sorely diminished in numbers, but covered with glory. The Russian army, badly defeated but by no means routed, made good its retreat during the night to Sivokhino, where it halted. St. Cyr did not pursue. He was not strong in light cavalry, and Corbineau's brigade was obviously demoralised. Still it seems that more use might have been made of Merle's Swiss regiments, which had scarcely fired a shot; several of Verdier's and Wrede's regiments also had not been heavily engaged.

The losses on both sides had been very heavy. Wrede gave the Bavarian loss as 118 officers and 1161 men killed and wounded. That of the 2nd Corps, which had 190 officers *hors de combat*, can hardly have been less than 3500. The Russians admitted a loss of 5000 killed and wounded. St. Cyr claimed 1000 prisoners; and 14 Russian guns were captured.

On the French side General Deroy was mortally wounded. Oudinot, St. Cyr, Verdier and Wrede were wounded. Of the brigade leaders the Bavarian Sieben was killed, and two French and two Bavarians wounded. The Russians had Generals Berg, Kozakovski and Hamen wounded.

Polotsk was hardly a very glorious victory, St. Cyr having some 35,000 men on the field against Wittgenstein's 23,000 or 24,000 at most, but it had important results in freeing Napoleon from anxiety for his left flank. He showed his satisfaction by at last giving St. Cyr his Marshal's bâton.

CHAPTER VII
SMOLENSK TO BORODINO

The battle of Lubino concluded the bloody fighting about Smolensk; and, though there was practically no pause in the operations, it marked the term of another stage in the campaign, as poor in results as the preceding ones. At Vilna the Russians had deliberately refused to fight, and had withdrawn out of reach. At Vitebsk they had almost accepted the chance of battle, but then, on better information, had slipped out of their great opponent's closing grasp in the nick of time. At Smolensk it seemed that the desired great battle would at last be delivered and elusive victory crown the eagles of Napoleon. Whatever be thought of the wisdom of the Emperor's manœuvres, they had been admirably carried out, and his troops had fought splendidly. Yet the results of the great effort had been completely negative. The Russian army had wrought its way out of the great conqueror's clutches, and had inflicted decidedly more damage that it had itself received. A few guns, a few prisoners and a ruined and nearly deserted city—these constituted the poor reward of so much skill and courage.

It may be regarded as certain that Napoleon had originally intended to conclude the campaign of 1812 at Smolensk. When he first began to contemplate a change of plan cannot be determined, but it is possible that it was at a comparatively early period of the campaign. The elusive strategy of his opponents cannot but have kept before his eyes the probability either of being forced to extend the area of his operations, or of taking up winter-quarters with his self-imposed task unfinished. Jomini points out that the fact that he did not then disclose his purpose may merely indicate that he wished to encourage his weary troops by the prospect of a speedy end of their toils. On the other hand, it is highly probable that his decision was not formed until after the battle of Smolensk. The absolutely negative results of that engagement forced him to consider the necessity of pushing on to strike a crushing blow. Had he succeeded in disorganising the main Russian army by a heavy defeat he would probably have stayed his advance, and devoted the rest of the campaigning season to solidly organising his communications, and crushing Tormazov and Wittgenstein.

So much for the time at which Napoleon decided to continue his advance. His reasons fall under three headings—military, political and personal.

Napoleon played many parts on the stage of history, but he was in the first instance and before everything a soldier. Military reasons may therefore justly take priority of place. Since crossing the frontier in June he had kept steadily before him

CHAPTER VII

the crushing of the principal forces of Russia in a great battle. This purpose he had failed to effect. The Russian armies were yet unbroken, and had suffered, relatively to their numbers, less heavily than their opponents. They were retiring upon their resources, and, slow and difficult as was the organisation of reinforcements, the Russian national spirit was thoroughly roused, and the vanguard of the new levies was beginning to reach the fighting line. But for the moment this fighting line was much weaker than the forces immediately under Napoleon's command, and would probably succumb to them in a pitched battle. Were it allowed to manœuvre rearwards, and rally and assimilate the new levies which were being collected and drilled, the chances of Napoleon's success would be greatly diminished. His lines of communication were already troubled by Cossacks, and time would mean the increase of these vexatious irregulars both in numbers and efficiency, thus compelling larger detachments and weakening the striking force upon which everything really depended. It was practically certain that the elusive Russians would never abandon "White-Walled Moscow" without a battle, and it was necessary to go forward to seek it while the striking force was yet strong enough to deal a decisive blow. It would also appear that the halt on the Düna and Dnieper had permitted the accumulation of supplies sufficient to subsist the army as far as Moscow, at any rate with the addition of what might be obtained by foraging.[5] Finally, the victory of Schwarzenberg at Gorodeczna on August 12th, and that of St. Cyr over Wittgenstein at Polotsk on the 17th and 18th, appeared to assure the immediate security of Napoleon's flanks.

Political reasons also must have weighed much with Napoleon. The continuance of his empire, as he himself probably understood better than anyone, depended upon continued military success. His own position rested almost solely upon the force of his own personality. To remain for several months, perhaps a year, away from France might lead to his downfall. Moreover, whatever the dynasts might say or do, Germany was full of discontent; and in his absence revolt might break out in his rear. To confess failure by a retreat was not to be contemplated. In short, there was practically no alternative to an advance.

To the influence exercised by sound military and political argument must be added that of Napoleon's personality. He had never yet experienced failure so far as his own personal enterprises had been concerned, and exasperated as he was by the lack of success, up to the present, of the campaign, every prompting of his fierce and impetuous nature impelled him to go forward.

On the other hand, the Russians—in so far as there was any public opinion in Russia—were by no means contented with the progress of the campaign. Alexander, before leaving the army, had issued two proclamations, one to the people at large, the other to the city of Moscow, calling upon the nation to make great efforts to expel the invaders. He then hastened to Moscow, where, on July 27th, an assembly of nobles and merchants was convoked under the presidency of the Governor-General, Count Rostopchin. The nobles offered for war a levy of one man in

---

[5] This is not absolutely certain, but appears to be proved by the statements of eyewitnesses of the campaign. De Fezensac, for example, says that the 3rd Corps had not yet exhausted its supplies when it entered Moscow.

ten from the population of their estates. The merchants volunteered a contribution by an assessment upon the capital of each; and a special subscription opened on the spot realised in an hour nearly £200,000. In the midst of these enthusiastic proceedings the Tzar entered the assembly, and ended a speech, in which he set forth the national peril, by a declaration that he intended to continue the struggle until the bitter end.

Alexander wisely restricted the new levies to provinces which were not yet the seat of war. He also decided that a proportion of 2 per cent. generally, and 1 per cent. in Siberia, would be sufficient. Men were not lacking, but arms and equipment were deficient, so also were officers capable of organising and training the new recruits. The collection of the levies was an operation requiring much time and trouble: it was even more difficult to realise the money contribution, part of which was not finally received until the following year. But considering the vast extent and poverty of the empire the immediate results were exceedingly creditable. We shall soon have occasion to note the rapid strengthening of the Russian army.

With all this enthusiasm and patriotic endeavour there was not unnaturally mingled a good deal of distrust and discontent among the nobles, who voiced such public opinion as existed. These feelings were justified to a great extent by the foolishness of the Government, which reported non-existent military successes, and misrepresented the operations which were in progress. A certain amount of reliable news, however, filtered through from the front. It gradually became clear that, despite the so-called successes of the Russians, the armies were steadily retreating, and that cities and provinces were being abandoned to the invader.

The general results of all this was a more or less openly expressed desire that the conduct of the war should be changed. To a certain extent it was the outcome of genuine conviction that the command might be in better hands, but it was also largely the reflection of the insubordinate discontent among the army officers, which had reached its height at Smolensk. The outcry was chiefly against Barclay, whose foreign name was made the platform for every kind of unjust accusation. It appears to have chiefly been the sentiments of Bagration and his adherents which made themselves heard in the capital. Barclay had few friends—Löwenstern says that Konovnitzin was almost the only general officer attached to him—and had neither leisure nor talents for defending his reputation against intriguers. Alexander apparently always trusted and liked him; but on the abandonment of the offensive early in August the clamour became so loud that he was constrained to give way, though he angrily declared that he would not assume responsibility for any evil consequences. He appointed a committee consisting of Arakcheiev, the Vice-Chancellor Count Kotschubey, and Prince Lopukhin, to consider the question of a different conduct of the war. The action was probably merely nominal, for both the remedy and the man to apply it had been practically agreed upon. The committee met on the 17th of August. It recommended the appointment of a commander-in-chief of all the Russian field armies, and for the post submitted to the Tzar the name of General Prince Golénischev-Kutuzov.

There were practically only two candidates for the onerous position. One was

CHAPTER VII

Kutuzov. The other was Bennigsen, who in his own estimation was fully equal to the responsibility. Others, however, did not think so highly of his merits, or of those of his campaign of 1807 against Napoleon. Alexander knew him as one of his father's assassins, and probably distrusted his vain and selfish character. Besides, he was a foreigner. Kutuzov's military reputation was estimated as highly as Bennigsen's; his laurels were recent; and, above all, he was a native Russian, popular with the army and believed to be the exponent of the hard-fighting tactics of far-famed Suvórov.

On the 18th Alexander nominated Kutuzov to the position of commander-in-chief. Bennigsen was appointed chief-of-staff. The reasons are somewhat obscure. Clausewitz considers that Bennigsen procured his appointment in the hopes of succeeding to Kutuzov's place if, as seemed not unlikely, the old man's health should break down. Bennigsen himself says that, at Vilna, Barclay informed him that Alexander wished to employ him again. It is possible that Alexander appointed him in view of such a contingency as Clausewitz suggests; certainly he was senior to all the generals with the army, so that, in the event of Kutuzov's retirement, he would naturally assume the command. He seems to have regarded himself rather as his chief's colleague than his assistant. Kutuzov did not take his appointment very kindly, and the yoking together of the two veterans, one a Russian noble and the other a German soldier of fortune, was not a happy expedient.

While at Smolensk, Napoleon regulated his main line of communications, which was now to run by Vilna, Minsk, Borisov and Orsha, to Smolensk. Smolensk became the advanced depôt of the army, and Vitebsk being of only secondary importance, Charpentier was transferred to the former place with the greater part of his garrison. Winzingerode, however, was so active in the neighbourhood of Vitebsk that on the 21st Napoleon detached Pino's Italian division thither to support Pajol. The alarm was a false one, for Winzingerode had, as we know, only a weak detachment of cavalry. On receiving intelligence of the retreat of the Russian main army he fell back towards Moscow, and Napoleon called Pino, Pajol and Guyon towards him, but only the cavalry were able to rejoin in time for the battle of Borodino.

Orders were given to construct bakeries at Smolensk, and to form magazines and hospitals. The city, however, was little better than a heap of ruins. Nearly all the inhabitants had fled, and artificers and materials were lacking to carry out the works ordered by Napoleon. It is a favourite saying of the Emperor's apologists that his orders were neglected. The truth is that they were too frequently impracticable. The hospitals, choked with some 15,000 sick and wounded, were in a frightful condition. So great was the dearth of supplies that the parchment of the city archives and gun-waddings were utilised for bandages.

Nor was the condition of the army at large satisfactory. Food was for the moment sufficient; but clothing and equipment were already wearing out. Nansouty declared that he had never seen cavalry in so wretched a condition as his own 1st Corps; there were Cuirassiers half naked. The number of broken-down horses was alarmingly large. Discipline was worse than ever. Napoleon declared in a moment of depression that two-thirds of the army were stragglers. There was small prospect of these evils being remedied. The army, having made an all too brief halt about Vitebsk and Orsha, and a yet briefer one at Smolensk, was about to be pushed forward for another 250 miles. Napoleon had, in a sense, provided for everything; that is, he had issued orders which anticipated most contingencies. But De Fezensac, himself a soldier of merit, puts his finger on the weak point of the elaborate arrangements, and sums up the situation in a single damning paragraph: "Mais il ne suffit pas de donner des ordres, il faut que ces ordres soient exécutables; et avec la rapidité des mouvements, la concentration des troupes sur un même point, le mauvais état des chemins, la difficulté de nourrir les chevaux, comment aurait-il été possible de faire des destributions régulières et d'organiser convenablement le service des hôpitaux?" The army swept the country through which it was moving clear in a few hours; it became literally and without exaggeration a wilderness. Stores of every kind were being poured into Vilna and pushed forward with all diligence to Minsk and Smolensk, but bad roads, lack of horses and sometimes mismanagement delayed the advance of the convoys. The main army, for whose benefit they were intended, was constantly moving forward, and they could never attain it. When on October 19th, Napoleon turned back from Moscow his nearest considerable magazine was at Smolensk, and it contained only six or seven days' supplies.

There was depression and growing discontent among the generals. Napoleon noticed it and made angry and bitter comments thereupon. Ney alone seems to have been undaunted. Just after Lubino he wrote to the Emperor suggesting that an attempt should be made to overtake the Russians by three or four forced marches.

In the rear also events were far from answering to Napoleon's expectations. He complained bitterly that Lithuania did nothing. It was to some extent true. Lithuania was a poor country; it had been wasted by the passage across it of the bulk of the *Grande Armée*, and it could furnish practically no supplies. The levies ordered by the provisional government existed largely upon paper, and the troops actually enrolled were of very poor quality. Had Napoleon frankly re-established the Kingdom of Poland better results might have been obtained, but it is not very probable. It is impossible, after reading his minute directions to De Pradt, his agent at Warsaw, and his ambiguous replies to the Polish deputies who waited upon him at Vilna, not to perceive that he was deliberately trading upon the hopes and enthusiasm of the Poles. Moreover, he had on entering Lithuania committed a blunder by proclaiming liberty to everyone. The serfs naturally interpreted this as granting permission for plunder and general licence. The nobles, whom Napoleon should certainly, from the point of view of his own interests, have conciliated, were alienated, as were the Jews, who practically monopolised such trade and industry as existed. At best it can scarcely be said that Lithuania was actively favourable to Napoleon. It was necessary to garrison the principal towns and to escort all convoys as if the country had been hostile instead of nominally friendly. For all practical purposes Napoleon's base continued to be on the Niemen and Vistula, and supplies had to be brought up thence.

On the 20th of August, apparently, Napoleon finally made up his mind to continue his advance, and on the 21st and 22nd the army was set in motion. Ney's shattered corps could no longer fulfil the duties of support to the advanced guard, and Davout's took its place. Murat led the way with the 1st, 2nd and 3rd Corps of Cavalry, and the light horse of the 1st and 3rd Army Corps. Behind Murat marched the 1st Corps, with Compans' division leading; the 3rd and 8th Corps and the Imperial Guard followed. The 4th Corps formed the left flank-guard; the 5th and Latour-Maubourg's Corps (less three Polish regiments left on the Dnieper) that on the right. On the 23rd intelligence arrived that the Russians had taken up a position for battle near Dorogobuzh, 22 miles east of Solovievo. Eugène and Poniatowski were drawn in towards the centre and the muster-rolls called. They showed an effective strength of 147,000 men, of whom 31,000 were cavalry, with nearly 590 guns—exclusive of the head-quarters troops.

On leaving Lubino Barclay had sent forward Toll to look for a favourable field of battle. While the First Army was marching to Solovievo, Bagration moved on towards Dorogobuzh. Toll, who was accompanied by Clausewitz, found a position, which he considered satisfactory, about 5 miles west of the town, behind the small river Uzha, which here flowed into the Dnieper from the south. It was open in front, giving free play to the action of the powerful Russian artillery, and woods behind afforded cover for reserves. On the right, however, a hill beyond the Uzha commanded part of the main position, and thus appeared to Barclay and Bagration, who met to confer, a cardinal defect. Barclay, whose temper had probably scarcely been softened by persecution, blamed Toll, and the latter, always gruff to the verge of rudeness, growled a reply to the effect that he could not *make* positions—if they were not to be *found* that was the fault of the country. Barclay, recognising that there was reason in the answer, if little courtesy, refrained from an angry reply; but Bagration was furious, and his natural generosity impelled him to praise the very man whom he had recklessly assailed.

"If you cannot choose positions," he told the luckless young Quartermaster-General, "that is not to say that others cannot! How dare you, you unlicked cub, address the commander-in-chief so? He owes his position to his great qualities, and deserves every consideration. I am his senior, but I set the example by serving under him. You and your blue riband! (Toll was a Knight of St. Andrew.) You think that you honour him by serving under him; but it is the other way about. It is disgraceful that a young swelled-head like you should hold such language towards the man on whom depends the fate of the army and the empire. Thank his generosity that worse does not befall you, for if I had my way I would change that blue riband for a common soldier's belts!"

The threat was by no means an empty one, for a Russian commander-in-chief had power to degrade officers to the ranks. Bagration's words certainly afford food for reflection, seeing his remarks of a few days since, but it is good to know that one of the last actions of his honourable life was to endeavour to make some amends to his ill-used colleague.

The position being deemed unfavourable, Bagration suggested another in front of Dorogobuzh. Clausewitz describes this—perhaps partly out of pique—as very bad. It at any rate appears that it was intersected by the Dnieper, though the river was not here a very formidable obstacle.

The rear-guard, under Platov, consisting of 3 regiments of Hussars, 1 of Lancers, 6 of Chasseurs and some Cossacks, had on the 22nd a brisk action with Murat, rejoining the main army on the 23rd. On the same day Napoleon himself left Smolensk, and Eugène and Poniatowski were called in. Poniatowski's march to the south of the road indicated an intention to turn the Russian left; and Bagration counselled a retreat. It seems obvious that he had at last definitely ranged himself on the side of Barclay. His example may have served to improve the sense of subordination among the other generals. It had fallen so low that Platov personally insulted Barclay a few days after the evacuation of Smolensk. The position was evacuated in the night of the 23rd-24th and the retreat continued, the main body retiring to Brazhino on the Moscow road, Baggohufwudt and Uvarov proceeding level with it on the north bank of the Dnieper. The rear-guard fell back to Dorogobuzh.

Barclay's resolution to give battle before Dorogobuzh was bold to the verge of rashness. His entire strength was probably not more than 107,000 men, of whom 3000 were raw militia-men from the province of Smolensk, and certainly neither of the positions in advance of the town was strong enough to compensate for a numerical inferiority of 40,000 men. It almost appears as if he had grown desperate at the persecution to which he was subjected, and had resolved to stake everything on a single throw of the dice.

On the 27th the two armies reached Viasma. Napoleon on the same day was at Slavkovo, about 27 miles westward. There was a rear-guard fight between Murat and Platov, as the result of which the latter, to avoid being turned, retired to Semlevo, nearer Viasma. Platov, being indisposed, was succeeded by Konovnitzin. On the 28th Napoleon entered Semlevo; and on the 29th Barclay and Bagration reached Tzarévo-Zaïmichi. On the same day General Miloradovich was at Gzhatsk with 14,466 infantry and 1123 cavalry—depôt troops, convalescents and recruits. Barclay and Bagration now decided that with this reserve force within reach, they might safely stand to fight, and took up a position. It appears to have been fairly strong in the centre, but, like most positions in Central Russia, its flanks were exposed. This weakness the generals proposed to remedy by entrenchments. In the evening Kutuzov arrived and assumed the supreme command.

Kutuzov decided not to give battle in the Tzarévo-Zaïmichi position. The decision was a perfectly sensible one. The responsibility was now his, and he as yet knew nothing of his army. He would naturally desire to become better acquainted with it, and as it was still some 130 miles from Moscow he might hope to find a stronger position. Toll and his staff were sent on ahead, and the army resumed its retreat, Konovnitzin with a force now augmented to 26 battalions and 72 squadrons covering the rear.

GENERAL OF CAVALRY COUNT PLATOV
Ataman of the Don Cossacks

Meanwhile the French were doggedly following, suffering much from fatigue and heat, and troubled, as usual, by internal dissensions. Davout accused Murat, apparently with great justice, of wasting the cavalry, and exhausting them by useless manœuvres and lack of proper care for their subsistence. He said that it wrung his heart—not a very tender organ—to see the wretched state of the reserve cavalry divisions, and declared that he would not allow his infantry to be so over-worked. Matters came to a head on August 28th in an open quarrel between the two leaders in Napoleon's presence. Murat retorted to Davout's accusation by a counter-charge of over-caution, and declared that they had better settle their differences by a duel! Napoleon rather added fuel to the flames, for he insinuated that had Murat been in Davout's place in July he might have intercepted Bagration. Davout was also on bad terms with Berthier. There is no discovering the real cause of this, but it is certain that Davout's fierce temper and rough manners made him many enemies.

The march of the army was toilsome. The wide road was occupied by the artillery and trains, five or six vehicles abreast, while along both sides tramped the infantry in heavy columns of companies or "divisions." They suffered much from heat, which was aggravated by the dense clouds of dust raised by the marching columns; and the supply of water was scanty. Even the Russians occasionally felt the want of it, and it was naturally worse for the French, who found the wells drunk dry and the streams trodden into mud. At the same time it does not appear that the diminution in the ranks owing to these causes was exceptional, though it was certainly serious. The worst losses were among the horses, which suffered at once from lack of proper forage and from thirst. Corn and hay became more and more difficult to procure, and the rations of the unfortunate animals were made up with rye straw. The wastage among them was all the more serious because there was little hope of being able to replace them.

The villages along the route, and the few small towns, were for the most part deserted by their inhabitants, and in part at least destroyed. This was not invariably the case. Dorogobuzh—"Cabbage-town," as the French soldiers called it from the cabbage fields amid which it lay—was uninjured, and three months later still contained some of its inhabitants. Gzhatsk also was uninjured. Viasma was partly destroyed, owing to fire spreading from a depôt of flour and spirits which the Russians had fired before retreating. Otherwise it is difficult to decide whether the destruction of houses and villages was due to French or Russians. It may be attributed to both at various times according to circumstances.

The Russians retired eastward through Gzhatsk, covered by their powerful rear-guard. On September 1 they were about Kolotskoï, a great monastery about 75 miles from Moscow, the rear-guard being a day's march behind. At Kolotskoï Toll and Vistitski II, Bagration's Quarter-master-General, recommended a defensive position at Borodino, a few miles farther on—probably in despair of being able to find anything better between it and Moscow. Napoleon either learned on the same day that the Russians had definitely turned to bay, or inferred that they were about to do so, for he stayed his advance at Gzhatsk in order to rally his forces for the impending struggle. The musters for the 2nd of September, including men temporarily detached or straggling who might rejoin within two or three days, and exclusive of head-quarter troops, showed nearly 135,000 sabres and bayonets. Two battalions of the 8th Corps were garrisoning Dorogobuzh and Viasma.

CHAPTER VII

Before the battle Napoleon was rejoined by Pajol's division and by the 1st and 12th Light Cavalry Brigades—nearly 4000 sabres in all. For the head-quarters troops 3000 is a conservative estimate.

Napoleon made great efforts at this time to grapple with the disorder in his rear, and especially to reduce the vast trains of vehicles which impeded the march. There is abundant evidence that they were out of all proportion to the strength of the army, and the superfluity consisted chiefly of private carriages. Napoleon's efforts produced little effect. He issued stringent orders, and himself directed the firing of some vehicles; but Baron Girod tells of at least one instance in which the fire was extinguished as soon as the Emperor's back was turned, and in general the order remained a dead letter.

During the halt there was a good deal of rain, which did not improve the indifferent roads, but relieved the distress for water. The 4th, however, was fine, and early in the morning the French army resumed its advance. The order was as before, but, to Davout's disgust, Compans' division was placed under Murat's direct orders. A provisional battalion of the Vistula Legion was left to garrison Gzhatsk. Konovnitzin made a stand at Gridnevo, about half-way to Borodino, withdrawing when Murat's infantry turned his flank, his cavalry skirmishing steadily with the leading French squadrons. On the 5th he made another stand at Kolotskoï, and it was not until he saw Eugène's corps marching past his right flank that he fell back into the main army behind the Kolotza.

The Borodino position has often been spoken of as an admirable one for defence. Clausewitz, who knew it, is of a very different opinion; and in all probability it was selected simply because there was no likelihood that anything better would present itself in the endless plain-lands. It had one grave strategic defect. Some way to the west the great road forks, the branches uniting again at Mozhaïsk, about 6 miles east of Borodino. It was therefore necessary to hold two roads instead of one, and to be strong on both. At Borodino they are 2½ miles apart, the new road, on which Borodino stands, lying to the north.

The Kolotza rivulet makes a very acute angle with the new road, running for a considerable distance nearly parallel with it, always in a gully with steep banks. After passing Borodino, which lies on its left bank, it flows north-eastward with a very sinuous course to join the Moskva, about 2¾ miles farther on. The Moskva itself flows south-eastward to the high-road at the village of Uspenskoïe, three miles from Borodino, where it turns eastward towards Mozhaïsk.

In the angle formed by the two streams lies a low partly wooded plateau, its base formed by a rivulet which joins the Kolotza at Borodino. At its south-western angle stood the hamlet of Gorki, about a mile from Borodino. A few hundred yards higher up another streamlet joined the Kolotza from the south-east. This streamlet, called after the hamlet of Semenovskoï, about a mile and a quarter south of Borodino, flows in a little ravine, and the ground between it and the Gorki rivulet forms another low plateau, not more than 30 feet high, but with a fairly steep western drop. It descends very slightly towards the east for about a mile, until it is crossed by another brook flowing in a gully. The eastern bank of this gully is the higher, and the ground extends eastward in another low plateau on which lies the village of Tzarévo, a mile and a half east of Semenovskoï. Just west of Gorki there is a low knoll, and another a mile due south-east of Gorki, and about 1100 yards north of Semenovskoï. From Semenovskoï to the old road at the village of Utitza is about a mile and a quarter, and from the latter village extended northward for about 1000 yards a thick wood. Three-quarters of a mile east of Utitza is a knoll, and a little eastward again another low plateau. South of the old road extended marshy woods, though a little south of Utitza there was a clearing round the hamlet of Michino. Patches of wood were scattered over the whole position. The villages were all log-built and useless for defence. From Utitza by Borodino to the junction of the Kolotza with the Moskva is a distance of almost 5 miles.

To the west of the Borodino-Utitza line the country is of the same character, only slightly lower. At the village of Shevardino, a mile westward from Semenovskoï, is a low knoll. The villages were of so little consequence that it is superfluous to name them.

It will probably be gathered from this description that the general position afforded no great advantages to the weaker side. Clausewitz, indeed, says that in places it was difficult to tell which had the advantage of the ground. The northern plateau was fairly advantageous for defence, but the Kolotza ravine in its front prevented the troops posted on it from making counter-attacks. The old road afforded opportunities to an enterprising foe of a turning movement. It was therefore necessary to hold it strongly, but the wood south of Semenovskoï almost cut the troops about Utitza from the main line farther north. Bennigsen criticises the whole position most bitterly, as far too extended, but represents it as being 2 miles longer than it really was. He was himself an advocate of very narrow positions, and French critics declared that his line at Eylau was far too close and heavy. He says in his memoirs that he perfectly understood that Napoleon's concentrated attacks could only be repulsed by a concentration of defence. In principle he was no doubt right, but the defensive concentration, as Wellington had been teaching an unappreciative Europe for years, should have been one of effective muskets, not of crowded columns. Bennigsen was too self-satisfied to see this; but it is perhaps fair to add that probably the British army was the only one in Europe sufficiently highly trained to execute linear tactics. The Russian soldiers were extremely steady and accurate in manœuvre, but not rapid, and scarcely highly trained; French observers criticise their clumsiness. Clausewitz thinks that the reserves were too near the front. The bulk of the army was massed on a front of four miles; both flanks were covered by Cossacks.

The Kolotza entered the Moskva amid marshy ground; the right was accordingly supported on a wood a mile and a half further south. In front of this and on its left towards Gorki were various field works. In front of Gorki was a parapet with redans, and on the knoll south of Borodino a large earthwork, called by the French the "Great Redoubt." Semenovskoï had been destroyed, the houses being mere shell traps. At its western end a parapet had been marked out, and to the south three *flèches* or redans. The Gorki work, the Great Redoubt and the Semenovskoï redans were the only entrenchments at all complete, and they were very hastily finished and of poor profile. Engineers and sappers were few in the Russian army, and tools seem to have been lacking.

The strength of the army gathered to defend this very mediocre position cannot be exactly estimated. Russian figures vary, and none seem to be accurate in details. Bogdanovich, for example, reckons 14,500 artillery and sappers present, which, allowing for 1000 of the latter, gives an average of 250 per battery—more than in June!

The only very certain fact about the Russian strength is that when the army reached Gzhatsk it cannot have contained much over 100,000 men, of whom 3000 were militia and 7000 Cossacks. Miloradovich's 15,500 men were drafted into the regiments, presumably with a view to bringing them up as far as possible to equal strength. On the 4th the army was joined by 7000 militia from Moscow under Count Markov, the vanguard of the great national levy. The total may be fairly estimated at nearly 125,000 men. The militia were absolutely raw troops; some of them were merely employed on police and fatigue duties. There were over 17,000 excellent regular cavalry, 7000 Cossacks, and 640 guns and howitzers, admirably appointed and horsed.

Napoleon had left perhaps 700 men in Gzhatsk, and allowing 1000 men for casualties at Gridnevo and Kolotskoï, and 2000 for stragglers or men who failed to rejoin, he had still over 131,000 men on the 5th of September, exclusive of the head-quarters guard, at least 3000 men, who must be counted as present no less than the Russian militia. Between the 5th and 7th the army was reinforced by 4000 cavalry, giving a total of 138,000 men available. There were about 32,000 cavalry, but their superiority in numbers hardly compensated for the inferior condition of the horses. The weight of metal thrown by the 584 guns was slightly superior to that projected by the 640 opposing pieces; and the former—with the exception of the regimental artillery—were undoubtedly more efficiently served, but here also the horses were in poor condition.

After the fight at Kolotskoï the French moved forward,—the main column by the new road, Eugène to the left rear, Poniatowski by the old road on the right—Konovnitzin and his troops retiring steadily before them. The Russian army was not yet definitely ranged for battle, the direction of Napoleon's attack being still uncertain. Barclay, with the 2nd, 4th and 6th Corps, was behind Borodino, Bagration about Semenovskoï with an advanced guard, under his second in command Prince Gorchakov, at Shevardino, where a redoubt had been thrown up and armed with 12 heavy guns. Gorchakov's force comprised the 27th Division, Sievers' cavalry corps, the 2nd Cuirassier Division, and a light infantry regiment from the 2nd Corps. The 3rd and 5th Corps, with the militia, were for the present held in reserve.

It was not until 3 p.m. that Konovnitzin retired from Kolotskoï, and probably not before 5 that Murat attacked Gorchakov. The 3rd Chasseurs were ejected from the hamlet of Doronimo by the 61st Regiment, which marched at the head of Compans' division; and the French infantry attacked the redoubt. It was a hastily constructed work; but the 27th Division fought with steady determination and contested its possession fiercely, the cavalry co-operating by means of repeated charges, in one of which the Russian Cuirassiers captured 5 guns. The position was taken and retaken three times, and Bagration seems to have contemplated holding it definitely, for at 8 he relieved Neverovski's troops by the division of Karl of Mecklenburg. But by this time Poniatowski was well advanced along the old Moscow road on the left; and about 10 p.m. Bagration, by Kutuzov's orders, withdrew to the main position. The losses on both sides had been considerable. Bagration, who had exposed himself in his usual reckless fashion, was slightly wounded, as were also Gorchakov and St. Priest.

The French army was not yet fully concentrated, and Napoleon occupied the 6th in reconnoitring the Russian position and arranging his plan of attack, while the troops already on the field rested. On the Russian side the army was placed in position, and the day was for the most part spent in religious exercises, culminating in the progress of the Virgin of Smolensk, which had been rescued from the city, through the camps.

The Russian commanders realised that they ran the risk of being turned by the old Moscow road. Tuchkov's corps was therefore withdrawn from the general reserve and posted at Utitza, with the Moscow militia behind it in support, and 6 regiments of Cossacks under Karpov on its left near Michino. On the plateau to the north of the new road were the 2nd and 4th Corps, the 2nd on the right and the latter to the left, near Gorki. Dokhturov, with a brigade of Voronzov's Grenadiers attached, stood between Gorki and the Great Redoubt. Raievski's weak corps occupied the space between Dokhturov and Semenovskoï and garrisoned the Great Redoubt, while the 8th Corps (less Voronzov's detached brigade) and the 27th Division held Semenovskoï and the redans. The wood between Borozdin's left and Tuchkov was occupied by 4 regiments of light infantry. Every corps had its Chasseur regiments thrown out in front. Borodino was garrisoned by the Chasseurs of the Imperial Guard. Kutuzov and Bennigsen were stationed between Gorki and Tzarévo, whence they could overlook nearly the entire field.

Behind the first line stood the cavalry, each reserve corps having attached for the day a regiment of Corps-Hussars. Uvarov, having also the Cossacks of the Guard, was with Baggohufwudt, Korff behind Ostermann-Tolstoï, Kreutz (*vice* Pahlen invalided) in rear of Dokhturov, and Sievers behind Semenovskoï, with Duka's Cuirassier division. Platov had 5 Cossack regiments watching the right flank, and 9 more in rear of the 2nd Corps. The 5th Corps, now under General Lavrov, was at Tzarévo, with an artillery reserve of about 240 field and horse guns.

These dispositions have not escaped criticism. Clausewitz considers that there were too many troops on the right, and as they had eventually for the most part to be brought over to the left he was probably correct. Bennigsen says that he saw that the left would be attacked in force, and that Bagration needed reinforcing. Both opinions have rather the air of wisdom after the event, and the manœuvre proposed by Clausewitz of forming a huge reserve, allowing Napoleon to drive back Bagration, and then attacking his advancing line in flank, seems rather a hazardous one.

CHAPTER VII

The Russian line comprised four sections. Miloradovich commanded the 2nd and 4th Corps and the 1st and 2nd Cavalry Corps; Dokhturov the 6th Corps and the 3rd Cavalry Corps; Gorchakov the 7th and 8th Corps and Sievers' cavalry; and Tuchkov the 3rd Corps and the Moscow militia. Finally, Barclay was in charge of the right half of the line, Bagration of the left. This multiplicity of generals was a nuisance. Barclay and Bagration sent orders direct to the divisional and brigade commanders.

The precise part which Kutuzov took in the battle is uncertain: the general impression is that he left Barclay and Bagration to direct the movements of the troops, except in a few instances.

It is a little doubtful if the Russian commanders intended nothing but a mere obstinate defensive. As has been already mentioned, Borodino was garrisoned and the bridge left intact; and from Barclay's actions and remarks, as recorded by Löwenstern, he seems to have contemplated a counter-offensive on the right. The vigour of the French attack, however, in any case rendered this idea, if entertained, fruitless.

As regards the French plans, there is little information to be gathered from Napoleon's orders, which merely provide in the simplest manner for massing batteries and opening infantry attacks, after which directions would be given according to circumstances. Poniatowski was to turn the Russian left by the old Moscow road—a task for which he had not enough troops. Probably, owing to the interposing woods, the Russian force on the old road had not been estimated at its real strength. Davout endeavoured to be allowed to make a strong flanking movement, but Napoleon characterised it as too hazardous. Probably his real fear was that the Russians would evacuate their position under its menace, and so rob him of the battle which he anxiously desired. The battle resolved itself into a general assault of the bulk of the French army upon the Borodino-Utitza line, which, to withstand the attacks upon it, was ultimately manned by the greater part of the Russian host. It is certain that Davout was in a state of sullen rage at the rejection of his advice, as well as at the fact that Morand and Gérard were detached from the 1st Corps, and placed for the day under the orders of Eugène.

Napoleon was certainly unwell. To say that he had a cold appears little to those who do not reflect that a cold may be very troublesome. Whatever the precise degree of Napoleon's sickness there can be no doubt as to his lack of activity, and for a circumstance so remarkable there must have been strong reasons. It was no small cause that could keep the great conqueror, during a battle upon which his fortunes depended, lying listlessly on a rug behind his line.

During the 6th the French sappers raised three battery-emplacements in front of the 1st, 3rd and 4th Corps, each for 24 guns; but they were placed at too great a distance from the Russian line and played no part in the battle.

The night of the 6th-7th was foggy. Early on the 7th, while the troops were forming, the usual Imperial proclamation was read by the Colonels. It was a brief and uninspiring document, which can hardly have done much to raise the spirits of the men. De Chambray says that it was coldly received. Kutuzov's proclamation, which was read to the Russian troops after the religious services on the 6th, was a much more effective production.

The French army was disposed in the following order from right to left. The 5th Corps was on the old Moscow road. Davout, with the divisions of Friant, Compans and Desaix, stood opposite Borozdin's position and the wood to its south. Ney continued the line to the Kolotza with Ledru's and Razout's divisions; the relics of Scheler's Württemberg division, now consolidated into only 3 battalions, were in reserve. North of the Kolotza, communicating with the other troops by means of five trestle bridges, was Eugène with the 4th Corps (less Pino's division), Morand's and Gérard's divisions, Grouchy's cavalry corps and Preising's Bavarian horsemen.

In rear of Ney were the 8th Corps and Latour-Maubourg's cavalry. Nansouty's cavalry corps supported Davout. The Imperial Guard, with Montbrun's cavalry corps, just rejoined by its light division, formed the general reserve, its final position being about the Shevardino redoubt captured on the 5th, near which Napoleon stationed himself.

About 6 a.m. the artillery of Davout's corps, speedily supported by that of Ney, began a furious cannonade of the Russian left centre. Very soon afterwards Davout opened the infantry attack, sending forward Compans' division against the Semenovskoï redans, while Ney supported by moving forward Ledru on Compans' left. The Russian entrenchments were so slight that there was little difficulty in entering, but to hold them was a very different matter. Redan No. 2 was carried by the 24th Léger and the 57th of the line, but Voronzov, charging with his six Grenadier battalions formed in square, supported by Neverovski and some of Sievers' dragoons, drove them out again, and the fight raged fiercely about the almost useless earthworks, which were taken and retaken as the generals on either side threw in reinforcements.

Bagration, seeing the heavy masses advancing against him, and fearing that he would be overpowered, ordered Tuchkov to send Konovnitzin's division (now commanded by Tuchkov IV, Konovnitzin being on Kutuzov's staff) from Utitza. This reinforcement was necessary, for by 8 Voronzov and Neverovski, no longer able to bear up against superior numbers, were evicted from all three redans, Voronzov being wounded. Tuchkov came up in time to rally the retreating battalions, and Bagration promptly led forward a fresh counter-attack which was successful in recovering the lost position, though Compans was now supported by Desaix. Already the terrible "Battle of the Generals" was earning its name. Compans was disabled first, then Desaix, while Rapp, sent by Napoleon to succeed Compans, received four wounds in about an hour.

On the left Eugène had attacked Borodino with Delzons' division of the 4th Corps. The attack was made under cover of the mist which still hung over the field, and the village was carried with a rush. The Guard Chasseurs lost 30 officers in a quarter of an hour, and were driven in wild confusion to and across the Kolotza. The bridge was taken, and the 106th French Regiment poured across it in pursuit. The garrison would have been destroyed but for the 1st Chasseurs, under Colonel

CHAPTER VII

Karpenko, who hurried up to the rescue. Charged by them, and smitten by the fire of Ostermann-Tolstoï's guns from the farther bank, the 106th lost heavily. General Plauzonne was killed as he endeavoured to rally it, and its remains were driven back across the stream. Karpenko's charge was stopped by the 92nd Regiment, but he succeeded in destroying the bridge. Eugène left Delzons to watch the Kolotza north of the village, placed the Royal Guard in reserve, stationed the cavalry of the 4th Corps and Preising's division, now united under General Ornano, to cover the left flank, and turned Morand's, Gérard's and Broussier's divisions, supported by Grouchy, against Dokhturov and Raievski.

On the right Poniatowski captured Utitza, held only by the outposts, without difficulty; but on the knoll beyond Tuchkov had massed a strong force of artillery, supported by Strogonov's division, while the Chasseurs in the wood to the north brought a flanking fire to bear upon the Poles. Poniatowski ranged 40 guns in advance of the village, but they failed to silence Tuchkov's artillery, and for some hours the action in this quarter was reduced to cannonading and skirmishing.

Kutuzov, seeing that nearly the whole French army was moving against his centre and left, about 7.30 a.m. ordered Baggohufwudt to march the bulk of his corps to the support of Bagration. But as the movement would take some time, and Bagration appeared to need immediate support, the Ismailovski and Lithuanian Guards, some Grenadiers, and a brigade of Cuirassiers, were sent forward, much to the disgust of Barclay, who held strong views about depleting reserves until the last moment. He hurried to Kutuzov, and begged him not to use up the Guard until things became critical, and Kutuzov assented. His action during the greater part of the battle indeed seems to have been confined to approving his lieutenants' measures.

Davout and Ney, after being forced from the redans, reformed their troops for another assault. Friant's division was called up in support, and Tharreau's division of the 8th Corps sent forward by Napoleon against the wood to the south, from which the Russian light infantry were keeping up a heavy fire. When the Westphalians began to penetrate the wood matters appeared critical for Bagration, exposed to attacks in front and flank at the same time; but at 9 a.m. Baggohufwudt's corps arrived to his support. Eugen's division was placed in reserve behind Semenovskoï; two of Olsuviev's regiments reinforced Tuchkov IV, while the remaining four pushed into the wood and drove the Westphalians out again.

The attack on the wood had, however, caused the cessation of the flanking fire which had annoyed the Poles; and Poniatowski attacked and carried the knoll behind Utitza. The success was but momentary. Strogonov rallied his broken division; Tuchkov I himself led forward the Pavlovsk Grenadier regiment; while Olsuviev broke out of the wood with two regiments of Chasseurs. Attacked in front and flank, and charged by Olsuviev in the rear, the Poles were unable to stand and were thrust back to Utitza. The Russian success was achieved at the cost of the life of Tuchkov, who was mortally wounded as he led on his Grenadiers.

The arrival of Baggohufwudt enabled Bagration to steady his line against the renewed advance of Davout and Ney. The struggle on the low heights was indescribably close and desperate. Behind the furiously fighting masses of infantry hovered the cavalry, charging again and again as opportunities presented themselves. By 10 a.m. the French had once more taken the redans; and the 15th Léger, of Friant's division, fought its way into the ruins of Semenovskoï. Borozdin, charging with four regiments of Grenadiers, drove it out again past the redans, but was then set upon by Nansouty's cavalry and forced back; and the struggle raged more furiously than ever as the French once more stormed the redans, to be hurled out again by a counter-attack of Tuchkov IV's division, led by Konovnitzin. Already the losses had been fearful. Romœuf, Davout's chief-of-staff, had fallen, and on the Russian side General Tuchkov IV, the second of his family to die for Russia on the field of Borodino.

Eugène, having crossed the Kolotza by the temporary bridges, placed batteries in position to bombard the Great Redoubt, and formed Morand's division opposite that of Paskievich, which held the knoll. Broussier moved forward in support on Morand's left, while Gérard was still crossing the stream. Paskievich's troops outside the redoubt were so shattered by the fire of the French batteries that they sought refuge behind the shoulder of the knoll; and General Bonami, with the 30th of the Line, saw his chance. As the regiment advanced up the knoll it suffered fearfully in its close formation, but nevertheless pressed on dauntlessly and stormed the work, after a furious struggle with the Russian infantry and gunners, who proved, as Captain François says, worthy antagonists.

This sudden piercing of the centre of the Russian line produced an immediate counter-attack, while Morand's other regiments appear to have been too busy with Kolubakin's division to support Bonami. A message was hurriedly sent to Barclay; but without waiting for orders all the officers on the spot immediately did the right thing. Yermólov, who was at hand, picked up a battalion of the Ufa regiment (Likhachev's division) and was joined by Colonel Löwenstern, Barclay's aide, with one of the Regiment of Tomsk. Likhachev hurried up the 19th and 40th Chasseurs. Vassilchikov promptly turned a battalion of Kolubakin's division against the lost redoubt, and Paskievich, rallying his broken division, again pushed forward. The improvised attack was completely successful. Unsupported, except by one battalion of the 13th Léger, the gallant 30th was lost. The redoubt was recaptured and Bonami desperately wounded and taken. As the remains of the regiment streamed away down the knoll, Barclay came upon the scene, and let loose a brigade of Kreutz's Dragoons. The 30th was almost completely destroyed, only 11 officers and 257 men being able to rally. The Russians had not come off scatheless. Count Kutaïsov was killed as he led the charge with Yermólov, and the latter was wounded. To cover the escape of the remains of the 30th Eugène concentrated a tremendous artillery fire on the redoubt, in which Barclay replaced Paskievich's shaken division by Likhachev's.

The Great Redoubt was retaken at about 11 a.m., and at the same time Ney, Davout and Murat made a last and determined assault on Bagration's position about Semenovskoï. The last reserves of the 1st and 3rd Corps were thrown into the fight; Napoleon sent up the rest of the 8th Corps; behind the infantry were ranged Nansouty's and Latour-Maubourg's corps and the Corps Cavalry, and the attack was covered by the fire of over 250 guns.

This final assault was made by the French and Germans with magnificent courage. Under the furious fire of the Russian artillery and musketry the attacking columns pressed steadily on. The sight of their advance roused Bagration to generous admiration. Believing that it could not be stayed by artillery and infantry fire, he determined to make a counter-attack, and sent forward every available battalion. Again the opposing forces closed in deadly strife—Frenchmen, Russians and sturdy Germans, Spaniards and Portuguese enlisted in a quarrel not their own, fighting to the death around the blood-stained derelict redans. The cavalry joined in the conflict, individual regiments and squadrons striking in whenever an opportunity occurred. Bagration was desperately wounded in the leg; and Löwenstern tells how he found him lying among his staff behind the line, while Sir James Wylie, Alexander's surgeon, attended to his wound. He said to Löwenstern, "How goes it with Barclay? Tell him that the safety of the army depends upon him. All goes well here at present"—and then seeing that Löwenstern was himself wounded, he kindly added: "Get yourself bandaged." This touch helps one to understand the personal admiration which Bagration undoubtedly inspired in nearly everyone who came in contact with him; and it is certain that his fall caused a serious slackening in the vigour of the defence. Once more the stubborn Russians were driven from the redans and past Semenovskoï; and this time they were not to regain their lost positions.

After Bagration's wound the temporary command devolved upon the brave soldier Konovnitzin; but he was unable to check the retreat which had now definitely set in. The whole of the defending force gave back towards Tzarévo, and upon it Murat launched his great masses of cavalry. Still there appear to have been no signs of demoralisation, and little real disorder; and, though clearly worsted, the Russian infantry maintained a desperate resistance. Behind Semenovskoï the Ismailovski and Lithuanian Guards, which had not yet been seriously engaged, were drawn up in squares; and, their heavy fire checked the advance of the French cavalry. Murat brought up some batteries which opened fire against them, while in the intervals of the cannonade Latour-Maubourg's corps charged their shattered battalions. The Guards suffered fearfully, but closed their ranks and held firm, repelling three charges of the Saxon Cuirassiers, who were almost annihilated. The two regiments must, however, have been destroyed also but that Borozdin II came to their rescue with a Cuirassier brigade, checking the French horsemen by countercharges and enabling the Guards to follow in the retreat, leaving their position outlined in squares of dead and dying.

In the rear of Semenovskoï the ground was covered with struggling hordes of infantry and cavalry. Out of the confusion at length emerged some sort of order, the Russians taking up position along the Tzarévo plateau, covered by the fire of batteries from the reserve, while Davout and Ney reformed in front of Semenovskoï. Davout had been hit four times, but declined to leave the field, though obliged to withdraw for a short time, during which Ney and Murat exercised the command. The King of Naples behaved with all his usual reckless bravery; and Baron Lejeune speaks with admiration of the splendid figure presented by Ney, as he stood directing the battle from the parapet of a redan. And on the other side Barclay, now practically in sole command of the Russian army, was setting an example no less heroic, apparently wishing to meet his death on the field of Borodino. As the stress of battle grew, the Russian generals for the most part concealed the insignia which made them conspicuous; not so the slandered War-Minister, who faced the storm wearing full-dress uniform and all his decorations. It is impossible not to appreciate the heroic impulse that prompted him, like Nelson and many another fiery spirit, to expose himself to death decorated with the badges won on the field of honour. His staff were almost all killed or wounded, and he had two horses shot under him, but escaped with the slightest injury.

MARSHAL NEY
Commander of the 3rd French Army Corps. The hero of the Retreat

CHAPTER VII 137

After the picture by Langlois at Versailles

As he saw Bagration's line driven in, Kutuzov had ordered the 4th Corps also to draw in to the centre. By noon the Russian position was peculiar. Dokhturov on the right and Tuchkov on the left still faced the French in nearly their old positions, while the rest of the army stretched in a convex between them. To drive back Dokhturov and Tuchkov was Napoleon's next object, and he was about to order forward part of his Guard when, apparently a little after noon, he received intelligence that his left was being attacked.

Early in the day Platov, reconnoitring towards the right, had ascertained that there were comparatively few French troops north of the Kolotza, and had proposed to the commander-in-chief a cavalry attack on their flank and rear. Kutuzov assented, and for the purpose detailed Uvarov's cavalry corps,[6] some 3500 sabres strong. Clausewitz, who was then on Uvarov's staff, criticises the movement severely. Certainly 3500 regular, and 4000 irregular, horsemen could not of themselves effect much; but it is a little difficult to concur in his opinion that the detachment of Uvarov's corps was a rash weakening of the line. It is easier to agree with him when he says that the movement was made too early in the day. Uvarov, however, was very slow and did not cross the Kolotza until past eleven. About 11.30 he approached the Voïna (a little stream which enters the Kolotza at Borodino), at Besubovo, about a mile and a half from the former village. On the Russian side of the stream stood Guyon's cavalry brigade and a regiment of the Italian Guard, which withdrew over a mill dam before the fire of Uvarov's artillery to join the rest of the Guard and Delzons' division, which occupied Borodino. Platov now came up, and his wild horsemen dashed through a ford and among the Italian infantry, followed, without orders, by the Cossacks of the Guard, who lost heavily in charging the squares. Uvarov, however, would not risk his regulars, halted, sent for orders and finally withdrew. Clausewitz's comment is that he was not the man to lead such an attack. Löwenstern fumes at his slowness and hesitation. More, undoubtedly, might have been achieved with a bolder commander. Even so his feeble diversion brought Eugène back across the Kolotza with Broussier's division, and delayed the advance against the Great Redoubt. He finally withdrew about 3 p.m., but before this Eugène had returned across the Kolotza.

All this time a tremendous and unprecedented cannonade was being kept up. Between Borodino and Utitza some 900 guns were in action. The Great Redoubt was being furiously bombarded by Eugène's artillery, while Ney's batteries brought a converging fire to bear upon it from the southward. To storm it Eugène detailed Gérard's division, hitherto but lightly engaged, while Morand and Broussier supported; and Napoleon ordered Montbrun, with his Cuirassier divisions, to charge the Russian line on Gérard's right. Montbrun was killed as he led forward his men, and General Caulaincourt, brother of the Duke of Vicenza, came hastily from the Emperor to take up the command. "Don't stop to lament!" he said to the dead general's aides. "Follow and avenge him!" The mass of mail-clad horsemen broke through the Russian line south of the redoubt, wheeled to the left and came thundering upon its rear, just as Eugène's infantry reached it in front. For the four

[6] Uvarov had 32 squadrons in all.

regiments of Likhachev's division which held it there was no escape—at least as regards the major part. Some of them who were outside the work succeeded in saving themselves; but those within were trapped and, after maintaining a desperate resistance against the charges in front and rear, were almost all cut to pieces. Likhachev, who was very ill, flung himself among the assailants, and had almost found the death which he sought when some French soldiers, attracted by his insignia, took him prisoner, severely wounded. Caulaincourt was struck down as he led the triumphant charge of his Cuirassiers—one more victim of the fatal "Battle of the Generals."

The capture of the redoubt opened a huge gap in the Russian line, through which Eugène's and Grouchy's cavalry poured to complete the victory. Against them Barclay hurled all the horsemen whom he had under his hand—the 2nd and 3rd Cavalry Corps and the Cuirassiers of the Guard—leading more than one charge in person, while Ostermann-Tolstoï's corps, supported by the yet unengaged portions of the 5th Corps, was ordered to make a counter-attack towards Semenovskoï. Ostermann-Tolstoï, as he had shown at Ostrovno, was not the man for an emergency; Löwenstern says that he appeared to have entirely lost his head. He moved forward so slowly that Ney, Davout and Murat were able to make preparations to receive him. The French infantry were almost fought out; the cavalry had literally "foamed themselves away" in endeavouring to shatter the resistance of the stubborn Russian infantry; the fire of the Russian artillery was as steady and effective as ever. The Marshals sent again and again for some part of the Guard to support their weary men, but Napoleon refused to risk it. The Russian writers express astonishment at his caution. All that he would do was to send forward the reserve of heavy artillery, under Comte Sorbier. Sorbier swore at Lejeune, who brought the order to advance. "I ought to have had it an hour ago!" was his comment.

The Marshals had got together 80 guns wherewith to oppose the Russian advance; and when Sorbier came up the 4th Corps was overwhelmed with a crushing cannonade, against which it could not make way. Its losses were terrible. General Bakhmetiev had his leg carried away; Ostermann-Tolstoï himself and several of his staff were wounded. The supporting cavalry charged with splendid audacity, and some of them actually re-entered the Semenovskoï redans. All was in vain. Sorbier's battery had turned the scale against the Russians, and by about 4 o'clock they were in full retreat. The infantry and cavalry on both sides were fairly fought out, and the struggle was maintained only by the artillery, except on the extreme left of the Russian line, where Tuchkov's force, now commanded by Baggohufwudt, was practically isolated. The Polish Corps, supported by the Westphalians on the left, succeeded about 5 p.m. in carrying the Utitza knoll, and Baggohufwudt, still barring the road, drew back into line with the centre and left. There was a last flicker of hostility near Semenovskoï, where the Finnish Guards repulsed an advance of some French battalions, and then the battle died away in a dwindling cannonade, until a thick fog shrouded in a merciful veil the awful scene of slaughter. The Russian line, reformed by Barclay, stretched from beyond Gorki along the edge of the Tzarévo plateau to the old Moscow road. Four Chasseur regiments, under Colonel Potemkin, were on the right with Platov's Cossacks. The remains of Dokhturov's corps, supported by Uvarov, held Gorki. Next came Ostermann-Tolstoï's corps; and thence Raievski and Borozdin, with Prince Eugen's and Shakovski's (late Tuchkov IV's) divisions, continued the line to Baggohufwudt's position. The cavalry was in rear, and the 5th Corps in reserve behind the centre. The French lay opposite, Delzons and Lecchi north of the Kolotza and, to the south of the river, the 4th, 3rd, 1st, 8th and 5th Corps in succession from Borodino through Semenovskoï to a point about 1200 yards east of Utitza.

The consensus of opinion of eyewitnesses on the Russian side is that the spirit of the Russians was unbroken, and that there was little confusion in the ranks. Löwenstern says that he offered to attack the Great Redoubt at break of day, and that Barclay approved. Kutuzov, however, when he learned the extent of the slaughter in his army, decided to retreat. It is quite certain that he must have retired in a day or two, since he had no reserves, while Napoleon had 11,000 fresh troops (Laborde and Pino) approaching the field. Barclay, however, was bitterly angry; and when he received the order to retreat broke into a fierce invective against Bennigsen, to whose influence he attributed Kutuzov's resolution.

Under cover of darkness the Russian army quietly withdrew, and on the 8th took up a position in front of Mozhaïsk. The retreat was effectually covered by the Cossacks, who displayed great audacity, and in the night of the 7th-8th repeatedly disturbed the French bivouacs. The French cavalry, shattered and exhausted, could do little or nothing, and the Russians remained all through the 8th at Mozhaïsk, employing the time in reorganising, and in evacuating towards Moscow as many as possible of their wounded. Nevertheless many were left to inevitable death on the field, and thousands more abandoned at Mozhaïsk to the mercy of the French, who, themselves in a sorely distressed condition, simply cast them out to die of misery in the fields.

Regarding the major tactics of the battle of Borodino there is little to say. Napoleon had deliberately chosen to make a frontal attack upon the Russian army in place of turning it; and in the practical absence of his personal supervision the battle almost fought itself. The idea of taking advantage of the extension of the Russian right by overwhelming the left was an excellent one. It was foiled by the determination of Bagration's resistance, which permitted Baggohufwudt's corps to be moved across to his support. On the part of the Russians the occupation in force of the position north of the new road proved a blunder, which the remarkable solidity of the Russian resistance enabled the generals to repair in time.

As regards what is often considered Napoleon's fatal error in not throwing in the Guard it is very doubtful whether it was an error at all. It must be remembered that Ney's and Davout's troops were almost, if not quite, fought out, that the Russians were still solid and undemoralised, and holding a position quite as strong as that from which they had been evicted; and that Kutuzov still had some almost untouched reserves. The Guard would have had no easy victory, and Napoleon was probably right when he refused to expose it to severe and perhaps fatal losses. He knew that the Russians were neither routed nor in disorder; and if they stood to fight again nearer Moscow he might yet have sore need of his Guard. He was

1200 miles from the frontier of his dominions, and in case of disaster all must depend upon it.

Of the minor tactics little need be said. On both sides they were crude and wasteful. There was a deficiency of infantry on the French side, and the cavalry was freely employed to supplement it, with the result that it was half destroyed. The infantry formations were dense and clumsy, it was a case of heavy mass pushing against heavy mass, with cavalry mingled in the melée, and all under the fire of a thousand or more pieces of artillery. It is no wonder that the losses were unprecedented on both sides.

Napoleon gave his loss at 10,000. French writers admit the suspicious round number of 28,000—6547 killed and 21,453 wounded—but Martinien's lists show 49 generals and 1934 officers killed and wounded, and even allowing for the fact that many of the effectives were now low, and the proportion of officers to rank and file therefore higher than usual, this can scarcely imply less than 43,000 casualties. Even the troops which had never been sent forward had suffered somewhat from the cannonade.

CHAPTER VII

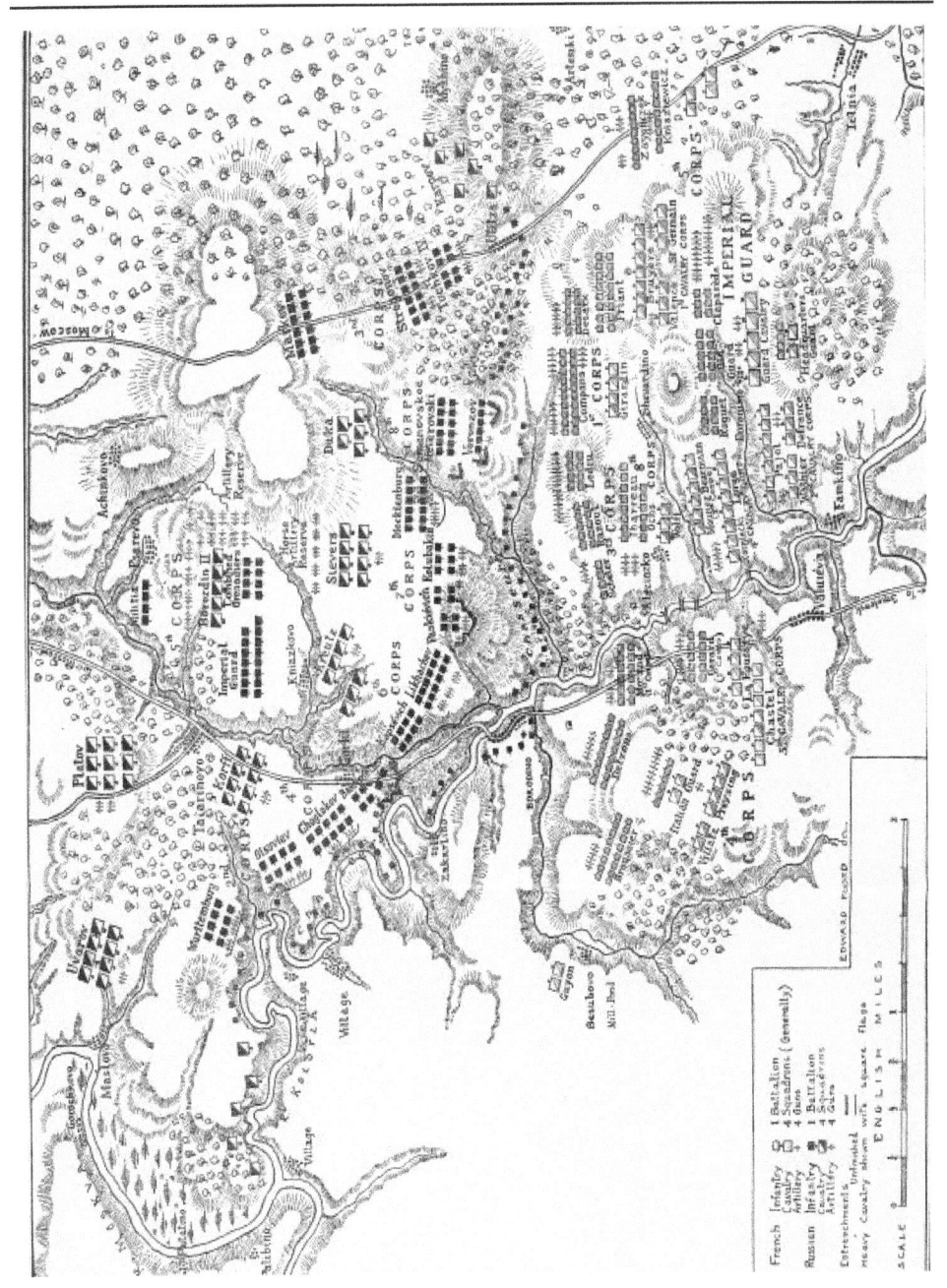

BATTLE OF BORODINO
(September 7th, 1812)

The losses of the First Russian Army from the 4th to the 7th of September are stated by Bogdanovich at 9252 killed and 19,226 wounded. Those of the Second Army may perhaps, since it contained only 54 battalions and 52 squadrons as against Barclay's 122 battalions and 112 squadrons, be estimated at 12,000. Adding the losses of the militia, a total is obtained of possibly 41,000 or 42,000. Sir Robert Wilson estimates it at 1500 officers and 36,000 men. Buturlin gives 15,000 killed and 30,000 wounded.

Prisoners there were few — perhaps 1000 or 1200 French and 2000 Russians. The estimates of guns captured are somewhat vague. Kutuzov's official figure of French guns taken and carried off by the Russians is 8. There may, of course, have been others disabled. The Russians seem to have lost about 18 in all.

On the field Borodino can scarcely be described as anything but a drawn battle. Napoleon had gained a little ground, but the Russian army was unbroken and apparently quite willing to renew the contest next day. Strategically the French appeared to have obtained a slight success, since they were able to continue their advance to Moscow. On the other hand, the battle, which ruined the cavalry and seriously shattered the infantry, brought ultimate ruin distinctly nearer. Perhaps its most noteworthy result was the extent to which the morale of the Napoleonic army was broken.

CHAPTER VIII
THE OCCUPATION AND DESTRUCTION OF MOSCOW

The morning of the 8th of September found the army of Napoleon bivouacked among the dead and wounded on the field of Borodino. Only the Guard was really ready for further combat. The corps of Davout and Ney were terribly cut up; the 17th, 30th and 106th Regiments were nearly destroyed. The cavalry, which had to compensate for Napoleon's comparative weakness in infantry, had suffered fearfully. Nearly all its corps and divisional commanders were killed or wounded; several regiments were almost annihilated. The four corps of the reserves counted some 19,000 men on September 2nd; on the 20th they could muster little more than 10,000. Thousands of horses had been killed, and there was no present possibility of being able to replace them, while the wounded animals were mostly doomed to perish from lack of forage and proper care. The cavalry of the Guard alone was in a state for serious combat.

The fate of the wounded was horrible. Means of every kind for tending them were lacking, and fortunate were those whose end was hastened by the incurable nature of their hurts, or thirst and starvation. Days elapsed before all had received so much as first aid; and this was but the commencement of their miseries. The great monastery of Kolotskoï became the principal hospital, and in its buildings the victims of Borodino were huddled literally in heaps, without beds even of straw, without food or fire, and without a tenth of the medical aid that was needed. Some of the wounded officers were able to buy food, at enormous prices, from the convoys which passed these dens of horror; but for the unhappy rank and file, who possessed little or no money, there was no hope. Sanitation there was none, and the unfortunate beings died in thousands, amid filth, pestilence and neglect. François says that in one hospital a dead officer was found who, in the agonies of starvation, *had devoured his own arm to the bone*. It is a painful task even to touch upon these sickening details, but to fail to do so is to neglect the primary duty of an historian.

Besides the enormous diminution of the effective strength, the state of the ammunition-trains was by no means reassuring. There is reason to believe that the artillery had fired 90,000 rounds during the 5th and 7th; the infantry must have expended millions of cartridges. It is certain that, immediately after Borodino, Napoleon was anxiously pressing for fresh supplies of ammunition; and it is doubtful if he could have delivered another pitched battle before they arrived.

Worse than all, the spirit of the troops was grievously depressed. The gaiety which commonly characterises Frenchmen, even in untoward circumstances, had vanished. Gloomy silence reigned during the march and in the bivouacs. The negative results of the great battle had completed the discouragement of the troops. The French soldiers, at any rate, were too intelligent not to have some inkling of the disasters that might too probably lie before them.

On the whole Kutuzov might perhaps have remained longer on the field of battle. It is, however, probable that his withdrawal to Mozhaïsk was wise. He had dealt a tremendous blow at the efficiency and morale of Napoleon's army, but in doing so his own forces had been fearfully shattered. Had he remained in position the circumstance might have decided Napoleon to use the almost untouched Guards, and so at the last moment wring a victory from frowning Fortune.

When the sun dissipated the autumn fog which had enwrapped the field, the Russian position was seen to be guarded only by the hovering *pulks* of Platov's Cossacks. Against them Murat moved such of his exhausted horsemen as could be rallied; and before the advance of regular squadrons the riders withdrew. Behind them, however, were supports of infantry—the four Chasseur regiments of the 2nd Corps. They gave back very slowly, and did not reach Mozhaïsk until 4 p.m. By that time a large number of the Russian wounded had already been evacuated. The town, however, was still choked with disabled men, many of whom were in a state to be moved, and to cover this operation Kutuzov directed Platov to hold it as long as possible. The Russian main body was in position behind it.

Napoleon, as soon as he was assured that the Russians had really retired, ordered Murat to press their retreat. The King had the four reserve cavalry corps and the light horse of Ney and Davout as before,—a total now of not more than 14,000 lances and sabres—but Compan's shattered division was replaced by that of Dufour (*vice* Friant wounded). The Emperor apparently at first believed that Kutuzov was in full retreat, and the head-quarters baggage was directed on Mozhaïsk; but Murat, as aforesaid, made little or no headway against Platov; and the head-quarters could not be transferred. Desultory skirmishing and cannonading went on until nightfall, when Platov was still in possession of Mozhaïsk.

The firm front shown by Platov must have convinced Napoleon that the spirit of the Russians was unbroken. He spent a part of the day in going over the battle-field, examining the positions and reviewing the troops according to his custom. In the afternoon he went forward to join Murat, and on the way received another unpleasant reminder of the unabated courage of his foes, some foragers being driven in by Cossacks, and an alarm caused. On this day, however, a much needed reinforcement arrived in the form of Pino's Italian division.

At about 10 a.m. on the 9th Platov was fiercely attacked by Murat, expelled, and driven along the Moscow road. Murat's pursuit was checked by a reinforcement of twelve battalions and a heavy battery sent back by Kutuzov, but Mozhaïsk was lost, and Napoleon transferred his head-quarters thither. Some thousands of the most seriously injured of the Russian wounded were still there; and there were hideous scenes as they were cast out of the houses for those of the French army,

CHAPTER VIII 145

who, in carriages and waggons, or dragging themselves along on foot, streamed in piteous procession in rear of the leading troops. The Russian main body retired deliberately to Semlino (or Shelkovka) about 12 miles east of Mozhaïsk.

Napoleon himself remained for three days at Mozhaïsk recovering from his cold, and transacting arrears of business. Already on August 27th he had sent orders to Victor to bring the 9th Corps from the Niemen up to Smolensk; and from Mozhaïsk fresh directions were despatched for him. From Mozhaïsk also was sent the bulletin announcing the battle of Borodino. As his cold rendered him speechless Napoleon wrote it with his own hand; and, being at best an execrable writer, the result may be imagined. The French losses are stated in it at 10,000. This would, according to Napoleon's usual standard, indicate from 40,000 to 50,000 casualties.

Meanwhile the Russian army was still steadily retiring on the high-road to Moscow, and Murat deliberately following. Eugène, as before, marched on the north by a track running roughly parallel with the main road by the towns of Rusa and Zvenigorod, while Poniatowski formed the right flank guard on the south. Junot remained at Borodino and Kolotskoï to guard the hospitals. In support of Murat marched Mortier with the divisions of Roguet and Claparède; and behind him Davout and Ney in the order named.

Kutuzov was displeased with Platov for abandoning Mozhaïsk prematurely, as he considered, and superseded him in the command of the rear-guard by Miloradovich. On the 10th the Russian main body made another deliberate march of about 8 miles, while Miloradovich stood to fight at Krymskoïe, some 3 miles short of Kutuzov's evening position. His force consisted of six weak regiments of Chasseurs, four line regiments, Uvarov's nearly intact cavalry division, and some Cossacks. He occupied a low, partly wooded ridge; his left was covered by a marsh, his right by woods, while in the centre the high-road approached the ridge by a narrow gully which was commanded by the Russian guns. Clausewitz, however, who was present, does not consider that the position was particularly advantageous. The twenty defending battalions can hardly have mustered over 6000 bayonets. Murat came up towards 5 p.m., and developed a fierce attack by Dufour's division upon the right of the position, defended by three Chasseur regiments under Colonel Potemkin. After a hard struggle Potemkin was forced back from the summit of the ridge, but he held firm, supported by three regiments sent to his support by Miloradovich. Uvarov's horsemen succeeded in keeping Murat's broken regiments at bay; and the Russians fought on doggedly until darkness put an end to the contest. The Russian loss is stated, probably with some exaggeration, at 2000. As Martinien's lists show 71 officers killed and wounded between the 8th and 10th, the French can scarcely have lost less than 1200.

On the 11th the main Russian army marched 16 miles to Viazema (Viazma on modern maps). Miloradovich retired to Kubinskoi, 8 miles from Krymskoïe, unpursued by Murat. Eugène and Poniatowski were nearly level with Murat on the north and south, Mortier and Davout some distance behind, and Ney only a short way past Mozhaïsk. On the 12th Kutuzov retrograded to Momonovo, a bare ten miles from Moscow, while Miloradovich withdrew to Malo Viazema, 12 miles to the westward, leisurely followed by Murat. On the same day Napoleon left

Mozhaïsk for the front.

MOSCOW FROM THE SPARROW HILLS
This is practically the scene which Napoleon contemplated in 1812

The question of the fate of Moscow was now imminent. It is at least possible that Kutuzov would have risked another battle had there been a fair prospect of success. But it cannot be said that this was the case. All the way from Mozhaïsk the militia had been steadily joining, but even so the army mustered less than 90,000 men, and of these only 65,000 were regulars, as against over 90,000 still under Napoleon's hand. Many of the militia were as yet unequipped with fire-arms, and all were raw and without training. Kutuzov could expect no further reinforcements of regulars for weeks, whereas Napoleon would be joined within ten days by Laborde's division as well as by some *régiments de marche*. The defective state of his ammunition Kutuzov did not know. The spirit of the Russian troops was indeed excellent, but against it was the greatest military genius of modern times, backed by an army wearied indeed, and in part much disheartened, but not yet demoralised, and including 20,000 untouched and undiscouraged veterans.

On June 10th Count Feodor Vasilievich Rostopchin, a former favourite and confidant of the ill-fated Emperor Paul, and a fanatical opponent of the French alliance, had been appointed Governor-General of Moscow. Whether he was the right man for his position must be questioned. It does not appear that anything was done to organise and arm the inhabitants or fortify the city. Nevertheless Rostopchin was furious at the idea of abandoning Moscow. According to Wilson he never forgave Kutuzov for keeping him in ignorance of the critical state of affairs.

As a fact he must have known that the evacuation of the city was to be expected; and he appears to have been steadily clearing it as far as possible of its inhabitants. This was the more practicable because in the summer Moscow was considerably less populated than in the winter, the nobles and their large households of serfs and retainers being absent on their estates. Otherwise the Governor, who was not a soldier, seems to have considered a good many rather wild plans of resistance. It would have been perfectly feasible to defend Moscow with the 90,000 troops of Kutuzov, but its destruction would thereby have been rendered inevitable. As regards Rostopchin's project of arming the inhabitants, it is certain that such muskets as were available were obsolete and of bad quality. For the rest, 200,000 human beings cannot abandon their homes in a day, and since the French found the city nearly deserted it is obvious that the exodus of the Muscovites had long been in progress.

On the 13th the Russians fell back to Fili, and took up a position on the east side of Moscow, chosen by Bennigsen, who eulogises it in his memoirs, saying that its only defect was that it was rather long. On arriving Barclay proceeded to inspect it, while Kutuzov, who could ill support the fatigue of the campaign, rested. Dokhturov, who apparently had a touch of the courtier about him, proceeded to serve him a meal, but the little picnic was quickly interrupted by Colonel Löwenstern asking for Dokhturov, with whom Barclay wished to confer.

"As usual!" said Barclay as he sent off Löwenstern. "There they all are, dancing attendance on the Prince, and not troubling about what *they* (the French) may do. Fetch Dokhturov here, even if his mouth is still full."

Kutuzov apparently rather enjoyed Dokhturov's disappointment on being thus interrupted. "You must not keep General Barclay waiting," he remarked. "I shall manage very well by myself," and therewith proceeded with his meal, while poor Dokhturov was obliged to go. Barclay and he studied the position and came to the conclusion that it was too weak.

A council of war was called for four o'clock in the afternoon. Bennigsen, still busy examining the position, kept the other generals waiting until six. There were present Kutuzov, Barclay, Bennigsen, Dokhturov, Konovnitzin, Raievski, Uvarov, Ostermann-Tolstoï, Yermólov, Toll, and, later on, Platov. Bennigsen opened the discussion by asking whether it was better to give battle or to abandon the capital. Kutuzov interrupted him, pointing out that the question was not of Moscow, but the salvation of all Russia, and that this clearly depended upon the preservation of the army.

Barclay strongly supported Kutuzov, and he was followed by Raievski, Konovnitzin, and Ostermann-Tolstoï. Barclay appears otherwise to have had no great confidence in the ability of the Russian troops, diluted with militia, to manœuvre. When fighting generals such as Raievski and Konovnitzin ranged themselves with him the question was practically decided. According to Bennigsen he was supported by Dokhturov and Platov; but his claim to have had the votes of Konovnitzin and Yermólov is elsewhere contradicted. To his suggestion that battle should be delivered Ostermann-Tolstoï replied with a blunt question as to whether he was ready to answer for victory. Bennigsen evaded this embarrassing query; but Kutuzov, who had perhaps already made up his mind, ended the discussion by deciding upon retreat. As to its direction Barclay appears to have considered that it should be to the eastward on Vladimir and Nizhnii Novgorod; but Toll, thinking more of the question of supplies, suggested a retirement towards Kaluga. A direct retreat on the latter place would have exposed the army to one of Napoleon's dreaded flanking attacks. Strategically Barclay's suggestion was sound enough, if perhaps over-cautious. Clausewitz points out that Napoleon's offensive power was exhausted, and that he could scarcely have pursued.

Kutuzov decided that the line of the retreat should be by Kolomna on Riazan, thus intermediate between that suggested by Barclay and that proposed by Toll. By taking it no opening was afforded for a flank attack; and it would be easy to manœuvre on either wing should occasion arise. The commissariat of the army would be assured since it would have at its back the fertile "Black Soil" provinces; and it would furthermore be in easy communication with the manufactories of arms at Tula and elsewhere. Orders were therefore issued for the retreat of the army by the Kolomna road. Bennigsen was extremely discontented, and showed his displeasure by leaving the council. He attributed it to Barclay, and their relations, already strained, became more hostile than ever.

There can be no doubt that Kutuzov and Barclay were correct in their resolution to retreat, but it was no light thing to make it. Kutuzov was greatly agitated; he passed a sleepless night, and more than once tears were seen to roll down his cheeks. No Englishman can perhaps fully understand what it meant to a Russian to leave "White-Walled Moscow," the mother of the Russian land, to the mercy of an enemy.

Barclay, though now in bad health, took executive command of the evacuation. At 2 a.m. on the 14th the army began its passage through the city. The troops, in the deepest dejection, tramped through the streets with furled standards and silent bands, many of them, officers and men, sobbing with rage and despair. The foreign commandant of the Kremlin garrison regiment began the evacuation with band playing, according to the usages of war, and there was a violent outcry among the retreating soldiery. They indignantly shouted that he was rejoicing, and the music had to cease.

CHAPTER VIII

NAPOLEON'S FIRST VIEW OF MOSCOW
The Emperor is standing on the Sparrow Hills, from which an imposing view of the old Russian capital is obtained.
From the painting by Verestchagin.

Barclay stationed his staff-officers along the line of retreat to enforce order. Knowing the especial weakness of the Russian soldiers, he issued strict orders that anyone found in a beer-shop or intoxicated was to be summarily punished. He worked himself to death in directing the march, and was on horseback for eighteen hours. He complained bitterly of the inefficiency of the staff, which, as usual, did little or nothing to facilitate the march. There was frequently disorder among the retiring columns. None the less it must be said that the operation was remarkably successful. By 9 o'clock in the evening, after eighteen hours of incessant toil, 90,000 fighting men, more than 600 guns and thousands of vehicles, had been passed through the great city and were on the Kolomna road. Kutuzov himself traversed Moscow in the morning. An eyewitness states that he saw him near the Kolomna gate sitting in his carriage quite alone, resting his head on his hands, silent and sad, while before him troops, guns, and waggons poured in an endless stream. The head of the army halted for the night at Panki, a village about ten miles from the city, where Kutuzov established his head-quarters.

Meanwhile, early on the 13th, Napoleon halted his army, fearing that Kutuzov was manœuvring to attack his right flank. That he could conceive such an eventuality shows how completely, and not for the first time in the campaign, his cavalry had failed to keep touch with the enemy. At 10 a.m., however, he became convinced that the Russian army was still in his front, and resumed his march. At 1 p.m. on the 14th Murat's vanguard crowned the Sparrow Hills, about a mile and a half west of Moscow, and saw before them in the plain the Russian rear-guard, and beyond it the widespreading city — the goal which they had toiled so strenuously to attain.

The Russian army was still pouring through the streets, and Miloradovich sent an officer to Murat to propose a short armistice, adding that if it were not granted he should defend the city step by step, and fire it as he fell back. After a while a sort of informal suspension of arms until 7 p.m. was made between Miloradovich and Sebastiani, now commanding the 2nd Cavalry Corps. The Russians evacuated the Dorogomilov suburb at 3 p.m., and Murat quietly followed. At about the same time Napoleon reached the Sparrow Hills. He is said to have gazed long and eagerly upon the goal of his wishes, now spread out before his greedy eyes; but he may well have muttered the words attributed to him: "It is full time!"

The Emperor approved of the informal truce concluded by Murat. The peaceful occupation of Moscow was an end bought cheaply enough at the price of the quiet withdrawal of the Russian rear-guard. Mortier was to be Governor, General Durosnel Military Commandant, and M. Lesseps, who had formerly been French Consul-General at St. Petersburg, Intendant of the province of Moscow. Orders were issued to prevent the ingress of plunderers. Eugène and Poniatowski were ordered to halt some miles short of the city. Mortier was directed to occupy the Kremlin, and to maintain order by severe methods. As the day wore on the 1st and 3rd Corps and the old Guard closed up on Murat. It is a characteristically French touch that the men had decked themselves out in their parade uniforms to take part in the triumphal entry.

As Miloradovich evacuated quarter after quarter of the city Murat advanced, dreading surprise, and taking great precautions against it. The streets were deserted; silence reigned everywhere. Near the Kremlin a tumultuous gathering of citizens and stragglers opened a scattering fire. They were dispersed by cannon shots, and Murat moved on, only to find silence and apparent desertion. Miloradovich marched through the city and established himself for the night some 4 miles from the Kolomna gate. Winzingerode's detachment, which had been falling back be-

CHAPTER VIII

fore Eugène, was on the St. Petersburg road, and another cavalry detachment was escorting the public treasure and the archives of Moscow to Vladimir.

When at last it became evident that Moscow was indeed deserted by most of its native inhabitants, a deputation of foreign residents was collected to be presented to Napoleon. His mortification was extreme. He quartered himself in the Dorogomilov suburb, and, between his anxiety and the dirt and vermin of an ill-kept abode, spent a restless night.

Mortier had duly occupied the Kremlin with Roguet's division, sending Claparède to support Murat. The silence of the city impressed even the reckless soldiery of Napoleon. Sergeant Bourgogne naïvely expresses it by remarking how disappointed they were to see not even a pretty girl listening to the regimental bands. With darkness disorder broke forth everywhere. It was impossible to prevent ill-fed and ill-clad men from pillaging when all that they needed, not to speak of wealth, which appeared to their ignorance inconceivable, lay ready to hand. In the evening fires were already breaking out. In the morning of the 15th Napoleon, escorted by the Old Guard, took up his residence in the Imperial Palace in the Kremlin.

It should here be said that the *Kreml*, or citadel, commonly known in Western Europe as the "Kremlin," was the original fortress or walled town of Moskva, fortified in 1147 by Prince Yurí Dolgorúki (Long-handed George), the son of the famous Great Prince Vladimir Monomakh. Around it grew up in the course of ages various suburbs, and these were in their turn walled. As the streets were wide, and there were many very large buildings—palaces, monasteries, and the like—often standing in spacious gardens or enclosures, the city covered an enormous area. It had the characteristics in general of a vast country suburb rather than of a city.

A volume might be written concerning the burning of Moscow. The catastrophe has been described in the works of numerous eyewitnesses, and lengthy reference to the event itself hardly falls within the compass of this work. Three points must, however, be dealt with: the causes of the conflagration; its extent; and its effects upon the fortunes of Napoleon.

As regards the origin of the fire it may be regarded as certain that it was not the outcome of Russian patriotic frenzy. The whole evidence is to the contrary; and the fury and grief of the Russians at the destruction of their holy city were obviously genuine. It was equally not due to the deliberate action of the invaders, who had every motive for preserving the city for their own convenience. It remains to be considered whether it was the act of Rostopchin or due to mere accident, assisted by a fortuitous combination of circumstances.

Public opinion at the time attributed the conflagration to Rostopchin. Two of his own residences were destroyed, and a few weeks later he deliberately fired his country mansion at Voronovo in order to prevent its seizure by the French. Sir Robert Wilson, who had means of knowing, says that Rostopchin's design was notorious, and that in order to prevent him from carrying it into execution Kutuzov repeatedly announced his intention of delivering battle before Moscow. Buturlin, the contemporary Russian historian, also attributes the fire to the Governor.

Rostopchin's own testimony cannot unfortunately be trusted. He, at the time, admitted the responsibility of having burned Moscow. Nevertheless later, as a voluntary exile abroad, he repudiated it. All that can be said is that either he was really responsible, or that if not he claimed the credit in the belief that the burning of Moscow would be regarded as an heroic action, and only disowned complicity when he found that it was generally considered atrocious.

The French believed that the fire was caused by Rostopchin's incendiaries, and hundreds or thousands of the Muscovites remaining in the city were hanged, bayoneted, or shot as such. The French, however, as all their history goes to show, have an unhappy tendency to lose their heads at a crisis, and it is certain that during the burning of Moscow they were wellnigh insane with panic. For the rest, they were utterly ignorant of their victims' language.

Certain facts appear to emerge from the confusion as proved:—

(1) The city was by no means entirely deserted by the more respectable classes. Tutulmin, the director of the foundling hospital, remained at his post; and a certain number of merchants and gentlemen, some of Francophil leanings, did not leave. The foreign colony—chiefly French—also remained.

(2) The lowest of the lower classes naturally remained; and the disreputable elements probably preferred to take their chance of making their profit out of the invaders. The criminals in the prisons had also been released.

(3) Whatever may have been the case as regards the mass of ordinary private dwellings, the palaces and mansions, of which Moscow was full, as well as most of the many warehouses and shops, were abandoned, as a seaman might say, "all standing."

(4) The fire was beginning as the Russian rear-guard left the city.

(5) Plundering on the part of the invaders commenced almost immediately after their entry.

(6) The wind changed its direction more than once.

(7) The French captured and utilised a vast quantity of gunpowder.

(8) Several thousand Russian wounded were left in the city.

The obvious deduction from (1) and (3) is that Moscow was hurriedly evacuated, and this is further supported by the evidence of (7) and (8). Had there been any settled plan of destruction one does not see why the powder-magazines were not fired, and the buildings of most importance to the invaders ruined. Nothing of this description was attempted, and the ammunition was for the most part saved by the French, to their great advantage. For the rest, with a mob of soldiery, together with a mixed horde of camp-followers of all nations, beggars, criminals, and prostitutes, plundering indiscriminately, there was every opportunity for wanton destruction. The frequent changes of the wind helped to spread the conflagration, and it was further assisted by the fact that the great majority of the private dwellings were wooden constructions.

On the whole, regarding the question solely from the standpoint of the established facts, it seems at least possible that the conflagration of Moscow, like most events of the kind recorded in history, was accidental in its origin.

It is probable that four-fifths of Moscow vanished in the conflagration, but it is doubtful if the material injury inflicted upon the invaders was very serious. In the city itself some 500 secular buildings of stone and brick survived, besides many churches and convents. The Kremlin was little injured. It is also clear that there were available great stores of food and other supplies. Forage alone was lacking. De Fezensac, who now commanded the 4th Regiment of Ney's corps, which was generally encamped outside the city, speaks of trouble in obtaining supplies, and of poor and coarse fare, but not of actual want. In Moscow itself there appears to have been a superfluity of food, though flour was less abundant than other less necessary supplies. Clothing and materials for manufacturing it were seized in quantities, and no doubt the whole army could have been refitted had organised attempts been made to that end.

It was the possession of Moscow which exercised a disastrous influence upon the fortunes of Napoleon. Having failed to crush the Russian field-army, and thereby force Alexander to make peace, he had now become obsessed with the idea that the occupation of Moscow would bring about the desired consummation of his hopes. There was, indeed, hardly ever the slightest chance of their fulfilment, but Napoleon could not bring himself to admit this, and lingered among the ruins for week after week.

It is certain that fires were already commencing as the Russians evacuated the city; but the first serious outbreak appears to have occurred at a Government spirit store. It was extinguished, but soon afterwards the great bazaar in which, as at Constantinople and other Oriental cities, the bulk of the retail trade of Moscow was concentrated, was found to be on fire. Both spirit stores and shops would be natural marks for plunderers. The wind rose, drifted inflammable wreckage across the city, and scattered it among the wood-built suburbs, through which the conflagration spread with terrifying rapidity. The stories that the fire engines had disappeared, and that the ropes of the wells had been cut, may be taken for what they are worth. It is obvious that little organised endeavour to control the conflagration of a vast and largely wood-built city was, or could be, made. The Guards in the central quarters soon abandoned all efforts to fight the flames in order to devote themselves to plunder, and the officers of the corps encamped outside, convinced that it was vitally necessary to fill their nearly empty store-waggons, permitted, or connived at, the entry of their own men to take part in the sack.

Napoleon himself remained in the Kremlin until the 16th, when a change in the wind brought the conflagration from the suburbs to the inner quarters of the city, and rendered residence in the Imperial Palace dangerous, more especially since the larger part of the captured powder-magazines were within the citadel. The Emperor left by the river gate—the land fronts of the walled enclosure being practically encircled by the flames—and proceeded along the quays, eventually reaching the Imperial palace of Petrovski, some 2 miles on the Petersburg road.

With Napoleon's departure pillage became universal. Some officers endeavoured to induce their men to take food and clothing, but apparently with little success, and that vast quantities of food were saved was due to the fact that the half-famished troops naturally turned to it. Murder and outrage went hand in hand with pillage. Many inhabitants were massacred by the soldiery, maddened with licence and intoxicating liquor; many others perished in the flames of their homes, or in attempting to escape from them. The miscellaneous horde of female camp-followers behaved as badly as the men. Paymaster Duverger relates how he knocked down a ruffianly *cantinière* who was robbing a sick and helpless Russian lady. There is unhappily evidence that many of the officers set a disgraceful example. Some pillaged openly; others made a levy upon the plunder of their men. The Guards had the best opportunities and gained an unenviable pre-eminence in misconduct. Drunkenness was everywhere rife. The men of the 1st Corps were almost as bad as the Guards, and probably this carnival of licence was the event which contributed most to the destruction of their discipline early in the retreat. It is worthy of note that Ney's corps, which took little direct share in the sack, was the one which kept the best order amid the horrors of the retreat. Marshal Lefebvre was furious at the disorder in the Old Guard, and issued a severe order on the subject.

NAPOLEON WATCHING THE BURNING OF MOSCOW

CHAPTER VIII

From the picture by Verestchagin

On the 19th the conflagration began to die away, partly owing to the equinoctial rains, and on the 20th Napoleon returned to the Kremlin. Useless efforts were made to induce the inhabitants to return to the ruined city, and the peasants to bring their produce to market. For payment Napoleon had provided a supply of forged Russian paper rúbles; but opportunities for uttering them were not forthcoming, though some were distributed to the surviving inhabitants and to charitable institutions. A few merchants and tradesmen accepted office under the French, but after the destruction of Moscow the Russians who entertained any feeling towards the invaders but that of bitter hatred were few indeed.

On evacuating Moscow the Russian army made two leisurely marches on the Kolomna road to where it crossed the Moskva, about 20 miles from the capital. Kutuzov appears at first to have intended to continue his march to Kolomna; but a conference with the Intendant-General Lanskoï convinced him that there would be difficulty in diverting the line of supply, and he decided to manœuvre towards Kaluga. On the 17th, therefore, leaving Raievski's corps to cover the rear, he turned westward, and marched along the Pakhra, a rivulet which here joins the Moskva, until he reached the Moscow-Kaluga road. On the 21st he took up a position behind the Pakhra, with an advance-guard, composed of the 8th Corps and the 1st Cavalry Division, under Miloradovich at Desna, only some 10 miles from Moscow. At the same time Dorokhov, with the hussars of Yelisabetgrad, the Dragoons of the Guard, and three regiments of Cossacks, was detached towards Mozhaïsk. This last movement was perhaps premature, since it gave Napoleon early warning of an intention to operate against his communications.

During the night of the 15th the glare of a vast conflagration had reddened the sky to the north-west. All through the next four days the bivouacs of the Russians were illuminated by the flames of their burning "Mother City," while by day dense banks of smoke lay upon the horizon, and charred fragments were frequently borne by the fierce gales among their marching files. The effect upon the soldiers may perhaps better be imagined than described. Whether the destruction of Moscow were deliberate or accidental in its origin, it kindled in the Russian army a flame of vengeful desire that endured until it marched triumphantly into Paris in 1814.

Murat, with his advanced guard, strengthened by Claparède's division, and supported by Poniatowski, was following the Russians. At the Pakhra he lost touch, and not until the 23rd was the true direction of Kutuzov's march ascertained and followed up, Raievski retiring on the main army. Napoleon apparently did not believe that Kutuzov's whole force was to the south of Moscow—at all events he adopted a dangerous half-measure, which might have resulted in disaster. Murat was to press the Russians' right, while a column under Bessières marched from Moscow against their front. Bessières' force comprised the infantry division of Friederichs (*vice* Desaix), now increased by the 33rd Léger, a brigade of light cavalry, Colbert's Lancers, and the 3rd Cavalry Corps detached from Murat. Its strength cannot have exceeded 11,000 men, while Murat certainly had not more than 25,000. Barclay and Bennigsen urged an attack, and it is clear that Murat must have been destroyed, or forced to retreat in haste. The cautious Kutuzov, however, inferred that Bessières was merely Napoleon's advance-guard — as a fact the Emperor did on the 28th issue orders for a general advance on the Pakhra. As Kutuzov envisaged the situation, he would have the whole *Grande Armée*, enormously superior in regular troops, upon his own weakened forces. The superior condition of his cavalry and artillery could scarcely be relied upon to give him more than a doubtful success. On the other hand, every day would bring the winter nearer and ensure the steady increase of the Russian numbers. He accordingly decided to retire towards Kaluga. The 4th Corps was detailed to strengthen Raievski, and Miloradovich took command of the rear-guard. On the 27th there was a brisk encounter of cavalry on the Pakhra. On the 29th another engagement took place at Czerikovo. Poniatowski's infantry were checked; General Ferrier was wounded and taken, and the advantage was, on the whole, with Miloradovich, who retired very slowly, contesting every mile of country.

On October 2nd the main Russian army reached Tarutino on the Nara, some 50 miles from Moscow, and took up a position, to protect which entrenchments were immediately commenced. Next day Sebastiani, always unlucky, experienced a slight check near Voronovo, but when Murat's main column began to arrive Miloradovich retreated to Spas Kuplia, 10 miles north of Tarutino. The 4th and 7th Corps were drawn back towards the main army, covered by the 8th and most of the cavalry. Early on the 4th Murat and Poniatowski surprised the Russians. Spas Kuplia was carried and the 8th Corps driven back behind the Chernishnia rivulet, half-way to Tarutino. Konovnitzin, with whom was Sir Robert Wilson, was nearly captured, but he rode out of the danger-zone, his night-cap, in which he had been surprised, showing under his cocked hat, puffing coolly at his pipe all the time. So Löwenstern describes the scene. The 8th Corps rallied and held firm upon the Chernishnia until night, and eventually retired across the Nara to Tarutino. The 2nd, 3rd and 4th Cavalry Divisions (the first two now amalgamated) and some Cossacks remained in observation of the French north of the Nara. Murat's offensive power had exhausted itself, and he halted, disposing the bulk of his force along the Chernishnia, with his advance troops at the village of Vinkovo.

Meanwhile the presence of Dorokhov south-east of Moscow had caused Napoleon to send some twenty miles on the road to Mozhaïsk, Broussier's infantry division, the light cavalry of the 4th Corps, and the Dragoons and Chasseurs of the Guard. This for the moment relieved the road to Mozhaïsk, but the whole route to Smolensk was infested by Cossacks; and Napoleon was obliged to issue an order that no body of troops less than 1500 strong was to be risked along it. Kutuzov's withdrawal to Tarutino seems for a short time to have improved matters near Moscow. Murat, with the reserve cavalry, the bulk of the light horse of the 1st and 3rd Corps, the 5th Corps, Dufour's and Claparède's divisions, remained on the Chernishnia. Broussier was stationed about 9 miles west of Moscow; Friederichs on the Pakhra; the Guard Cavalry returned to Moscow. Foraging detachments were despatched over the surrounding country to gather in food and fodder — with poor results — and in this manner a fortnight passed away.

CHAPTER IX
THE FRENCH SOJOURN IN MOSCOW

For almost a month after Napoleon's return to Moscow on September 20th, the main French army lay almost inactive about the city. The Emperor's anxieties on the score of supplies had been to some extent relieved by the quantities of food and ammunition captured. He says himself in a letter to Lariboissière, the Chief of Artillery, that he has taken 300,000 pounds of powder, and an equal amount of sulphur and saltpetre, besides an immense number of cannon-balls and 2,000,000 cartridges. It can scarcely be imagined that, however much the habit of lying had become ingrained in him, he would wilfully mislead the man whom, most of all, it was necessary to furnish with correct information.

A number of cannon were captured, but all practically useless. The Kremlin, in fact, was and is a museum of ancient weapons, mostly preserved as trophies of Russia's victories over her enemies. Among them now are hundreds of the guns of the Napoleonic *Grande Armée* of 1812. The cannon had no carriages, but about twenty of them were mounted by the French artillerymen on the walls of the ancient citadel. The captures of ammunition were of extreme value. Napoleon exultantly declared that he could fight four battles of the magnitude of Borodino.

Forage, however, was seriously deficient. The cavalry and artillery of the Guard, which received supplies in advance of the other corps, remained in fair condition, but that of the rest of the army rapidly deteriorated. The horses died in great numbers. At the beginning of October De Chambray estimates that already 4000 troopers were dismounted. The misery in the advance-guard was great; breadstuffs could hardly be obtained, and the men lived chiefly upon horse-flesh.

In Moscow matters were by no means satisfactory. The troops had indeed shelter and food; but these advantages were dearly bought at the price of a fatal relaxation in discipline. The privileged Guards were bad offenders, and Napoleon himself had at last to complain of their misconduct. The 1st Corps was little better. The 3rd and 4th Corps were mostly outside the city. They lived chiefly from hand to mouth as before, and though a considerable amount of flour had been warehoused at Moscow Napoleon would not permit it to be issued, even when Berthier reported Pino's division as being completely destitute. No issue was made of clothing material until October 17th, nor were any preparations made for rough-shoeing the horses. In the general relaxation of discipline little was done by the men themselves. In the face of proven facts such as these the statements as to Napoleon's unerring and all-pervading foresight and activity, made even by respectable witnesses such as Rapp and Fain, make somewhat foolish reading.

In a sense, indeed, Napoleon did provide for much—that is, he issued orders which had they been at all applicable to the situation might have effected a great deal. Such an order was that for the provision of hand-mills for the troops. The need for them had been apparent during the advance, and had they been provided earlier they would doubtless have been invaluable. As it was the first convoy of them only came to hand during the retreat, when they were useless.

THE KREMLIN, MOSCOW
On the extreme left is the Great Red Staircase—the State entrance to the Palace. Next is the Uspanski Sabor, or Cathedral of the Assumption, in which the Tzars are crowned. Behind it appears the Bell Tower of Ivan Velikii

Others of the Imperial orders were simply incapable of execution. One of them, for example, gives directions for exploring the country for two or three leagues on each side of the highway so as to find parallel roads passing by villages and cultivated tracts. It would have been extremely difficult to find such roads in fertile and well-peopled Germany, and to expect to discover them in Russia was merely absurd. As a fact, had they existed, the country was laid waste for a breadth of forty or fifty miles by the destructive passage of two great armies. The only criticisms that can be made in reading this order is that Napoleon's intellect was either failing or so affected by pride and over-confidence as to be fatally debilitated.

Yet in spite of his fatal optimism Napoleon was growing uneasy. On his return to Moscow he induced Tutulmin, the director of the Foundling Hospital, to be the bearer of a letter to Alexander. It was a diplomatic document after Napoleon's

CHAPTER IX 159

fashion, compounded of blandishments and threats; a characteristic touch is the careful detailing of the war material which has been captured. The Tzar would not deign to reply. Napoleon waited for a fortnight and then sent General Lauriston to endeavour to open negotiations with Kutuzov.

However, gloomy as the prospect might appear to intelligent observers, the bulk of the army was at rest, and, save in the vital matter of horses, increasing in strength. During the latter half of September there entered Moscow Laborde's division, the 1st battalion of Hesse-Darmstadt Guards, three battalions of the 33rd Léger, and several *régiments de marche*—in all some 10,000 infantry and over 4000 cavalry. In the first half of October there arrived nearly 17,000 men—*régiments de marche*, mostly infantry, and the battalions which had been left in garrison at Orsha, Dorogobuzh, Viasma, and elsewhere. The muster rolls were also swelled by a certain number of convalescents. The fighting strength of the 5th and 8th Corps, which were harassed by constant skirmishing, remained stationary or declined; and the number of mounted horsemen steadily dwindled. But in the 1st and 3rd Corps there was a steady increase in the numbers of the infantry and artillery. Reinforcements of artillery also arrived; there were, indeed, more guns in Moscow than the enfeebled teams could draw.

The movements of the French main army during this period of comparative quiescence were not very important. Eugène early in October pushed an advance-guard to Dmitrov, some miles north of Moscow, while Ney moved to Boghorodsk, about 25 miles eastward on the road to Vladimir. The Russian cavalry screen, under Winzingerode, gave back before the advance of the French columns, and there was little fighting. Ney ordered the construction of barracks for winter quarters at Boghorodsk, but De Fezensac pessimistically remarks that the sham deceived nobody. Ney and Eugène were soon recalled to Moscow, and the entire army, except Murat's advance-guard, was concentrated there on the 15th.

Meanwhile Murat, isolated on the Chernishnia at a distance of nearly 50 miles from the main army, and with a vastly superior army in his front, was in a position of great danger. The peril was aggravated by the scantiness of supplies and by the lack of forage, which was steadily killing the over-worked horses. Skirmishing was continually taking place, with general ill fortune to the invaders. Foraging parties had to be pushed farther and farther afield, and needed larger and larger escorts to protect them against the enterprising regular and irregular cavalry of the Russians. On one occasion a foraging party of Dragoons of the Guard, under Major Marthod, accompanied by a detachment of the 33rd Léger, was attacked and cut up. On October 9th Colonel Kudachev with two regiments of Cossacks made a successful attack upon a large foraging party, and carried off 200 prisoners. Similar skirmishes were continually occurring. On October 10th Dorokhov, who had been reinforced by five battalions and some more cavalry and artillery, stormed Vereia, killing or capturing its garrison of 500 Westphalians, and thus establishing himself dangerously near the Moscow-Smolensk road.

It has been seen that on October 4th Kutuzov had begun to entrench himself at Tarutino. Bennigsen criticises the position severely. The Nara in its front was everywhere fordable, and on the left there were some unoccupied heights which might be seized by an assailant. However, as matters went, there was little fear of an immediate attack, and the Russians were so strong in cavalry that they could obtain early warning of any move of the French from Moscow.

Soon after reaching Tarutino Barclay left the army. He had been deeply wounded by the rancorous attacks made upon him by the ultra Russians, and his relations with Bennigsen were very strained. Kutuzov had treated him with great respect, and after Borodino had given him the chief command of both Russian armies. But when a supreme commander is present at the head-quarters of an army difficulties are certain to arise. In 1864 the presence of General Grant with Meade's army of the Potomac did not make for unity of command, though both officers were men of the finest character. Barclay soon found his position intolerable, and resigned. He was bitterly hurt, and told Clausewitz, who had just been appointed to a post on Wittgenstein's staff, that he might thank heaven that he was well out of it. It is impossible not to sympathise with him, and at the same time not difficult to see that his departure made for unity of command. Whether Kutuzov was the right man for the post of commander-in-chief is another question. Barclay was abominably ill-treated and insulted by the populace on his way to St. Petersburg, but Alexander never lost confidence in him, and he emerged from his retirement in 1813 to take command of the Russian armies in Germany. His departure occasioned a show at least of regret among the officers of the army, many of whom perhaps felt conscience-stricken at the memory of ill-conditioned murmuring and mutiny. Most of the generals came to bid him farewell; and Yermólov, who had been his worst and most treacherous enemy, actually wept—an episode to which allusion has elsewhere been made.

On the 24th of September, at a mansion on the road to Vladimir, Bagration died. It is probable that travelling on the bad Russian roads had brought on gangrene. On his death-bed he was visited by Wilson, who was returning from his visit to Alexander. The Tzar, very wisely, had judged it best to overlook the insubordination of the generals, and had sent by Wilson the strongest assurances of his determination to continue the resistance. He would, he said, sooner let his beard grow to the waist and eat potatoes in Siberia, than permit any negotiations so long as an armed Frenchman remained in Russia. The language may perhaps be thought a little high-flown, but it possesses dignity in that it was the expression of the firm resolution of the united Russian nation. To the dying soldier Wilson repeated the brave words of the Tzar. Bagration pressed his hand convulsively. "Dear general," he said, "you have made me die happy, for now Russia will assuredly not be dishonoured. *Accipio solatium mortis.*" So passes from the scene the fine Georgian soldier whose life had been spent in faithful service to his adopted country. Wilson eulogises his good qualities, the kindness and graciousness which his fiery temper perhaps at times concealed, his generosity and chivalrous courage. Wilson was his devoted admirer—the two had much in common. But in sober fact Bagration, whatever his faults, had ever proved himself a worthy descendant of the warrior-kings of the Bagratid line; and having adopted Russia, the steady protector of the Caucasian Christians, as his country, he had served her faithfully to the end. It is difficult not to feel a sense of decline in passing from Barclay, the simple, devoted servant of his country, and Bagration, the chivalrous descendant of kings, to the caution and cunning of the pleasure-loving old aristocrat Kutuzov, and the hardly disguised self-seeking of the soldier of fortune Bennigsen.

Kutuzov, from the field of Borodino, had sent a first brief and hasty despatch stating that he had held his own and captured some guns. As has been seen, the statement was only true in a general sense, since the Russian troops had certainly been driven back a short distance. This report was perhaps hurriedly penned in the exultation of finding that he had fought the terrible conqueror for a long day without real ill-success. A second despatch told the truth or something near it, describing the battle as a drawn one—which it tactically was—estimating Napoleon's loss as probably the greater, and insisting upon the necessity of retreating in order to reorganise after the tremendous losses. A third despatch attributed the chief merit of the balanced success of the day to Barclay and Bennigsen. Alexander did not publish the second despatch—whether wisely or not it is difficult for an Englishman to judge. Kutuzov was promoted Field Marshal, and received a grant of 100,000 rúbles. Barclay was decorated with the order of St. George (2nd Class), and Bennigsen with that of St. Vladimir (1st Class). Bagration, who wore all the Orders of Russia, received a grant of 50,000 rúbles. Miloradovich, Dokhturov, Ostermann, and Raievski received the order of St. Alexander Nevski. Each soldier was awarded a gratuity of 5 rúbles—which, it may be hoped, was paid in silver, not in the depreciated paper currency.

When in the midst of announcements of victory and of rewards the news arrived that Moscow had been abandoned, the discouragement was naturally great. In the army itself Kutuzov certainly felt very dubious of success. At St. Petersburg the state archives were sent into the interior, and the fleet was sent to winter in England. The Empress Dowager, the Grand Duke Constantine, and the Grand Chancellor Rumiantzev, were strongly in favour of peace; but neither domestic nor political pressure, nor public alarm, appear to have shaken for a moment the stern resolution of the commonly yielding, sensitive, and dreamy Tzar.

Alexander's reply to the fall of Moscow was a proclamation to his people calling upon them to rise superior to the loss, and to overwhelm the invaders, whose position was painted in colours perhaps darker than the reality. Preparations for continuing the war were energetically pushed forward. Count Lieven was despatched as ambassador to London, and with an assurance of Alexander's immovable determination to continue the struggle at all hazards. For the present he asked nothing but munitions of war. Later, when he had saved Russia, he intended to do his best to free Europe from French domination, when he hoped that Britain would not be sparing of her wealth. At this moment, be it remembered, Napoleon was encamped among the ruins of the sacred capital of Russia.

Meanwhile at Tarutino the reorganisation of the Russian army was being energetically proceeded with. The man immediately responsible for it, who justly received the major part of the credit, was Konovnitzin, who has already been repeatedly met with in his country's battles. Konovnitzin was a strong adherent and admirer of Barclay, and seems to have possessed his chief's virtues of modesty and devotion to duty.

Borodino and the subsequent actions had grievously shattered all the regiments, and some had been practically destroyed. These were either dissolved or sent back into the interior to reform; the combined Grenadier battalions were broken up and distributed; and the militia and new recruits then drafted in. The experienced Russian generals did not make the mistake committed by the leaders of the Spanish uprising in 1808-1809 and swamp the battalions with raw levies. Only the picked men who had received some training were sparingly introduced among the war-seasoned soldiers. Even so Kutuzov was very distrustful of his infantry.

Horsemen cannot be trained so easily as foot-soldiers, and the Russian cavalry could not be greatly increased in strength. Such reinforcements as it received must have consisted of small drafts and rejoining convalescents. It included the same regiments as had fought at Borodino, but all were in a greatly reduced condition. The men, however, were in high heart and the horses in excellent condition. The artillery was also in admirable order.

Alexander had made an appeal to the loyalty of the Don Cossacks, which was seconded by the great personal influence of Platov. By the middle of October there were present in the Moscow theatre of war some fifty regiments of irregular horsemen.

Reorganisation and steady reinforcement had their effect. The numerical strength of the Russian army at Tarutino began to rise at once, and its efficiency steadily increased. The number of battalions had fallen to 147 by October 18th, but they had all been brought up to an average strength of over 500 bayonets, except those of the Guard, which, having no depôts at hand, were rather weaker. By October 23 the strength of the Russian Grand Army, including its detachments, had risen to 105,000 regulars, including 12,000 cavalry, and nearly 20,000 Cossacks, with an artillery train of some 650 guns excellently appointed and horsed.

Kutuzov made certain changes in the organisation. The entire regular cavalry was massed in four unequal "Corps," one of which consisted of Cuirassiers. Lieutenant-General Prince Golitzin I received the command of the Cuirassier Corps, and the 1st and 3rd were given to Major-Generals Baron Müller Zakomelski and Vassilchikov respectively. Baron Korff continued to command the 2nd, which was increased to 8 regiments of Dragoons, and 1 or 2 of light cavalry. The various army corps still retained their old leaders, except the 3rd, which was now commanded by Strogonov.

At the same time some changes were made in the higher commands. Miloradovich practically took the place of Bagration—by no means unworthily—while General Tormazov was called from the west to succeed Barclay.

Strategically the army was organised by Kutuzov into an advanced guard, under Miloradovich, a *Corps de Bataille,* under Tormazov, six Flying Columns, and six Cossack detachments. The advanced guard included the 2nd and 4th Army Corps, the 2nd and 3rd Cavalry "Corps," and 4 regiments of Cossacks. The *Corps de Bataille* consisted of the 3rd, 5th, 6th, 7th, and 8th Army Corps, and Golitzin's and Müller-Zakomelski's cavalry. The Flying Columns were: (1) Platov's, compris-

CHAPTER IX

ing 13 regiments of Cossacks, 1 of light infantry, and a horse battery; (2) Winzingerode's, of 1 regiment of Hussars, 1 of Dragoons, 7 of Cossacks, and a battery, observing Moscow on the north; (3) Dorokhov's, observing Mozhaïsk, ultimately increased by detachments to 5 battalions, 16 squadrons, a battery, and some Cossacks; (4) Orlov-Denisov's, consisting of 6 regiments of Cossacks and 6 guns; (5) Karpov's, comprising 7 regiments of Cossacks; and (6) that of Major-General Count Ozharovski, composed of 4 regiments of Cossacks, 1 of Hussars, a regiment of light infantry, and 6 guns. The Cossack detachments which infested the Moscow-Smolensk road, were those of Colonel Kaisarov (3 regiments), Colonel Prince Kudachev (2 regiments), Colonel Yefremov (2 regiments), Lieutenant-Colonel Davidov (2 regiments), Captain Seslavin (1 regiment), and Captain Figner (1 regiment).

The Russian army at Tarutino experienced little or no privation. Supplies of food were plentiful. Forage after a time grew scarce in the immediate neighbourhood, and it was necessary to send to some distance to obtain it, but the horses remained in excellent condition. Löwenstern says that the army had never fared better; it was even possible to obtain luxuries from the merchants who visited the camp. Dry fuel alone was lacking. To obtain it the villages within the Russian lines were almost entirely demolished.

While making a show of preparations for the fortification and provisioning of Moscow the French Emperor, on October 4, sent his aide-de-camp, General Lauriston, who had been Ambassador at St. Petersburg before the war, on a mission to Kutuzov. Lauriston's real object was to ascertain the chances of peace. It was certain that his mission could have no success. Apart from the firm resolve of the Tzar the generals at Tarutino were bitterly determined, and kept a close watch upon their commander-in-chief. Kutuzov consented to receive Lauriston; and thereupon his subordinates requested Wilson to inform him that if he conferred privately with Lauriston he would be deposed from the command. Kutuzov himself, not very confident of the ability of his army to beat Napoleon's, persisted in his determination to receive Lauriston, but consented to do so publicly in the first instance. He then had a private conversation with the French general, of which he afterwards gave an account to Count Langeron. He ultimately consented to pass on a letter brought by Lauriston to St. Petersburg; but declared that he had no power to conclude an armistice.

The successes of Schwarzenberg and St. Cyr appeared to make the French line of communications fairly safe, and the calling up of Victor's 9th Corps to Smolensk was an additional measure of security. The 9th Corps crossed the frontier on September 3. It was increased by the addition of four German regiments to a strength of 33,500 men. Victor left Coutard's German brigade at Vilna, and with the rest of the corps marched for Smolensk, where he arrived on September 27. Napoleon had ap pointed Comte Baraguay d'Hilliers Governor-General of the province of Smolensk, but he could do little to collect supplies and keep the roads clear. The country was infested by small parties of Cossacks and of armed peasantry on the one hand, and on the other by numbers of stragglers, disbanded troops and marauders belonging to the invading army.

Until the arrival of the 9th Corps troops were entirely lacking wherewith to suppress the disorder, and it will soon be seen that Victor could make but a brief stay at Smolensk. Baraguay d'Hilliers, worried and distracted by Napoleon's angry complaints, gave his master the facts of the situation in two letters, which enable us to appreciate the precise state of things in rear of the *Grande Armée*.

The armed peasants and Cossack detachments checked foraging operations and cut off detachments. At Smolensk, indeed, there was a strong garrison. A provisional administration had been organised, on paper, under the superintendence of M. de Villeblanche; but the town was ruined and nearly deserted. General Charpentier could organise strong foraging parties, but had no artisans to construct barracks and bakeries, or to manufacture clothing and equipment. From Smolensk to Gzhatsk there was hardly any protection for the road. Baraguay d'Hilliers declared that, after providing for the necessary garrisons of the posts, he could dispose of only 600 men, in three detachments, for police and foraging operations on a line of some 200 miles! As to establishing markets as Napoleon ordered, he frankly exposed the utter absurdity of the idea. For removing wounded and forwarding supplies there were not a fifth of the vehicles required.

MARSHAL VICTOR, DUKE OF BELLUNO
Commander of the 9th French Army Corps
From the painting by Gros at Versailles

Detachments on the march to Moscow straggled for many miles north and south of the high-road in order to forage, and it was impossible to keep them in hand. One officer, in charge of a convoy, reported that his escorts melted away one after another; and he entered Moscow alone! The marauders committed nameless atrocities, which amply explain and to some extent justify the terrible retaliations of the peasants during the retreat. It is an ungrateful task to allude to these horrors, but one hideous incident given by Löwenstern must be mentioned, if only to afford a proper impression of what a state of warfare in Napoleonic days implied.

Among the Russian leaders of irregulars Captain Figner early acquired a terrible reputation for blood-thirsty cruelty towards his French and Polish foes, to whom he gave no quarter in battle, and whom, when captured, he massacred without pity. His savagery was strongly reprobated in the Russian army, except in the case of a number of fierce spirits whom the sufferings of their country had maddened. Even the wild irregulars looked askance at Figner; and for the execution of his savage orders he could not always rely upon them.

Figner himself declared that he acted from conscientious motives. While on one of his expeditions he surprised a marauding party—evidently consisting of Frenchmen and Poles—in a village which they had sacked. In the church they had penned a number of women and girls, and outraged and tortured them with horrible barbarity, crucifying them about the building—partly in order the more easily to gratify their brutal lust, partly no doubt from sheer love of cruelty. Into this hideous orgy burst Figner and his Cossacks. Most of the ravishers were captured. The unhappy victims—such of them as survived—were rescued; and there and then, before the desecrated altar, the Russian leader swore a solemn oath never to spare a Frenchman. He shut his prisoners up in the church and fired it over them; and thereafter, until he was killed in the following year, Frenchmen were to him but as vermin to be exterminated. It is futile to comment upon the moral ethics of his determination. It is only evident that in Russia, as in Spain, the brutality and lust of the French conquerors sowed the seeds of a terrible harvest of vengeance.

In spite of the disorder in Napoleon's rear there is no doubt that the French numbers rose steadily during the halt. Presumably the stragglers therefore—or such of them as survived the Cossacks and armed peasants—drifted in eventually. But it is hardly necessary to point out that such a method—or lack of method—of marching was the worst possible preparation for a retreat in which strict discipline and careful order would be before everything necessary.

What Napoleon's own plans were is extremely doubtful. The troops generally anticipated that they would winter in Moscow—but this of course implies nothing. Count Daru certainly suggested doing so, positively stating that to his knowledge the supplies were sufficient and shelter ample. But on the other hand the lines of communication were already seriously threatened, and though the army in Moscow might have been preserved it must have lost most of its horses, and Napoleon would have been cut off from France for several months.

The Emperor is credited by Fain with the intention of advancing upon St. Petersburg. This project was a most extraordinary one, and it passes human comprehension how Napoleon could have imagined it. It is useless to give it in detail. The essential part is that the army is to march upon Velikii Luki, about 90 miles northeast of Polotsk, and 300 from Moscow, through a fertile country (it is actually quite the reverse), and thus threaten St. Petersburg—200 miles farther on, over barren and sparsely-peopled country. The time allowed for accomplishing the movement appears to be about fifteen days! Farther comment is surely unnecessary.

Clausewitz considers that Napoleon must always have intended to retreat by the direct road to Smolensk, the only one in any sense guarded and furnished with magazines. On the Kaluga road, he says, the army would have starved within a week. He therefore infers that in marching upon Kaluga, as he eventually did, Napoleon merely intended to manœuvre or push Kutuzov out of the way.

The facts, of course,—which Clausewitz may not at the time have known accurately—were that the country along the Smolensk-Viasma-Moscow road was absolutely devastated, that forage could not be obtained upon it, while farther south matters were better; and that east of Smolensk there were practically no magazines.

Jomini is of opinion that Napoleon would have done best to retreat upon Vitebsk. The country, however, was poor and thinly peopled, and the roads were very bad; the only advantage of the plan was that the army would have gained a considerable start of Kutuzov.

Finally, there was the design of retiring by Kaluga on Smolensk. The roads were bad, but probably better than those on the north, since there were upon them some considerable towns. The country was tolerably fertile and—for Russia—fairly well peopled; there were, besides, magazines at Kaluga and elsewhere which might be captured. Further, there was the opportunity of destroying the factories of arms and ammunition at Tula.

How long Napoleon would have remained at Moscow is doubtful. His orders during October for the evacuation of the hospitals show that he meditated departure; but he still waited, hoping against hope that the stubborn Tzar would at length give way, until on October 18th came the news that Kutuzov had taken the offensive.

Kutuzov himself appears not to have had very much confidence in the solidity and ability to manœuvre of his army. Murat's position, however, was such as to tempt even a cautious commander; and Kutuzov gave way to the energetic representations of Bennigsen and Toll. An attack was fixed for October 17th, but bad staff arrangements compelled it to be postponed until the 18th. Bennigsen gives no reasons. Bogdanovich and Löwenstern both blame Yermólov. Löwenstern says that recalling the horses from their distant foraging grounds caused great delay and that Yermólov did not inform General Baron Löwenstern, the artillery commander, in time.

The Nara, flowing from the west, turns sharply to the southward some 5 miles north of Tarutino; and soon after is joined on the left by the Chernishnia rivulet. Close to Tarutino it again turns abruptly eastward. The road from Kaluga runs northward through Tarutino for nearly 5 miles to Vinkovo, a village about 2 miles

CHAPTER IX

from the mouth of the Chernishnia, and then proceeds for 5 miles to Spas-Kuplia, where it passes between two woods.

Murat's line stretched from the confluence of the Chernishnia with the Nara to the hamlet of Teterinka, some 5 miles to the westward, and about 4 south of Spas-Kuplia. Vinkovo, which lay south of the Chernishnia, was occupied by Claparède's Poles, supported by the 3rd Cavalry Corps, under General St. Germain, and a division of the 1st. To the left rear of Vinkovo lay Dufour's division, with the rest of Nansouty's cavalry corps on its left. Still farther to the south of the Chernishnia stood Poniatowski's corps, with Sebastiani's cavalry on the extreme left. Latour-Maubourg was watching the Nara on the right rear. Murat's whole strength hardly exceeded 25,000 men; he was encumbered rather than supported by about 180 miserably horsed guns; and his 9000 or 10,000 cavalry were in a wretched state.

PLAN OF BATTLE OF VINKOVO,
OCTOBER 18TH, 1812
General position at moment when Murat's retreat began

The Russian plan contemplated a demonstration by part of the bulk of the army against Murat's extended front, while Bennigsen, with a force composed of the 2nd, 3rd, and 4th Corps, Müller Zakomelski's cavalry, and 10 regiments of Cossacks under Orlov-Denisov, turned his left. Miloradovich was to move towards Vinkovo with Korff's and Vassilchikov's cavalry, while behind him the rest of the army debouched from Tarutino.

Orlov-Denisov and Müller Zakomelski fell, about 7 a.m. on the 18th, upon Sebastiani's bivouacs, while Baggohufwudt attacked the 5th Corps in front. His advance had been revealed by the growing light and some premature shots, and the Poles were able to form and oppose a vigorous resistance. One of the first shots from their artillery killed Baggohufwudt, and his fall rather dashed some of his young troops, especially when the remains of the French Carabiniers, led by Murat himself, gallantly charged the 48th Russian Chasseurs. The Russian cavalry on the right, however, swept away Sebastiani, capturing most of his baggage and artillery, and pushed on towards Spas-Kuplia, which they occupied, thus cutting Murat's line of retreat. The position would have been critical had the Russian horsemen been supported by infantry. The whole of the French line gave back in haste, but the Russian 2nd Corps, imposed upon by Murat's bold charge, and shaken by the fall of its leader, followed very cautiously. Ostermann-Tolstoï failed to advance with the necessary speed; and Bennigsen thought himself obliged to hold back the 3rd Corps until the arrival of the 4th. The result was that the entire French army, in great disorder, indeed, and suffering considerably from the Russian artillery fire, succeeded in effecting its retreat. Orlov-Denisov and Müller Zakomelski were obliged to abandon Spas-Kuplia as infantry came up; and the line of retreat was clear. Meanwhile Kutuzov was executing his part of the programme very slowly or not at all. Only Miloradovich›s cavalry, supported by five infantry regiments, crossed the Chernishnia and pressed the rear of the retreating columns towards and through Spas-Kuplia, where the pursuit ceased. Murat retreated to Voronovo, where he rallied his shaken troops, while the Russian main body tranquilly returned to Tarutino. Miloradovich with the now formally constituted advance-guard was stationed at Vinkovo.

The French returns, which are manifestly incomplete, show a loss of 2795 men, of whom 1151 were prisoners or missing. The bulk of the diminution was in the 5th Corps and Sebastiani's cavalry; Claparède and Dufour were scarcely engaged. Two generals were killed and two wounded. The Russians claim to have lost only 502 killed and wounded. They captured 37 guns, a standard, and a mass of baggage.

Bennigsen was exasperated at Kutuzov's tardy and slight support, though his own conduct had not been too energetic, and the breach between them widened. It was already great, Kutuzov relying upon the retiring and hard-working Konovnitzin far more than on Bennigsen.

The Russian success at Vinkovo, incomplete as it was, none the less dealt a heavy blow to the already shaken *morale* of the Napoleonic army.

As the period of Napoleon's evacuation of Moscow has now been reached, it appears necessary to survey the positions occupied by the various sections of the opposing forces.

Dealing first with the invaders—

The Imperial Guard, Grand Head-quarters, the Cavalry Reserve, and the bulk of the 1st, 3rd, 4th, and 5th Army Corps were encamped, under Napoleon's personal command, in the environs of Moscow. About Mozhaïsk was the 8th Corps, under Junot, the total combatant strength of this, the original Grand or Central Army, including engineers, gendarmerie, etc., being nearly 125,000 men.

At Viasma was a column of drafts under General Evers, which with the garrisons at Gzhatsk and elsewhere may be estimated at about 5000 men.

About Smolensk there were the 129th and Illyrian regiments from Ney's corps, three 3rd battalions of the Vistula Legion, and some of the Hesse-Darmstadt Guards belonging to the Imperial Guard, a Mecklenburg regiment and a battalion of the 33rd Léger (1st Corps); a Polish cavalry regiment (5th Corps); and about 8000 men in *régiments de marche*—say 16,000 in all, including 1500 cavalry under General Baraguay d'Hilliers.

In the neighbourhood of Smolensk also was cantoned the 9th Corps, under Victor, some 26,000 strong.

At Vitebsk and in its neighbourhood were a battalion of the 9th Corps and a few drafts—say 1000 men.

Between Smolensk and Orsha there were in garrison perhaps 3000 men—drafts, convalescents, engineers, and Polish levies.

At Mohilev were 1 infantry and 1 cavalry regiment of Dombrowski's division, about 1500 men. The rest of the division, about 5500 men with 20 guns, was spread to the south-westward.

At Minsk and Borisov and scattered about the neighbourhood there were 2 weak French battalions, some depôt troops of various nations, a weak Württemberg infantry regiment, and 4 battalions and 4 squadrons of untrustworthy Lithuanian levies—less than 6000 in all, under General Bronikowski. At Slonim General Konopka was organising the new Lithuanian Lancer Regiment of the Guard, which with a few other levies may be estimated at 1000 men.

Between Minsk and Kovno there were various depôts, *régiments de marche*, and a number of Polish and Lithuanian levies, totalling perhaps 14,000 men, and Coutard's brigade of the 9th Corps, 2500 strong.

In Kurland and before Riga Macdonald's 10th Corps now numbered perhaps 26,000 men.

In and about Polotsk lay the 2nd Corps, the remains of the infantry of the 6th, and Doumerc's Cuirassier Division—about 30,000 combatants—under Marshal St. Cyr.

Schwarzenberg had at Wengrow, Bielostok, and elsewhere about 37,000 men, comprising 22,000 Austrians, nearly 10,000 Saxons, and about 5000 Poles. Marching to join him were 5000 Austrians, and a French division (Durutte) of the 11th

Corps, 13,000 strong.

At Königsberg and in the neighbourhood was Loison's division of the 11th Corps, 13,000 men, French, German, and Neapolitans.

In addition there were in Poland and Prussia, in garrison or moving up to the front, about 21,000 men of various arms.

The total force of the Napoleonic army, therefore, on Russian soil or about to move across the frontier was, in the middle of October, some 351,000 men.

In Germany, for the most part along the line of the Oder, was the rest of the 11th Corps, under Marshal Augereau. It consisted of two provisional divisions under Generals Heudelet and Lagrange, a Neapolitan division in Danzig under General d'Estrées, Cavaignac's cavalry brigade, and some detached troops, amounting, with artillery, to about 40,000 men; besides perhaps 27,000 drafts. Of these troops, 67,000 in all, about 55,000 were on the Vistula at the close of the campaign. Adding these to the 351,000 troops already beyond that river the total of Napoleonic troops still bearing on Russia was 406,000. As the aggregate employed during the campaign has been elsewhere estimated at 674,000, it results that 268,000 men had already disappeared from the fighting line. Some, no doubt, had returned home invalided, some had been taken by the Russians; a certain number had no doubt fallen into good hands in the country and ultimately recovered from their injuries. But by far the larger number were already dead.

To these 406,000 actual and prospective enemies Russia opposed the following forces:—

At and near Tarutino and around Moscow, under Field-Marshal Prince Golénischev-Kutuzov, were 105,000 regulars and 20,000 irregulars. Under Wittgenstein, near Polotsk, were 40,000 regulars, irregulars, and militia. Marching to reinforce Wittgenstein was Count Steingell with 10,000 men, almost all regulars. At Riga, under Essen I, there were perhaps 15,000 troops.

Admiral Chichagov had under his general command about 70,000 men in all, including General Lüder's division coming from Serbia. Ertel at Mozyr now had about 14,000, while Bobruisk was garrisoned by 6000. Finally, in small regular detachments, drafts of recruits and militia, and Cossacks, there were perhaps 30,000 men on the march to reinforce the various armies. The Russian total therefore was nearly 310,000 men.

CHAPTER X
THE FIRST STAGES OF THE RETREAT

The battle of Vinkovo put an abrupt end to any hopes which Napoleon may yet have cherished as to a speedy conclusion of peace. It is fairly obvious, however, that he had already made up his mind that Moscow must be abandoned. On October 14th orders were reiterated to evacuate the hospitals at Mozhaïsk and elsewhere by the 20th. Junot was also directed to destroy arms which could not be carried away. Evers' column of reinforcement, which had already passed Viasma, was turned back to that town; and other régiments de marche were ordered to remain at, or return to, Smolensk.

The condition of the army needs careful consideration. Montholon, who may be regarded as speaking for his master, says that it was strengthened and revivified by its long rest, that it had twenty days' supply of food, that it was abundantly provided with ammunition.

It is to be observed that this categorical *apologia* does not mention the vitally important matters of discipline, clothing, and horses. Of these something will presently be said. The points noted by Montholon may be discussed one by one.

In the first place a distinction must be drawn between the troops in and about Moscow and those belonging to Murat's advance-guard.

Of the former, it may be said that they were, as regards the men, in fair physical condition. Even here, however, a distinction must be made. The Guards and the 1st Corps had been lying inactive for four weeks. They had had the benefit of the best that Moscow could afford; and certainly should have been in first-rate condition. But, on the other hand, they had been living freely, upon food not always as nourishing as attractive to rough men, and upon the wines and spirits which abounded in the palaces and warehouses, and were probably hardly prepared for new and terrible hardships. The 3rd and 4th Corps had been generally encamped outside Moscow, had obtained little by pillage, and had been uselessly fatigued and over-worked by constant foraging and outpost work. Yet it is possible that these unpampered men were really better prepared for what lay before them than the Guards and Davout's corps.

As to the question of food supplies it is difficult to express an opinion. It is certain that food was not lacking, and probably the troops might have carried with them twenty days' rations had discipline been good and transport abundant. As it is, it is clear that the army was short of supplies within ten days of its departure from Moscow.

There is no reason to doubt Napoleon's statement that the supply of ammunition was abundant.

Napoleon having, according to his custom, dealt entirely with material matters, it may be well to follow in his footsteps before considering things moral. The evidence of survivors is all to the effect that the troops were badly and inadequately clothed. Except in so far as some of them were supplied from the pillage of Moscow the men had only the worn and tattered uniforms which had served them all through the advance. The footgear was much worn, and the underclothing in a deplorable condition. Bourgogne, a sergeant in the Young Guard—one of a favoured corps, therefore—speaks of wearing a shirt until it rotted upon him. Only on the 17th of October were leather and linen issued, and it was then too late to make up the material.

THE CHURCH OF VASILII BLAGORENNYI AT MOSCOW
Built by the famous Tzar Ivan the Terrible in the latter half of the 16th century

CHAPTER X

Whatever might be the state of the army's supplies it lacked transport for them. The horses were dying steadily from fatigue, sickness and, above all, lack of food. The state of the cavalry has been noticed, and the artillery and trains were naturally in equally bad condition. Napoleon refused to abandon any of his vast and wretchedly horsed artillery in order to lighten the dead weight which encumbered the march. It would have been wiser to leave behind a part of the enormous mass of ammunition and to fill up the artillery waggons with food or forage. The commander of the artillery of the Young Guard did do something of the kind, with good results, but for the most part the dread of Napoleon effectually hindered such common-sense action. The draft horses, in bad condition, and overloaded in any case, without considering non-military and unnecessary further additions, began to die at the very beginning of the retreat, and the artillery and trains were lost piecemeal. Much of what food and forage the army took with it was lost early, owing to the failure of the transport.

One fact is curious and inexplicable. It might have been thought that the most strenuous exertions would have been put forth to provide the individual soldiers with plenty of breadstuffs, when the deficiency of the transport was well known. There is evidence that food was left in Moscow. De Fezensac states that he made a present of the flour which he could not carry away to some Muscovites whom he had fed during his stay in the city. The incident does honour to his humanity. Yet one wonders why he did not distribute it among his soldiers, who were ere long dying of want. It is clear that little food was carried by the soldiers themselves, and the reason for this is probably connected with the low *morale* of the army.

A long course of excess of every kind had weakened such sense of honour as the bulk of the men possessed, and the scattered barracking necessitated by the destruction of the greater part of the city rendered the maintenance of order very difficult. So far as can be judged, constant drill was by no means a feature of the Napoleonic army, and inspections of kits were apparently often perfunctory. It is, at any rate, certain that they were so during the sojourn in Moscow. Haversacks and knapsacks, instead of being stored with necessaries, too often contained plunder. The officers either made no determined attempt to check the evil, or their efforts were without avail. It is probable that the former discreditable condition of affairs actually obtained. Brigandage was rife in the Napoleonic armies, and numbers of officers had their private vehicles laden with plunder. Generals were often no better. Napoleon himself added to the encumbrances of the army two convoys of spoils, one of gold and silver bullion, the presence of which may be justified, the other of objects of purely sentimental value, for which excuse can hardly be made. It was but another example of the paltry spirit which impelled Napoleon to desecrate the tomb of Frederick the Great. It is difficult to blame subordinate officers when their ruler and their generals set so evil an example, still less is it possible to find fault with the ignorant soldiery. Be this as it may, lack of discipline, fostered by a low sense of honour among the officers, and greed of plunder, was not the least of the causes of the destruction of the *Grande Armée*.

Finally, the pernicious practice of permitting the troops to march in disorder was soon to be productive of fatal consequences. Officers and men had grown so accustomed to it that its extent was probably not at first realised, and it soon became impossible to check it. The results were terrible. The worse element among the suffering troops had every opportunity for disbanding, and the Russian irregulars, who could achieve little against closed bodies of infantry, were able to commit immense havoc.

Over and above all this the army was encumbered by a disproportionate throng of non-combatants. Besides the ordinary camp-followers, male and female, it has already been observed that there were with the army a number of persons—partly women—who should not have been permitted to accompany it. There were sick and wounded to the number of at least several thousands at the outset. The French colony at Moscow mostly fled with the army. Also a number of Russian prostitutes, and even a good many women and girls of better stamp—including some of the upper classes—accompanied men who had formed connections with them.

The precise state of feeling in the army cannot be ascertained. There is no doubt that the struggle at Borodino had badly affected its *morale,* and the French troops at least with their quick intelligence must have looked forward to the future with dread. On the other hand, their natural light-heartedness and their belief in Napoleon probably sustained their spirits. The foreign element was, doubtless, even less hopeful. That the more reflective among the officers were filled with misgiving is indubitable; and there was much discouragement among the generals, many of whom, besides, were war-weary and yearned for rest.

Thus, disorganised, with discipline shattered, ill clothed, ill supplied, deficient in transport but laden with useless plunder, encumbered with sick, wounded, and helpless non-combatants, and with demoralisation latent everywhere, the *Grande Armée* set out from Napoleon's Farthest to fight its way home. It is perhaps difficult to see things in their true light, every effort at so doing being naturally affected by knowledge of succeeding events. But the conclusion can hardly be avoided that the fate of the *Grande Armée* was already sealed, and that the shadow of impending disaster lay darkly upon its disorderly columns.

The numbers of the Napoleonic host on leaving Moscow can only be approximately computed. The dates of the muster-rolls collected by De Chambray vary so much that they can only be taken as a general guide. There are also errors in the published tables, the 8th Corps having 4916 infantry and artillery instead of 1916. De Chambray also, with all his merits, has the failing, natural enough indeed, and entirely excusable, of rather under-rating French numbers. An example of this may be seen in his estimate of Napoleon's strength at Borodino.

On the whole, working upon the muster-rolls collected by De Chambray, the marching-out strength of Napoleon's army from Moscow would appear to have been approximately as follows:—

CHAPTER X

Corps.	Infantry, Artillery, Dismounted Cavalry.	Mounted Cavalry.	Total.	Guns.
Grand Quarter-General	3,000	1,000	4,000	?
Imperial Guard	19,000	4,000	23,000	
1st Army Corps	30,000	1,000	31,000	
3rd " "	10,500	1,000	11,500	
4th " "	26,000	1,500	27,500	
5th " "	5,000	1,000	6,000	
8th " "	5,000	750	5,750	
Cavalry Reserve	1,000	5,000	6,000	
Brigade of Dismounted Horsemen	4,000		4,000	
Artillery Parks, Engineers, Pontonniers, Gendarmerie, etc.	5,000	500	5,500	
	108,500	15,750	124,750	600

The precise number of guns is not very certain, and to compute it is a somewhat unnecessary task. But, including the spare pieces in the reserve parks, and allowing for losses and reinforcements, the total must have been in the neighbourhood of 600. There were over 2000 artillery vehicles, for the most part heavily laden and very inadequately horsed.

The trains, already enormous, were now still further augmented by quantities of carts and carriages of every kind taken in Moscow, and requisitioned to transport food, wounded, refugees, and plunder. The bulk of the troops had made additions to their worn uniforms in the shape of garments of all kinds, often female ones, ransacked from the shops and warehouses. The effect must at the time have appeared fantastic and comical; but the humour of the sight was soon to be quenched in horror.

It has been seen that on the 14th orders had been issued which foreshadowed the evacuation of Moscow; and on the 16th Napoleon wrote to Maret at Vilna, setting forth his intentions. He would march against and defeat Kutuzov, take Kaluga, and then act according to circumstances. He would probably eventually go into winter quarters between Minsk and Smolensk, as Moscow did not afford a satisfactory military position. The Emperor made a final attempt to induce Kutuzov to open negotiations, but, of course, without result. He was in one of his worst moods, raging at his want of success, and the savage side of his nature displayed itself in all its nakedness in the disgraceful orders to blow up the Kremlin and its sacred and historic buildings.

From Moscow two roads led to Kaluga. The western one went by the towns of Fominskoïe, Borovsk and Maloyaroslavetz, that to the east by Voronovo and Tarutino. The eastern road is the more direct of the two, and is roughly the chord of the shallow arc of a circle described by the other. From Borovsk a cross-road leads by Vereia to Gzhatsk. From Maloyaroslavetz a fairly good highway goes eastward and south-eastward by Medyn to Yukhnov, and thence by Ielnia to Smolensk. The two Moscow-Kaluga roads are farthest apart between Tarutino and Borovsk, the latter place being some 20 miles distant from the former and slightly to the northeast of it. Maloyaroslavetz is about 11 miles south of Borovsk, and some 22 by road from Tarutino. It is thus evident that it was a point of great strategic importance.

The positions of the opposing armies were as follows: On the French side Murat's force was near Voronovo, some 18 miles north of Tarutino. At Fominskoië, 15 or 16 miles west of Voronovo, was Broussier's division of the 4th Corps, which had been sent thither a few days earlier. Junot, with the 8th Corps, was about Mozhaïsk. The rest of the *Grande Armée* was in and around Moscow.

Marshal Kutuzov was encamped with his *Corps de Bataille* about Tarutino, while Miloradovich with the advance-guard was pushed forward to observe Murat. Platov's Flying Corps and other light detachments were in the vicinity of Tarutino; Dorokhov was at Vereia; and Winzingerode's cavalry observed Moscow, as before, on the north and east.

Marshal Mortier was left by Napoleon to complete the evacuation of Moscow and to execute the abominable order to destroy the Kremlin. He had under his command Laborde's division of the Young Guard, Charrier's brigade of dismounted troopers, a brigade of light cavalry, and some artillery and sappers—about 9000 men in all. He was to hold the Kremlin for a few days and to give out that Napoleon would soon return, while clearing the ruins of such wounded, non-combatants and refugees.

The rest of the Guard, the 1st, 3rd and 4th Corps, began to evacuate Moscow in the night of October 18-19. There was great confusion, owing to the crowding of the trains into the Moscow-Kaluga road, and the march was slow. Recklessness and the breakdown of discipline were everywhere apparent. When the 3rd Corps reached its rendezvous at the monastery of Semenovski it was found to be in flames, and it is astounding to read that quantities of provisions were burned in it. It is useless to seek for excuse for the commission of such an act; it was simple insanity.

The army advanced along the eastern road directly upon Tarutino. Eugène opened the march, and behind him came the 1st and 3rd Corps and the Guard. The advance by the western road appeared to threaten a frontal attack on the position of Tarutino, but on reaching the Pakhra, the Emperor diverted the columns on to the western route. Murat's force was broken up. The King himself with the relics of the 1st, 2nd and 3rd Cavalry Corps was directed upon Fominskoië; Poniatowski's corps on Vereia, to recover that place from Dorokhov. Ney was to take Murat's place at Voronovo, the Vistula Legion, the remains of the 4th Cavalry Corps and the cavalry of the 1st Corps being also placed at his disposal. He had in all about 16,000 men and over 100 guns—sufficient under his resolute leadership to hold Miloradovich in check. There was also the possibility that his presence at Voronovo would induce Kutuzov to believe that the whole French army was advancing by the eastern road; and in any case it would divert attention from the flank movement by the western one.

The diversion of the advance to the western road was a well-conceived manœuvre, and had it been carried out with greater rapidity it might have achieved brilliant results. The distance to Maloyaroslavetz by the French line of march is about 72 miles, which the leading troops covered by the evening of the 23rd. As the roads were poor and the cross-tracks unspeakable, and there was besides some rain to make them worse, the army cannot be said to have done badly. But its march, encumbered as it was by interminable trains of artillery and baggage, was not speedy enough for the emergency. The attention of the Russian staff, indeed, appears to have been riveted upon the eastern road, for it was not until the 22nd that Kutuzov learned that there were French troops at Fominskoië. Considering that it was probably merely a powerful screen for foraging operations, Kutuzov directed Dokhturov, with the 6th Corps and the light cavalry of the Imperial Guard, to attack and drive it back. Miloradovich was ordered to demonstrate against the force in his front so as to prevent it detaching succours to the division at Fominskoië. This was on the evening of the 22nd. Eugène's corps, with Delzons' division leading, was between Fominskoië and Borovsk; Davout and the Guard were about Fominskoië. At midnight on the 23rd Ney started from Voronovo for Borovsk in pouring rain which simply obliterated the tracks and seriously impeded the march. He was also harassed by detachments of Cossacks. Poniatowski arrived at Vereia early on the 23rd and, after some fighting, drove out Dorokhov, who retired by cross-roads towards Maloyaroslavetz. Late on the same day Delzons occupied Maloyaroslavetz with his advanced guard of two battalions.

Dokhturov, accompanied by Yermólov and by Sir Robert Wilson, left Tarutino early on the 23rd. The 6th Corps, owing to its terrible losses at Borodino, was only 10 regiments strong, even with the addition of one or two from corps which had suffered less. One of them, moreover, was detached to Ozharovski's column. Dokhturov had, therefore, only 18 battalions, 7 batteries and the 3 regiments of the light cavalry of the Guard—about 12,000 men in all, with 84 guns. By the afternoon he had arrived at a point 5 or 6 miles from the western road, between Fominskoië and Borovsk, and there received information that 12,000 French troops were in his front. He consulted with his subordinates and with Wilson, and it was decided, rightly, to halt and await events, since if this body were isolated it would probably remain on the defensive. If, on the other hand, it continued to advance it was probably the head of a formidable force—perhaps the entire French army. Very soon intelligence came from Seslavin that Moscow was evacuated and the French army marching across from the eastern road to Fominskoië; and immediately afterwards a report from Dorokhov announced that a Cossack post at Borovsk had been expelled by Delzons. Dokhturov promptly took his decision. He could no longer hope to intercept the French at Borovsk, so must make a dash for Maloyaroslavetz, and there bar the road. He sent off word to Tarutino of his intelligence and intentions, and started his force for the vital point, arriving there in the night of the 23rd-24th.

Napoleon himself reached Borovsk on the 23rd. Thence he despatched orders to Baraguay d'Hilliers to move out from Smolensk towards Ielnia. He evidently expected to carry out his manœuvre without hindrance. In a letter to Eugène, dated at 7.30 p.m., he appears to have discovered the presence of Dokhturov, but to have anticipated an attack on the flank of his columns rather than an attempt to bar his way. As he dictated this despatch all the Russian commanders in touch with him had full information of his manœuvre, Kutuzov had been warned, and Dokhturov was marching hard for Maloyaroslavetz!

At 1 a.m. Mortier in Moscow ordered the firing of the mines which had been laid under the buildings in the Kremlin and elsewhere. They were charged with 183,000 pounds of powder, and great damage was wrought, but by no means the complete destruction intended by Napoleon. Mortier, who hated the ignominious task which he had been set by his master, is said, doubtless with truth, to have been by no means sorry at the comparatively small results of the Emperor's vandalism.

Winzingerode, who was already in the suburbs with his troops, pressed forward rather inconsiderately to reoccupy the Kremlin, riding himself in advance without an escort, attended only by a single aide-de-camp. The result was that he was taken prisoner, though he made a dishonourable, if not entirely inexcusable, attempt to escape by waving his handkerchief and pretending to have come on a parley. Mortier quite rightly declined to listen, and detained him. The evacuation was then completed. The Marshal made the most strenuous efforts to save all the invalids and to alleviate their sufferings as far as possible, but so great was the deficiency of transport that many hundreds had to be left behind. Eighteen guns, doubtless rendered unserviceable, were also abandoned. The gigantic convoy, guarded by Mortier's small force, moved not by the main road to Smolensk, but by cross roads on Vereia.

At Tarutino Kutuzov during the 23rd received the intelligence sent by Miloradovich and Dokhturov. The hour is a little doubtful, but he cannot have received Dokhturov's report until late in the day, and it was not possible to march at once owing to the absence of a large part of the artillery horses, which, as before the action of Vinkovo, had been led far away to obtain forage. The blame freely lavished upon Kutuzov for dilatoriness seems to be without foundation; there was no unnecessary delay. To set forth to encounter Napoleon without the artillery would have been unwise to the verge of insanity. As a fact, supposing the final information to have reached the camp about 4 p.m., six or seven hours was not too long in which to call in the parties and make preparations for the march. Platov was sent off at once with 15 regiments of Cossacks to observe and harass the march of Napoleon's column, and at 11 p.m. the rest of the army started for Maloyaroslavetz. The distance, allowing for deviations, was about 25 miles, mostly over an execrable byway rendered almost impassable by the pouring rain. Nevertheless, the Russians pushed doggedly forward, and by 11 a.m. on the 24th the head of the column was within reach of Maloyaroslavetz. Seeing that Ney, who on this same night was moving across from the eastern road, did not reach Borovsk until the evening of the 26th, having occupied three days in covering about 36 miles, the

CHAPTER X

greatest credit is due to the Russian army.

Dokhturov with his force reached Maloyaroslavetz in the night of the 23rd-24th. Either now or soon after daylight on the 24th he was joined by Dorokhov from Vereia. His troops must have been nearly dead beat, but he managed to spread them round the town so as to hold the outlets of all the roads which led out of it. He, of course, did not know that there were only two battalions holding the town; but Buturlin's blame of him for not carrying it is unreasonable. His men had been marching for nearly an entire day and night, and it was indispensably necessary to allow them some rest.

Maloyaroslavetz, an ordinary Russian country town built almost entirely of wood, lay on the southern bank of the small river Luzha, at the point where it was crossed by a bridge carrying the Moscow-Kaluga road. The river, like most streams in the region, flows in a deeply sunk channel. Below the bridge there were, according to Wilson, fords, but the Russians did not need them, and the French knew nothing of them. In any case, neither side attempted to use them. The country was very broken and also wooded, and the banks of the river, especially the southern one, were very steep. There were a few isolated buildings near the stream, while the town proper lay some hundreds of yards farther on, spreading over the top of the rise on to a plateau with a slight descent to the southward. The only good artillery position on the Russian side was eastward of the town, but though from it the opposite bank of the Luzha, down which the enemy must come, could be commanded, the ground was so broken and wooded that the bridge could nowhere be seen, and it was never apparently seriously injured.

Early on the 24th some fugitive inhabitants made their way to Dokhturov, and informed him that there were as yet only two battalions of French troops in the town. Accordingly soon after daylight, his men having by this obtained a little rest, he sent forward the 6th and 33rd Chasseur Regiments to carry the town. They expelled the garrison from nearly the whole of the place, but the buildings near the bridge formed a sort of *tête du pont*, which the French held desperately. Dokhturov supported the attack by two more Chasseur regiments, but the resistance was stubborn, and the Russians could not advance against the deadly fire kept up upon them. Delzons could at first only reinforce the gallant garrison by fragments and driblets, for when his main body endeavoured to defile down the northern bank Dokhturov rapidly brought a line of batteries into action east of the town and effectually checked them. About an hour later some batteries of the 4th Corps, which were toiling along the miry road, were ranged by the Viceroy opposite the Russian artillery, and thus covered Delzons' division crossed the bridge and recaptured the town.

Dokhturov thereupon restored the fight with three line regiments, which rallied the Chasseurs and stormed through the streets of Maloyaroslavetz, driving the 13th Division back towards the bridge. Baron Delzons was killed in the midst of the struggle, and as his brother and aide-de-camp endeavoured to carry his body to the rear he also was struck down. Baron Guilleminot, Eugène's chief-of-staff, took the command, rallied the division and, supported by part of Broussier's, which was beginning to arrive, again stormed the now burning town, only to be forced out again as Dokhturov sent in fresh reinforcements. Once more the Russian charge was checked at the bridge; and Broussier and Guilleminot, with their united divisions, again drove the 6th Corps through the blazing town, but could not debouch from it in the face of the Russian artillery fire.

The main armies were approaching the scene of action. Davout's corps was advancing from Borovsk to the support of Eugène; the main Russian army was nearing the field from Tarutino. Raievski's corps marched at the head of the long column, and behind him came in succession the 8th, 3rd, 5th, 2nd and 4th Corps, and Korff's, Golitizin's and Vassilchikov's cavalry. The aged commander-in-chief travelled during the night in his carriage. When about 3 or 4 miles from Maloyaroslavetz he halted and ordered Colonel Löwenstern to see Dokhturov to report. The whole of the 6th Corps was now engaged and forced on the defensive by Broussier and Guilleminot; and of this Löwenstern informed the commander-in-chief. Kutuzov sent Raievski forward at once to the assistance of Dokhturov, ordered the other corps to march upon the held with all speed, and himself mounted his horse and hurried to the front to range his oncoming troops in line of battle.

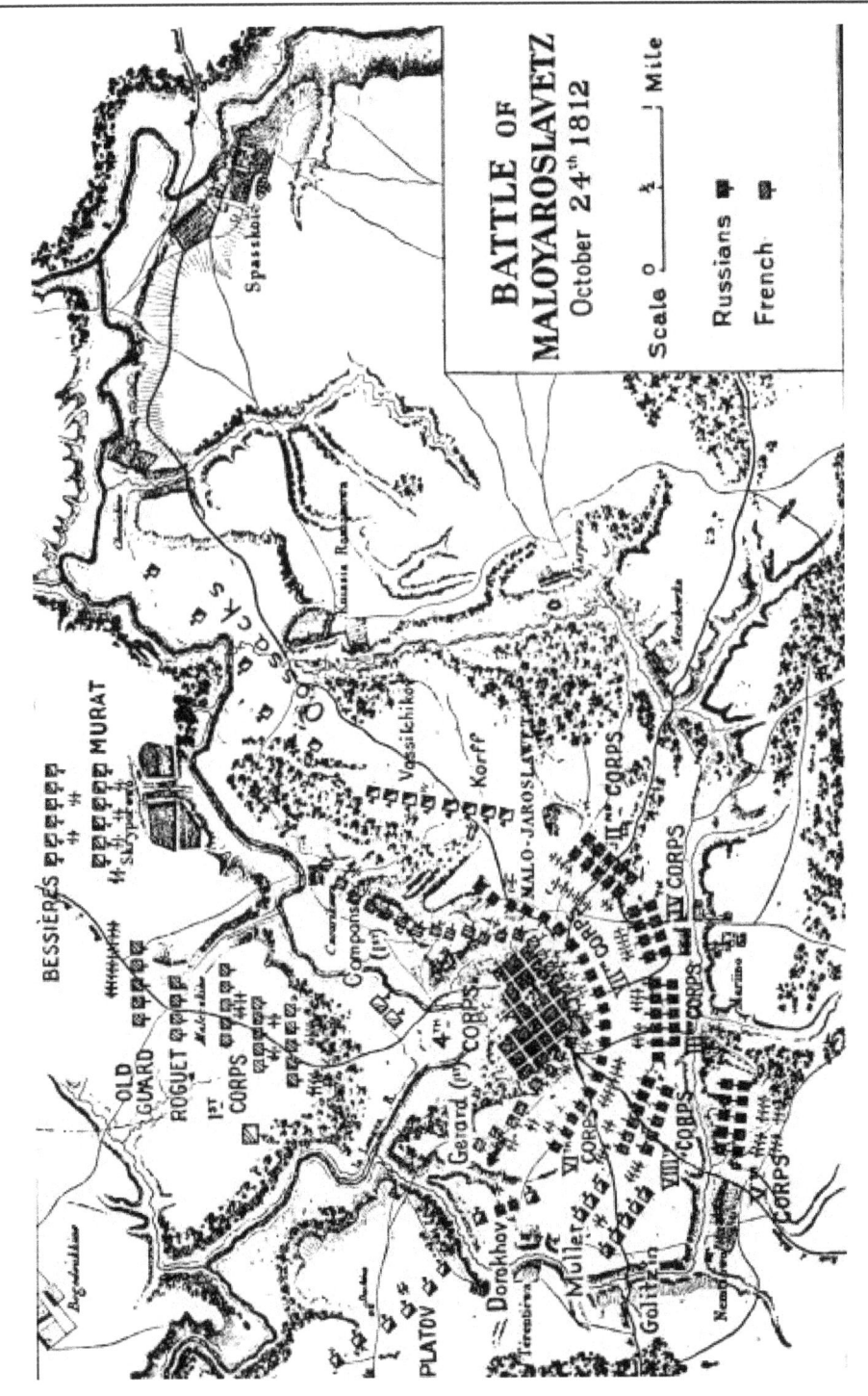

PLAN OF BATTLE OF MALOYAROSLAVETZ,
OCTOBER 24TH, 1812

Raievski's leading division, personally led by the corps commander and by Konovnitzin, reached the front about 12.30 p.m., gathered up Dokhturov's weary divisions, and the united force stormed Maloyaroslavetz for the sixth time, driving Broussier and Guilleminot into the bridge-head for shelter, until Pino's Italians sustained and rallied them. The three divisions beat back the oncoming Russians and once more gained possession of the awful heap of blood-stained ruins that now represented the town. The conflict was horrible beyond description; the opposing soldiery fought to the death amid conflagration and ruin; the wounded were suffocated, trodden underfoot, burned alive in the blazing houses, or hideously mangled by the opposing guns and artillery waggons as they forged their way backward and forward through the chaos.

To repel the three French and Italian divisions Dokhturov was now obliged to send in Raievski's second division. Once more the Russian infantry poured into the ruins of Maloyaroslavetz, driving their opponents before them and thrusting them down the slope towards the bridge. But the head of Davout's corps was at length arriving, and Eugène accordingly sent in his last reserve, the Royal Guard of Italy. Its six battalions finally turned the scale against the Russian 6th and 7th Corps, which, still fighting furiously, were driven back upon and through the ruins of the town. Davout's corps artillery forced the batteries on the east to retire; the entire artillery of the 4th Corps was pushed to the front over the dead and dying to support the infantry, while Compans' and Gérard's divisions crossed a temporary bridge and took up positions, the former on Eugène's left, the latter to his right.

The French were masters of the blood-stained ruins of Maloyaroslavetz, and that was all. While the battle was raging Kutuzov had stationed his whole army just south of the town and commenced to entrench himself. He relieved the 6th Corps by the 8th and the 3rd Division, and directed Borozdin and Raievski once more to assault the dreadful ruins of Maloyaroslavetz. Borozdin's leading troops entered it, but were driven out again, and, realising that the French hold was now too firm to be shaken, the Russians finally withdrew; but their immense artillery commanded every exit, and their skirmishers were everywhere close up to those of their opponents. The 7th and 8th Corps and the 3rd Division were in front line; the 2nd, 4th, 5th and 6th with the rest of the 3rd in second and third, while the powerful cavalry covered both flanks as far as the Luzha.

So far as a single event can be fixed upon as the decisive point of Napoleon's career that event is undoubtedly the battle of Maloyaroslavetz. Dokhturov's swift decision, splendidly seconded by the desperate fighting of the 6th and 7th Corps, had definitely ended all hope of carrying out the retreat with success. It may be doubted whether, even by marching by way of Kaluga, the army would have succeeded in retaining much discipline and cohesion; but, at any rate, it would have been the only chance, and now the attempt had failed. Napoleon knew it. He established his head-quarters in a peasant's hut at Gorodnia, about 5 miles north of Maloyaroslavetz, and to him in the evening he called Murat, Berthier and Bessières. He was seated at a table on which was spread a map of the country, and began to detail the situation to the generals. Suddenly the full extent of his immi-

CHAPTER X   183

nent ruin seemed to burst upon him, and, dropping his head upon his hands and his elbows upon the table, he re mained for more than an hour staring at the map, the comrades of his sixteen years of victory waiting for him to speak, silent and mournful. Rising at last he dismissed them without further comment, apparently resolved on a final desperate throw of the dice. He sent word to Davout to relieve Eugène's weary troops at the front, and that he would himself bring up the Guard in support. Ney, who had now reached Fominskoië, was ordered to bring Ledru's and Razout's divisions to a point between Borovsk and Maloyaroslavetz, leaving Claparède and Scheler to guard the vast assemblage of trains at the former place.

Meanwhile Kutuzov had also been deliberating. He had announced his intention of standing to fight on the ground which he held; but as the hours wore away his resolution failed him. He is not perhaps to be blamed; it was no light thing to meet Napoleon—never so dangerous as when he appeared completely baffled. He knew that the quality of his army, diluted with raw militia-men and recruits of a few weeks' training, left much to be desired; another battle like that of Borodino would completely cripple it. At any rate, he decided not to accept battle where he stood, but to fall back to another position about 3 miles in rear. This appears to have been strong enough; but it left uncovered the road from Maloyaroslavetz to Medyn, which Napoleon might have used for his retreat. The anger in the Russian army was great. Wilson was furious, and practically accuses Kutuzov of treachery. This is, of course, absurd. The Russian commander-in-chief and the English commissioner were on very bad terms, the latter being apparently rather tactless and too urgent in his efforts to induce the former to take the offensive. There is no question that Kutuzov was too old for his post; but, after all, he was the responsible chief of the Russian armies, and he knew, what Wilson did not, the internal condition of his own. Wild enthusiasm, assisted only by pikes, hardly constitutes a very firm stay against veteran and well-armed warriors led by a great military genius. Nevertheless, it is certain that Wilson and the bellicose Russian corps commanders were correct. The position behind Maloyaroslavetz was a better one than that which had been held with such desperate obstinacy at Borodino, and to defend it Kutuzov, after deducting the losses on the previous day, had 100,000 regulars and 15,000 irregulars with over 600 guns. Against these Napoleon could bring only the Guard (less Claparède's division), the 1st and 4th Corps, the bulk of the 3rd and the remains of the reserve cavalry. Mortier was on the march from Moscow to Vereia, Junot near Mozhaïsk, Poniatowski moving westward from Vereia. Allowing for these detachments Napoleon could place in line of battle by the 27th little more than 80,000 men, including the Head-quarters Guard. He would have 12,000 cavalry, mostly in very bad condition, and about 450 badly horsed guns as against at least 620 excellently appointed Russian pieces. This, however, Kutuzov did not accurately know, while he did know that Napoleon was in his front with the bulk of his army. He pointed out that any reverse would be fatal, since behind the present position was a very difficult defile. To Wilson's heated expostulations he replied angrily that he did not intend to win victories of which only England would reap the benefit! This outbreak may be charitably attributed to ill-temper at Wilson's worrying of him. The withdrawal was carried out. There was considerable disorder during the passage of the artillery through the defile, but the movement was successfully accomplished, well protected by Miloradovich's skilful handling of the rear-guard.

THE COUNCIL OF WAR AFTER THE BATTLE OF MALOYARO-SLAVETZ
Napoleon in the peasant's hut at Gorodnia remained for over an hour gazing at his map before making the fatal decision to retreat by the devastated route to Smolensk

Davout in the morning was able to debouch unopposed from Maloyaroslavetz, but his advance was soon checked by the sight of the Russian army, now established in its new position. Meanwhile, Napoleon had started from Gorodnia. He was attended by his usual escort of three or four squadrons. The cavalry of the Guard was some distance behind when, on the road to Maloyaroslavetz, a mass of Cossacks poured out of the woods on the left and raced at the escort. They were riding in good order, says Rapp, so that it was at first thought that they were regulars. They were, in fact, Platov's own corps, the Ataman having crossed the Luzha early that morning to raid Napoleon's line of communications. He was now aiming for a park of 40 guns of the Guard near Gorodnia. Rapp seized Napoleon's bridle and turned his horse, and the escort formed in haste, Rapp thrusting himself before the Emperor to shield him from the lances of the wild moss-troopers. His chivalrous devotion had wellnigh cost him dear, for his horse was killed, but the staff and escort rescued him, and, the cavalry of the Guard coming up, the Cossacks dispersed. They seized the artillery park, however, but the horses being at a distance watering, only 11 guns could be carried off. The bold attempt spread alarm through the army, which was almost all called under arms to resist an expected attack.

Napoleon, probably greatly exasperated, returned to Gorodnia until the way should be safe. At ten o'clock he again started, examined the battle-field and then returned to Gorodnia, having practically wasted a whole day—this when every hour was precious. This may have been because he was still undecided as to what he should do. At his quarters he held a final and stormy council. Murat, bold to the last, advocated advance, and offered to clear a way if the Guard cavalry were added to the remnant of his horsemen. Bessières, however, opposed him, observing that the transport was already failing and that the advance could not be rapid enough to be effective. Davout advised that the Medyn-Smolensk road should be adopted as the main line of retreat, but this was sufficient to provoke the opposition of Murat, who insisted that it was not safe from Russian flank attacks. The end was that Napoleon decided to fall back by the main road to Smolensk, and ordered the whole army to move on to it by way of Mozhaïsk. The road by Medyn, Yukhnov and Ielnia is about 40 miles shorter than the route adopted; the country which it traversed was not yet entirely devastated, and it is strange that Napoleon did not take it, braving the chance of a flank attack by the cautious, and by no means confident, Russian commander-in-chief. It is possible that, whichever route the army might take, it would have been prevented from foraging by the Cossacks. Perhaps also Napoleon hoped to give Kutuzov the impression that he was retreating upon Vitebsk—as, in fact, he at first did.

Kutuzov was, indeed, so little confident that on the 26th he retreated towards Kaluga. His decision has been violently criticised, and not without much show of reason. The only reply is that what we know very well to-day was not so plain to Kutuzov in 1812. He did not believe that his army was a match for Napoleon's, and that the correct policy was to "play hide and seek" with the invaders, as Clausewitz expresses it, and so wear them out. Having come to this conclusion, Kutuzov proceeded to carry out his design regardless of opposition. He was perhaps wrong, but it cannot be pronounced on the evidence which lay before him at the time that he was. Had Napoleon followed, his army would but have been weakened; had he turned westward the Russians would still have been on his flank. Wherever he went his line of march would be infested by Cossacks. Kutuzov was undoubtedly too cautious; he might have risked more, but he might equally have exposed himself to the counter-strokes of his mighty antagonist, now driven to desperation, and have lost everything. His operations were conducted on the basal idea that Napoleon was not to be beaten by open force, but by steady evasion and constant harassing. From this point of view his retirement was natural. His really serious blunder was com mitted two days later, and was the direct outcome of Napoleon's retreat by Mozhaïsk.

On the 26th, while Kutuzov's exasperated generals were ordering the retrograde march on Kaluga, Napoleon was commencing the fatal movement which was the beginning of his downfall. The 8th Corps about Mozhaïsk naturally formed the advance-guard; Ney was directed on Mozhaïsk from Borovsk, while the Guard moved back to that place. Mortier was to reach Vereia by the evening, and next day would be rejoined by Roguet's and Claparède's divisions. Eugène was to follow in the track of the Guard, while Davout with the 1st Corps and the relics of the 1st and 3rd Cavalry Corps covered the rear. Poniatowski was to move by cross-roads to Gzhatsk to cover the left flank. Finally, Evers, who had moved some way southward towards Yukhnov, was to return to Viasma, and there await the army.

While the French army lay about Maloyaroslavetz it had received repeated proofs of the activity and audacity of the Russian light troops. All the columns had in their turn been alarmed and harassed. On the 25th a body of Cossacks executed a *hourra* (alarm) upon Borovsk. On the same day Colonel Ilovaïski IX with three regiments of them surprised the advance-guard of the 5th Corps, consisting of a regiment of infantry and two of cavalry under General Tyskiewicz near Kreminskoië, between Vereia and Medyn. Tyskiewicz was captured, and of his force of about 1300 men, 500 were killed, wounded and captured. Ilovaïski also took 5 guns.

In the actual battle of Maloyaroslavetz the forces engaged were nearly equal in number. On the French side there were successively sent into line the 4th Corps and the 3rd and 5th Divisions of the 1st—about 35,000 men in all. The Russians successively engaged about the same numbers—Dokhturov's force, Dorokhov's detachment, the 7th Corps, the 3rd and 27th Divisions, and some regiments of Cossacks. The Russians admitted a loss of 4412 killed and wounded and 2753 missing. Very many of the latter, it is to be feared, perished in the burning town, and the actual total cannot be reckoned at less than 6000, quite five-sixths of which fell upon the 20,000 infantry of the 6th and 7th Corps. A heavy loss was that of General Dorokhov, who, being somewhat deaf, miscalculated the distance of musketry fire and was mortally wounded in consequence. Martinien's lists show something over 300 officers killed and wounded on the French side, and the total of casualties, therefore, would also be about 6000—the vast majority falling upon the 4th Corps. Of its four infantry division commanders, Delzons was killed, and Broussier and Pino were wounded. Two generals of brigade were killed and three wounded. The losses in the various Cossack alarms were probably slight on both sides. The Russians, as aforesaid, captured 11 guns.

CHAPTER XI

THE OPERATIONS IN NAPOLEON'S REAR DURING SEPTEMBER AND OCTOBER

The result of the operations on the Düna and in Volhynia had been that by the end of August, Wittgenstein was standing on the defensive at Sivokhino faced by a considerably superior force under St. Cyr, while in Volhynia Tormazov had been driven to cover behind the Styr. He also was opposed by forces considerably larger than his own, but Admiral Chichagov was now advancing fast from Moldavia, and within a few weeks the scale would be turned heavily against the invaders. On August 28th the Tzar and the Crown Prince of Sweden met at Abo. The result was the treaty of Abo, which freed Count Steingell's Russian army of Finland for service against Napoleon. Reinforcements to the number of about 15,000 men, of whom 10,000 were St. Petersburg militia, were ordered to join Wittgenstein.

To co-ordinate the movements of the widely scattered forces which from Finland to Moldavia were converging upon the theatre of war an elaborate plan of operations was worked out by Alexander and his council. It was far too detailed, required an impossible exactness of co-operation from the commanders, and assumed as complete the processes of reinforcement which had often hardly commenced. In its main lines it was as follows:—

MARSHAL GOUVION ST. CYR
Commander of the 6th (Bavarian) Army Corps and victor of first battle of Polotsk, Aug. 18th, 1812
From the picture by H. Vernet at Versailles

Chichagov was to concentrate at Ostrog, in Volhynia, and reach Pinsk by September 20th. He was to march upon and capture Minsk and then occupy the line of the Berezina in conjunction with Wittgenstein, while Tormazov held in check or drove back Schwarzenberg.

Wittgenstein, reinforced by 19,000 militia and 9000 regulars, was to cross the Düna, supported by Steingell, attack St. Cyr in the rear and, having beaten him, was to push on to co-operate with Chichagov.

CHAPTER XI

Steingell, with 14,000 men of the army of Finland, was to go to Riga. The Riga garrison, 20,000 strong (it was actually much less), was to attack and contain Macdonald, while under cover of this demonstration Steingell advanced on Polotsk to co-operate with Wittgenstein. Then, while the latter moved on to effect a junction with Chichagov, Steingell was to pursue St. Cyr towards Vilna.

General Ertel's force at Mozyr was to move northward and join Chichagov in the neighbourhood of Minsk.

The main object of the operations is clearly to bar Napoleon's homeward march from Moscow by a competent force. But the orders were too minute in some respects and vague in others. They spoke of such events as the defeat of Schwarzenberg by Tormazov as if they were certain to materialise, were clogged with superfluous regulations of detail, and took little account of the practical difficulties of organising and moving troops in a country like Russia. The strategy in broad outline was executed; no more could have been expected.

The efforts and intrigues of Andréossy, Napoleon's Ambassador at Constantinople, failed to induce the Turks to repudiate the Treaty of Peace concluded at Bukharest; and thus Admiral Chichagov was, after long delays, enabled to start his army for the north. He had under his personal command five divisions of all arms commanded respectively by General Count Langeron, Lieutenant-Generals Voïnov, Essen III and Sabaniev, and Major-General Bulatov. In all there were 50 battalions, 56 squadrons, 17 batteries and 11 regiments of Cossacks. The troops generally were of excellent quality and largely veterans, but the units were weak. The total of regulars was perhaps 34,000, with 204 guns; there were also between 3000 and 4000 Cossacks. A division of about 6000 men and 12 guns under Major-General Lüders, which had been supporting the famous Serb chief, Black George, was following from the west.

The original idea had been that the Army of the Danube should invade the French possessions in Illyria; but this was soon abandoned. Chichagov was much disappointed, but to penetrate through wild and rugged Balkania would have certainly meant the destruction of his army.

Chichagov had been placed in charge of the Russian army of the Danube and of the peace negotiations with Turkey by the express command of Alexander, who was angry at the slowness of his predecessor Kutuzov. The Admiral was also a strong advocate of the policy of arming the Serbs against Napoleon and invading Illyria. The Tzar considered him an able and energetic man, and he certainly should have known, for Chichagov had been for some time Minister of Marine. Wilson, who visited him at Bukharest, was much impressed with his ability, and regretted that he had not been placed earlier in command.

Wilson remarked that the Admiral's ability might not necessarily be equal to independent command, but, as a fact, Chichagov did quite as well as any of the other Russian generals. His lack of experience made him occasionally too slow; but his comments upon the plans submitted to him show that he really possessed very sound military judgment. Above all, he was of a remarkably independent temper, and did not shrink from expressing his opinions. He criticised the elaborate Imperial plan of operations with vigour and acumen, telling the Tzar bluntly that he should act as if the orders were more definite than they actually were, and would answer for his deviations from them!

Chichagov's position in his own army was not too pleasant. The military officers were sulky at being commanded by a seaman; his second-in-command, the Frenchman Langeron, was bitterly hostile, and in his memoirs loses no opportunity of attacking him. Even Langeron, however, admits his remarkable probity and scorn of personal profit—very rare virtues in a Russian of that period—and once or twice, despite himself, has to remark upon his chief's energy.

Chichagov left Bukharest on August 3rd, and on the 9th concentrated his army at Fokshani. The weather was very wet, and the result was the flooding of the rivers Putna and Sereth beyond Fokshani, which destroyed the existing bridges and retarded their re-establishment, so that it was not until the 17th that the Army of the Danube was able to resume its march. The battle of Gorodeczna had been fought; Tormazov was in full retreat for the Styr, and soon his anxious messages began to reach the Admiral, who, in reply, hastened up to the rescue at a pace, considering the difficulties, perhaps never equalled in war. The weather was hot; the roads were almost non-existent; the army, after the bad fashion of Russian forces, was encumbered with immense trains; nevertheless the speed of its march was remarkable. From the Sereth to Jassy, from Jassy to Choczim and Kamenetz-Podolski, thence for the Styr by Staroï-Konstantinov and Zaslavl, it took its way, marching rapidly but methodically, halting for one day in every six in order to rest and close up its straggling columns. Every effort was made to hasten the march, especially after passing the Dniester; weakened infantrymen were carried in waggons, while the cavalry and artillery pressed forward with all speed. On September 14th, as Miloradovich was withdrawing his rear-guard from Moscow, Chichagov in person entered Ostrog; and on the same day Voïnov's division reached Krymniki-on-Styr to the support of Tormazov. Langeron was at Dubno, one march behind Voïnov, Essen and Sabaniev at Ostrog, while Bulatov had not yet passed Zaslavl. From Fokshani to the Styr is a distance of over 450 miles, which had been traversed by the leading divisions in 29 days, including 5 of rest—a sustained average of over 15 miles a day and an actual marching average of 19! The army reached the Styr in excellent order, ready to take the offensive immediately.

At Dubno Chichagov was joined by two infantry regiments from the Crimea. The united Russian armies now amounted to about 67,000 men, including 18,000 cavalry and Cossacks, with over 300 pieces of artillery.

Schwarzenberg had about 42,000 troops under his command, but some thousands of them were raw Polish levies, and he possessed only 102 guns wherewith to oppose the immense park of his opponents. The marshy and malarious country was causing much sickness among his troops. Very likely also he was withheld by orders from Vienna, and the disaffection among his subordinates must have counted for much. But, in fact, he had not troops sufficient to force the passage of the Styr against an army not very inferior to his own in numbers, and much stronger in artillery. On September 15th, just as Chichagov was closing up to the front, he wrote to Berthier and explained his difficulties. On the 17th he made a demonstration along the river and became convinced that the Army of the Danube had now joined Tormazov.

Chichagov, having relieved Tormazov from fear of being overwhelmed, could now allow his troops to move more leisurely. For some days, therefore, his divisions were merely quietly ranged along the Styr; and the river was bridged. Schwarzenberg, realising that he was about to be attacked, drew back his detachments and prepared to retreat as soon as the Russians moved forward. Early on the 20th Lambert crossed the Styr and surprised 14 squadrons of German and Polish cavalry, capturing 300 prisoners. On the 22nd the general advance of the Russians began.

It is rather characteristic of the Imperial orders that they provided for no subordination of one general to another in the combined operations which they contemplated. In the present instance no trouble arose, as Chichagov and Tormazov agreed well together; and when on the 24th orders arrived from Kutuzov for Tormazov to march to reinforce the main army the latter quietly disregarded it. A few days later came another order, this time directing Chichagov to go, and Tormazov to remain to check Schwarzenberg. The Admiral declined to abandon his comrade, and comments sarcastically upon these contradictory directions. In any case, neither Chichagov nor Tormazov could have reached Tarutino in time. At the end of September the Imperial instructions were brought by the Tzar's aide-de-camp, Colonel Chernishev. Chichagov observes that their object was clearly to range a strong force along the line of the Berezina; and, having despatched his outspoken reply to his master, proceeded to attain the end in his own way. At the same time Tormazov was called by Kutuzov to succeed Bagration, leaving Chichagov in supreme command.

On the 22nd the Russian armies crossed the Styr, Schwarzenberg's outposts falling back before them. Schwarzenberg retired upon Luboml, a little east of the Bug on the Lublin-Kovel road, where he concentrated on the 28th. By the evening of the 29th Chichagov and Tormazov had collected most of their forces in his front; but in the night he evacuated his position and retreated towards Brest-Litovsk, sending at the same time Siegenthal's division to Pruzhani. Chichagov pursued him with the bulk of his forces, only detaching Voïnov to follow Siegenthal. On October 9th Chichagov reached Brest-Litovsk and called in his detachments to give battle; but Schwarzenberg wisely decamped in the night and retreated on Warsaw. He took up a position at Wengrow, about 42 miles east of Praga, and awaited events, while Siegenthal fell back to Bielostok. Chichagov, having driven Napoleon's extreme right wing across the Bug, halted at Brest-Litovsk with his main body in order to prepare to carry out the instructions brought by Chernishev.

The losses in these operations were not very heavy. There had been a good deal of skirmishing, but no general action; and it is unlikely that Schwarzenberg's army lost more than 3000 to 4000 men. The diminution in the Russian forces must have been even less.

Chichagov now, according to various critics on both sides, committed a great blunder. He remained halted for 18 days at Brest-Litovsk. But, as Bogdanovich has justly pointed out, he was about to advance through a country which, never rich, had been devastated by the passage across it of several armies. He had to divide his army for its new operations, leaving a competent force to observe Schwarzenberg, and to collect supplies sufficient to feed his own corps. Besides, the Army of the Danube had been marching and fighting for more than two months, and may well have needed time wherein to repose and refit.

During the halt at Brest-Litovsk General Sacken joined the army from the south, bringing with him about 4000 dépôt troops, who appear to have been drafted into the weaker units.

While the Admiral himself remained at Brest, preparing for the march to the Berezina, he sent out detachments to overrun Warsaw and sweep the country towards Minsk. The detachments sent towards Warsaw were supported by Essen III's division, which, on October 18th, came in contact at Biala with Reynier and was driven back, with a loss of several hundred men and a gun, upon Brest-Litovsk. On the other hand, General Chaplitz on the 20th destroyed the new Lithuanian regiment of Napoleon's Guard at Slonim, only about 120 men escaping out of 600. Chaplitz's detachment was supported by Cherbatov's (formerly Markov's) division. Eastward of Slonim there were very few invading troops to cover the long line of communications, threatened on the south by Russian forces at Bobruisk and Mozyr. The garrison of Bobruisk was not strong enough to make effective sorties, but the force at Mozyr had been gradually increased to about 12,000 men and over 30 guns. To guard against the menace of this force and to observe Bobruisk, Dombrowski's infantry division and three regiments of cavalry had been left by Poniatowski in August. Dombrowski's whole force, even after the junction of some Lithuanian levies, can never have exceeded 9000 men, and was barely sufficient, after garrisoning Mohilev, to observe Bobruisk, much less to oppose any effectual resistance to Ertel. On September 11th a column from Mozyr forced an Austrian detachment to abandon Pinsk, while a second, under Ertel himself, defeated Dombrowski's Lithuanians on the 15th and threw some reinforcements into Bobruisk. Then, however, he retired to Mozyr.

From Riga on August 7th Essen again made a sortie and captured Schlock, which was then retaken by the Prussians. On the 23rd Essen decided to make a general attack upon the Prussians, who lay observing the city, extended from Schlock to Thomsdorf on the Düna, a distance of 42 miles. A column under Lewis was to make the real attack upon Eckau, while a detachment under Major-General Veliaminov demonstrated towards Mitau, and Rear-Admiral von Müller with a flotilla of sloops attacked Schlock. The Prussian posts at Dahlenkirchen on the Düna were driven back, with some loss, by Lewis, but Veliaminov's demonstration had no results, though von Müller captured Schlock. On the 26th Grawert, having collected his scattered detachments, drove Lewis back into Riga; and Schlock and Dahlenkirchen were reoccupied. The losses in these actions, combined with sickness, considerably weakened the garrison. On the other hand, they proved that the Prussians were not strong enough even to blockade the place. Macdonald sent a brigade of Grandjean's division to reinforce them, and prepared to bring up the rest of it at need.

CHAPTER XI 193

After this both sides lay inactive until September 18th, when there was some more indecisive skirmishing about Schlock. The Prussians were now commanded by Lieutenant-General Yorck, Grawert being invalided. Between the 20th and 22nd, Count Steingell's corps from Finland, which had landed at Revel on the 10th, entered Riga. It had sustained some losses by shipwreck, and part of the troops were detained by contrary winds, so that Steingell had with him only a little over 10,000 men and 18 guns. Nevertheless, the force in Riga was now over 20,000 strong, and an attempt could be made to execute the Tzar's orders.

On the 26th accordingly Steingell with his own troops and a division under Lewis moved out upon Dahlenkirchen. It was easily occupied, and on the 27th Steingell advanced upon Eckau, where Yorck had collected several regiments. His superiority in artillery enabled him to hold Steingell in check until the arrival of Lewis, when he retired behind the Aa, abandoning Bausk.

While Steingell was pushing back Yorck, Essen directed a column of 2000 men and 6 guns upon Mitau from Riga, while a flotilla came up the Aa. Essen's hope was to destroy the siege train, which, however, was not there. He ordered Steingell to support the advance with 3000 men and 6 guns, under Colonel Ekeln. On the 28th Yorck, being not yet joined by Hunerbein's brigade (Grandjean's division), ordered General Kleist to abandon Mitau and come to reinforce him. This Kleist did, and on the 29th the Russians occupied the place without opposition. But meanwhile Yorck, reinforced by Kleist and Hunerbein, took the offensive against Steingell's weakened force and began to drive it back. There was some not very vigorous fighting along the Aa, as the result of which the Prussians gained a foothold on the farther bank.

Hunerbein, coming from the right, had retaken Bausk, and on the 30th Yorck made a general advance, driving Steingell back all along the line. The fighting was not at all severe, Steingell merely gave way deliberately before the advance of Yorck's now superior columns. On the other hand, Yorck was probably not anxious to do more than his strict military duty required. Steingell retired towards Riga with no serious loss and re-entered the lines on the 2nd of October, Essen at the same time evacuating Mitau. The losses on neither side were heavy.

The result of the action was that Macdonald decided to come himself to the support of Yorck. Leaving a Polish regiment in Dünaburg he marched for Mitau with the rest of Grandjean's division, but when he arrived the Russians had retreated into Riga. The Marshal increased Hunerbein's brigade to 8 battalions, rearranged the positions of the troops, and sent Grandjean with one brigade back to Illuxt, near Dünaburg. To draw closer to Riga with his feeble forces was evidently impossible, and week after week wore itself away without any fighting except some occasional skirmishing at the outposts.

After his victory at Polotsk, on August 18th, St. Cyr had been unable to follow in pursuit of Wittgenstein owing to his weakness in cavalry fit for the purpose. Wittgenstein therefore was able to withdraw unmolested behind the Drissa. On the 22nd Wrede made a strong reconnaissance towards Sivokhino, but the Bavarians were repulsed by a detachment under Colonel Vlastov with a loss of about 300 killed and wounded and 150 prisoners.

Both sides now settled down into cantonments. Both had suffered very severely and neither was in a state to resume hostilities. Wittgenstein entrenched his position at Sivokhino, and his cavalry were able to circumscribe the French foraging operations on the right bank of the Düna. Wittgenstein also fortified his advanced base of Sebezh. Meanwhile, St. Cyr threw up entrenchments round Polotsk. The troops were distributed around the town, and, being largely in quarters or in barracks and tolerably well supplied, were soon in good condition. The effectives were increased by drafts and convalescents, but it is doubtful whether there was any great rise in the numbers owing to the diminution occasioned by constant petty skirmishing. The Bavarians were apparently unable to recover from the blighting effects of the sickness planted in their midst by their terrible hardships in July, and, though they were at rest and better supplied than they had hitherto been, their numbers continued to diminish. Maret and Hogendorp did their best to forward supplies from Vilna, but bread was often scarce and already, on October 7th, St. Cyr was writing to express his anxiety at the difficulty of procuring forage. The numerical strength of St. Cyr's force by the middle of October appears to have been about 30,000 men—2nd Corps 21,000; Doumerc about 2200; 6th Corps perhaps 7000 or 8000.

Meanwhile, Marshal Victor, having crossed the Niemen on September 4th, reached Smolensk on the 27th. On October 6th Napoleon gave him his instructions. Besides his corps and the Saxon and Westphalian brigades of Löw and Coutard he was given control of Dombrowski's division. He was informed that he was to act as the general reserve of the *Grande Armée*, and would move to support either Schwarzenberg, St. Cyr, or Napoleon, according to circumstances. Napoleon greatly underestimated the pressure on his flanks. He says in the despatch that Chichagov is only 20,000 strong, that his junction with Tormazov will only raise his force to 40,000, and that Schwarzenberg can easily deal with him. As a fact, both Schwarzenberg and St. Cyr were opposed by greatly superior numbers. Even when the former had been joined by his reinforcements he was still outnumbered by Chichagov, who might be further strengthened by Ertel from Mozyr. On the north Wittgenstein and Steingell had 50,000 men against St. Cyr's 30,000. To afford adequate support to the wings Victor would have needed 80,000 men.

A few words must here be said upon the diplomatic situation. Prussia, trodden into the dust by Napoleon's iron heel, was in the last stages of destitution, while Austria, though sorely humiliated, was still independent, far less wasted, and, in addition, was more or less afraid of a revival of Prussia. These circumstances are reflected in the despatches of the Prime Ministers, the Prussian, Hardenberg, being eager to take vigorous steps and inclined to believe in the rumours of French defeats; while Metternich is pessimistic and obviously playing for his own—or Austria's—hand. He seems after the fall of Moscow to have considered that Napoleon might win, and accordingly a reinforcement of about 5000 men was despatched to Schwarzenberg. Otherwise there were signs that Napoleon's vassals were beginning to falter at the never-ending drain of human life. Bavaria and Württemberg sent drafts to refill the wasted ranks of their contingents; but the King of Württemberg spoke of his uneasiness at receiving no news. The Grand Duke of Baden professed himself unable to add to his treaty contingent. In his growing anxiety Napoleon actually went to the length of politely asking the King of Prussia to replace two weakened cavalry regiments. He also directed that every reinforcement despatched was to be stated in all newspapers at double its strength, so as to impose upon the Russians should the tidings reach them!

After the failure of the sortie from Riga Count Steingell made up his mind to waste no more time in attempting to execute the official plan of operations, but to join Wittgenstein without delay. On October 5th he left Riga, and proceeded by forced marches up the right bank of the Düna. On the 15th he reached Druia, having marched over 180 miles in ten days.

On October 10th Wittgenstein's first column of reinforcement, over 5000 strong, arrived at Sivokhino. On the same day the 9000 men of the second column reached Nevel, and on the 14th its junction with the main force was practically complete. Wittgenstein had now under his hand about 40,000 men, including 5000 cavalry and Cossacks, with 154 guns.

Wittgenstein distributed the militia battalions among the infantry, one to each regiment, and his staff issued special orders as to how these enthusiastic but raw troops were to act in battle. The effect was excellent; and though the men were imperfectly clothed and equipped, and almost untrained, they rapidly gained efficiency and cohesion.

The unfortunate effect of the elaborate and too minute Imperial plan of operations now became evident. Steingell had acted upon his own judgment in marching to reinforce Wittgenstein; but he felt himself obliged to act upon his master's orders as far as possible, and so crossed the Düna at Druia to operate on the left bank. He was thus completely separated from Wittgenstein, and the latter could only endeavour to remedy the strategic defect by bridging the river nearer Polotsk. As he had no pontoons the operation was likely to prove a lengthy one. He ordered his chief of engineers, Colonel Count Sievers, to construct a bridge at Desna, detailing as his escort 4 battalions of infantry and a regiment of cavalry—2500 men and 4 guns.

So far as there was any concerted plan of operations on the part of the Russian commanders, it appears to have been that Wittgenstein was to attack Polotsk and Steingell to cut off St. Cyr's retreat. It was clear that the French general might choose to hold Polotsk merely by a rear-guard, and destroy Steingell's small force by concentrating upon him the bulk of his own army. To obviate this, Wittgenstein must attack Polotsk speedily and vigorously. Even so the outlook was not altogether promising. Polotsk was fortified; and St. Cyr was quite strong enough to hold it against the 37,000 men of whom Wittgenstein disposed after deducting Sievers' detachment.

Wittgenstein distributed his numerically strong but rather incoherent force into three large divisions of all arms, commanded respectively by Lieutenant-Generals Prince Iachvil and Berg and Major-General Beguichev, besides a flank detachment under Major-General Alexiev. On the 16th he began his march upon

Polotsk, while Steingell was moving from Druia.

COUNT WITTGENSTEIN
Commander of the 1st Russian Army Corps in 1812

St. Cyr did not believe that he could hold his own unaided against the united Russian forces; but determined to defend Polotsk if Wittgenstein should dash his head against its entrenchments. He detached Corbineau with his cavalry brigade and three weak Bavarian battalions to observe Steingell, passed his trains, escorted by Doumerc and Castex, across to the left bank of the Düna and posted the rest of his forces in the entrenchments which he had caused to be thrown up. Polotsk itself was covered by a palisaded parapet. Across the western part of the town a second palisaded parapet had been carried from the Polota to the Düna, covering the two bridges of rafts which had been thrown across the river. On the western bank of the Polota, north-west of the town were three redoubts, and to the north the Roman Catholic cemetery had been entrenched. On the east of the Polota the exterior chain of defence was less complete. Three redoubts and an outlying battery were under construction, but not yet finished. Below the town batteries had been thrown up to flank the entrenchments on the western side. The passage of the Polota had been rendered as difficult as might be, and at the village of Struria above Polotsk the ground near the river had been flooded by damming up a brook.

Merle's division held the entrenched western side of the town, and the first of the Polota redoubts. Wrede's Bavarians defended Nos. 2 and 3, the cemetery, Spas, and the line of the Polota. On the east side of the Polota stood Legrand, while Maison continued the line to the Düna. On the right flank were four squadrons of cavalry, all that St. Cyr had retained. Struria was occupied by a detachment of Bavarians.

On the 18th Steingell had not yet reached Desna; the bridge was scarcely commenced; and Wittgenstein decided to assault St. Cyr's position. He rightly directed the weight of his attack upon the French right and right centre, where the entrenchments were still incomplete. Prince Iachvil was ordered to contain Merle and Wrede, while Berg and Beguichev assailed Legrand and Maison.

The French outposts were driven back by the advance of the Russians; but when Berg and Beguichev assailed the main French line they could make little headway. The combat swayed backward and forward; the Russian militia behaved with splendid bravery; but the French troops, aided by their entrenchments, everywhere held their ground; the single redoubt carried by the Russians could not be held in the face of the furious fire poured into it from the entrenchments before Polotsk. Wittgenstein apparently lost his head; and though he had at first, according to Russian authorities, merely intended a demonstration, he had by the evening employed nearly the whole of Berg's and Beguichev's divisions in vain attempts to force the French right.

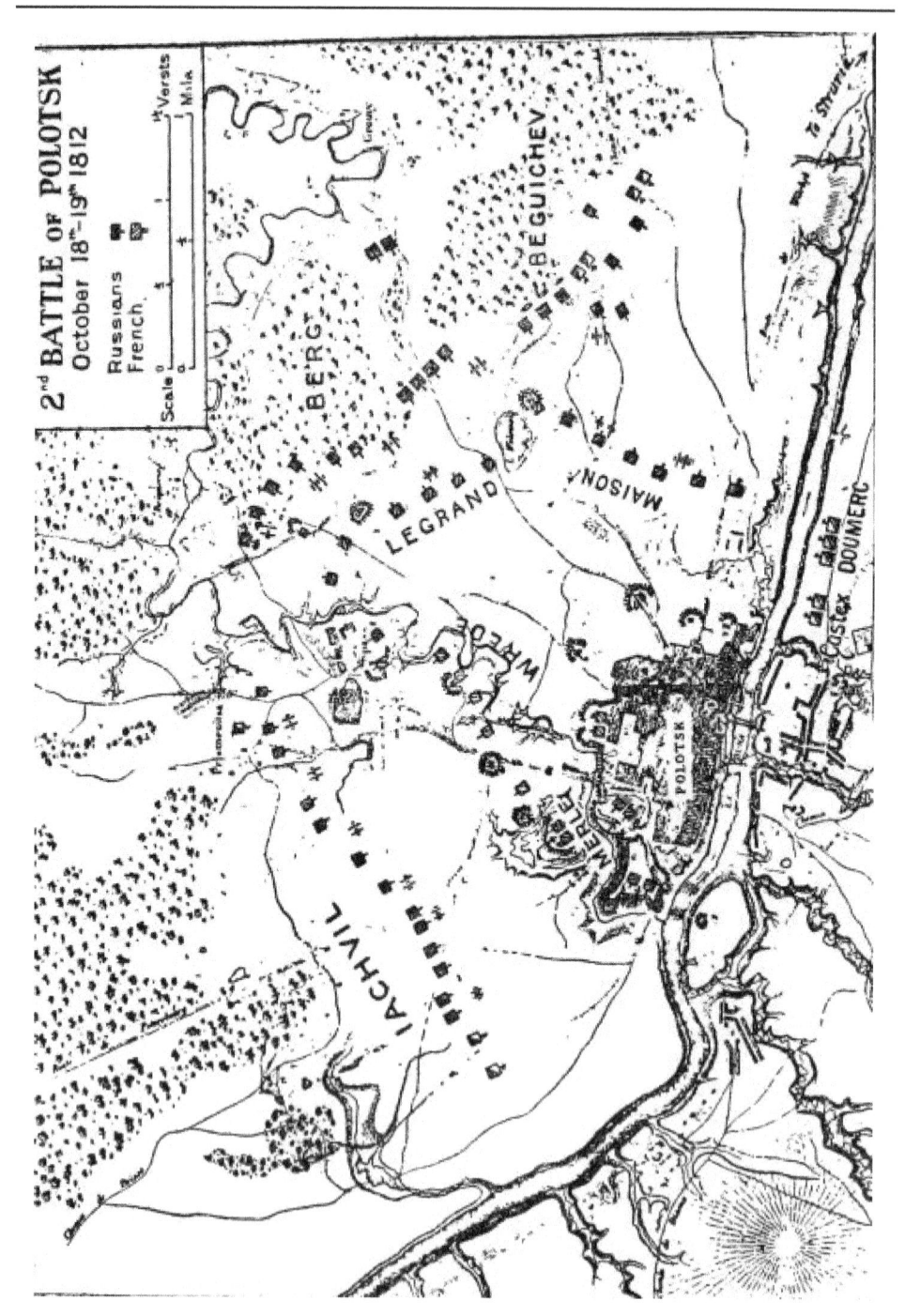

SECOND BATTLE OF POLOTSK
October 18th-19th, 1812

About 4 p.m., apparently on the hypothesis that St. Cyr had weakened his left to withstand the attack on his right, Wittgenstein ordered Iachvil to assault in earnest the western works. The attempt was hopeless, and could not for a moment have succeeded. Such advantage as the Russians gained was due to a rash counter-attack made by a Swiss regiment and a battalion of Croats. They suffered very heavily and were driven back upon the works, the Croats being mostly captured. But this was all that Iachvil could achieve, though his militia fought with fanatic fury. At nightfall St. Cyr's position was practically intact; and the Russians had certainly lost far more heavily than the French. While the battle was proceeding, Steingell was approaching by the left bank of the Düna, but was only able to reach the Uchach, 7 or 8 miles west of Polotsk, by the evening of the 18th with his advance-guard. De Chambray criticises him for his slowness; but as he only crossed the Düna on the 16th, and then had nearly 50 miles of bad road to traverse in order to reach Polotsk, the stricture appears unjust. On the 19th Steingell informed Wittgenstein that he was at hand. The bridge at Desna was hardly commenced, and had St. Cyr been a little stronger the position of the Russians would have been even more serious than it was. Wittgenstein's army had obviously been badly shaken by the fierce fighting of the day before; for he made no attempt to renew the attack until Steingell could join in from the south. This threw an awkward responsibility upon the commander of the weak Finland corps, and exposed him to the risk of destruction should St. Cyr decide to hold Polotsk only as a *tête de pont* and concentrate a superior force on the left bank of the Düna. To the writer it seems that St. Cyr might have abandoned his outlying works, and left the inner and continuous line to be held by about 14,000 men, while with the remaining 14,000 (allowing for losses) he attacked and defeated Steingell, who had scarcely 10,000 actually in hand. This, however, he did not do; and as the precise strength of the entrenchments is a matter of doubt he was perhaps right. He detached one regiment from each of his divisions, and sent them under General Amey to reinforce Corbineau. A Cuirassier regiment was also directed to the Uchach. Steingell's advance-guard, only four battalions under Colonel Turshaninov, naturally halted before this accumulation of force and waited for the main body, while Steingell apparently was listening for the sound of Wittgenstein's guns before advancing on Polotsk. The French containing force took up a fairly strong position among woods and broken ground, and effectually checked the advance of the Finland corps. St. Cyr, however, made up his mind that he was not strong enough to contend at the same time with both Russian forces, and in the evening began to evacuate Polotsk. Iachvil noted the withdrawal of troops and opened fire on his front, the Russian centre and left taking up the ball. The Russians were too late to molest the evacuation of the outer works, but they pushed forward against the inner line round the town. The houses everywhere took fire, partly ignited by the Russian howitzers, partly, as it would seem, burned by the French to clear the front of some of their works, which would otherwise have been masked. The Russian infantry attacks were everywhere repulsed; and during the evening Legrand's and Maison's divisions and the Bavarians defiled through the town and crossed the bridge, covered by Merle's Swiss and Croats. At midnight the Russians entered Polotsk; but the battle was far from its end. Merle and his gallant regiments disputed every inch of the streets with splendid valour, repeatedly repulsing the headlong charges of the Russian infantry. By 2.30 p.m. the whole French army was safe on the left bank of the Düna, and the bridges were destroyed. St. Cyr, as he directed the battle, was severely wounded in the foot, and disabled for the rest of the campaign. He had perhaps committed an error in not merely holding the inner works at Polotsk and thus concentrating a superior force on Steingell; but the steady and successful retreat did him much honour. It seems clear that he was throughout master of his operations; and that Wittgenstein could only press the withdrawal very slightly. The honours of the fighting rested chiefly with the gallant Swiss regiments of Merle's division, whose conduct in the rear-guard was truly admirable.

St. Cyr being now for the moment in safety, reinforced the force facing Steingell with another French regiment and placed Wrede in command. At 4.30 a.m. on the 20th he fell unexpectedly upon Steingell, whose advance-guard, surprised in its bivouacs, was seized with a panic and dispersed. Buturlin says that 1800 men of 2 regiments of Chasseurs were captured, but as this would appear to be almost their whole strength, and they figure later as at least 2 battalions strong, this is doubtless an exaggeration. Steingell's main body was not closely supporting the unlucky vanguard, and on its dispersal he hastily collected the remainder of his troops and retreated on Desna, where he crossed the Düna, while Wrede, having disposed of him, rejoined the main body of the French army. Besides St. Cyr, Legrand, the senior divisional commander, was wounded, and the temporary charge of the 2nd and 6th Corps devolved upon Merle. On the 21st he finally retreated from before Polotsk. Wittgenstein, hampered by lack of engineers and bridging material, could not establish a passage over the Düna until the 23rd. Only a detachment of cavalry under Colonel Rüdiger forded the river and skirmished with Merle's outposts. To make the best of things Wittgenstein detached a division of all arms under General Sazonov to Desna to reinforce Steingell. The latter thereupon on the 23rd repassed the Düna, detached Major-General Vlastov with a force of 8 regular battalions, 1 militia battalion, 3 squadrons of Hussars, a regiment of Cossacks and 12 guns—about 5000 men in all—to observe Dünaburg, and with the rest of his force moved once more up the left bank of the river. On the same day Wittgenstein completed a bridge at Polotsk and began to cross. He had just been joined by two battalions of Novgorod militia, which he left with another militia battalion, 2 batteries, a detachment of regulars and some cavalry and Cossacks to garrison Polotsk.

Merle retreated from before Polotsk in 3 columns, Legrand's division moving on Bechenkowiczi, Wrede, with the remains of the 6th Corps and Corbineau's cavalry, on Glubokoië to cover the road to Vilna, the remainder of the 2nd Corps and Doumerc's Cuirassiers on Chasniki by way of Uchach and Lepel.

Martinien's lists, probably not quite complete, show 238 officers of the 3 "combatant" arms, almost all of the 2nd Corps, killed and wounded during the three days' fighting round Polotsk. The French loss would therefore have been in the region of 5000. The number of unwounded prisoners was apparently about 1000. The French lost also 1 gun. The Russians only admit a loss of 3000 killed and wounded, but, seeing the character of the fighting, and that the French were acting on the defensive and covered by entrenchments, this estimate is certainly far too low. Probably, allowing for Steingell's losses, 8000 would not be too low a figure.

CHAPTER XI

Among the wounded were Major-Generals Balk, Hammen and the Prince of Siberia; and Privy Councillor Bibikov and Chamberlain Mordvinov, who commanded militia battalions.

Marshal Victor cannot long have had Napoleon's instructions in his hands when he was called upon to act upon them. On reaching Smolensk he cantoned his corps between that place and Orsha. His troops appear to have maintained good discipline; and a commencement was made of establishing order in the vicinity. Some officers, at least, succeeded in instilling confidence into the villagers and obtaining supplies by regular methods; and more might have been done had the 9th Corps remained longer in the district. Upon learning from St. Cyr of the large reinforcements which were joining Wittgenstein, Victor sent Dändels' German division to Vitebsk, and four battalions to Bechenkowiczi to watch the line of the Düna. Then he heard of the abandonment of Polotsk; and it was clear that he must assist the overmatched army of St. Cyr. He accordingly directed Dändels upon Bechenkowiczi; and with the rest of his corps moved towards Chasniki.

The result of the operations about Polotsk therefore had been that the French had been forced to abandon the line of the Düna, and that to sustain them Napoleon's sole powerful reserve had to be diverted to sustain the retreating 2nd and 6th Corps. Only the small force at Smolensk was now available to reinforce the retreating army of the centre; and there was hardly anything to oppose the advance of Chichagov on the Berezina. On October 25th Napoleon was 70 miles south-west of Moscow, just about to retreat on Smolensk, with the Grand Army of Russia on his left flank able to reach his goal before him. Wittgenstein was advancing from the Düna towards the Berezina, but was faced by an equal or superior force, and might be kept from the main line of communications. Chichagov was at Brest-Litovsk, ready to march on Minsk, with nothing in his front but feeble detachments.

Therefore, in the last days of October, the focus of operations became the Berezina near Borisov. Upon it were converging: (1) Napoleon, nearly 400 miles distant, with an equal or superior enemy attending him on the flank and able to reach Smolensk before him; (2) Wittgenstein, 90 miles away, with an equal French force in his front; (3) Chichagov, 262 miles distant, with hardly anything to oppose him. Schwarzenberg was in rear of Chichagov, and watched by a force at least able to seriously hamper any attempt at pursuit made by him. So the curtain rose upon the last act of the great tragedy, as from every side Napoleon's armies and those of his enemies set their faces towards the Berezina, soon to acquire a terrible renown in the history of the world.

CHAPTER XII
THE FRENCH RETREAT. MALOYAROSLAVETZ TO ORSHA

On October 26th the French retreat by the Moscow-Smolensk road definitely commenced. Napoleon with the Guard and 4th Corps moved back to Borovsk. Ney was directed by Vereia on Mozhaïsk, while Davout with the 1st Corps and the relics of the 1st and 3rd Cavalry Corps remained near Maloyaroslavetz until the evening. And, while Napoleon was retracing his steps, Kutuzov, also, was retreating upon Kaluga. He apparently feared that the French, having the road open, would move westward to Medyn and thence south-eastward upon Kaluga. This hypothesis is a direct reflection upon his action in abandoning his position outside Maloyaroslavetz. As matters stood, Kutuzov's inference was not unreasonable; Poniatowski's corps was actually on the march from Vereia to Medyn, and appeared to be the advance-guard of a turning movement. Miloradovich remained in observation on the original Russian position, and Platov continued to hover about Davout's corps. The Corps de Bataille retrograded to Gonsherevo, about 12 miles from Kaluga. Paskievich's division was sent to bar the Medyn-Kaluga road at Adamovskoë, some miles to the westward. There he was joined by Ilovaïski IX and his Cossack detachment. Miloradovich was about to fall back on the Russian main body when it was discovered that Maloyaroslavetz was evacuated. Kutuzov was informed, and the advance-guard reoccupied the line of the Luzha.

Kutuzov appeared to have inferred that Napoleon's intention was to retreat upon Smolensk—as, in fact, it was. He accordingly directed his main body upon Adamovskoë, evidently with the purpose of following on the flank of the French retreat, while Miloradovich was ordered to Medyn. The latter, however, disquieted by reports that the French army was moving from Borovsk by cross-roads upon Medyn, hesitated, delayed, and finally also moved to Adamovskoë. Kutuzov remained at the latter place during the 29th, endeavouring to envisage the situation, and finally appears to have decided that the *Grande Armée* was retreating on Vitebsk. The conclusion was reasonable enough. The march of the French along the Borovsk-Mozhaïsk road might certainly indicate an intention to cross the Smolensk road at Mozhaïsk and take a route to the northward for Vitebsk—as Jomini considers that they should have done. Consequently upon the 30th Kutuzov marched northwards upon Mozhaïsk. Platov with his Cossacks and Paskievich's division was to follow the French rear-guard. The advance-guard would move parallel with the French left flank, while the *Corps de Bataille* kept to the left of the advance-guard, generally at about a day's march distance. On the 30th the main

CHAPTER XII

army had reached Kremenskoë, but by that day the French rear-guard had arrived at Mozhaïsk and all the corps were moving along the highway to Smolensk. Kutuzov and Miloradovich therefore turned to the westward, while Platov and Paskievich harassed Davout.

The result, therefore, was that the French army had at the outset gained a start upon their pursuers. Bennigsen says that he advised that the march should be directed from Adamovskoë on Yukhnov, thence by a broad road to Slavkovo. It seems clear that this direction would have been an excellent one. But Kutuzov knew that Napoleon was free to use the Medyn road, and indeed expected him to do so. He had, however, fallen back by Vereia, a direction which rather indicated an intention of retreating upon Vitebsk. If he had hoped by taking this route to deceive the Russians as to his line of march he had certainly succeeded.

From Mozhaïsk to Viasma the Moscow-Smolensk road proceeds generally in a shallow arc of a circle, often describing a very sinuous course. Miloradovich marched steadily to the south of it, gradually closing in, and moving much faster than the already dwindling and straggling French army with its immense trains. Still farther to the south and far to the rear the Russian *Corps de Bataille* had turned in the right direction and was also marching for Viasma. The roads by which it was forced to proceed were wretched, but none the less the troops marched at a very creditable pace, covering some 74 miles in 4 days.

Meanwhile the Napoleonic host was making its way into and along the Moscow-Smolensk high-road. Junot's corps being actually on it when the retreat from Maloyaroslavetz began of course led the way; behind it came in succession the Guard, the 2nd and 4th Cavalry Corps, and the 3rd, 4th, and 1st *Corps d'Armée*, while Poniatowski covered the left flank. At Vereia, on the 27th, Mortier rejoined, bringing with him his prisoner, Winzingerode. Napoleon treated the general with gross insolence and brutality, overwhelming him with abuse, and actually condemned him to death as a traitor because he was a German and therefore a subject of one of his vassals! It is difficult to say whether he was or was not in earnest. When he was enraged his manners were brutal beyond words; and at this time he had every cause for being exasperated. In any case, he gave way to the remonstrances of Berthier and Murat. His conduct was otherwise inexcusable. Winzingerode had entered the service of Russia previous to the formation of the Rhine Confederacy. After being kept in suspense for some days Winzingerode was sent in custody to France; but he was rescued in Lithuania by Cossacks, as we shall have occasion to mention.

On the 28th Napoleon, at Mozhaïsk, received a report from Davout that he had as yet seen no enemies but Cossacks. He thereupon inferred that the main Russian army was marching to cut his line of retreat. Its natural objective would in that case be Viasma, and the Emperor decided to push for that place with all speed with the Guard.

ARMED RUSSIAN PEASANTS IN AMBUSH IN THE WOODS WAITING TO CUT OFF FRENCH STRAGGLERS
From the picture by Verestchagin

On the evening of the 28th Davout was near Vereia. He reported that the Russians were already showing infantry—these were of course Paskievich's division. He begged the Emperor to put a stop to the wholesale burning of villages by the corps ahead of him. Demoralisation was spreading fast, and the men were abandoning the ranks in crowds. The usual straggling array of march of the Napoleonic hosts was a bad preparation for a retreat in face of an enemy. The field of Borodino was crossed by the Guard at daybreak on the 29th. It still presented a fearful spectacle. Junot's men had been unable to bury many even of the French dead; and the ground was strewn with rotting corpses mingled with the wreckage of the terrible struggle. The hospitals at Kolotskoï and elsewhere were mere charnel-houses in which the dead lay heaped with the living, amid pestilence, filth, and destitution. About 1500 unhappy creatures still remained, Junot having been unable to remove them. Napoleon issued an order that every private carriage or other non-military vehicle was to carry one or two. Its effect was simply to hasten the end of the unfortunate invalids, who were so much additional encumbrance to men already beginning to feel the pinch of want. They were abandoned by the drivers at the earliest opportunity: some apparently were murdered outright; not one, probably, lived to reach Smolensk. Food was becoming scarce. As far as Mozhaïsk the country was not entirely devastated, and the leading troops had been able to feed their horses; but there was nothing for the rear-guard, whose plight was rendered all the worse by the reckless destruction of shelter by the corps ahead of them. After Mozhaïsk the wasted countryside afforded little or no forage; the horses, already exhausted and over-worked, were reduced to such substitutes for fodder as thatch and autumn leaves, and died by hundreds every day. The destruction of the means of transport meant the loss of much of the already too scanty supply of food. When it was not lost outright it was pillaged by the stragglers and simply served to keep alive these useless beings, while better and braver men died of starvation. By November 3rd such supplies as had been brought were almost entirely exhausted; the only resource of the starving horde was the flesh of the horses which were continually breaking down. The officers, of course, and the head-quarters, were better provided; and some of the men had still remains of their plunder, but these were the exceptions.

The weather was still fine, but it was steadily growing colder, and the half-famished men, ill-clothed, ill-shod, weary with marching, obtained little rest in their chilly bivouacs, and became day by day less able to endure their trials. Those who left the line of march were commonly slaughtered or captured. Capture was often the same thing as lingering death. The peasants, naturally half barbarous, and maddened by the excesses of the invaders, showed little mercy. Sir Robert Wilson tells from his own knowledge how they burned and buried alive their prisoners. Sometimes they were massacred by the women. Even when their lives were spared they were often wholly or partially stripped, and the effect upon frames enfeebled by privation was generally fatal. It is useless to dwell in detail upon the hideous barbarities perpetrated, still less is it profitable to reprobate them. It must be said that if there be but too much testimony to the barbarity of the infuriated Russians, there is also plenty of evidence as to their frequent kindliness and humanity. At their worst be it remembered that they were but retaliating for their own wrongs.

The mass of disbanded troops, which every day grew at the expense of those who remained faithful, consisted in the first place of men already weakened, who therefore fell out early and of course died. Then there were many who had not the spirit to bear up under their misery and wandered along in the crowd until they also fell and died. Lastly, there were large numbers who were simply deserters—often of the worst kind—men who left the ranks before they were disabled and subsisted by murder and robbery. They did more than anything to destroy the army. Some of the leaders of the faithful troops were aware of it. De Fezensac tells how he ordered that no mercy or consideration was to be shown them.

On the other hand, there were very many gallant soldiers of every rank who kept their ranks and did their duty to the bitter end. Russian eye-witnesses were full of admiration at the martial bearing of the scanty and ever dwindling battalions which, with eagles in their midst, moved doggedly on through the miserable horde of skulkers. The officers, with few exceptions, remained firm to their duty. Their intellectual and educational level was upon the whole naturally higher than that of their men, and general good conduct among them was to be expected. They were, too, generally better supplied with food and clothing, and exercised more judgment in providing themselves.

The extent to which demoralisation affected the strategic units of the army is difficult to decide; and the task is a somewhat invidious one. The 3rd Corps certainly appears to have kept the best order and discipline. It had taken a very small part in the demoralising sack of Moscow; but a great deal of its persistent good conduct must be attributed to the personal influence of its chief. The 1st Corps, on the other hand, seems to have crumbled early. Davout was not a very sympathetic personage, and perhaps the care which he had always taken of his men, and his firm discipline, really unfitted them to bear the strain of being in a condition of inferiority to the enemy. At any rate the early demoralisation of the 1st Corps is an established fact. The 4th Corps also rapidly disbanded, as did also, apparently, the 5th and 8th. Of the cavalry we hear little. The Guard took the lion's share of whatever food and shelter was to be had; nevertheless its conduct was not relatively better than that of the 3rd Corps—perhaps not so good, since it never experienced the same trials.

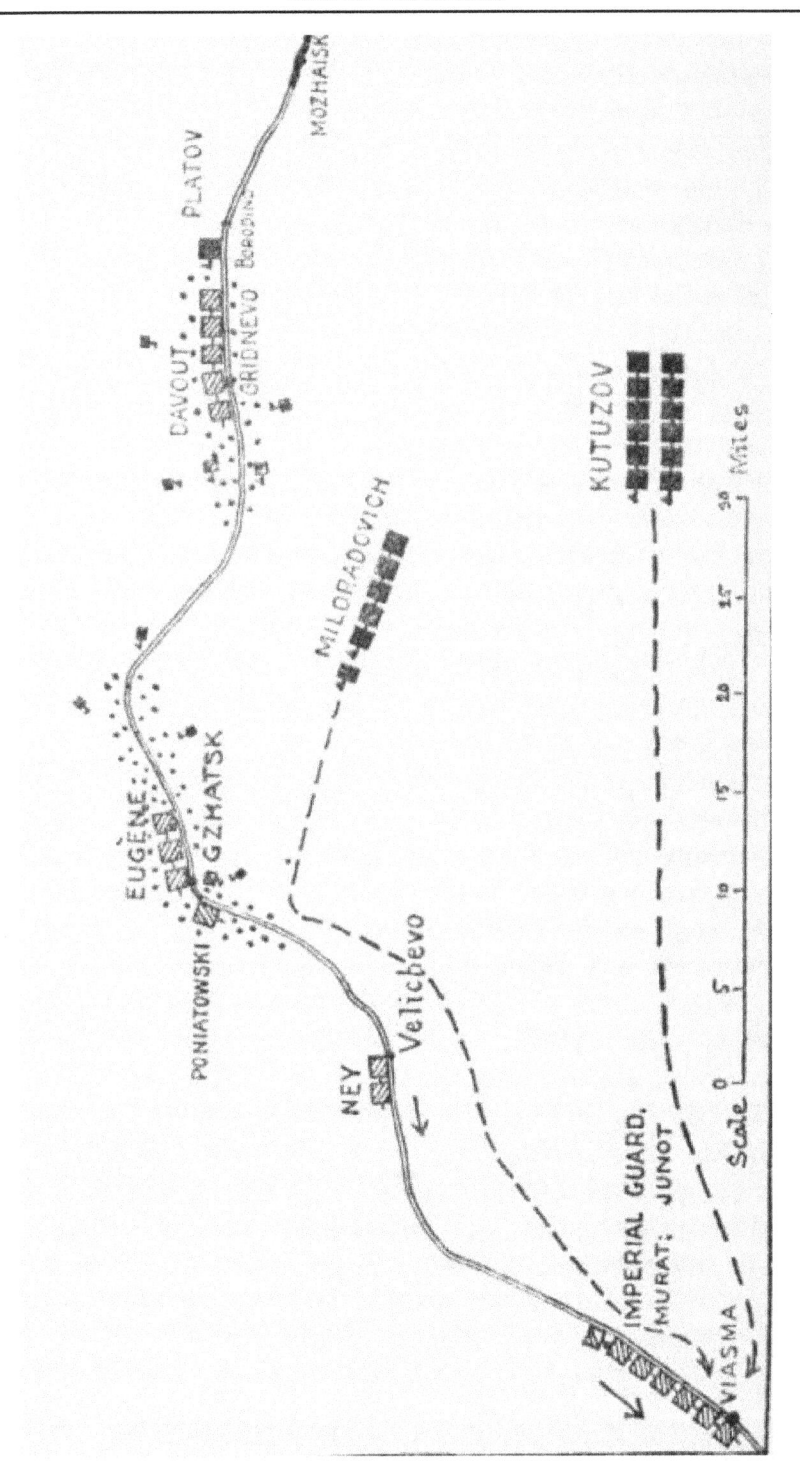

PLAN OF THE APPROXIMATE POSITIONS OF THE FRENCH AND

RUSSIAN MAIN ARMIES ON OCTOBER 31ST, TO INDICATE THE DANGER INCURRED BY NAPOLEON'S EXTENDED ORDER OF MARCH

Napoleon, with the Guard, reached Viasma on October 31st. The cold on this day was greater than it had hitherto been; and the Emperor donned a Polish dress of green, heavily furred, and a fur cap. At Viasma was General Evers' column of drafts. There was also in the place a small magazine of bread, biscuit, flour, and rice. It was pillaged by the leading troops, and so great was the demoralisation that much of the town was destroyed, though thousands tramping painfully behind were thus deprived of shelter. On this day the Guard, the 2nd and 4th Cavalry Corps, and Junot's Corps were about Viasma; Ney one march short of it; Eugène and Poniatowski about Gzhatsk, and Davout at Gridnevo. The line was nearly 70 miles long from front to rear. Miloradovich was near at hand with his cavalry, but his infantry could not arrive before the 3rd. Kutuzov also was marching for Viasma, but was still 60 miles distant.

Davout's slow withdrawal was doubtless dictated by a desire to save as much as possible of the artillery and trains; but in the circumstances it was impossible to do much, and it would have been better to abandon at once everything that fell behind. Lack of shelter, inadequate food, and the steady harassing of Platov was rapidly breaking up the 1st Corps. It had already abandoned 20 guns and much of its trains; the roads were dotted with men and horses dead of fatigue.

Napoleon remained for 36 hours at Viasma, principally occupied with deskwork. He informed the generals in the rear of his retrograde march, representing it as a purely voluntary movement made to come into touch with his wings. From Baraguay d'Hilliers he learned that he had advanced to Selnia, and despatched orders for him to return to Smolensk. From Victor he became aware that the 9th Corps had been forced to support St. Cyr.

General Ilovaïski IV, temporarily commanding Winzingerode's detachment, had reoccupied Moscow on October 23rd. He found there some 1500 sick and wounded whom Mortier had been unable to evacuate, and 42 mounted guns, of which 24 were French.

Ney's corps reached Viasma on November 1st. Miloradovich continued to move parallel to the road, hastening the march of his infantry and anxious to strike a blow. At 11 a.m. on the 2nd Napoleon left for Semlevo. Davout in the evening arrived at a point about 9 miles from Viasma and a little more than 1 east of the village of Federovskoië. Eugène and Poniatowski were between Viasma and Federovskoië. Ney was to take over rear-guard duty as soon as Davout should pass Viasma. Napoleon was angry with the slowness of the latter; but the orders which he issued to hasten the march of the trains could not be executed owing to the deplorable state of the horses. The orders to prevent straggling were equally impossible of execution. None the less, Davout had certainly moved very slowly, and there was some excuse for the Emperor's irritated remark that "the Prince of Eckmuhl keeps the Viceroy and Poniatowski waiting for every band of Cossacks that he sees." In justice to Davout it must be said that the young and inexperienced

CHAPTER XII

Eugène appears often to have delayed him by his own lack of speed.

At 8 a.m. on the 3rd Miloradovich with Korff's and Vassilchikov's divisions reached Maximovo, a village some 2 miles from Federovskoië, and about 1 mile south of the high-road. Davout was passing through Federovskoië, his leading division—Gérard's—being nearly abreast of Maximovo. The Hussars of Akhtyrka, supported by a brigade of dragoons, boldly charged the head of Gérard's column, while the Russian horse artillery opened a brisk cannonade on his flank. The 2nd Corps could not come into action before ten; while Kutuzov was only just leaving Dubna, nearly 30 miles from Viasma.

Gérard's division, attacked without warning, was checked in its march upon Viasma. Platov was close on Davout's rear, and as soon as he heard the sound of Miloradovich's cannonade he pressed home his advance, Paskievich marching straight upon Fedorovskoië, while Platov turned it on the left. Davout saw that there was not a moment to lose in clearing the way before the arrival of Miloradovich's infantry, and hurried his divisions up at the double to support Gérard. Eugène turned back to his colleague's support, while Poniatowski took up a position in advance of Viasma to support Eugène. Ney posted his corps to the right of the town, behind the Viasma river; he threw a bridge across it in order to facilitate the retirement of his colleagues' trains. The river makes an acute angle a little south of the town, so that Ney had it both before and behind him; he threw a second bridge over it to assure his own retreat.

Miloradovich had available for the conflict the 2nd and 4th Army Corps, Paskievich's division of the 7th and Platov's Flying Corps, perhaps 30,000 or 32,000 combatants in all, with some 120 guns. The estimates of the French force vary. Davout may have had 20,000 infantry and artillery, Eugène perhaps 15,000, Ney probably 8000, Poniatowski about 3500. The remains of the corps cavalry and of the 1st and 3rd Reserve Corps probably could not muster 4000 mounted men. The artillery could still count over 300 guns, but the worn-out state of their teams rendered them incapable of manœuv ring. The troops, with the exception of those of Ney, were demoralised.

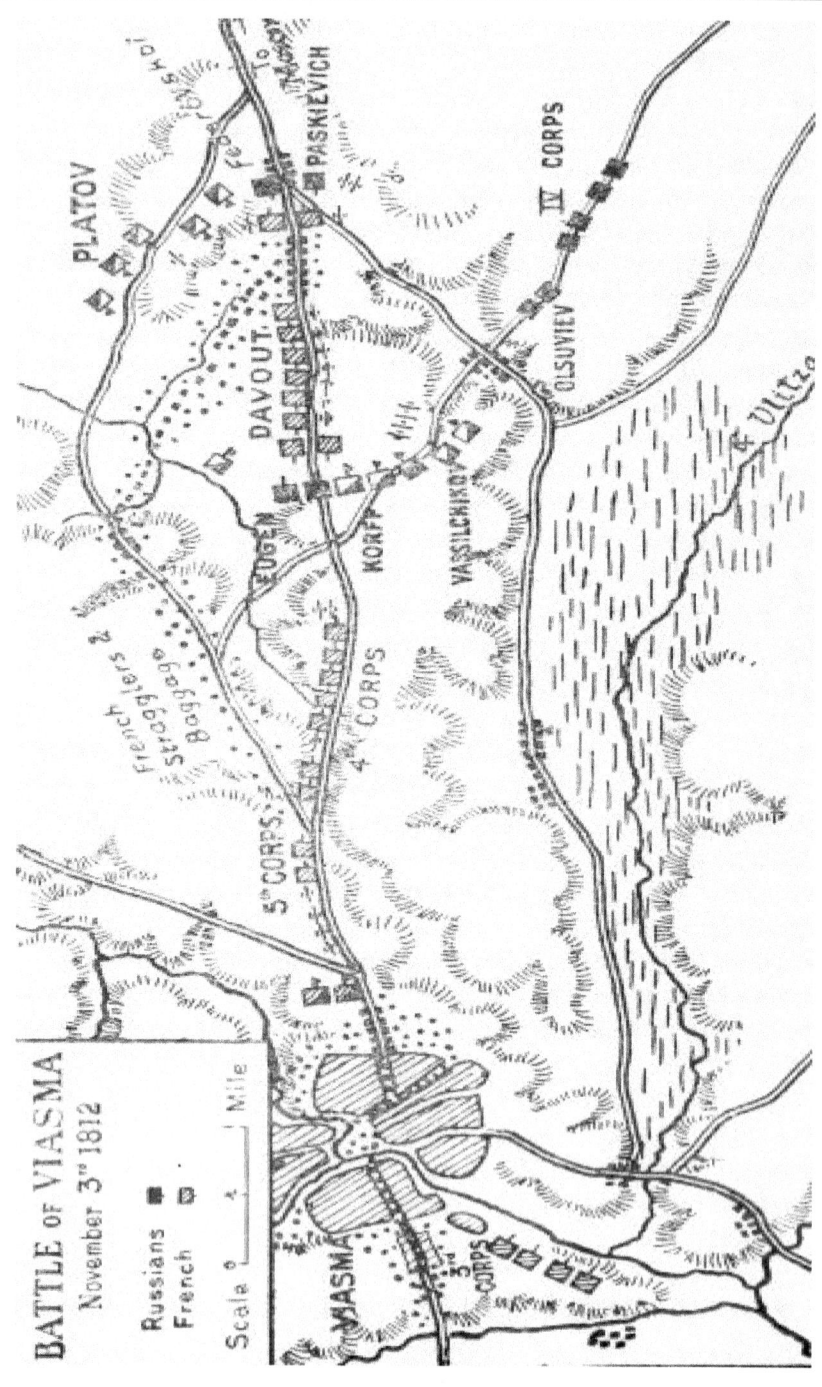

BATTLE OF VIASMA
Positions about 10 a.m.

Davout's troops, ranged in dense battalion columns, attacked the Russian

CHAPTER XII

cavalry on the road and broke through, scattering the hostile squadrons, some of which had to retreat towards the north to join Platov. This appears to have occurred at about 10 a.m. Paskievich meanwhile had carried Federovskoië, and Platov was harassing the French on the right; while Prince Eugen's division of the 2nd Corps formed across the road just as the Russian horsemen gave way and poured a heavy fire into the head of Davout's column. The Marshal's position was extremely critical. The Viceroy, however, was now close at hand with Broussier's and Guilleminot's divisions and the 5th Corps. He cannonaded the flank and rear of the 4th Division and attacked it with a cloud of skirmishers. Its commander believed that he could hold his own, but Miloradovich was of a different opinion, and, seeing the force which was coming from Viasma, he was probably correct. Eugen drew back into line with the rest of the Russian infantry on the south of the road, and Davout's troops were able to defile past. But they had suffered considerably, and the disorder among them was increased by the cannonade beneath which they had to march. The trains streamed away to the north of the road to reach Viasma, while the 1st Corps inclined to the south to come into line with the 4th and 5th Corps. Eugène formed across the road with Poniatowski in support; but as Platov spread to the north he threw back his right wing. Davout's troops were on Eugène's right, nearly parallel with the line of the road. To support and steady them Ney advanced Razout's division, while Ledru's remained to check Uvarov, who was now coming up with Kutuzov's advance-guard. Uvarov, however, who had only the bulk of Golitzin's Cuirassiers under his command, could only confine himself to a desultory cannonade. The head of Kutuzov's column reached Bykovo, 5 miles from Viasma, in the afternoon, but it had marched 22 miles already and could hardly engage that day.

Miloradovich, after Davout had passed, deployed his whole force across the road and marched forward, Eugen's, Paskievich's and Choglokov's divisions in first line, the remaining two in reserve, Platov pushing forward on the right, Korff and Vassilchikov in reserve and on the left. The French generals, fearing that at any moment Kutuzov might debouch in their rear, held a conference on the road, and decided to retreat. The final withdrawal commenced at about 2 p.m. Eugène and Poniatowski succeeded in passing through the town in fair order; but Davout's shaken troops fell back in confusion, hotly pressed by Paskievich and Choglokov. Ney covered the retreat of his colleague to the utmost of his power, and retired through Viasma, burning such of it as remained intact. The French bivouacked in the woods on the west of the town. The night proved bitterly cold.

The French losses are usually stated at 4000 killed and wounded. Those of the Russians may have amounted to 2500. Miloradovich captured 3 guns and about 2000 prisoners, besides some thousands of the disbanded mob. Among the prisoners was General Pelletier, commanding the artillery of the 5th Corps. The French writers attribute the defeat mainly to Davout's error in inclining to his right as he fell back instead of his left, but it is doubtful whether this was more than a subsidiary cause.

On the 4th Kutuzov remained inactive at Bykovo. His troops may have needed rest, but it is extraordinary that he made no attempt to crush or at least to harass the weary, half-starved and beaten French army behind the Viasma. Perhaps he was imposed upon by Ney's bold show in the rear, and the good order of the undemoralised 3rd Corps. It is perhaps difficult to judge him, since we can scarcely appreciate the vast influence exercised by the prestige of the Napoleonic army upon the minds of its opponents everywhere save in Britain. But to say the least, he could and should have done much more.

Ney, early on the 4th, took up a strong position on the edge of the woods. Beurmann was detached to the right to observe Uvarov, whom he held in check during the day. Meanwhile the 1st, 4th and 5th Corps defiled on the road to Dorogobuzh. All were in the greatest disorder. The men were worn out with fatigue and appeared hopelessly discouraged, only the Royal Guard of Italy still marched in fair order. The number of stragglers, of whom the majority had thrown away their arms, was enormous. Ney was much impressed by the disorder of the 1st Corps, and his despatch upon the battle contained some bitter remarks upon it, as well as the haphazard conduct of the engagement.

The substitution of the 3rd Corps for the 1st rear-guard duty was another proof that Napoleon did not really understand the critical state of affairs. Ney was an ideal rear-guard leader, and the 3rd Corps was an intact and undiscouraged force, but it consisted of only two divisions (the Württemberg troops having been amalgamated with the other two) as against the five of the 1st.

At daybreak on the 5th the 3rd Corps withdrew in good order, but followed and impeded by at least 4000 disbanded men of the other corps. De Fezensac, in bivouac that night, ordered all able-bodied skulkers to be driven away by force from the fires. Near Semlevo there was an action with the leading troops of Miloradovich, but the 3rd Corps was not molested on the 6th. Kutuzov, had he pushed forward on the 4th, would certainly have destroyed Ney and probably Eugène also. The Russians were so strong in cavalry that they could always retard the French retreat by employing it vigorously to harass the moving columns. However this may be, Kutuzov on the 5th bent south-westward to Ielnia, while Miloradovich and Platov continued to follow and harass the French rear-guard. Many stragglers were slain or taken by the Cossacks and waggons were abandoned in numbers; but no impression was made upon Ney's corps, which continued its march to Dorogobuzh and there took up a position.

Napoleon had intended to receive battle east of Dorogobuzh. His plan appears in his correspondence, and it can only be characterised as utterly impracticable. It assumed that the whole Russian Army was following on the main road, and also counted upon being able to ambuscade their advance-guard. Even had the army been less reduced and demoralised this would have been impossible, the Russians being so strong in cavalry. The plan was not executed; by the time that he had drawn it up Napoleon had probably read Ney's despatch of the 4th, in which the marshal stated his conviction that only a part of the Russian army was at Viasma. Next day Ney reported that he had learned that Russian columns were passing him on the right; and Napoleon retreated with the Guard upon Mikalevka.

On the 6th and 7th the weather, which had hitherto been by day comparatively mild, changed for the worse, with violent gales and heavy snowstorms. After this the destruction of the army proceeded apace. The horses were the first to suffer; it was impossible to obtain any forage with the ground covered deep with snow. No provision had been made for rough-shoeing the horses, except by the Polish cavalry; and on the slippery surface of the trodden snow they fell in hundreds, to be preyed upon by the starving troops. Vehicles of every kind had to be abandoned; and each was instantly plundered by a group of wolfish stragglers, often to the accompaniment of murder. The number of disbanded men rapidly increased, and their lawlessness and savagery grew even more quickly. Had it been possible to maintain better discipline the state of the army might have been less intolerable. Terrible as the conditions were, they could have been somewhat ameliorated had there been a better sense of comradeship among the troops, which might have prevented so many of them from disbanding and degenerating into veritable wild beasts.

But in truth the misery was so great that the finest loyalty and steadiness could not greatly have alleviated it. Had there been a sufficiency of even the coarsest food, the troops might have withstood the cold. But almost the only resource remaining was the unwholesome flesh of the worn-down horses. Even the officers were often little better off as regards meat, though they could still procure small quantities of biscuit or flour. The troops as a whole were insufficiently clad and, above all, ill-shod; those who succeeded in obtaining a little food were often disabled by frost-bite or injuries to their ill-protected feet. In the hope of guarding against the deadly cold the men overloaded themselves with clothing of every kind and quality, often filthy rags torn from the dead and dying. In their fear of taking a fatal chill they never removed them even for necessary purposes, and dared not wash. In their ravening hunger they ate like wild beasts, tearing the raw or half-cooked horse-flesh with their teeth, and covering themselves and their wretched garments with blood and offal. Their appearance soon became indescribably hideous, and the result of their panic-born neglect was, of course, loathsome disease. Selfishness increased with misery; men thrust their weaker comrades from the bivouac fires, and fought for the wretched carrion on which they strove to maintain their existence; while those who fell were robbed and stripped by passers-by.

THE RETREAT OF THE FRENCH FROM MOSCOW
From the painting by Adam

Amid all this misery and lack of self-respect there was much that redounds to the credit of human nature. Many soldiers added to their hardships by endeavouring to assist the women and children who followed the army. Officers who possessed private carriages gave them up to these unhappy fugitives; those attached to the head-quarters, which was better provided than the rest of the army, succeeded in saving many. Unhappily the most necessary requisite was food, and this the chivalrous protectors could not often give their charges. The hardy female followers could protect and provide for themselves to some extent, but too many of the officers' wives or connections were utterly helpless, and their fate was a piteous one.

One of the most awful incidents of the retreat was the fate of the Russian prisoners, of whom some 2000—stragglers, convalescents, and civilians—were dragged with the army, under a guard made up of fragments and detachments of every nation. From the first the captives were treated with gross cruelty and neglect. The weakly ones who fell behind were done to death without mercy. Every night the survivors were huddled together, fireless, on the bare ground, without food save a little raw horse-flesh. Before long even this was not forthcoming, and the miserable prisoners, driven along and herded together like wild beasts by men who were losing the traces of humanity, perished amid horrible misery. Cannibalism is said to have raged among them. There is no darker stain on the escutcheon of Napoleon (who must be held ultimately responsible) than this treatment of men who were at any rate open enemies, and some of whom were not even combatants.

Day by day the number of men in the ranks dwindled. Every bivouac was the graveyard of hundreds of men and thousands of horses; the line of march resembled a long battlefield. The roads were strewn with dead or dying men and horses, abandoned guns and vehicles, and wreckage of every kind. Amid this streamed westward in wild confusion the endless procession of disbanded men and male and female camp-followers, accompanied by vehicles of all kinds, through which the troops still with the colours could scarcely force their way. Many men were already so weak that they could hardly stumble along. Some became idiotic with privation and the spectacle of the misery about them. The plight of the troops in the ranks was no better; their devotion to duty only prolonged their sufferings. Ill-clad, starving, stricken with cold and disease, often half-blind from the effects of the glaring snow by day and the smoke of the fires at night, it is wonderful that they ever managed, as they did, to make some kind of fight. Their duties, when they had strength to carry them out, were confined to beating off the hovering Cossacks, and to destroying guns and waggons that would otherwise have been abandoned.

From Dorogobuzh Eugène's corps was diverted towards Dukhovchina with the intention of directing it thence upon Vitebsk to relieve the pressure upon Victor by Wittgenstein. The result was its practical destruction.

On November 7th Eugen of Württemberg attacked Razout's division before Dorogobuzh and after some obstinate fighting, partly owing to the indecision of its short-sighted commander, forced it to retreat through the town with a loss of several hundred men and 4 guns. Ney, who had hoped to delay Miloradovich for a day, was obliged to fall back towards Smolensk. Dorogobuzh was choked with disbanded men, who were ruthlessly murdered or stripped by the exasperated inhabitants. A watchmaker boasted of having killed 11 Frenchmen with a knife which he had concealed for the purpose! Miloradovich, however, was then obliged to draw off his infantry towards the south for the sake of food and shelter against the cold. He left the pursuit of Ney to Major-General Yurkovski with a brigade of dragoons and some Cossacks, while Platov followed Eugène towards Dukhovchina.

At Mikalevka Napoleon learned of Malet's audacious conspiracy in Paris, and the tidings doubtless did not tend to relieve his mind. On the 8th Junot's corps arrived at Smolensk; but the day before that ruined town had been invaded by crowds of disbanded troops. Junot was not allowed to pass his corps into it, and cantoned it in villages on the Mstislavl road. Napoleon himself arrived on the 9th, only to be met by bad news from every side.

Victor was proving unable to hold back Wittgenstein. Baraguay d'Hilliers' division, as has been related, had pushed out to Ielnia, and was retiring upon Smolensk, when on this day his rear-guard brigade, 2000 strong, under General Augereau, was surrounded in the village of Liakhova by Orlov-Denisov, with his own flying detachment and those of Davidov, Seslavin, and Figner. Augereau was without artillery, and not being supported by Baraguay d'Hilliers, who showed great irresolution, was forced to surrender. Baraguay d'Hilliers retreated hastily to Smolensk with the rest of his division, and was very properly ordered home for trial. Besides Augereau's brigade several depôts or posts of troops were captured by the Russian advanced detachments. Kutuzov reached Chelkanovo on the

Smolensk-Mstislavl road, about 25 miles from Smolensk, on the 12th. He had not marched very rapidly—some 120 miles in 9 days—but it is true that both roads and weather were terrible. The Russians were well clothed and fairly well fed; but many of the Russian troops were young, and the snowy bivouacs had disastrous effects upon their unformed constitutions.

On this same disastrous day, the 9th, Eugène's corps, after 3 days' struggling through the snow, reached the small river Vop, only 30 miles from Dorogobuzh. The Viceroy had already lost 1200 of his remaining horses and much of his artillery. He had sent on a detachment to bridge the stream, but materials were lacking, and the wretched soldiers were forced to wade. The Royal Guard led the way, with Eugène in their midst, with ice and water up to their waists, formed on the opposite bank and drove away Platov's vanguard, which was already across. Platov himself was tormenting the rear-guard with his light artillery, and threatening the unhappy column in flank and rear. When Eugène had crossed an effort was made to bring over the artillery and baggage. The steep banks of the stream had been hurriedly made practicable for vehicles, but the inclines were quickly covered with ice; the ford was soon choked by guns and waggons sticking fast in the mud, and eventually all but the small proportion which crossed first had to be abandoned. There were terrible scenes on the bank when this became known. A turmoil of fighting, pillage and murder reigned. Many worn-out soldiers, struggling through the icy water, were overcome by the cold and drowned: many others died in the night. Broussier's division covered the rear against Platov all night, and only crossed on the morning of the 10th, leaving behind them many sick and wounded, a vast quantity of baggage and some 60 guns. Hundreds of men, overcome by cold, threw away their arms. The bulk of the corps streamed along the road to Dukhovchina completely disorganised; only the Royal Guard and Broussier's division still moved with some show of order. Dukhovchina was already occupied by Cossacks—the leading regiments of Winzingerode's old detachment, now under Major-General Golénischev-Kutuzov. They, however, of course had to retire before the advance of the Royal Guard, and Eugène occupied the town. It had not yet been plundered, and the exhausted remnants of the 4th Corps were able to obtain food and a little rest. On the 12th Eugène set fire to Dukhovchina and retreated on Smolensk, where he arrived on the 13th, surrounded and harassed all the way by the indefatigable Cossacks. He had with the colours only 6000 or 7000 armed men, and 20 guns at most out of over 100.

Davout's and Poniatowski's[7] troops made their way from Viasma to Smolensk with little opposition from the Russians, but disintegrating day by day under the influence of cold, fatigue and hunger. The Poles seem to have completely broken up, and only about 800 privates reached Smolensk. On the other hand, they saved a large proportion of their artillery, owing to their sensible precautions in rough-shoeing their horses.

Ney reached the Dnieper at Solovievo on the 19th. The approach to the bridge was choked for more than half a mile with abandoned guns and waggons; and be-

---

[7] Poniatowski had met with an accident, and General Zayonczek commanded the 5th Corps.

fore passing Ney ordered his men to fire them. In doing so they came upon some remnants of food supplies and some spirits. In the woods on both sides of the road were thousands of stragglers, largely wounded, whom the omnipresent Cossacks massacred and plundered under the very eyes of their comrades. In the evening the 3rd Corps passed the river and destroyed the bridge. It defended the passage against Yurkovski's brigade, the Cossacks, and some supporting infantry, until the 12th, and then retreated on Smolensk, in weather so awful that even the Russian Löwenstern speaks of it as something exceptional. It was impossible to halt for fear of freezing, while the icebound road was fatal to hundreds of exhausted men. A terrible night in bivouac put the capstone on the sufferings of the devoted 3rd Corps. On the 4th it entered Smolensk—some 4000 men left of more than 11,000 who had marched from Moscow.

It is now necessary to turn aside to follow the fortunes of Napoleon's wings. On October 29th Victor joined Merle at Chasniki, at the junction of the little river Lukomlia with the Ula, about 17 miles south-west of Bechenkowiczi. Dändels had already joined Legrand. Wittgenstein and Steingell united at Lepel on the same day and reached the Ula on the 30th. They were, however, owing to the detachment of Vlastov's division, not more than 33,000 strong, while the 2nd and 9th Corps, even in the absence of Corbineau, mustered 36,000 infantry and 4000 cavalry. Victor therefore decided to attack, and sent to call in Dändels and Legrand. Owing to misunderstandings, however, neither Legrand nor the cavalry of the 9th Corps arrived, and Victor hesitated to attack. Wittgenstein drove Victor's advance troops over the Lukomlia, and brought a mass of artillery into action, which gained the advantage over the French guns. After a long cannonade the action died away, and before dawn on November 1st Victor retreated upon Sienno, about 25 miles east of Chasniki. He had suffered no reverse, and, indeed, had hardly engaged his troops. He may have thought, as De Chambray says, that it would be better to temporise until he was reinforced by Napoleon. Wittgenstein did not pursue, but moved Harpe's division towards Bechenkowiczi to observe Victor's movements. The latter, after remaining for two days at Sienno, turned south-westward to Chereia, about 20 miles north of the Smolensk-Minsk road at Bobr. Whether this move was due to his fear for the highway cannot be determined, but the result was disastrous. On November 7th Harpe attacked Vitebsk, which was now uncovered. The small garrison, under General Pouget, was either killed or captured.

On October 29th, Chichagov started from Brest-Litovsk for Minsk. To hold back Schwarzenberg he left with Sacken the divisions of Bulatov, Lieven, and Essen III, a total of about 27,000 combatants, with 96 guns. Under his own command were the 2 corps of Voïnov and Sabaniev, forming together the *Corps de Bataille* under Langeron, and two advance-guards commanded by Lambert and Chaplitz—33,000 men with 180 guns. Chichagov sent orders to Ertel to advance from Mozyr to meet him. General Musin Pushkin was left with 4000 or 5000 men to guard the Volhynian frontier. The Admiral left Pruzhani on the 30th and reached Slonim on November 3rd. He might have moved more rapidly, but he explained to the Tzar that he hoped to draw Schwarzenberg upon him and be able to strike hard at him before marching upon Minsk. He waited about Slonim until November 8th in this expectation, then, feeling that further delay would be dangerous, started for Minsk. He had, in fact, waited too long already.

Schwarzenberg, having left Kosinski's Poles to cover Warsaw and one of Durutte's regiments to garrison that capital, concentrated the rest of his army at Bieloslok, and marched for Volkovisk, which he reached on November 8th, Chichagov being nearly 60 miles in advance with his way clear before him. On the 14th Schwarzenberg was at Slonim with his Austrians, while Reynier and Durutte were at Volkovisk. Sacken broke up from Brest-Litovsk on November 1st. He left Colonel Witte with 3 battalions and 2 newly joined Cossack regiments to cover his base, and marched for Volkovisk. Between him and his objective lay the extensive forest of Bielovezhi, which he had to skirt, but on November 12th he was nearing Volkovisk, throwing forward his right in order to interpose between Schwarzenberg and Reynier. The latter, fearing to be assailed in flank, fell back upon Volkovisk.

Volkovisk lies upon the right bank of the river Rossi, which flows northward to the Niemen. Hard by the town a rivulet entered the Rossi. Both were now frozen. North of the town are some low heights, and on these the bulk of Reynier's army was posted; but his head-quarters were in Volkovisk itself.

Sacken decided that his best course was to vigorously attack Reynier, so as, at least, to bring back Schwarzenberg to his assistance. It was a bold but perilous resolve, since Sacken was not greatly superior even to Reynier in numbers, and might be taken in rear by the Austrians. In the night of the 14th-15th his advance-guard surprised Volkovisk, driving out its garrison and nearly capturing Reynier. The advance of the Russian column, however, was then checked by Durutte.

On the 15th Reynier took up a position behind the town, his right, consisting of Saxons, resting on the wooded bank of the Rossi, Durutte in the centre, and more Saxons on the left. Sacken was drawn up south of the town, with Bulatov on the right, Essen in the centre, and Lieven on the left.

Early on the 15th Durutte retook Volkovisk. Sacken did not attempt to recover it. The day passed in desultory cannonading, except on Reynier's left, where the Russian cavalry of Bulatov's corps, under Melissino, endeavoured to take advantage of a movement of Saxon infantry to charge, but was handsomely repulsed by their horsemen.

Schwarzenberg, informed of Sacken's advance, left Frimont with about 7000 men at Slonim, and returned towards Volkovisk with the remaining 18,000. On the 15th his advance-guard was already well on the way; but Sacken, misled by the false reports of some prisoners, decided to press home his attack upon Reynier. On the 16th he recaptured Volkovisk, and about midday developed a heavy attack upon Reynier's left, when guns were heard on the road to Slonim nearly in rear of Sacken's centre, and fugitives from the guards of baggage which had been sent there announced that Schwarzenberg was at hand. Sacken at once began to withdraw towards the left, first Lieven, then Essen, finally Bulatov. It was dark before even Essen began his march, and the army retreated safely to Svislozh on the Brest-Litovsk road.

He was hotly pursued by Schwarzenberg and Reynier, the latter following

CHAPTER XII

him on the main road, while Schwarzenberg threatened to turn his right, and interpose between him and the Bielovezhi Forest. During the next ten days there was constant rear-guard fighting, though never of a very severe description, as Sacken made his way back towards Brest-Litovsk. On the 25th he took up a position to cover that place, but his opponents were manifestly too strong for him, and on the 26th it was reoccupied by Reynier. The net result of Sacken's operations was that he had drawn Schwarzenberg far away from the decisive point on the Berezina. On the 25th the Austrian general received a letter from Maret at Vilna, bidding him turn back to support Napoleon. This he at once did, but whatever he might or might not wish it was now far too late. On the 27th, when he set out to remeasure his steps, Napoleon was already crossing the Berezina, threatened by Chichagov and Wittgenstein. Sacken's losses during his brief campaign had been heavy, though certainly they had not approached the figure of 10,000, at which the French estimated them. He had lost also a considerable part of his trains. The losses of his opponents were perhaps about 3000 killed, wounded, and prisoners. The importance of the strategic success of the Russians is not, however, to be expressed in terms of losses.

The remains of the central Napoleonic army were collected at Smolensk by November 13th. The leading troops had thus some five days' rest from marching, but little alleviation of their misery. There had been some 1500 beef-cattle in the villages round the town, but most of these were swept up by the Cossacks who preceded the march of the main Russian army. In Smolensk itself there were considerable stores of flour, grain, and brandy—probably enough to supply the remains of the army for several days. There was also a certain quantity of biscuit, rice, and dried vegetables. The Guard as usual was unduly favoured. Napoleon ordered that it should have 15 days' supplies issued to it, while the other unhappy corps were only to have six. Judging, however, from narratives of members of the Guard, it never received anything like the amount ordered. The men, hungry and improvident, seem to have largely gorged themselves on their rations; a good many sold them at exorbitant prices to others; in this way the survivors of Preising's Bavarian horsemen were able to obtain a little food. Portable mills, which had by this time begun to arrive, were also issued. Even in their misery the soldiers made bitter jests at this provision for grinding flour which was not to be had. Shelter there was little. Eyewitnesses give grim accounts of the wretchedness within the walls. As corps after corps reached the town in their misery the hospitals were choked with sick and wounded, who were literally heaped into these dens of horror without provision of any kind. The cold was worse than it yet had been, and the men were frost-bitten by hundreds. It was fortunate for Napoleon that a thaw set in on the 14th. While in the town the troops had at any rate food enough for immediate needs, the troops of Junot and Zayonczek in the villages outside were left unprovided for, with the result that they pillaged such convoys as passed near them, and ate hundreds of serviceable horses.

The army received indeed considerable reinforcements at Smolensk. Baraguay d'Hilliers' column was distributed among the corps as they arrived. The Vistula Legion was joined by its 3rd battalions, Ney's corps by the 129th Regiment and that of Illyria. It is difficult to state the strength of the army on the 14th, but it may be perhaps estimated at nearly 60,000 men. The Guard still retained about 2500 badly mounted horsemen; all the other cavalry divisions did not muster more than 3000 mounted men between them. The remnant of the Cavalry Reserve—some 2000 sabres—was collected under the command of Latour-Maubourg. Much of the artillery, which had been so far dragged along, could no longer proceed, and 140 pieces were abandoned in Smolensk.

RUSSIAN GRENADIERS PURSUING THE FRENCH ARMY
From the picture by Verestchagin

On the 13th the remains of Eugène's corps poured in wild confusion into the town. An issue of rations was commenced, but the starving men broke from control and pillaged the magazines. Order was restored by desperate exertions, but there had been much damage and waste of precious food. Next day the 1st Corps flooded into Smolensk in a state as pitiable as that of the 4th, and the disorder of this erstwhile best disciplined of the army corps could not be restrained. The storehouses were broken open amid frenzied scenes of disorder and violence; the miserable wretches murdered one another at the doors and in the streets. The provisions were pillaged, a great part of them being of course destroyed in the confusion. Nothing was left for Ney's brave men, who were sacrificing themselves to save the rest of the army, except such remnants as they could obtain by searching for them.

Kutuzov meanwhile was advancing with a slowness and caution which exasperated the more eager of his subordinates and caused some of them to mutter angrily about treachery. On the 14th he marched 13 miles from Chelkanovo to Jurovo, and halted for a day. It may well be, as Clausewitz reasonably remarks, that his firmness was shaken by the deteriorating condition of his own army, which was suffering severely from the cold, and perishing in bivouac at an alarming rate, though, of course, less rapidly than the *Grande Armée*, since the soldiers were fairly well fed. This, however, would probably have impelled a younger and more energetic man to deal a deadly blow at his opponents before his own force melted away. Kutuzov, however, was undoubtedly too old and infirm for the present crisis. Moreover, it is clear that the Russian scouts greatly overrated the French numbers largely because the stragglers were frequently mistaken for fighting men. A good many of them still possessed weapons. Miloradovich left Choglokov's division to watch Ney before Smolensk, and himself with the bulk of his force moved round the town to join his commander-in-chief, while Platov moved past it on the north. On the 16th Kutuzov moved on to Chilova, 4½ miles south-east of Krasnoï, and there halted.

On the 13th Napoleon directed Junot, with the 8th Corps and the remnant of the dismounted cavalry, and Zayonczek, with the 5th Corps, upon Krasnoï. Generals Eblé and Jomini had already been sent forward with detachments of sappers to repair bridges and facilitate the march. But already the disbanded troops had drawn ahead of the organised bodies and were streaming along the highway, pillaging convoys and spreading disorder everywhere. There were small magazines of food at Krasnoï, Liadi, Tolochin, and other places, and a larger one at Orsha. The situation was thus in one sense less unfavourable than before. Unfortunately, however, the Russian army at Chilova was within easy reach of the high-road; and now Napoleon, as though his evil-genius ever directed him in 1812 to do the wrong thing, moved the remains of his army along its front with a day's interval between its corps!

Claparède's Poles, escorting the treasure and head-quarters baggage, and the little left of the reserve artillery, followed Junot. On the 14th Napoleon left Smolensk with the Guard and Latour-Maubourg. Eugène was to leave on the 15th, Davout on the 16th, Ney on the 17th, after destroying the ramparts. Davout was to reinforce Ney with one of his divisions.

On the 14th Count Ozharovski's flying column entered Krasnoï, and began to destroy the stores collected there, but was driven out by Claparède's division, and withdrew to Uvarova, on the Lossmina, 2 miles to the south-east. Early on the 15th Miloradovich, with the 2nd and 7th Corps and the 1st Cavalry Division, reached Riavka, a little way west of Korythnia, just as Napoleon and the Guard were passing. He opened with his artillery, but did not venture to attack the infantry of the Guard, though the opportunity was surely worth seizing. He moved down into the road when the last closed bodies had passed, and picked up 11 abandoned guns and 2000 stragglers. He then moved along the road to Merlino, and took position across it with his front covered by a rivulet, flowing as usual in a difficult gully. Napoleon reached Krasnoï in safety, and the Guard camped about the little town.

Though a thaw was setting in this brought little relief to the sufferings of the *Grande Armée*. Snow fell heavily, and the fatigue of tramping through it was enormous, while the damp foggy weather told almost as heavily upon the men as the bitter cold of previous days. The horses appear to have completely broken down, when after some kind of rest they had to resume the road. The artillery of the Guard, the best appointed of the army, took 22 hours to cover the first 13 miles out of Smolensk, and on reaching Krasnoï 12 of the 24 horse guns had to be abandoned. Half of Latour-Maubourg's cavalry remnant were dismounted in 2 days, while divisions abandoned and destroyed their reserve parks wholesale, being utterly unable to get them through the broken country west of Smolensk. The ravine of the Lossmina, east of Krasnoï, was one of the most fatal to the trains; guns, waggons and vehicles of every kind were literally heaped together to the east of it, where the road passed through a defile.

Eugène left Smolensk on the 15th, but it was difficult to get the worn-down troops and their fatal incubus of non-combatants away from the town, and the 4th Corps by evening had only reached Lubna, about 7 or 8 miles on the road to Krasnoï. On the 16th it continued its march, harassed all the way by clouds of Cossacks. On the afternoon of the 16th it found its way barred by Miloradovich, Kutuzov on the same day reaching Chilova. Napoleon appears at last to have awakened to the necessity of uniting his scattered columns, and remained at Krasnoï in order to allow the 4th, 1st and 3rd Corps to close up. Davout on this day left Smolensk with 4 divisions, and Zayonczek arrived at Dubrovna. The shattered relics of the *Grande Armée* were thus scattered on a line of 60 miles. Even if the Poles and Junot be discounted, owing to their small numbers, the main force was spread over 30 miles of road, while Kutuzov, with his whole army, seriously reduced but in fine heart and fair condition, lay close to its head.

Miloradovich, at Merlino, had the 2nd Corps, under Prince Dolgoruki, drawn up across the road, while Raievski lay parallel with it on the south. Uvarov's cavalry were in reserve. The relics of the 4th Corps totalled only some 6000 combatants and a few guns, besides about 1200 armed stragglers, whom Guilleminot succeeded in collecting and forming. These latter, however, were quickly repulsed, and driven behind the remains of the 4th Corps, which, with Broussier's division on the left, Phillipon's (formerly Delzons') in the centre and Pino's on the right, steadily awaited destruction, cheering defiantly in answer to the heavy cannonade of the Russians. Eugène, of course, rejected with disdain Miloradovich's proposal of surrender, and moved forward. Paskievich's extreme flank brigade was for a moment disordered by Broussier's gallant advance, but the attack was speedily repulsed, and only darkness saved the survivors of the 4th Corps. Leaving Broussier to cover the rear, Eugène filed the other divisions to the right and reached Krasnoï early on the 17th. He had only about 4000 men left. The last guns had been captured, and Broussier's division almost annihilated.

On the 16th, before daylight, Roguet's division of the Young Guard had expelled Ozharovski's detachment from the villages which it occupied to the south of Krasnoï. Roguet, of course, could not pursue his slight success, as the whole Russian army was now nearing Krasnoï, but its effect was to render Kutuzov more than ever cautious and circumspect.

The arrival of Eugène convinced Napoleon that if Davout and Ney were to be saved he must make a stand in order to allow them to close up upon him. The 4th Corps was incapable of taking any part in the action, and he ordered it to defile on the road to Orsha. The infantry of the Guard was drawn up to the south of Krasnoï, Claparède's division in the town, Laborde in the centre, Roguet on the left near the Lossmina ravine. The Old Guard, the cavalry, and Latour-Maubourg's few remaining mounted troopers, with 30 guns were to move back towards Smolensk to meet Davout. Napoleon's total strength amounted to less than 18,000 men, of whom 2500 were cavalry in miserable condition; while only the light artillery of the Young Guard could manœuvre away from the road.

Davout had left Smolensk on the 16th, and his leading division bivouacked for the night about 2 miles past Korythnia. There the Marshal learnt of Eugène's disaster. Sending off messengers to warn Ney that he must hasten his march, he broke up at 3 a.m.

Kutuzov on his side had made up his mind to attack. Prince Golitzin, with the 3rd Corps and the 2nd Cuirassier division, was to attack the Guard in front. Miloradovich, strengthened by Korff's cavalry, was to take position about Larionovo, a little east of the Lossmina, and let Davout go by; but was then to fall vigorously upon his rear, and incline to the left to support Golitzin. Tormazov with the 5th, 6th and 8th Corps, and the 1st Cuirassier Division, was to move to the left and bar Napoleon's line of retreat. Ostermann and Vassilchikov were some distance to the rear, but could easily come up during the day. Exclusive of Platov, who was north of the Dnieper, and the various flying columns, Kutuzov probably disposed of nearly 70,000 regulars, with about 450 well-horsed cannon.

As regards his plan of action, one does not see why Miloradovich should not had attacked Davout directly, Golitzin was too weak to hold the Guard in check, while Tormazov's column was too strong for its purpose. None the less, had the over-elaborate design been vigorously executed, Napoleon's small available force of some 28,000 men might easily have been destroyed.

Early on the 17th Golitzin moved upon Krasnoï, but was checked by Roguet, who momentarily captured the village of Uvarova, driving Ozharovski's detachment across the Lossmina. Golitzin therefore decided to await Miloradovich's co-operation before pressing his advance; while Kutuzov, hearing that the whole Imperial Guard, whose strength and fighting power he enormously overestimated, was at Krasnoï, kept back Tormazov.

Davout's leading division (Gérard's) reached the Lossmina between 8 and 9 a.m., and came into line with Roguet; the remaining three followed. The confusion in the rear was frightful; the trains of the 1st Corps streamed away to the north of the road with the Russian cavalry and Cossacks ranging among them. The panic-stricken drivers cut the traces and fled with the horses, and much of the remaining baggage of the 1st Corps was taken, the spoil including Davout's private carriages, containing, amongst other things, his Marshal's bâton and a valuable collection of maps. Of organised resistance there was little except from small bodies of brave men, who formed here and there to face the cavalry, and for the most part met their death in the performance of their duty. The effect of Napoleon's diversion was that the 1st Corps succeeded in crossing the Lossmina, but its loss was very severe, for it had to defile in square or close column to withstand the charges of the Russian cavalry, exposed all the time to a heavy cannonade.

CHAPTER XII

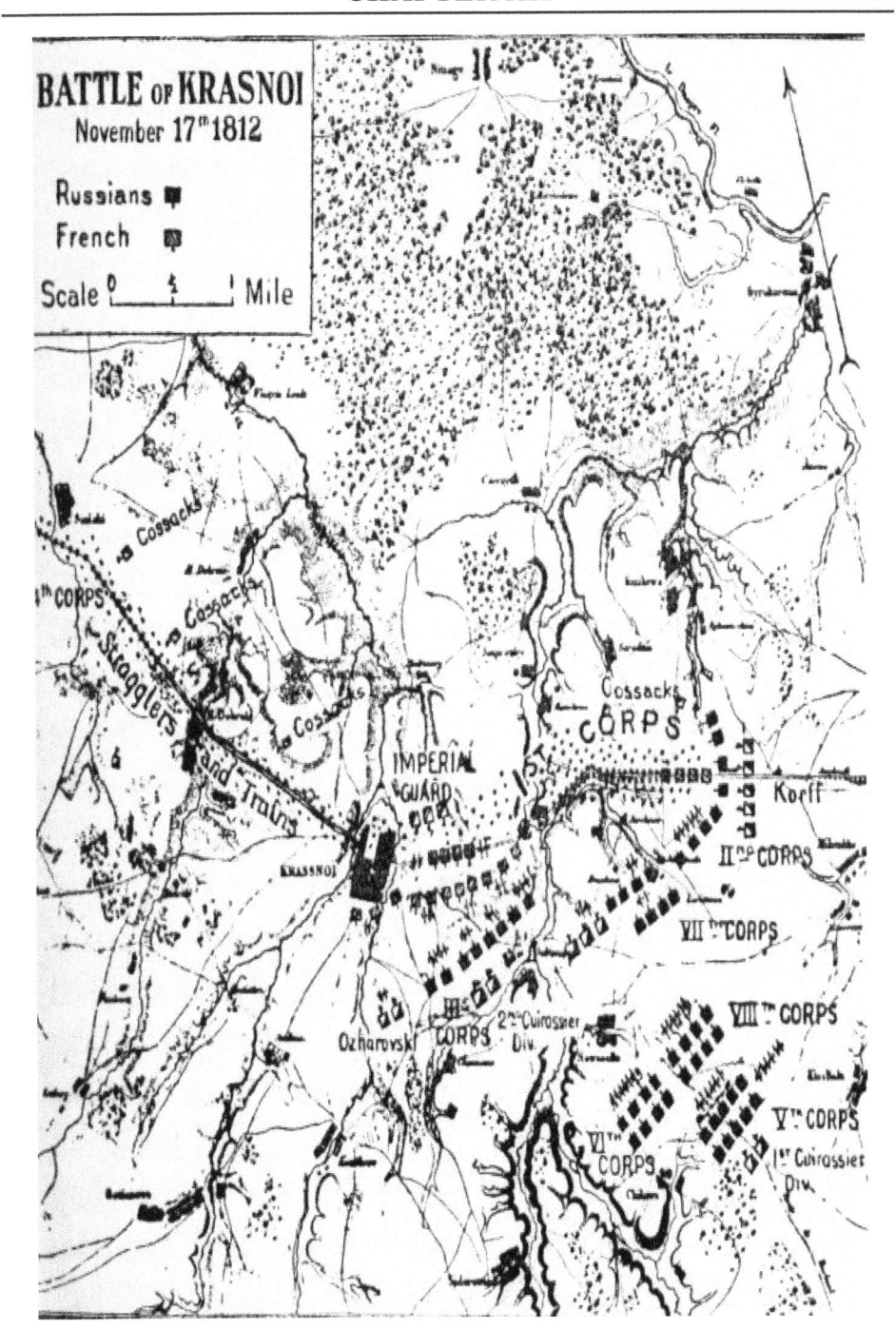

POSITIONS ABOUT 10 A.M. ON THE 17TH WHEN DAVOUT EFFECTED HIS JUNCTION WITH NAPOLEON

As soon as Davout and Mortier had established communication, Napoleon began to retire upon Liadi with the Old Guard and the cavalry, except the Dutch Grenadiers and Lancers, whom he left to support Mortier. Miloradovich and Golitzin were now in touch, and began to press vigorously. A murderous cannonade was directed upon the thin French line south of Krasnoï, and under cover of it the Russian infantry advanced. The Dutch Grenadiers, shattered by artillery fire, fell out of the line, and the young "Flanqueurs-Chasseurs," who were ordered by Roguet to take their place, could not bear up against the iron hail. To support them Roguet sent the 1st Voltigeurs and the Fusilier-Grenadiers. The Flanqueurs were extricated, but the Voltigeurs were charged by Duka's Cuirassiers and destroyed, only forty wounded men escaping. Nevertheless, it was already too late for the Russians to gain any decisive success. Tormazov did not receive his orders to advance until about midday, and the tracks were so bad and narrow that he could not reach the high-road in time to bar Napoleon's march. Some light cavalry were easily dislodged and the Head-quarters and Old Guard reached Liadi in safety. Mortier and Davout followed but, hotly pressed by Miloradovich and Golitzin, lost heavily. The Dutch Guards were nearly destroyed; several of the regiments of the Young Guard were cut up. Nevertheless, Mortier's troops and three of Davout's divisions succeeded in getting away to Liadi, but Friederichs' division, fiercely pressed in the rear, was assailed on the west of the town by Tormazov's vanguard, under General Rosen, and nearly destroyed. The 33rd Léger was all but exterminated, only 25 men remaining unwounded.

Ney had defended Smolensk until the morning of the 17th. On the 15th the 4th Regiment gallantly repulsed an attempt of Choglokov's Division to press the evacuation of the northern suburb. Early on the 17th the force left for Krasnoï. Nothing was known of what was occurring ahead, and Davout has been severely blamed for neglecting to inform Ney. It is probable that his messengers were intercepted. Ney had, including Ricard's division of the 1st Corps, perhaps nearly 9000 men, but with hardly any cavalry, and only 18 wretchedly horsed guns. He was also encumbered by a horde of 7000 non-combatants. Five thousand sick and wounded were left to perish in Smolensk, many being killed by the explosion of the mines which, in obedience to orders, Ney had laid beneath the ramparts. The first day's march was unmolested, but on the 18th Ricard's division, which was in advance, blundered in the fog against Miloradovich, who was in position behind the Lossmina. Surprised and outnumbered by six to one the division lost heavily, and was driven back in disorder along the road to Smolensk. This, however, might have helped Ney, for Miloradovich believed that Ricard's force was really the whole 3rd Corps, and was therefore taken by surprise when Ney, after rallying the remnants of the 2nd Division, came up towards 3.0 p.m. The Russians, on the advice of Paskievich, formed line as they stood, a battery of 24 guns being placed across the road. Ney's force, which looked very formidable through the fog, was much overestimated, and the promptitude with which the marshal cleared away some cavalry from a bivouac on his left impressed the Russians. He, on his side, hoped that he had to deal only with a detachment, though Miloradovich sent an officer to summon him to surrender, and informed him that he had the whole Russian army in his front. Ney detained the officer, shots having been fired during the parley, and ordered the attack. Razout's division went forward with splendid heroism, entered the ravine, breasted its further bank under a furious fire, and almost reached the Russian front when it was crushed by the cannonade and musketry and driven back in wild disorder by a counter-attack of Paskievich's division. The Uhlans of the Guard charged the relics of the 18th Regiment and captured its eagle. General Razout was wounded, General Lanchantin captured; and only a mere remnant of the gallant force succeeded in withdrawing under cover of Ledru's division, which sacrificed itself nobly to cover the retreat. At 4.0 p.m. Ney retreated, and so impressed had Miloradovich been by the magnificent audacity of the attack that he made no effective pursuit.

Ney retrograded a short distance on the road to Smolensk, and then turned to the north. He resolved to cross the Dnieper on the ice and make his way to Orsha by the right bank. He had the ice on a streamlet broken to ascertain its direction, and followed its course until the Dnieper was reached. He made a show of bivouacking at a village, but left his fires burning, and, guided by a captured peasant, found a place where the ice on the great river would bear. A thaw was, however, setting in, and though the fighting men mostly succeeded in crossing, the ice broke under the first vehicles. Guns, trains, and wounded were left to their fate on the farther bank; there remained with Ney about 3000 exhausted and starving foot-soldiers. The only favourable circumstance was that the cold had ceased. But on the 19th Platov was upon them with his Cossacks, and all the way to Orsha they marched in the midst of his squadrons, repeatedly cannonaded by his sledge-artillery. The details of the daring march are vividly related by De Fezensac, but in a work such as this there is little space for them. Ney kept the weary handful of troops together by the sheer magnetic force of his personality. On nearing Orsha the road was found to be barred by fires, but the Marshal ordered the charge, and they were found unguarded, having been lighted in order to terrorise him into halting. At midnight on the 21st the force reached the Vitebsk road about 8 miles from Orsha, where a column which Eugène had led forth to succour it was encountered. So the heroic episode ended. Of the 3rd Corps and Ricard's division there survived not 1500 armed men.

While Ney was making his way to Orsha by the north bank of the Dnieper, Napoleon had arrived there on the 19th. Krasnoï, ill-planned and ill-fought as it was, was Kutuzov's last—or only—serious effort. He remained in the neighbourhood of the battle-field until the 19th, made two marches, halted for a day, and then made two easy marches to Kopys on the Dnieper, south of Orsha. His army was certainly greatly weakened and fatigued; but he might have achieved much by a persistent and resolute advance. The result of his practical inaction was that the small remains of Napoleon's fighting force were able to make their way to Orsha unmolested by the enemy.

In spite of mismanagement and timidity the fighting round Krasnoï was fearfully disastrous. The Napoleonic army had lost probably 10,000 men in action. The Russians claimed 26,170 prisoners, but at least half of these were the disbanded fugitives; over 100 guns were taken on the field, and 112 more had been abandoned. Baggage had been taken literally in heaps. As against this the Russians only admitted a loss of 2000 men; and it is possible that this is not a gross misstatement.

CHAPTER XIII
ORSHA TO THE BEREZINA

Napoleon reached Orsha on November 19th, and at once set strenuously to work to restore order. Stringent orders were given that all stragglers were to rejoin their respective corps in specified localities. What effect these orders produced cannot easily be estimated; demoralisation was so advanced and the mass of disbanded troops so great, that it appears that little could be done to reform the skeleton units.

Something, however, could be done to rally and refresh the scanty relics of the fighting force. There were in the town stores sufficient to supply the troops with food for some days. There were, apparently, fifty guns, some hundreds of horses, and Eblé's reserve train of sixty pontoons with all its equipment. Six batteries were organised out of the artillery, each of six guns. Two went to Davout, who had saved only eight guns out of 150; two to Eugène, who had not one left; two were assigned to Latour-Maubourg—for what reason is not very clear. Mounted cavalry officers were collected into what was called the Sacred Squadron, under Grouchy. It has been stated that it was destroyed as soon as created; but it was certainly in existence a week later.

Severe orders were issued to destroy superfluous vehicles, and to hand over the horses thus freed to the artillery. Generals were restricted to a single vehicle, and soldiers were forbidden to possess carts or pack-horses. These orders were largely non-effective; there were not gendarmes and faithful troops enough to execute them, and too many people interested in resisting or neglecting them—as the passage of the Berezina was soon to show.

Reasonable and necessary as it undoubtedly was to diminish the mass of baggage and assist the artillery, it was surely the height of imprudence to destroy the bridge-train. Eblé, alive to the danger, pressed to be allowed to keep fifteen pontoons, but in vain, and he could only save 2 field forges, 2 waggons of charcoal and 6 of implements. At Smolensk he had seen to it that each man carried a tool, and a supply of clamps and large nails. To his wise precautions the piteous remnants of the *Grande Armée* were to owe their salvation. When Napoleon gave the order to burn the pontoons, Chichagov had been four days in possession of Minsk, and was already close to Borisov with his advance-guard! Comment is needless.

Victor remained at Chereia until November 10th. Oudinot, who had now recovered from his wound, resumed the command of the 2nd Corps. The army at Chereia was thus commanded by two independent generals who would probably disagree. Victor was the senior officer, but not definitely the commander-in-chief; and Napoleon in his orders merely bids him to concert measures with Oudinot. Probably on the 9th, Victor received an urgent order written by Napoleon at Mikalevka, to take the offensive and drive back Wittgenstein. He was told that the safety of the *Grande Armée* depended upon him. The Emperor admitted that it was much fatigued and that the cavalry was dismounted. "March!" ordered the falling giant. "It is the order of the Emperor and of necessity!"

On receipt of this pressing order Victor and Oudinot got under way. But the army was no longer what it had been a fortnight previously. The troops appear still to have been well clothed; they had availed themselves of convoys intended for the Poles. Food does not appear to have been lacking. But the weather was bitterly cold, the ground covered with snow, and the numbers were steadily dwindling. It is probable that the two corps did not muster over 30,000 men on November 14th. Wittgenstein, exclusive of Vlastov, had as many, and his position behind the Ula and the Lukomlia was strong. His army was now distributed in four small corps under Lieutenant-Generals Count Steingell, Prince Iachvil, Berg, and Major-General Fock.

Oudinot is said by De Chambray to have advocated a direct attack, but Victor considered it too risky, and it was decided to endeavour to turn the Russian left. On November 11th, therefore, the French army, the 9th Corps leading, advanced to Lukoml, about 10 miles south of Chasniki, and thence moved eastward across the Lukomlia and the Usveia upon Smoliani, a village lying beyond Wittgenstein's left flank. On the 13th Partouneaux's division, which formed the advance-guard, found that of Wittgenstein in position across the road and drove it back upon Smoliani with heavy loss, including several hundred prisoners. Wittgenstein, seeing that his left was threatened, changed front in that direction and sent forward Prince Iachvil to reinforce and rally the advance-guard. With the rest of his army he took up a position along the Lukomlia. His line extended for about a mile and a half, generally in advance of the frozen stream, its front being covered by three large ponds, beyond which lay Smoliani. Steingell's troops were on the right and Berg's on the left. Iachvil's would form the centre. Fock's division was stationed in the bend of the Ula below Chasniki.

On the morning of the 14th Partouneaux's division moved upon Smoliani, Iachvil retiring steadily before him into the Russian main line. Partouneaux developed an attack on the village, and easily captured it, but was checked by the fire of the Russian artillery. Steingell then sent forward some troops and retook Smoliani. Round this outpost of the Russian line a brisk conflict lasted through the rest of the short winter's day. Its possession was, indeed, of slight importance; and, since the Russians declined to be cowed by the threat of a turning movement, Victor's bolt was practically shot. Except for an attempted demonstration by Victor's cavalry on his right, the fighting elsewhere was confined to a cannonade. The 2nd Corps and the bulk of the Russian army were not engaged at all. On neither side were the losses heavy. Victor may have had about 1400 killed and wounded. The Russians claimed 900 prisoners—probably a great exaggeration. Their own losses during the two days probably totalled 2000.

Victor could now only retreat. He did not know the real state of the central army, but he did know that his dwindling force was Napoleon's last reserve. On the 17th the two corps were once more about Chereia. There they might at least hope to hold back Wittgenstein from the vitally important high-road.

Wrede, after Polotsk, had, as has been seen, fallen back to cover Vilna. He retired through Glubokoië to Danilovichi, and was there reinforced by Coutard's brigade, Lithuanian levies, and various drafts, until on November 18th he had some 11,000 men. Vlastov, after the action of Smoliani, had been drawn in by Wittgenstein, and Wrede reoccupied Glubokoië on the 19th, having previously sent Corbineau to rejoin Oudinot.

At Riga Essen had been succeeded in the command by Paulucci. The field force of the garrison was spread out on the left bank of the Düna. Its line was very extensive, and the troops on the left, under Lewis, were dangerously exposed. On November 15th, therefore, Macdonald made an attack upon them with Massenbach's Prussian cavalry division, a brigade of Prussian infantry and one of Poles. Lewis, cut off and hotly pressed, only succeeded in escaping by crossing the Düna on the ice. This sharp lesson made Paulucci cautious, and some weeks passed away in tranquillity, Macdonald growing more and more uneasy at the bad news which began to filter through to him, and not at all on good terms with Yorck.

While Schwarzenberg was following Sacken, Admiral Chichagov pursued his way to Minsk. The town was full of vast magazines of every kind, besides thousands of sick and wounded. Yet no attempt had been made to fortify it, and the force immediately available for its defence consisted only of two small French battalions, a weak Württemberg regiment, some depôts, and 4 Lithuanian battalions and 4 squadrons newly raised and untrustworthy. Instead of keeping his troops united near Minsk and Borisov, Bronikowski formed a field force under General Kossecki, which he sent forward on the road to Slonim. Dombrowski, hearing of Chichagov's advance, hastened to collect his division, but it was so scattered in his effort to fulfil his multitudinous duties that it could not arrive in time.

Having once made up his mind to ignore Schwarzenberg and push on to Minsk, the Admiral wasted no time. He sent off Colonel Chernishev with a regiment of Cossacks to explain the situation to Wittgenstein, and on November 9th started Lambert and Sabaniev for Minsk. In defence of his slowness hitherto it must be said that, besides the menace of Schwarzenberg in his rear, he was much pestered by orders from Kutuzov, which were usually too old to be applicable to the situation. He was directed to entrench himself on the Berezina, and he had only a single competent engineer officer. He was ordered to reinforce the garrison of Kiev, lest Napoleon should follow the example of Charles XII and move southward! To further weaken his army was madness, but Chichagov diverted some drafts to Kiev, and held on for Minsk, Lambert leading, Sabaniev and Voïnov following, and Chaplitz bringing up the rear. At Nesvizh, on the 12th, General Lüders joined. On the 13th Kossecki's column was found by Lambert holding the bridge over the Niemen at Novi-Svergen. Kossecki had only 4 Lithuanian battalions and a solitary gun. He had vainly represented to Bronikowski the strength of the advancing enemy, and begged permission to retire. Lambert easily carried the bridge, capturing the gun and about 1000 prisoners. Kossecki fell back towards Minsk, and on the way was reinforced by a small battalion of the French 46th, 300 French cavalry, 150 Württembergers and 2 guns. On the 15th he was overtaken by Lambert at Koidanow, 18 miles from Minsk, and, after a running fight of several miles, his force was destroyed, only the remnant of the French cavalry, which had fought splendidly, reaching Minsk. The consequences were fatal. Dombrowski was still over 20 miles distant with his advance-guard; not 1500 troops remained in Minsk and Borisov; and Lambert was already half-way from Koidanow. Dombrowski, who had himself hurried on in advance of his troops, saw nothing for it but to abandon Minsk. Next day Bronikowski, with about 1000 men, retreated on Borisov, while Dombrowski turned his troops back to Berezino, hoping thence to reach Borisov before the Russians. Minsk was occupied by Lambert in the afternoon, and there he found no less than 2,000,000 rations of food and 4700 sick and wounded. The hospitals were found to be in a shocking condition.

Chichagov's whole army was in Minsk by the 18th, and a halt was made to rough-shoe the horses and rest the men. Ertel should have been at hand with his corps; but on pretext of sickness he was still at Mazyr, and only a detachment of 6 battalions, 4 squadrons and a Cossack regiment had been sent forward to Igumen. Chichagov at once despatched Major-General Tuchkov II to supersede him.

On the 19th the Admiral started Lambert for Borisov and Chaplitz for Zembin. Next day Sabaniev marched in the track of Lambert, and Voïnov after Chaplitz. Chichagov accompanied Voïnov, while Langeron was with Sabaniev. A small garrison was left in Minsk, and the Cossack Colonel Lukovkin sent towards Igumen to observe Dombrowski.

Bronikowski had at Borisov and Vseselovo less than 2000 men. Dombrowski reached Borisov at midnight on the 20th, bringing with him 6 battalions and 6 squadrons of his division; his other infantry regiment and 2 squadrons were still behind. Arriving in the dark he bivouacked on the left bank. A French battalion occupied the *tête du pont*, the 7th Württembergers Borisov; the rest of Bronikowski's force was at Veselovo, several miles higher up the river opposite Zembin.

Lambert had with him 5 infantry regiments, 28 squadrons and some Cossacks—about 8000 men and 36 guns. Against him Dombrowski could bring less than 5000 in all, with, apparently, 34 guns.

Lambert attacked the bridge-head early on the 21st. The French battalion was driven out, but the Württembergers hurried up from the rear, repulsed the Russians, and gave Dombrowski time to arrive. Again and again Lambert assaulted the works in vain; and the fight raged obstinately well into the afternoon, the 1st and 6th Polish regiments, with their French and German comrades, resisting with magnificent courage. Lambert himself was dangerously wounded. Towards evening, however, the 14th Chasseurs succeeded in turning the works on the right by slipping through a gully, while the bulk of Lambert's division again assailed them in front. They were finally carried, and the adventurous 14th pressed on so impetuously that they passed the bridge with the flying foe and saved it from destruction. The remains of Dombrowski's force were hurled through the town in utter confusion, despite their desperate attempts to rally, and pursued by the Russian cavalry towards Lochnitza, on the road to Orsha. Langeron arrived with his leading troops towards the close of the action, and in the evening was joined by Chichagov and Voïnov.

On the Russian side more than 1500 men were killed and wounded, General Engelhart being among the former and Lambert among the latter. Dombrowski's force lost over 3000 men killed, wounded, and prisoners. Twenty-four guns were taken by the victors.[8] Dombrowski's rear-guard regiment was attacked on the march by Colonel Lukovkin, and severely mauled before it could recover from the surprise and beat off the Cossacks.

The position of Napoleon now appeared desperate. Seventy thousand men, inspirited by success, were preparing to bar his retreat to the frontier; Minsk and Vitebsk with their magazines, Borisov with its all-important bridge, had passed into the enemy's hands, and Schwarzenberg, with the one powerful force that remained at Napoleon's disposal, had been drawn far away to the south-west. The Emperor had with him about Orsha only some 25,000 demoralised men, surrounded by a helpless mob of 40,000 non-combatants of both sexes, the majority in the last stages of misery and despair. He had scarcely any effective cavalry, and not more than 110 badly horsed guns, while to his left rear was a pursuing army three times his strength. So must the position of the defeated conqueror have presented itself to his dismayed followers. It now remains to review the circumstances which rendered it, terrible as it undoubtedly was, somewhat less critical than it might have been.

After Krasnoï, Kutuzov had practically abandoned the pursuit. The condition of his army was very serious; the number of men in the ranks was diminishing daily, while the horses were rapidly breaking down under the effects of hard marching, little forage, and constantly remaining saddled. Buturlin states that the loss by fatigue and hardship since October 24th already amounted to 30,000 men.

In direct pursuit of Napoleon, Kutuzov sent forward the various flying columns and Cossack detachments, and a special force under Yermólov, consisting of the Chasseurs of the Guard, six battalions of Dokhturov's corps, 2 regiments of Cossacks and 12 guns. The united force of these detachments may be estimated at 20,000 men and 40 guns. The vanguard of Miloradovich, which was to follow in support, totalled also about 20,000 men. A regiment of Chasseurs had been left to garrison Smolensk. With the rest of the army Kutuzov marched slowly to Kopys, which he reached on the 24th, Miloradovich being about two marches farther on, and Yermólov and Platov were in advance of the vanguard. Kutuzov left the guns of 12 batteries at Kopys, using their men and horses to complete weakened units, and detailed to escort them the remains of the light cavalry of the Guard. On the 26th he left Kopys with a force reduced now to about 40,000 men and 200 guns. Napoleon was already at the Berezina, and for all practical purposes the Russian Grand Army was off the board at the decisive moment. What was worse, though his information was naturally out of date, Kutuzov still endeavoured to control the operations of Chichagov and Wittgenstein.

[8]   Langeron.

CHAPTER XIII

Chichagov on the Berezina was in a state of great uncertainty. His army was not now more than 33,000 strong, and his 10,000 cavalry were almost useless on the wooded and marshy banks of the river. He was without information of the main armies later than the evacuation of Moscow. On the evening of the 21st the Comte de Rochechouart, one of the Admiral's French *émigré* staff-officers, found among Bronikowski's half-burnt papers a despatch from Victor, stating that Napoleon would probably reach Borisov on the 23rd. The news must have been something of a shock to Chichagov, since he naturally expected to be attacked by greatly superior numbers. His conduct at this juncture has been sharply criticised, yet one does not well see what else he could have done. He moved forward the advance-guard, now commanded by Major-General Pahlen II, towards Lochnitza, on the Orsha road, to give warning of any hostile advance, established his head-quarters in Borisov, and kept the bulk of his force on the right bank of the river. His errors appear to have been that he allowed too much of his baggage trains to cross, and permitted a large detachment of his cavalry to disperse to forage; the latter step may, however, have been necessary. The point is that Chichagov was ignorant of the deplorable condition of the Moscow army, and rather expecting to be himself attacked.

Wittgenstein, on his side, possessed very scanty information about the general state of affairs, and his staff estimated Napoleon's strength as at least 60,000. The result was that his movements were extremely slow and circumspect.

In other words, while the destruction of the remnant of Napoleon's forces was inevitable if all his adversaries showed energy, it was already becoming apparent that this would not be the case, and that he would have an opportunity of escaping.

Napoleon learned of the fall of Minsk while on the march to Orsha, and despatched orders to Oudinot to march to Borisov to secure the passage. On the 20th Victor was directed to cover the march on Borisov, which he was to reach on the 26th.

Oudinot was timed to arrive on the 24th, and since he had only about 50 miles to march, the Emperor did not imagine the position to be desperate. Oudinot, perhaps more alive to it, reached Borisov on the 23rd. On the 22nd he was rejoined by Corbineau, who, after a skirmish with Chernishev's Cossacks, found himself cut off from Borisov by Chichagov's army, and was guided by a peasant to a ford at Studianka, about 8 miles higher up.

Napoleon, with the Guard and head-quarters, left Orsha on the 20th and arrived on the 22nd at Tolochin. There were in the place considerable stores, and Napoleon halted for 24 hours. There he was joined by Ney with the relics of his command, Davout now resuming rear-guard duty. Platov occupied Orsha on the afternoon of the 21st. He captured 21 abandoned guns, some stores, a mass of trains, and thousands of sick and wounded, all of whom perished. The Russians had not the means of succouring them, even had they possessed the will to do so.

Junot and Zayonczek, with the remains of the 5th and 8th Corps and the dismounted cavalry, were in advance; then came the Guard and head-quarters, Ney,

Eugène and Davout. Davout may have had remaining about 6000 men, Eugène perhaps 3000, Ney 1500, Junot and Zayonczek possibly each 1000; to the former were attached about 1000 dismounted horsemen. The Guard may have been 9000 infantry and artillery and 1500 cavalry strong. A few hundred only of the line cavalry still retained horses. It was with the greatest difficulty that the fighting troops could force their way through the helpless horde of stragglers and disarmed fugitives which covered the road. The armed soldiers themselves presented a miserable spectacle. A mournful silence reigned in the shattered ranks; the men plodded along mechanically, huddling themselves in their rags; little was heard save the shuffling of feet in the snow and slush. Vaudoncourt records his feelings of horror when he met the advance-guard and saw the dismounted Cuirassiers, ragged, bare-footed, emaciated, wretched beyond belief, dragging themselves painfully along the roads.

An incident typical of the absolute callousness to which misery had reduced everyone is related by Lejeune, who had succeeded Romœuf as Davout's chief-of-staff. At Krupki, near Borisov, Davout's staff found two babies in the house occupied by them. Lejeune begged the Marshal's steward to try and give them a little broth. None was forthcoming, and the steward at last, distressed by the continued wailing of the little creatures, drowned them! Wilson, too, tells how the Grand Duke Con stantine, out of sheer humanity, as he declared, "put out of his misery" a stripped and perishing French officer.

NAPOLEON, BERTHIER, MURAT, AND RAPP (IN THE ORDER NAMED) ROUND CAMP FIRE
Russian peasants brought in prisoners by French Chasseurs-à-cheval

CHAPTER XIII

From the picture by Verestchagin

On the 22nd Napoleon heard from Oudinot that Chichagov had captured Borisov and that he himself was on the way to retake it. The Emperor replied in a somewhat incoherent letter, instructing him to seize a point of passage, and interspersing orders and intelligence with agitated appeals to the Marshal's energy and devotion. The last were not needed. Oudinot's intellectual capacity was not great, but his devotion was undoubted, and he never served Napoleon so well as in the terrible days that followed.

Oudinot on the 23rd picked up Dombrowski and the remains of his force. He placed the remains of his cavalry at the head of the advance, with Legrand's division in support; and in the afternoon fell upon Pahlen near Lochnitza. The Russians were taken entirely by surprise, largely apparently because of their leader's negligence, and, veterans as they were, broke and fled headlong. They poured in mad panic into Borisov just as Chichagov and his staff were dining. Everybody seems to have lost his head, and the place was abandoned in haste and complete disorder. All the baggage which had crossed the river was left behind as the prey of the 2nd Corps—much to its benefit. Voïnov hurried up 4 battalions, which occupied the houses near the bridge, and enabled the panic-stricken mob to crowd across in safety. The bridge was then broken, and despite their really brilliant success the passage of the river was closed to the French. The Russians had lost in their panic flight about 1000 men in all and a quantity of baggage, including the Admiral's camp service and portfolio; but no guns were lost—probably rather owing to good fortune than good management. Langeron sneers bitterly at his chief, but the fault was obviously that of Pahlen and his advance-guard, who should not have permitted themselves to be surprised by a small force of cavalry.

On November 23rd Napoleon with his leading troops reached Bobr, a town of 300 houses, about 35 miles from Borisov. Victor was falling back towards the road from Chereia, and on this day Billard's brigade of Partouneaux's division had a sharp encounter with Wittgenstein's advance-guard under Vlastov. Billard was driven back with considerable loss, which was, however, much exaggerated by the Russians, though a battalion of the 126th Regiment was completely destroyed. Wittgenstein might have done much more, but he was very circumspect and timid, and Clausewitz hints that he was not greatly disposed to co-operate cordially with Chichagov. The latter expected him to unite with his own army behind the river, according to the Tzar's directions; and so also did Napoleon, who ordered Victor to endeavour to bar his march on Zembin. The Marshal could not obey, for he was already too far south, having acted upon previous instructions given when Napoleon was still uncertain as to the point at which he should cross the Berezina. Otherwise Napoleon till the last dangerously underestimated Wittgenstein's strength, and wrote as if Victor could easily defeat him.

At Bobr Napoleon received the crushing news of the failure to save the bridge of Borisov. All now depended upon the bridging of the river. Eblé, with his pontonniers and his inestimable convoy of implements, was ordered forward, while General Chasseloup was directed also to the Berezina with all the sappers and artificers who could be collected, but they were without forges and almost destitute of ordinary hand tools. Stringent orders were given to destroy superfluous vehicles and hand over their horses to the artillery. Needless to say, they were generally evaded. Davout was directed to hold firm as long as possible in order to give the miserable mob of non-combatants time to escape. It would have been better had the humane order never been issued. Most of the non-combatants were doomed, and the lives of devoted officers and soldiers were wasted in protecting them. At Bobr d'Alorna rejoined with the garrison of Mohilev. His 1500 men and the remains of the 5th Corps and Claparède's division were united to the relics of the 3rd Corps, thus giving Ney a force of about 6000 men and 30 guns.

Oudinot also, on the banks of the Berezina, was doing his best. He was, as usual with Napoleon's generals, timid of responsibility; but having made up his mind he acted with excellent judgment. Having obtained, despite all difficulties, information as to the points of passage, he, about midday on the 24th, selected Studianka, and directed thither his small, ill-trained, and ill-equipped force of artificers. He informed Napoleon frankly of the difficulty of his task; the enemy were keenly watching the course of the river. To distract Chichagov he made demonstrations above and below Borisov, and noted that the Russians seemed inclined to expect the French advance rather below than above. Napoleon, after a conference with Generals Dode and Jomini, who knew the course of the river, also decided to force a passage above Borisov, and indicated the ford at Veselovo, 15 miles above that town. When the order arrived, however, the Marshal had already selected Studianka.

The frost, which had ceased since the 18th, was now setting in again. On the one hand, the slightly alleviated misery in the army now again began to increase. On the other, it hardened the low, marshy banks of the Berezina and enabled the French to transport their artillery and trains. Opposite to Studianka, about a mile from the right bank, ran the Borisov-Zembin road, by which the army must defile in order to gain the Minsk-Vilna highway at Molodechno. Behind Studianka the ground rose, and artillery could be placed in position to command the low opposite bank. Studianka itself was a fair-sized village, and its houses afforded timber useful for the construction of bridges.

We must now turn to Chichagov, who has been made by Russians the scapegoat for the escape of Napoleon. In the first place, he believed that Napoleon had 70,000 or 80,000 men against his 32,000. Next, he had been informed by Wittgenstein that Napoleon was, in his opinion, retreating in the direction of Bobruisk. The Admiral was confirmed in this by intelligence that Austrian cavalry scouts were on the Minsk-Bobruisk road. Chichagov's dispositions in these circumstances were perfectly sound. Chaplitz, who had been watching the upper Berezina for some time, remained near Brelova, nearly opposite Studianka; while Voïnov and Sabaniev, with Pahlen's rallied force, were concentrated round Borisov, ready to act in force in any direction.

On the 25th he received a despatch from Kutuzov. It was not a direct order, but, coming from the commander-in-chief, it naturally had great weight with the Admiral. It suggested that Napoleon would probably move southward towards

Bobruisk to cross the lower Berezina. At the same time, Major-General O'Rourke and Colonel Lukovkin reported that they had found Polish troops lower down (these were Dombrowski's belated detachments).

Chichagov, assuming that Kutuzov had good reason for sending his despatch, and considering the intelligence sent by his detachment commanders, concluded that Napoleon's rumoured southern movement was a reality; and, on the 25th, leaving Pahlen at Borisov, and ordering Chaplitz to draw in to him, he marched off with Voïnov and Sabaniev to Chabachevichi, some 15 miles down the Berezina. Langeron says that both he and Sabaniev endeavoured to dissuade him—Sabaniev apparently losing his temper. Chichagov, however, persisted, and considering everything it is difficult to see what else he could have done, misled as he was by bad information from every side. On the 25th Napoleon himself reached Borisov, and was seen by Langeron and his staff, much to their consternation, as the only force at hand to oppose him was Pahlen's weakened advance-guard. The French Guards were in Borisov; the rest of the Moscow remnant between Borisov and Krupki, two marches to the rear. Oudinot was at Studianka; Victor rather to the north of Davout at Krupki, in order to cover him against Victor. Davout since Orsha had been only harassed by Cossacks. The bulk of Wittgenstein's slowly advancing force was at Kolopenichi, 27 miles north-east of Borisov: Platov was east of Krupki, and Yermólov at Maliavka, near Bobr.

General Aubry, Oudinot's chief of artillery, began to fell trees and construct trestles for bridges immediately upon arriving at Studianka, but unfortunately they proved too weak. As soon as it was dark Oudinot started his artillery for the selected point of passage, and as night drew its veil over the dreary banks of the Berezina, Generals Eblé and Chasseloup reached Studianka with their men and their slender equipment, and began in earnest to construct bridges. All night they laboured to prepare the supports, and at 8 a.m. on the 26th the first trestle was fixed in position. It had been hoped to throw three bridges, but there were scarce enough materials for two. Chasseloup soon saw that the hopeless deficiency of equipment of his engineers would prevent him from doing anything independently; he therefore brought his men to help Eblé, the engineers working at the preparation of trestles and floors while the pontonniers fixed them.

The fate of the relics of the *Grande Armée* now rested, humanly speaking, in the hands of a prematurely aged and physically broken man of fifty-five years of age, who had never, under Napoleon, received employment equal to his merits. The name of Jean Baptiste Eblé is one to be uttered with all honour and reverence as that of a man who, besides being a master of his profession, was in very truth a hero, upright, modest, self-sacrificing, and literally faithful unto death. One seeks not for purity or an exalted standard of duty among the rough and greedy fighters about Napoleon. Exceptions there were, but they were comparatively few; and so one turns with peculiar respect towards the simple, gracious figure of Eblé.

Early on the 26th Eblé verified the width and depth of the river. The latter had increased, owing to a freshet, since Corbineau's crossing from 3½ feet to 5.

Besides pushing on the preparations for the bridges, the engineers constructed three small rafts, by which some 400 infantry were ferried over to guard the bridge-head, accompanied by some of Corbineau's troopers, who forded the river with foot soldiers behind them.

The cold was bitter; the water was already freezing; and the pontonniers would have to work in it up to their shoulders. The ordeal meant certain death to almost all; but the men answered the call of their chief with a heroism as high as his own. They were relieved every 15 minutes and were promised special rewards, but five-sixths of them perished. There were 7 companies in all, about 400 men, of whom 100 were Dutch.

The bridges were placed 200 yards apart. Each had 23 sets of trestles (*chevalets*). That on the right was intended only for troops. It was terribly weak. Suitable wood for the roadway was lacking, but the engineers patched up one of planks nailed one upon another, and laid brushwood and twigs upon it to lessen the strain. The roadway was in places nearly level with the water; there were no rails. The left-hand bridge was intended for artillery and baggage. It was more solid than the other; but still very weak, and as there was no time to square them the roadway was constructed of rough logs, the passage over which of vehicles occasioned continued joltings which impaired the stability of the frail structure.

GENERAL BARON EBLÉ
Commander of the Bridge Trains of the Grand Army in 1812

CHAPTER XIII 239

Napoleon himself, with his Head-quarters and Guard, reached Studianka early on the 26th. He came to the head of the bridges and there remained until they were completed, personally supervising the construction. In the intervals when he could do nothing he sat on a pile of logs on the bank, gloomily gazing upon the slowly progressing structures on which his last hopes rested. More than once he asked Eblé to hurry. The General pointed to his devoted pontonniers working themselves to death in the icy stream, and the Emperor could say no more. What he could do to relieve them he apparently did, sometimes helping with his own hands to serve them out brandy.

The artillery of the Guard and of the 2nd Corps was massed behind Studianka ready to open fire as soon as the Russians should show themselves. But Chaplitz was already withdrawing through the woods to Borisov; only a weak rear-guard with 2 light guns remained opposite the village. Chaplitz's worst fault was to neglect to destroy the long wooden bridges on which the Zembin road crossed the marshes. He was a brave and a good officer, but on this occasion failed much in the performance of his duty.

At 1 p.m. the right-hand bridge was completed, and at once Napoleon gave the order to Oudinot's corps to cross. With the addition of Dombrowski's Poles it appears to have been nearly 11,000 strong. Some of its regiments were reduced to mere skeletons; but others were still relatively strong. They were generally well clothed and in good order, and their still unbroken spirit appeared in the lately unaccustomed cheers with which they hailed Napoleon as they defiled past him. The Swiss regiments were especially solid and eager. Only 2 guns were taken across for fear of injuring the bridge. The advance-guard easily cleared away Chaplitz's feeble rear-guard, and moved forward on the Borisov road until it found Chaplitz, reinforced by Pahlen, in position across its path. Reconnaissances despatched to Zembin found the Vilna road clear, and the Emperor decided to give up any intention of reaching Minsk and to move upon Vilna.

The heavier bridge was ready at 4 p.m., and the artillery of the Guard and Oudinot's corps began to pass. At 8 p.m. three sets of trestles gave way. Half the pontonniers were called upon and, worn out with desperate toil and sunk in sleep as they were, they answered Eblé's call. By 11 p.m. the breakage was repaired, and the rest of the artillery, the remains of the reserve park, and Ney's corps began to cross.

At 2 a.m. on the 27th the bridge broke in the centre; three sets of trestles were destroyed. The second half of the pontonniers were called upon. Eblé himself chose good sound wood and superintended the making of new ones, while the heroic pontonniers sacrificed themselves as nobly as before. At 6 a.m. the damage was repaired and the passage proceeded. The bridge broke again at 4 p.m., two trestles giving way. It was repaired by 6 p.m.

The supports of the troop bridge held firm, but the weak roadway was continually breaking, and the devoted engineers were at work upon it with little intermission. It was so frail and swayed so badly that it is remarkable that it did not collapse.

Napoleon, with the Head-quarters and the Guard (less Claparède), crossed about 1 p.m. on the 27th. As yet no very great number of the non-combatants had arrived, and they were mostly employees of the army who crossed with their corps. The disbanded mob was flocking into Borisov ahead of Eugène and Davout. It was amenable to no control, and, as aforesaid, Napoleon's order to the rear-guard to hold back was little likely to save it from destruction.

Chichagov, on reaching Chabachevichi, sent patrols across the river which failed to locate the enemy, and the Admiral became aware that he had been misled. He once more turned his troops towards Borisov, which they re- entered on the evening of the 26th. He directed Langeron to do what he could to reinforce Chaplitz, adding that he was coming up with all speed. Everybody, according to the bitter Langeron, was cursing "this miserable sailor." They, however, did not know the circumstances, and might have cursed the high and well-born Prince Golénischev-Kutuzov with better reason. Langeron took forward Pahlen's infantry to reinforce Chaplitz; he says—certainly with exaggeration—that there were only 1200 of them. Voïnov's and Sabaniev's troops, after a 30 miles march in frost and snow, were in no condition for battle, and the Army of the Danube had to remain at rest on the 27th. Without wishing entirely to absolve Chichagov, it appears to the writer that the chief blame must be laid upon Kutuzov, who lagged behind and sent misleading intelligence. Blame also attaches to Chaplitz for his negligence at Zembin. Yet it must be observed that he probably expected, with the rest of Chichagov's officers, that Napoleon would retreat upon Minsk, and therefore drew in the detachment, which might otherwise have been cut off. Chichagov cannot be blamed for resting during the 27th. Borisov was full of French, who might attempt to force a passage there. They were mostly non-combatants, but this could not of course be ascertained with certainty. For the rest his troops were weary.

Wittgenstein was probably more blameworthy than the much abused Admiral. His pursuit of Victor was unenergetic; despite his double superiority of numbers, he made no attempt to press. He was in fear that Napoleon would turn his own right flank and retreat by Lepel to Vilna; and this was in fact one of the Emperor's alternative plans. He moved so cautiously that on the 25th his advance-guard did not touch the rear-guard of Victor, who fell back unmolested towards the high-road at Borisov. Reconnaissances made it clear that Napoleon was not moving past the Russian right and Wittgenstein advanced to Kostritza, only 8 miles from Borisov and about 10 east of Studianka. Victor reached Borisov in safety; and Eugène and Davout moved on to Studianka, where they arrived at dusk on the 27th. Victor's move, however, had evil effects; his troops came upon the line of march of the unhappy fugitives from Moscow, and the awful condition of the latter spread demoralisation in the ranks of the 9th Corps. The 2nd Corps had already come in contact with the woeful relics of the Guard and Ney's corps, and their morale was affected. At Kostritza Wittgenstein learned that the French were at Studianka, but instead of marching thither he directed part of his troops on the 27th on Borisov, part on Staroï Borisov, some miles above the former place. Platov was in touch with Wittgenstein, and Yermólov was on the march to Borisov. There were thus, of Russian troops, on the Berezina the army of Chichagov, 32,000 strong with 180

CHAPTER XIII 241

guns, that of Wittgenstein at least 31,000, and Yermólov's and Platov's columns, say 12,000 men and 30 guns, in all 75,000.

As against this large and eager, if partly irregular, force Napoleon is said by De Chambray to have had barely 31,000 men. This figure is certainly too low. De Fezensac believes that he had 50,000 men; and on the whole it is possible that the total number of combatants was about 47,000. It was composed as follows: Guard (less Claparède) 8500, Ney about 5000, Davout 3000, Eugène 2000, Junot 1500 (including dismounted cavalry), Oudinot 11,000 (including Dombrowski), Victor 13,500, Head-quarters 2500. The last item is usually ignored by historians. There were between 250 and 300 guns, and perhaps 5500 effective cavalry, of whom 1500 belonged to the Guard and Head-quarters. But of these troops nearly a third were so worn down by hardship as to be hardly capable of making any great effort.

Eugène and Davout on reaching Studianka crossed in the night, the bitter cold of which went far to achieve the destruction of their few remaining troops. Even Oudinot's troops, still in comparatively good condition, suffered greatly in their wretched bivouacs in the woods of Stakhov. Behind the 1st and 4th Corps the horde of non-combatants came pouring down to the bridges. The road from Borisov to Studianka was choked with their throngs. Every age and sex was represented in the helpless mass; and there was to be seen human misery in its most hideous aspects. Even more harrowing than the misery and hideous aspect of the fugitives was their utter apathy and helplessness. The crowd heaved itself sluggishly along the tracks in whatever direction it chanced to take or was pushed by moving troops. Most of the wretches who composed it seem to have lost their senses no less than their appearance as more or less civilised human beings. The instincts of comradeship and humanity were almost extinct, and progress was constantly retarded by the brawling and fighting for places in the column of the mass of degraded savages which once had been Napoleon's *Grande Armée*.

Snow fell heavily during the night upon the unfortunates huddled shelterless among the woods and marshes. The non-combatants on reaching Studianka would go no further, despite the efforts of Eblé and Chasseloup to induce some of them to cross. Napoleon had issued orders that the passage was to be kept up day and night, but they probably could not be, at any rate were not, executed. The luckless people continued to stream down towards Studianka until the bank for miles was covered with them, and apathetically bivouacked as best they could among their vehicles. Very few appear to have attempted to cross; those who did probably created blockages and disorder, being amenable to no kind of control. The pontonniers and engineers were too few and too weary to enforce order in such a mass. More might have been done had Napoleon personally exerted himself to supervise the passage; unfortunately after the 27th he did nothing.

Victor's corps on the 26th became the rear-guard, Davout and Eugène passing in advance with the scanty relics of their troops. Victor left Borisov for Studianka on the 27th. The Baden brigade of Dändel's division marched first and crossed the bridges soon after Napoleon. Victor himself with the rest of Dändel's troops, Gérard's Poles and Saxons, and the artillery made his way out of Borisov towards midday, while Partouneaux's division with 4 guns and Delaître's cavalry brigade formed the rear-guard. It was to remain at Borisov until dark. Platov was marching upon Borisov; behind him came Wittgenstein with Steingell's and Berg's troops. Yermólov was behind. Vlastov's division was marching upon Staroï Borisov and Fock's reserve on the way to rejoin.[9]

The road from Borisov to Studianka was choked with non-combatants, sick and wounded barely capable of dragging themselves along, straggling soldiers, disbanded skulkers, fugitives from Moscow, camp-followers, men, women and children, huddled in a helpless mass, all streaming mechanically to Studianka with the last of the organised fighting men. Vlastov's division coming into the road at Staroï Borisov about 3 a.m., cut the line of retreat and the rearward portions of the mob fled back towards Borisov, whence Partouneaux moved out to fight his way through. His division was now only 4000 strong. Delaître had about 500 Saxon and Berg horsemen. Two tracks led from Borisov to Studianka, dividing a short distance west of the town. That to the left skirted the bank, but it was full of stragglers, and Partouneaux, believing that the right-hand one would take him directly to Studianka, struck into it. This movement brought him right against Vlastov's division. After a most gallant attempt to fight their way through the French were forced to give way. Partouneaux and Billard were taken prisoners with the poor remains of the latter's brigade, and the remaining three fell back towards Borisov, to find it occupied by Wittgenstein. They passed a fearful night in the snow, without food, fire, or shelter. Next day almost all the wounded and weaker men were dead, and the benumbed and starving survivors could only surrender. A single battalion, about 160 strong, which had luckily taken the left-hand track, reached Studianka. The French loss was over 4000 men, including 500 cavalry and 4 guns.

In the evening of the 27th Yermólov entered Borisov. As soon as the French left the town Chichagov repaired the bridge with pontoons, and direct communication being thus established, a general attack was concerted for next day. Wittgenstein was to complete the destruction of Victor's corps, while Chichagov, supported by Yermólov and Platov, pressed Ney and Oudinot, and endeavoured to throw them back upon Zembin.

The whole country was partially wooded except on the marshy banks of the Berezina, and in places the woods became very thick. On the western bank, about 3 miles south of Studianka and nearly half-way between the villages of Brilova and Bolshoï Stakhov, stood Ney and Oudinot. Their front was about a mile long, Ney's force being on the left, resting on the river, Oudinot on the right, supported upon a dense wood. Guns could not be brought into action on either side except on the road, where 8 pieces, equally divided between the two armies and continually replaced, fought each other all day. In reserve behind Ney and Oudinot stood the Guard.

At 8 a.m. Chaplitz and Pahlen began an attack on the 2nd Corps with 7 regiments of Chasseurs, and soon a furious conflict raged in the woods. At first the attack made headway, and the French and Swiss soldiers, who had passed a wretched night, began to give ground. When the roar of firing swelled up all the <u>disbanded men </u>took to flight, disordering and carrying away the reserves, while

[9] Iachvil's advance-guard was apparently distributed.

CHAPTER XIII 243

Oudinot was disabled by a wound. Ney, always at the point of danger, rushed to take his place, rallied the 2nd Corps and, calling up some of his own troops in support, checked Chaplitz's advance and began to drive him back upon Stakhov. Some hundreds of prisoners were taken. Sabaniev, who was moving up to support Chaplitz, stayed Ney's advance, but was suddenly charged in the most gallant fashion by Doumerc's Cuirassiers. They burst from the woods upon Cherbatov's division, broke through its skirmishing line, and charged its squares with desperate courage. Some 2000 Russians were sabred and captured. The Cuirassiers were of course nearly destroyed, but their splendid behaviour saved the army for the moment. Chichagov sent forward Voïnov to sustain Sabaniev, but though nearly twice as numerous the Russians could make no headway. The French losses were fearful. General Zayonczek, who had defended Praga against Suvorov in 1794, had his leg shattered; Legrand, Rapp, Amey, Dombrowski, and Kniaziewicz were also wounded. Half the survivors of the 2nd Corps were killed or disabled; but at night their shattered ranks still held their own, and if courage and devotion could have saved the *Grande Armée*, that end would have been achieved.

Meanwhile on the left bank Victor's corps, with equal heroism but less success, had been contending with Wittgenstein. Most of Victor's artillery and the Baden brigade were already across, but Napoleon now sent back the latter, adding to them apparently the Baden battalion at Head-quarters. The bridges were so blocked that the artillery could not return. Victor took up a position nearly perpendicular to the river, just south of Studianka, on some rising ground partially wooded. On the right, close to the river, there was a thick clump of wood. This was defended by the Badeners. Next on the left stood the Berg brigade when it arrived in line, then Gérard's 3 Polish regiments, with Löw's Saxon brigade beyond them. On the extreme left stood General Fournier with his two remaining cavalry regiments (Baden and Hesse). Victor had under his hand only 15 guns, and his entire strength was not more than 8000 infantry and 500 cavalry (according to his own account only 7400). The Berg brigade had moved forward to endeavour to rescue Partouneaux.

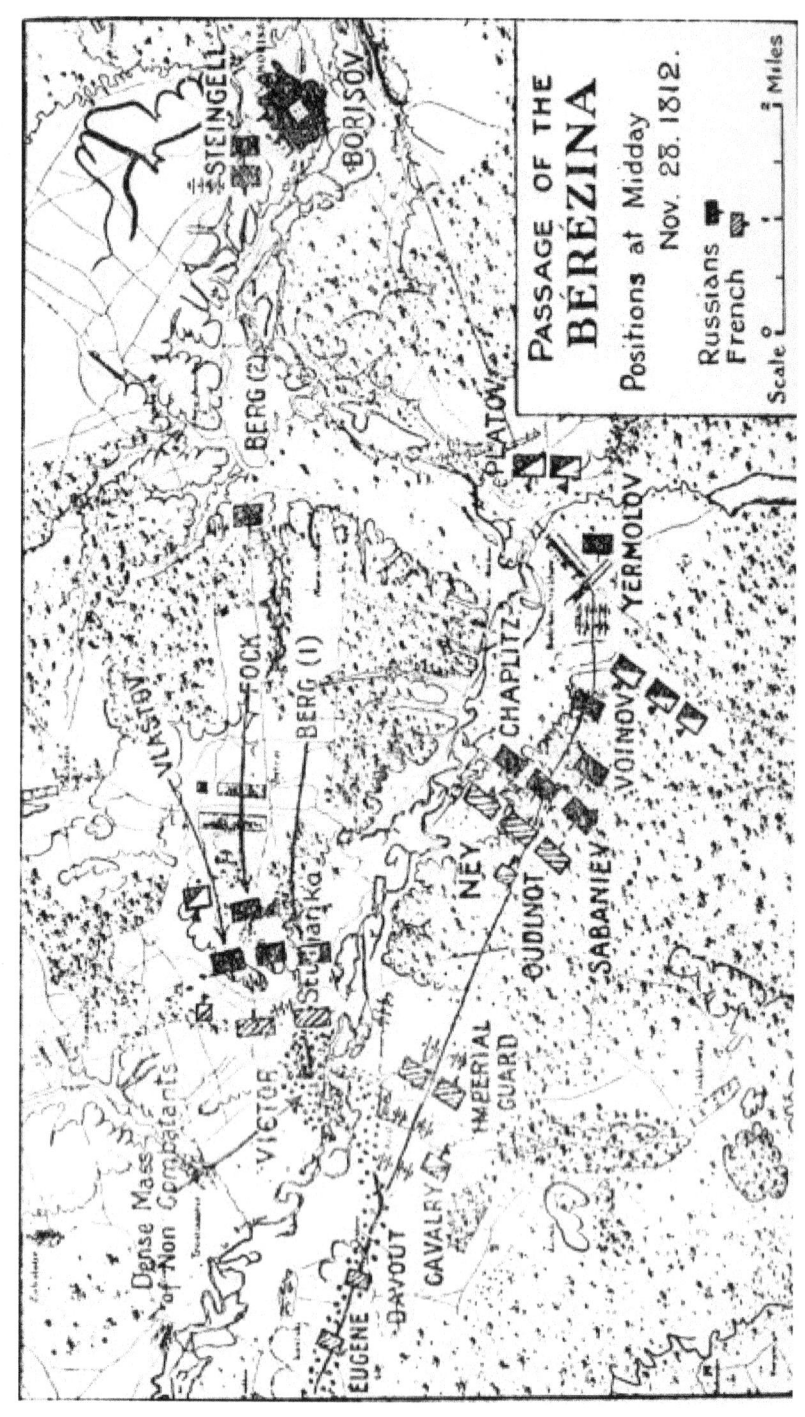

PASSAGE OF THE BEREZINA
Positions at Midday

CHAPTER XIII

Nov. 28, 1812.

Wittgenstein left Steingell at Borisov to disarm the prisoners; the rest of his army was directed upon Studianka. Vlastov drove back the Berg troops into the main line of the 9th Corps; but was then checked, though a battery established by Diebich made terrible havoc among the wild crowd which was surging around the entrance to the bridges. All the non-combatants, when the balls began to fall among them, crowded to the river marge in utter confusion and there remained, huddled in a mass more than 200 yards deep and extending for three-quarters of a mile. The panic was fearful, and the horrors that took place in the crowd will never be known. Men fought their way ahead by any and every means, and drove their vehicles remorselessly through the press. Men, women, and children were murdered, trodden down, and forced helplessly into the river, while all the while the Russian cannon-balls were falling with the snow. Many of those who reached the bridges were thrust off them and drowned or crushed beneath the wheels of vehicles. Many committed suicide to avoid a worse fate: there is at least one well-authenticated case of a mother who, herself mortally wounded, killed her child before she died. Yet carriages of Napoleon's staff and of the Generals of the Guard were laden with helpless women and children whom their protectors made every effort to save. Marshal Bessières and General Laborde in particular earned by their humanity laurels fairer than any which they had gained upon the field of battle.

CROSSING THE BEREZINA

The Baden Brigade crossing the upper bridge during the night of the 28-29th of

November, 1812
From the painting by J.A. Nikutowski at Carlsruhe

General Berg's first division quickly supported Vlastov. The Badeners on the right were driven back; but Napoleon at once took the Russians in flank by establishing a battery on the other side of the river. The Badeners reoccupied their position and held it all day against incessant assaults—at grievous cost to themselves. Further to the left Victor's Polish troops executed a fierce counter-attack, and were on the point of piercing the Russian centre when Fock arrived with his division and restored the conflict. Victor's men were now hopelessly outnumbered, but they fought on with magnificent tenacity until nightfall. An attempt to turn the left was checked by a gallant charge of Fournier's troopers and repulsed by the Saxons and a Polish regiment. Berg's second division, owing to some misunderstanding, did not arrive until the action was over. Victor's left was thrown back, but he still covered the bridges.

At 9 p.m. Victor received orders to cross, and began to withdraw. All round the bridges huddled the living mass of human beings and animals, heaving sluggishly with convulsive movements to escape, but practically inert. The eastern outlets were blocked by a hideous heap of broken vehicles and dead or dying human beings and horses piled one upon another in the trampled and blood-stained snow, through which it was impossible to make way. Eblé and his engineers literally had to make a cutting through the horrible heap and pile up the corpses on each side to keep back the unhappy mob. Through this ghastly passage, and along others like it made for them by the pioneers, the weary remains of the German and Polish regiments defiled, but even so they often had to fight their way. It was not until 1 a.m. on the 29th that they were at last across. Victor and Eblé vainly endeavoured to persuade some of the mob to follow, but most of them were torpid with misery and hopelessness and would not move. At dawn on the 29th a small detachment of the 9th Corps which had remained to the last was withdrawn. Eblé's orders were to fire the bridges at 8 a.m., but he waited until 8.30, hoping to save some more lives. A few of the non-combatants followed Victor's rear-guard, but the passages were soon blocked. At 8.30 Eblé fired the bridges, and there was a last scene of horror. Many of the unhappy wretches, at last alive to the situation, strove to dash through the flames, others endeavoured to cross on the thin ice between the bridges, many threw themselves into the icy stream to wade or swim. It is useless as well as painful to dwell longer upon the tragedy, the details of which may be gathered from countless works. Perhaps no event in history has ever so completely united in itself every element of misery.

The loss of life at the passage of the Berezina will never be exactly known. The *Grand Armée* lost 1200 officers killed and wounded, which may perhaps indicate a total of all ranks of 12,000 to 15,000. The 2nd and 9th Corps lost half their effective strength. Including prisoners and deaths from cold and misery during the three days the army was probably diminished by from 20,000 to 25,000 men. Enormous quantities of baggage were lost, but few guns—the Russians claimed 23. The loss of life among the non-combatants must have been enormous; almost all who were captured died of hunger or cold; their captors had little to spare them, and if the Russian regular soldiers often behaved with kindliness, the wilder Cossacks stripped their captives of everything. Perhaps the most awful incident was the fate of 500 women who were huddled in a barn at Borisov, without food for several days, and almost without fires. Only some 20 survived.

There is reason to believe that the Russian armies lost at the Berezina not less than 10,000 killed, wounded, and prisoners. Langeron says that Chichagov alone lost 7000. Of the 1500 prisoners many died of want before the survivors were retaken by the Russians.

It cannot be said that Napoleon showed to any advantage at the Berezina. The selection of the point of passage was due to the skill and energy of Oudinot; the credit for the splendid resistance on the 28th is to be attributed to Ney and Victor; while the true heroes of the episode were General Eblé and his pontonniers. Eblé died of his hardships a month later, and of his devoted 400 not 40 ever saw their homes again.

CHAPTER XIV
CONCLUSION OF THE CAMPAIGN. LOSSES AND RESULTS

The passage of the Berezina practically put an end to the existence as an organised body of the remains of the Grande Armée. Of the 45,000 or 47,000 combatants whom Napoleon had near Studianka on the 26th, there probably remained on the 29th little more than 25,000, a total which rapidly diminished through slaughter, fatigue, famine, despair and, above all, the steadily increasing cold. The 2nd and 9th Corps had sacrificed themselves heroically to cover the passage, but the double ordeal of battle and hasty retreat was too heavy for them to bear, and they began to disband like the rest of the army. They had already been reduced to a mere handful. In a report on the evening of the 30th Victor stated that he had only 60 mounted horsemen left. He believed that he still had 4000 infantry—the surviving half, as he explained, of the 2 divisions which had fought so gallantly on the 28th—but on calling the roll he found that they had already dwindled to 3300.

While the battles of the 28th were raging the corps of Davout and Eugène had defiled on Zembin. The effects of the neglect of Chaplitz to break down the long wooden bridges over the marshes were now apparent; the marshes were hardly as yet solid enough to bear vehicles, and had the bridges been destroyed nothing could have passed. Before daylight on the 29th Napoleon started with the Guard, followed by Victor and Ney, but the passage over the long narrow bridges was so slow that at 10 p.m. Ney was only at Zembin, 7 or 8 miles from Studianka. With him were Eblé and the remnant of his pontonniers, and when the last troops had passed they fired and blew up sections of the bridges to check the pursuit of the Russians.

On November 26th Kutuzov, who was then at Staroselie, 12 miles west of Kopis, seems to have awakened to the probability that Napoleon would escape. At any rate, he suddenly acted with convulsive energy, and during the next 2 days the *Corps de Bataille* marched 42 miles. The effort, of course, exhausted it, and on the 29th it could only cover 11. In any case it was too late. Napoleon himself was already safe, and, though only followed by a remnant of his once mighty host, was able and willing to give endless trouble to Europe.

Miloradovich reached Borisov on the 28th, too late to take part in the battles. Wittgenstein was retarded by the necessity of bridging the Berezina at Studianka, for which purpose he had to avail himself of Chichagov's pontoons from Borisov. He directed Kutuzov II, who had just joined him, to pursue Wrede towards Vilna,

CHAPTER XIV

and Orlov-Denisov, reinforced by some cavalry and mounted infantry, to follow Napoleon. Chichagov pushed forward Chaplitz, and prepared himself to follow with the bulk of his army.

For the relics of the *Grande Armée* there was now, as De Chambray says, no resource but in hasty flight. Wrede, after reoccupying Glubokoië, had moved southward to Dokchitsi, and was directed to cover the right flank of the retreating army; but his force, at first about 10,000 strong, rapidly dwindled from the ravages of cold and hardships, and the steady harassing of Kutuzov II. To expect that he could check Wittgenstein, who crossed the Berezina on the 31st, and began to pursue by roads roughly parallel to the main highway, was hopeless.

The country between the Berezina and Vilna had not been completely wasted; the towns still existed; there were small garrisons and magazines in some of them. But the increasing cold rapidly shattered every semblance of organisation. It rapidly became so fearful that all energy was absorbed in fighting it and endeavouring to preserve existence. The number of men actually with the colours dwindled fast. On December 1st Ney sent the eagles of the 3rd Corps with their guards and the regimental officers to take refuge with the head-quarters and the few thousand troops who still marched with it. When he had sent them off there remained to escort him only a company of 100 fighting men! The others, under General Ledru, tramped doggedly on for two days and three nights, only halting for necessary rest, and joined the head-quarters at Molodechno.

MARSHAL NEY SUPPORTING THE REAR-GUARD DURING THE RETREAT FROM MOSCOW
From the painting by Yvon

The flight to Vilna contains little of military interest. It was a mere rout of the most pitifully helpless condition, the mass of fugitives trailing mechanically along the road, followed, surrounded, and massacred by the Cossacks, while Chichagov's army and Yermólov's division marched steadily in the rear, ready to overwhelm any solid resistance that might be made. But, in truth, little could be offered. On November 29th Lanskoi's cavalry detachment seized Plechenitzi on the French line of retreat, nearly capturing the wounded Marshal Oudinot, whose staff heroically defended the house in which he lay. Chaplitz crossed the Zembin marshes by strengthening the ice with planks and brushwood, followed up the French rear-guard, and captured 7 guns and hundreds of stragglers. On the next four days there were further rear-guard actions, all much alike and all resulting in loss of guns and prisoners to the unhappy French, whose misery and demoralisation prevented them from responding to the splendid example still set them by their heroic leader. The hopeless condition of affairs may be gauged by the fact that on December 2nd there remained hardly 13,000 men with the colours (De Chambray says only 8800). With the head-quarters there were still perhaps 6000 or 7000; Ney had about 2500[10]; Victor perhaps as many; while the 1st, 4th, and 8th Army Corps and the cavalry could not muster 1000 armed men between them. There was still a considerable number of armed officers, but they fell sick or broke down daily. Disorganisation was complete. Disbanded men who had hitherto kept their weapons now threw them away. Forage could be procured; and food in quantity sufficient to support life was not lacking. But rest was now more necessary even than food, and it was impossible to obtain it. The bulk of the men were already broken by misery and fatigue, and were forced to continue their weary march amid a cold which grew ever more severe. On December 3rd it became intense; on the 5th the thermometer fell to 20° below zero (Réaumur); on the 6th to 24°; on the 7th to 26°; and it is said to have fallen still lower later on. Its severity struck even men like Löwenstern, accustomed to the winters of the Baltic provinces.

At Vilna Napoleon might expect his last powerful reinforcement—Loison's division of the 11th Corps, which reached the Lithuanian capital in the last week of November with two cavalry regiments of D'Estrée's Neapolitan division in Danzig. There were besides in Vilna 6000 or 7000 troops of all kinds—*régiments de marche* and Polish and Lithuanian levies. Maret, with the best intentions but disastrous results, ordered Loison's division forward to Ochmiana to take position and cover the retreat of the relics of the army into Vilna. It was composed of young French and German recruits, and three or four days of the cruel weather nearly destroyed it. How many men actually died and how many disbanded cannot be ascertained; it is only certain that on December 7th there remained in the ranks less than 3000 men!

At Molodechno on the 3rd, just as the cold was becoming deadly, Napoleon, who already contemplated leaving the army, issued practically his last direct orders. The remains of the Polish divisions were sent off south-west towards Warsaw, which they eventually reached in safety with such guns as they had preserved. Here Napoleon received the first posts which had reached him for several

---

[10]   2nd Corps 500 infantry; Claparède 200; Dombrowski 800; 5th Corps 323. Cavalry about 500. Artillery perhaps 200.

days, the others having presumably been intercepted by the Cossacks. Here also he composed and sent off the 29th Bulletin. It is so well known that little reference to it is necessary. It is, however, to be observed that it is as grossly mendacious as any of the Napoleonic series; and the Emperor's total lack of appreciation of the often heroic conduct of his troops throws a very disagreeable light upon his character. Certainly no one, reading its paragraphs, would conclude that the campaign had been an annihilating catastrophe. Every post brought shoals of letters to Maret, enquiring about the food supplies at Vilna, furiously attacking the Poles for not supporting him, and his own agents for not having urged them to do so! One most remarkable question is as to whether Vilna and Kovno are fortified. Surely Napoleon should have given orders on this point. The fact seems to be that at first he had been over-confident of success, and later had overlooked the necessity of protecting his bases—witness the case of Minsk. On the 29th of November he had ordered the minister to clear all the diplomatic body away from Vilna, lest they should be witnesses of the awful state of the army.

On December 3rd, Victor—much against his will—relieved Ney of rear-guard duty. He was weary of the war, and desired chiefly to save the relics of his corps. The result was a quarrel between the two marshals. The survivors of the 9th Corps succeeded in holding off Chaplitz in an engagement on the 4th, but next day Victor reported that it was completely used up, and could not receive the lightest attack. He hurried on to Smor goni with the few hundred frost-bitten men who remained to him.

Napoleon himself reached Smorgoni at 8 a.m. on the 5th. There he called to his presence Murat, Eugène, Berthier, Davout, Ney, Lefebvre, Mortier and Bessières, and announced to them his intention of proceeding forthwith to Paris. There can be no doubt that this was his wisest course of action. His presence at the capital was imperatively necessary to direct new levies, and to sustain public spirit. The army practically existed no longer, and could gain nothing by his remaining with it; finally, any longer delay might render it impossible for him to reach his own frontier across Germany.

Murat, by virtue of his rank, succeeded to a command which was merely nominal. It was no doubt wise to leave all the corps commanders with the army, since the circumstance might impose upon the Russians; but otherwise it was a measure of doubtful utility. Ney, the hardest fighter of them all, and apparently the only one who persistently held firm to his duty, was on bad terms with Davout and Victor, and Davout and Murat quarrelled whenever they met. As it was, there being hardly anything to command, their squabbles counted for less than they might otherwise have done.

Napoleon left in his carriage at 7 p.m., accompanied by Caulaincourt. Duroc and Lobau followed in a sledge; and on the box of the carriage were the Mameluke Rustan and Captain Wasowicz of the Polish Lancers of the Guard, who acted as interpreter. Believing the road to be clear, he was escorted only by a small detachment of Neapolitan cavalry—and thus the mighty conqueror stole away from the scene of his ruin, leaving the survivors of his gigantic host to the climate and the arms of Russia.

As a fact, he had a very narrow escape from capture, since Seslavin that day made a dash at Ochmiana. Loison's division, however, or what remained of it, had reached the town just before; Seslavin was driven out, and bivouacked for the night a little way to the south, so that the Emperor arrived in safety. At Medniki, the next stage, he met Maret, who had come out to meet him. The minister informed him of the enormous magazines which had gradually collected in Vilna. Presumably, as De Chambray suggests, Maret's returns under this heading had failed to reach the Emperor, for he expressed his great relief, and directed Maret to tell Murat to halt for eight days in the city, in order to restore the physique and morale of the army. He arrived at Vilna on the 6th, leaving again, after a brief halt, for Warsaw. There, on the 10th he had the interview with De Pradt which the latter has so graphically described. He started again in a few hours *via* Dresden for Paris, which he reached on the 18th.

At Vilna, indeed, there were 4,000,000 rations of biscuit and flour and 3,600,000 of meat, besides an immense quantity of grain; 27,000 spare muskets, 30,000 pairs of boots, and great stores of clothing and equipment. But little of this was destined to be of use to the unhappy victims of Napoleon's overweening ambition. The scenes on the road between Vilna and the Berezina would pass all belief were there not trustworthy witnesses, both French and Russian, to bear testimony to them. The road and its borders were strewn with dead men and horses and abandoned guns and vehicles, often broken and half-burned, the fugitives having endeavoured to utilise them as fuel. Along this way of sorrow trailed an endless stream of human beings of both sexes, falling at every step to mingle with the corpses upon which they trampled. Those who fell were quickly stripped of their wretched rags by the passers-by—themselves doomed to the same fate before long. To dwell upon the horrors which marked every mile of the flight is useless. They may be gathered from countless works composed by eyewitnesses. The sense of humanity had been in many cases extinguished, and there are well-attested incidents of canni balism. Langeron vouches for having seen bodies from which the flesh had been hacked. The intense cold produced insanity; men took refuge in heated ovens and were roasted to death, or sprang into the fires. To be taken prisoner brought no alleviation of the lot of the hapless fugitives. The Cossacks usually stripped them; often, too, the Russians, exasperated at the destruction of Moscow and the ravages of the invaders, gave no quarter even to those who surrendered. Besides, they could do nothing to provide for them even had they the will. Prisoners died, as before, by the roadside, stripped, famished, frozen; at Vilna they were packed into buildings where pestilence raged amid cold, filth, and lack of proper food.

On towards Vilna, to which they looked forward as a haven of rest, the wretched horde streamed. The Cossacks hung about the route, dashed at will into the huddled mass, mixed with the crowd, and killed and plundered with deadly dexterity. Around the head-quarters still moved a considerable but steadily diminishing body of fighting men, but discipline had vanished, and even the Guard marched in confusion, and paid little heed to orders. Here and there among the piteous crowd that followed were to be found groups of armed officers and men, often sick and worn out, but retaining spirit to sell their lives dearly when attacked, but these were few. Even the rear-guard was not an organised body—merely a band of desperate warriors held together, usually, by the personal influence of the one Marshal of France who returned from Russia with added renown.

On the heels of the French rear-guard marched Chaplitz's division, attacking at every opportunity, picking up abandoned guns and vehicles mile by mile and disarming prisoners, who were then left to live or die as they might. After Chaplitz, always between a piteous double stream of "prisoners" whom it could neither care for nor guard, tramped the Army of the Danube, everyone from the Admiral downwards marching on foot to escape frost-bite, and carefully taking every precaution against it. Sometimes the road was so choked with dead that the dismounted cavalry in the advance had to clear it before the guns and trains could be got forward. Langeron says that, despite the weather, fatal cases of frost-bite were almost unknown among these veterans of the Turkish War.

It is distressing, amid the stories of the universal misery and destitution, to read of the waggon-loads of luxuries belonging to Napoleon, Murat and other generals which were taken by the Russians. There is a grim humour in learning that the uncouth captors often took perfumes for spirits and liqueurs, and ate pomade in mistake for butter!

Victor on reaching Ochmiana found, instead of Loison's strong division, 3000 or 4000 half-frozen recruits who would waste away entirely in a couple of days. He continued his retreat in all haste, followed and harassed by Chaplitz and Platov, who picked up prisoners by thousands and cannon by scores. On the 9th, a little way short of Vilna, Wrede arrived. His force had dwindled from cold, dispersion, and losses in skirmishing to a remnant of less than 3000 men, but he still possessed several guns. Murat and the head-quarters had reached Vilna on the 8th; but as early as the 6th bands of ragged and destitute fugitives had begun to enter the city to the consternation of the inhabitants. Even in Murat's column there was panic and disorder, which was only checked for a while by the Chasseurs of the Old Guard, who held together in the mob and prevented a mad rush. But when they had entered the crush became terrible, and order impossible. The gates were choked and, amongst others, Davout and his staff could only enter by a gap in a wall. The fugitives poured through the streets seeking for food and shelter—often vainly, for the horrified inhabitants barricaded themselves in their houses—and when they could not obtain it, dropped down to die. The Jewish tradesmen sold food to the helpless wretches literally for its weight in gold; but when the city was evacuated, unless all accounts lie, they murdered and robbed them wholesale.

To stay in Vilna, even for a few days, was impossible. Seslavin and his Cossacks actually entered the city on the 9th, but were, of course, obliged to retreat almost immediately. But the action showed the absolute recklessness of the Russians, and the French army was destitute of power to resist. So many of the men dispersed in the city that on the 10th only 6000 or 7000 at most were under arms. A large part of the fugitives never left Vilna again. Many were worn out by sickness and fatigue, and having once lain down to rest had not power to rise. Many died through drinking spirits, in the hope of resisting the cold. Many more were frost-bitten, and sudden warmth added to neglect produced gangrene. Nearly 20,000 helpless creatures were left, mostly to perish, in the city when the remainder pursued their way to the Niemen. No news as to the actual state of affairs had been allowed to reach Vilna, and the consequence was that no preparations had been made for the reception of the army. Murat simply lost his head; at the first sound of the cannon at the advance posts he left the palace in which he had established himself and hurried to the Kovno gate to be ready to escape. Berthier issued hasty orders to destroy the arms and ammunition in the arsenal. Eblé, whose noble life was almost spent, and who had set the crown upon his reputation by his unfailing heroism and self-sacrifice during the last stages of the retreat, was charged with this melancholy duty, Lariboissière being even nearer his end. Directions were given to issue food and clothes to everybody abundantly and without attention to forms. Orders were sent to Schwarzenberg to withdraw to Bielostok, while Macdonald was instructed to retreat to Tilsit. The hopeless task of holding back the Russians was thrown upon the shoulders of Ney.

Wrede with his frozen and disorganised remnant was driven in upon Vilna by Platov on the 9th. The Cossacks were already all round the town skirmishing with the defenders. Apart from the destruction wrought by the cold the latter suffered considerable loss. The Lithuanian Tartar Squadrons, destined to form part of the Guard, were completely annihilated. In the night Murat evacuated Vilna, and next day Ney abandoned it, the Cossacks following him through the streets.

A few miles from Vilna the road to Kovno leads over a steep hill. The remains of the army trains and those from Vilna, which were following the army, found themselves blocked at the foot of the icebound slope, up which the horses were utterly unable to drag them. The last remaining guns and most of the waggons had to be abandoned. The army pay-chests, containing 10,000,000 francs, were abandoned and partly pillaged by the soldiers. Only Napoleon's private treasure and carriages, and a very small proportion of the trains, were by desperate exertions preserved, 20 horses being necessary to drag a single vehicle up the hill. In the midst of the disorder and pillage the Cossacks arrived. Platov opened on the crowd with his light guns, but his wild horsemen for the most part fell upon the spoil and apparently disdained to take prisoners. The disaster was due to sheer lack of management, since the Novi Troki road, which was level and little longer, turned the hill to the south, and might easily have been used for the retreat.

CHAPTER XIV

NAPOLEON'S TRAVELLING KITCHEN
It was taken to Moscow and afterwards captured on the field of Waterloo
Photographed for this work at the Royal Artillery Museum, Woolwich

It was as hopeless to attempt to hold firm at Kovno as at Vilna. There were 42 guns in the town, partly those of Loison's division, which had been left there, great magazines of food and clothing, and about 2,500,000 francs in cash. There was a feeble *tête du pont*, but the Niemen was frozen and could be crossed anywhere on the ice. On the 12th the main body poured into the town— about 20,000 men, mostly in the last stage of misery and despair and nearly all disarmed. The Guard mustered 1600 bayonets and sabres. Ney, who had been fighting with Platov all the way from Vilna, reached the town in the evening; with the garrison troops added to the relics of the rear-guard he had not 2000 men. Efforts were made to distribute the stores and re-arm the disbanded troops, but the men threw away the muskets. The magazines were pillaged, the miserable wretches naturally fastening upon the spirit stores. Men drunken and dying lay in heaps in the snow-covered streets. Most of the benumbed fugitives lacked even the sense to avail themselves of the ice on the river; they crowded mechanically over the bridge, fighting for precedence, stifling and trampling each other down, as at the Berezina and Vilna. Murat placed some guns in battery on the left bank of the Niemen, and left for Königsberg on the 13th, while Ney and the rear-guard occupied the town, which they held until dark. Platov sent across a detachment on the ice, which captured the guns on the left bank and barred Ney's retreat. His men were largely huddling in the houses; he had only a few hundred armed soldiers. He turned down the left bank of the river and then diverged to the left across the Pelwiski forest, eventually making his way by Gumbinnen to Königsberg. He abandoned in the forest Loison's 16 guns, almost the last artillery that the army retained.

The Russians did not immediately cross the political frontier, and bitterly as the Prussian peasantry hated the French they did not actively ill-treat them. Many isolated fugitives were disarmed, but their misery was such as to melt even hearts steeled by hatred and the memory of recent oppression. De Fezensac says that the happiness of being fed and lodged prevented them from noticing the hostility of the people. The bulk of the mob of fugitives reached Königsberg by the 20th, and thence cantonments were spread along the Vistula. On that day the infantry of the Guard counted about 2500 officers and men, of whom 1000 were sick. The 1st, 2nd, 3rd, and 4th Corps mustered between them on January 10th, 1813, some 13,000 men sound and sick, of whom 2500 were officers. As to the condition of the army, nearly all the troops were disarmed and had to be furnished with new muskets from the vast magazines at Danzig. On December 23rd Eblé, now in chief command of the artillery, reported that of all the vast train which had entered Russia with the Central Army there remained but 9 guns and howitzers, and 5 caissons!

Two days before Lariboissière had died, and on December 30th Eblé also passed away. Colonel Pion des Loches, a man who rarely has a good word to say for his superiors, expresses himself thus concerning them: "Both were victims of their zeal and devotion. Our army lost in them its pillars and supports ... and what are all our other generals worth beside them?" As his comrades in arms laid Eblé to rest in the Roman Catholic cemetery at Königsberg, Napoleon was signing the decree which created him First Inspector-General of Artillery. Eblé's grave has vanished, for the cemetery has been destroyed, but his glory far outshines that of thousands of better known men.

Marshal Kutuzov reached Vilna on December 12th to control the hitherto independent movements of Chichagov and Wittgenstein. His own troops were following under Tormazov, but they were so shattered by the long march from Moscow that their offensive power was for the time at an end, and they were cantoned about Vilna. Chichagov was to follow to the Niemen to support Platov and the advance-guards which hung on the heels of the retreating French. Wittgenstein was ordered to intercept Macdonald on his expected retreat to the Niemen, while Paulucci was to press him in rear. Sacken's army, supported by the Mozyr force, now under Tuchkov II, and a detachment from Bobruisk, was to deal with Schwarzenberg. The Emperor Alexander reached Vilna on December 22nd, and at once devoted himself to the task of endeavouring to save the lives of his captured enemies. The hospitals were choked with the Russian sick, and the French prisoners, almost all ill and helpless, were perishing wholesale. Biscuit and bread they received, but there was no other help for them. Gangrened wounds, frost-bite, and typhus produced by filth, hunger, and putrefaction, swept them away. In three weeks 15,000 are said to have died. Alexander and Constantine made magnificent efforts to cope with the awful mass of human misery. Reckless of personal danger, they personally superintended the relief operations; the Grand Duke nearly died of the fever which he caught in the midst of his labour of humanity. St. Priest was transferred from the work of collecting the Russian stragglers to that of superintending the hospitals of the prisoners, for which his French origin especially fitted him.

Macdonald, before Riga, received his orders to retreat on December 18th, and started next day in two main columns, he himself leading the way with Grandjean's division, a Prussian infantry brigade, and Massenbach's cavalry; while Yorck followed a day's march behind the rest of the Prussians. Wittgenstein himself could hardly intercept him; but the flying detachments of Kutuzov II and Diebich, thrown far forward, might hope to impede Macdonald's march. The Marshal on reaching Koltiniani divided his own column, taking advantage of two roads thence to Tilsit, and intending to reunite his whole corps at Tauroggen. Kutuzov II was too weak to intercept him; but Diebich, with his 1500 cavalry and a few sledge-guns, got between Macdonald and Yorck on the 25th, and boldly proposed to the latter a conference in order to prevent useless bloodshed. After some hesitation Yorck at last made up his mind, and on the 30th concluded the famous convention of Tauroggen, by which the Prussians were declared neutral. The results were incalculably important, but belong rather to the history of the German War of Liberation. The immediate consequence was that the wreck of the *Grande Armée* was weakened by 16,000 or 17,000 excellent soldiers and 60 guns.

Macdonald, meanwhile, was pursuing his retreat, and on the 27th repulsed Vlastov's divisions, which had come up to support Kutuzov II, capturing some prisoners and a gun. But at Tilsit, on the 31st, he was deserted by Massenbach and was forced to fall back on Königsberg. He marched rapidly and steadily, and reached the Prussian capital in safety. On January 3rd, 1813, his rear-guard, under Bachelu, was driven through Labiau, after a hard fight, by Wittgenstein's advance-guard under Chepelev. At Königsberg Macdonald was joined by Heudelet's division, but Yorck's defection ended all hope of being able to make a stand on the Pregel, and the retreat was continued to Danzig. When the blockade of Riga was raised, Paulucci sent Lewis with 8000 men to pursue Macdonald, and himself with 3000 made a dash for Memel, which he reached on December 15th, after an amazing march of 200 miles in 8 days. The place immediately surrendered.

While Schwarzenberg had been contending with Sacken, General Kosinski with his Poles had once more invaded Volhynia, but was repulsed after a little skirmishing by Musin-Pushkin.

Schwarzenberg, turning from his pursuit of Sacken, reached Slonim again on December 7th; but on learning of the catastrophe of the *Grande Armée* he retreated on the 14th to Bielostok, arriving there on the 18th. Reynier drew back behind the Bug. On the advance of Sacken and Tuchkov, to assist whom Kutuzov also directed a column under Miloradovich, Schwarzenberg steadily withdrew, there being nothing but the most insignificant fighting. The Austrians eventually fell back into their own territory, while Reynier retreated towards Saxony. The Polish troops remained in the Vistula fortresses, and were mostly captured in the following year. The little field army which Poniatowski was able to collect was allowed to join Napoleon in Saxony, since its blockade employed too many troops.

Thus in the last days of December the Russian territory had been freed from the vast host which had threatened to overwhelm it. The immediate result of the campaign was the all but complete destruction of an army nearly 700,000 men strong and its immense material. In all it would appear that, exclusive of Polish stationary troops and local levies other than those already mentioned, some 674,000 combatants crossed the Vistula against Russia, of whom about 640,000 actually took part in military operations. Of these 640,000 there remained as organised troops at the end of the campaign only the forces of Schwarzenberg and Macdonald, perhaps 68,000 combatants in all. All the other corps and divisions were represented by about 25,000 disorganised and generally disarmed men—largely officers—without cavalry and with scarcely any artillery. The number of guns which actually entered Russia is somewhat doubtful, but appears to have been over 1300, exclusive of the Riga siege train. Of these some 250 can be accounted for as having returned. The Russians claimed 929 as captured; the rest were no doubt abandoned and never recovered. More than 200,000 trained horses were lost; and it was the want of them which, even more than the deficiency of trained men, ruined Napoleon's chances in 1813. The total chasm in the Napoleonic ranks was over 550,000 fighting men. As prisoners the Russians claimed 48 generals, 3000 officers, and 190,000 men, but it is to be feared that half of them were captured only to die. Even without making allowance for this, more than 350,000 soldiers must have perished, besides the tens of thousands of camp-followers, refugees, and other non-combatants.

The Russian losses are extremely difficult to compute. It is impossible to work upon the number of men successfully put into the field, and those remaining active at the close of the campaign, since the deficiency does not, as in the case of the Napoleonic army, represent absolute loss. There are reasons for believing that the actual loss of fighting men was nearly 150,000. The number of non-combatants—largely peaceful inhabitants of the country—who perished must have been enormous.

The ultimate results of the Russian victory were the general uprising of northern Germany against Napoleon, the adhesion of Austria—after considerable hesitation—to the anti-Napoleonic coalition, and the complete overthrow within little more than a year of the empire of force which he had built in Europe. Britain had long since destroyed Napoleon's efforts at gaining power on the sea, and had struck heavy blows at his prestige on land. As the Russian army lay at Tarutino it was gladdened by the news of Wellington's victories. And the prestige of Napoleon, shaken in Spain, was now shattered in Russia, and his material military power so broken that he was never really able again to face his antagonists on equal terms. It is perhaps true to say that the enthusiastic uprising of Germany was the chief factor in Napoleon's downfall in 1813, but it was Russia who gave the impulse and cleared the way; and her military aid was of vital importance.

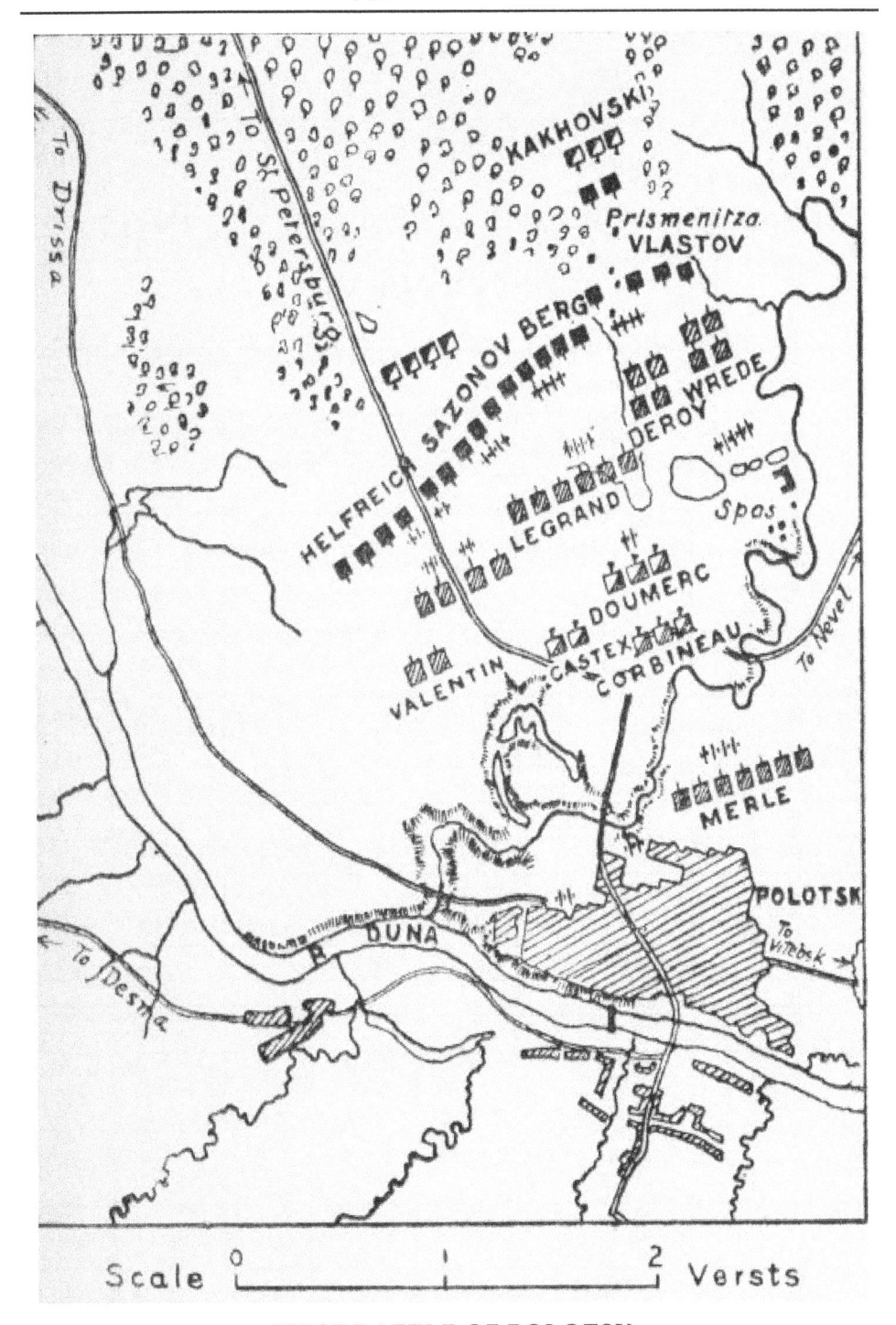

FIRST BATTLE OF POLOTSK
(August 17th and 18th, 1812)

APPENDICES, BIBLIOGRAPHY & INDEX
APPENDIX A

FORCES SUCCESSIVELY EMPLOYED BY NAPOLEON AGAINST RUSSIA IN 1812

	Date of Muster Roll.	Battal-ions.	Squad-rons.	Infantry and Foot Artillery.	Cavalry and Horse Artillery.	Total.	Guns.
Grand Head-quarters	June 24			3,075	908	3,983	(?)
1st Corps d Armée	" "	88	16	68,627	3,424	72,051	150
2nd " "	" "	48	16	34,299	2,840	37,139	92
3rd " "	" "	45	24	35,755	3,587	39,342	86
4th " "	" 30	54	20	42,430	3,368	45,798	116
5th " "	" 24	33	20	32,159	4,152	36,311	70
6th " "	July 1	28	16	23,228	1,906	25,134	58
7th " "	June 24	18	16	15,003	2,186	17,189	50
8th " "	" "	18	12	15,885	2,050	17,935	34
9th " "	Sept 3	43	12	31,663	1,904	33,567	80
10th " "	June 24	36	16	30,023	2,474	32,497	84
Austrian Corps	" "	26	44	26,830	7,318	34,148	60
Imperial Guard	Estimated (except Cavalry)	38	28	25,000	6,279	31,279	112
1st Cavalry Corps	June 24	—	54	—	12,077	12,077	30
2nd " "	" "	—	52	—	10,436	10,436	30
3rd " "	" "	—	50	—	9,676	9,676	30
4th " "	" "	—	40	—	7,964	7,994	24

APPENDIX A

32nd Division	Nov 2	18	—	13,592	—	13,592	20
34th "	Nov 18	19	6	13,290	700	13,990	16
Engineers, Artillery Reserves, etc.						10,000(?)	230
				410,849	83,279	504,128	1,372
Absentees who rejoined		—	—	—		37,100	—
Lagrange's Division (Drafts)		—	—	—		13,408	—
Foreign Guard Battalions}							
Kosinski's Polish Brigade}							
Austrian Reserve Brigade}		circa	—	—		70,000	18
2 German Regiments }							
Drafts of all kinds}							
						624,636	
In Duchy of Warsaw and on Vistula }							
5 Foreign Guard Battalions}							
Heudelet's Division (20 Battalions)}							
Destrée's Division (Neapolitans) at Danzig}		—	—	—		50,000	32
New Levies, Drafts, etc.}							
Garrisons on Vistula}							
						674,636	1,422

It is extremely difficult to compute the numbers of reinforcements, etc., since a proportion of them consisted of convalescents and rejoining stragglers.

No allowance is made for the large number of transport drivers and other non-combatants.

APPENDIX B

COMPOSITION OF THE NAPOLEONIC GRAND ARMY BY NATIONALITIES

Imp. Guard, Head-quarters, Army Corps 1-10, Austrians, 4 Cavalry Corps, 32nd and 34th Divisions.

	Battalions.	Squadrons.
French and New French	239	214
Poles	51	69
Italians	22	14
Croats and Dalmatians	7	—
Spaniards	4	—
Portuguese	6	3
Swiss	12	—
Bavarians	30	24
Saxons	22	32
Westphalians	22	20
Württembergers	12	16
Badeners	7	2
Berg Troops	8	4
Mecklenburg Troops	3	—
Hesse-Darmstadt	6	2
Small Rheinbund States	11	—
Austrians	26	44
Prussians	20	24
Various	(Mamelukes)	1

APPENDIX C

FORCES SUCCESSIVELY EMPLOYED BY RUSSIA AGAINST NAPOLEON IN 1812

FIRST ARMY OF WEST. APPROXIMATE STRENGTH

Force.	Battalions.	Squadrons.	Cossack Regiments.	Batteries.	Infantry and Engineers.	Cavalry.	Cossacks.	Artillery.	Total.	Guns.
1st Army Corps	28	16	1	8	17,100	2,250	880	1,620	21,850	96
2nd " "	24	8	—	7	14,400	1,120	—	1,340	16,860	84
3rd " "	26	4	1	7	15,360	600	550	1,340	17,850	84
4th " "	22	8	—	6	12,960	1,120	—	1,120	15,200	72
5th " "	26	20	—	6	15,840	2,880	—	1,400	20,120	80
6th " "	24	8	—	7	14,400	1,120	—	1,340	16,860	84
1st Cavalry Corps	—	24	—	1	—	3,480	—	220	3,700	12
2nd " "	—	24	—	1	—	3,360	—	220	3,580	12
3rd " "	—	20	—	1	—	2,800	—	220	3,020	12
Cossack Corps	—	—	—	1	—	—	6,160	220	6,380	12
Artillery Reserve	—	—	—	3	—	—	—	720	720	36
					95,060	18,730	7,590	9,760	126,140	584

SECOND ARMY OF WEST

Force.	Battalions.	Squadrons.	Cossack Regiments.	Batteries.	Infantry and Engineers.	Cavalry.	Cossacks.	Artillery.	Total.	Guns.
7th Army Corps	24	8	—	7	14,650	1,120	—	1,340	17,110	84
8th " "	22	20	—	5	12,000	2,800	—	1,040	15,840	60
4th Cavalry Corps	—	24	—	1	—	3,360	—	220	3,580	12
Cossack Division	—	—	9	—	—	—	3960	220	4180	12
27th Infantry Division	12	—	—	—	7,200	—	—	—	7,200	—
					33,850	7,280	3,960	2,820	47,910	168

THIRD ARMY OF WEST

Force.	Battalions.	Squadrons.	Cossack Regiments.	Batteries.	Infantry and Engineers.	Cavalry.	Cossacks.	Artillery.	Total.	Guns.
Kamenski's Corps	17	8	—	4	9,970	1,120	—	780	11,870	46
Markov's "	24	8	—	7	14,400	1,120	—	1,340	16,860	82
Sacken's Reserve	12	24	—	2	4,000	2,500	—	440	5,940	24
Lambert's Corps	—	36	—	—	—	5040	—	—	5040	—
Irregulars	—	—	9	—	—	—	3,960	—	3,960	—
Reserve Artillery	—	—	—	1	—	—	—	240	240	12
					28,370	9,780	3,960	2,800	44,910	164

ARMY OF THE DANUBE

APPENDIX C

Force.	Battalions.	Squadrons.	Cossack Regiments.	Batteries.	Infantry and Engineers.	Cavalry.	Cossacks.	Artillery.	Total.	Guns.
Langeron's Division	12	8	3	4	6,000	1,000	1,000	700	8,700	48
Essen III's Division	12	8	3	4	6,000	1,000	1,000	700	8,700	48
Voïnov's Division	11	12	3	4	5,500	1,500	1,000	700	8,700	48
Bulatov's Division	6	20	1	4	3,000	2,500	300	700	6,500	48
Sabaniev's Division	9	8	1	1	4,500	1,000	300	200	6,000	12
Lüders' Division	9	8	2	1	4,500	1,000	600	150	6,250	12
					29,500	8,000	4,200	3,150	44,850	216

ARMY OF FINLAND

Force.	Battalions.	Squadrons.	Cossack Regiments.	Batteries.	Infantry and Engineers.	Cavalry.	Cossacks.	Artillery.	Total.	Guns.
Steingell's Corps and Field Detachments	22	6	1	4½	—	—	—	—	14,000	54
Garrison Detachments	4	—	1	—	—	—	—	—	2,500	12
									16,500	66

RESERVES AND GARRISONS IN JUNE

Depôt, Troops, etc.	87	54	—	?	—	—	—	—	35,000	—

CRIMEAN GARRISON

Detachments	8	—	—	2	—	—	—	—	5,000	24

									90,000	
					Total				410,310	
									======	

APPENDIX D

STAFF OF NAPOLEON'S GRAND ARMY OF RUSSIA, 1812

Commander-in-Chief:	
H.I.M. THE EMPEROR AND KING NAPOLEON I.	
Chief of Staff	Marshal Berthier, Prince of Neuchatel
" Cavalry	H.M. the King of Naples (Marshal Murat)
" Artillery	Général de Division Comte Lariboissière
" Engineers	" " Comte Chasseloup
" Bridge Trains	" " Baron Eblé
Intendant General	" " Comte Mathieu Dumas

CHIEF MINISTERS, COURT OFFICIALS, ETC., ACCOMPANYING THE EMPEROR

Maret, Duke of Bassano	Minister of Foreign Affairs
Comte Daru	Secretary of State
General Duroc, Duke of Friuli	Grand Marshal of the Palace
" Caulaincourt, Duke of Vicenza	Grand Equerry
Baron Ménéval	Secretary of the Portfolio
" Fain	" " Archives
" Mounier	" " Cabinet
Colonel Baron de Ponton	" " "
State-Council Auditor Lelorgne d'Ideville	Chief Interpreter
Baron Bacler d'Albe	Director of Topographical Cabinet

THE GENERAL STAFF

General Officer.	Department or Command.
Général de Division Junot, Duc d'Abrantes	First Aide-de-Camp
" " Lebrun, Duc de Placentia	Aide-de-Camp
" " Mouton, Comte Lobau	"
" " Comte Rapp	"
" " Comte de Narbonne	"
" " Comte Durosnel	"
" " Comte Sokolniki	Polish Officer Attached
" " Comte Sanson	Topography and History
" " Baron de Caulaincourt	Grand Head-quarters
" Brigade Comte Bailly de Monthion	Chief of Berthier's Staff
" " Baron Guilleminot	Small Head-quarters
" " Baron Jomini	History
" " Comte Lauer	Gendarmerie

There were in Napoleon's train a large number of General Officers "disposable." Most of these were appointed to commands later, and mostly appear in the list of Commandants of districts.

GENERAL OFFICERS COMMANDING IN THE DISTRICTS OF THE ARMY (11TH AUGUST)

General of Division	Comte Hogendorp	Government of Lithuania
" "	Baron Durutte	Berlin
" "	Comte Dutaillis	Warsaw
" "	Comte Charpentier	Vitebsk
" "	Gomès Freyre	Glubokoië
" "	Marquis d'Alorna	Mohilev
" "	Baillet-de-la-Tour	Elbing
General of Brigade	Castella	Königsberg
" "	Corsin	Pillau
" "	Plauzonne	Plock
" "	Ferrière	Bielostok
" "	Tarayre	Kovno
" "	Voyezinski	Thorn
" "	Wedel	Wilkowiski
" "	Brun	Grodno
" "	Bronikowski	Minsk

Corps.	Division.	Division General.

APPENDIX D

1st Corps (Maréchal Davout, Prince d'Eckmühl)	1st Infantry	Morand
	2nd "	Friant
	3rd "	Gudin
	4th "	Dessaix
	5th "	Compans
	Cavalry	Girardin (Sept.)
	Artillery	Baron Pernety
2nd Corps (Maréchal Oudinot Duc de Reggio)	6th Infantry	Legrand
	8th "	Verdier
	9th "	Merle
	Artillery	Dulauloy
3rd Corps (Maréchal Ney, Duc d'Elchingen)	10th Infantry	Ledru
	11th "	Razout
	25th "	Prince Royal of Württemberg
	Artillery	Foucher
4th Corps (His Imperial Highness Prince Eugène)	13th Infantry	Delzons
	14th "	Broussier
	15th "	Pino
	Artillery	Danthouard
5th Corps (General Prince Poniatowski)	16th Infantry	Zayonczek
	17th "	Dombrowski
	18th "	Kamienicki
	Artillery	Pelletier
6th Corps (General Gouvion Saint-Cyr)	19th Infantry	Deroy
	20th "	Wrede
7th Corps (General Reynier)	21st Infantry	Lecoq
	22nd "	De Funck
8th Corps (General Vandamne) (later General Junot)	23rd Infantry	Tharreau
	24th "	Ochs
9th Corps (Maréchal Victor, Duc de Belluno)	12th Infantry	Partouneaux
	26th "	Dändels
	28th "	Gérard
10th Corps (Maréchal Macdonald, Duc de Taranto)	7th "	Grandjean
	Prussians	(1) Grawert
		(2) Yorck
	Cavalry	Massenbach
11th Corps (Maréchal Augereau, Duc de Castiglione)	30th Infantry	D'Heudelet
	31st "	Lagrange
	32nd "	Durutte
	33rd "	Destrées
	34th "	Morand

CAVALRY RESERVE

Commander-in-Chief:
The King of Naples.

Chief of the Staff:
General Belliard.

Corps.	Division.	Division General.
1st Corps	1st Light Cavalry	Bruyère
(Nansouty)	1st Heavy Cavalry	Saint-Germain
	5th "	Valence
2nd Corps	2nd Light Cavalry	Sebastiani
(Montbrun)	2nd Heavy Cavalry	Wathier
	4th "	Defrance
3rd Corps	5th Heavy Cavalry	Doumerc
(Grouchy)	6th "	Lahoussaye
	3rd Light Cavalry	Chastel
4th Corps	4th Light Cavalry	Rozniecki
(Latour-Maubourg)	7th Heavy "	Lorge

APPENDIX E

STAFF OF RUSSIAN ARMIES OPPOSED TO NAPOLEON, JULY, 1812
FIRST ARMY OF THE WEST

Commander-in-Chief	General of Infantry Baron Barclay de Tolly
Chief of Staff	Major-General Yermólov (July)
Quartermaster-General	Colonel Baron Toll (July)
General "of Service"	Colonel Kikin
Chief of Artillery	Major-General Count Kutaïsov
Chief of Engineers	Major-General Trusson

Army Corps.	Corps Commander.	Division.	Divisional Commander.
I	Lieut.-General Count Wittgenstein	5th Infantry	Major-Gen. Berg
		14th "	Major-Gen. Sazonov
		1st Cavalry	Major-Gen. Khakovski
II	Lieut.-General Baggohufwudt	4th Infantry	Major-Gen. Prince Eugen of Württemberg
		17th "	Major-Gen. Olsuviev
III	Lieut.-General Tuchkov I	3rd "	Lieut.-Gen. Konovnitzin
		1st Grenadier	Lieut.-Gen. Strogonov
IV	Lieut.-General Count Ostermann-Tolstoï	11th Infantry	Major-Gen. Choglokov
		23rd "	Major-Gen. Bakhmetiev
V	General H.I.H. Grand Duke Constantine	Imperial Guard	
		(Infantry)	Lieut.-Gen. Lavrov (July)
		Combined Grenadiers	
		1st Cuirassier	Major-Gen. Depreradovich
VI	General of Infantry Dokhturov	7th Infantry	Major-Gen. Kapsevich
		24th "	Major-Gen. Likbachev

		1st Cavalry Corps	LieutGen. Uvarov
		2nd Cavalry Corps	LieutGen. Baron Korff
		3rd Cavalry Corps	Major-Gen. Count Pahlen II
Cossacks	General of Cavalry Platov		

SECOND ARMY OF THE WEST

Commander-in-Chief   General of Infantry Prince Bagration
Chief of Staff   Major-General Count de St. Priest
Quartermaster-General   "   " Vistitski II
General of Service   Colonel Marin
Chief of Artillery   Major-General Baron Löwenstern
Chief of Engineers   "   " Förster

Army Corps.	Corps Commander.	Division.	Divisional Commander.
VII	Lieut.-General Raievski	12th Infantry	Major-General Kolubakin
		26th "	" " Paskievich
VIII	Lieut.-General Borozdin I	2nd Grenadier	" " Prince Karl of Mecklenburg
		Combined Grenadiers	" " Count Voronzov
		2nd Cuirassier	" " Knorring
		4th Cavalry Corps	" " Count Sievers
		27th Infantry	" " Neverovski
		Cossacks	" " Ilovaïski V

THIRD ARMY OF THE WEST

Commander-in-Chief   General of Cavalry Tormazov
Chief of Staff   Major-General Inzov
Quartermaster-General   "   " Renne
Chief of Artillery   "   " Sievers

Army Corps.	Corps Commander.	Division.	Divisional Commander.

	Lieut.-General Count Kamenski	18th Infantry	Major-General Cherbatov
		Combined Grenadiers	?
	Lieut.-General Markov	9th Infantry	?
		15th "	Major-General Nazimov
Reserve	Lieut.-General Sacken	Reserve Battalion &	" " Sorokin
		Squadrons (Skeleton)	
Cavalry Corps	Major-General Count Lambert	4 Brigades	?
		Irregulars	?

ARMY OF THE DANUBE (JULY 31)

Commander-in-Chief	Admiral Chichagov
Chief of Staff	Lieutenant-General Sabaniev
Quartermaster-General	Major-General Berg
General of Service	" " Tuchkov II
"Corps"	Divisional Commanders
I	General of Infantry Count de Langeron
II	Lieutenant-General Essen III
III	" " Voïnov
IV	Major-General Bulatov
Reserve	Lieutenant-General Sabaniev
Detachment	Major-General Lüders

ARMY OF FINLAND

Commander-in-Chief: Lieutenant-General Count Steingell

3 Divisions (about half brought to front in September)

STAFF OF THE MAIN RUSSIAN ARMY, OCTOBER 18, 1812

Commander-in-Chief	Marshal Prince Golénischev-Kutuzov (Commander—in—Chief of all Russian Armies)
Chief of Staff	General of Cavalry Baron Bennigsen

General of Service
Intendant-General
Chief of Artillery
Quartermaster-General
Commander of Corps de Bataille
Commander of Advance-Guard

Lieutenant-General Konovnitzin
Privy-Councillor Lanskoï
Major-General Baron Löwenstern
Colonel Baron Toll
General of Cavalry Count Tormazov
General of Infantry Miloradovich

BIBLIOGRAPHY

FRENCH AND GERMAN

BONNAL, GEN. *Le Manœuvre de Vilna.*
BERTIN DE LA MARTINIÈRE. *Campagnes de Bonaparte.*
BERTIN. *La Campagne de 1812 (Témoins Oculaires).*
BOURGEOIS, DR. RENÉ. *Tabléau de la Campagne de 1812.*
BOUSSET, L.F.J. DE. *Mémoires.*
BIGNON, BARON. *Souvenirs d'un Diplomat.*
BOURGOGNE, SERGEANT. *Mémoires.*
BOURGOING, BARON DE. *Souvenirs Militaires.*
BLAREMBURG, LT.-GEN. VON. *Erinnerungen.*
CASTELLANE. *Journal du Maréchal de.*
CHAMBRAY, MARQUIS DE. *Histoire de l'Expédition de Russie.*
" " *La Vérité sur l'incendie de Moscow.*
CHUQUET. *Collected Letters, etc.*
" *Human Voices from the Campaign of 1812.*
COIGNET, LE CAPITAINE. *Mémoires.*
DENRIÉE, LE BARON. *Itinéraire de Napoléon.*
FANTIN DE ODOARDS. *Journal du Général.*
FABER DU FAUR, MAJOR (Württemberg Artillery). *Camp of 1812.*
FAIN, BARON. *Précis des Événements de 1812.*
FABRY, CAPTAIN (Editor). *Campagne de Russie* (French Staff History, June 23-August 20, 1812).
FEZENSAC, DUC DE. *Mémoires.*
FRANÇOIS, CAPTAIN. *Mémoires.*
GIROD DE L'AIN. *Vie du Général Eblé.*
GRABOWSKI. *Mémoires Militaires.*
GOUVION ST. CYR, MARSHAL. *Mémoires.*
GOURGAUD, GEN. *Examen Critique* (of Ségur's *History*).
GRIOIS, GEN. *Mémoires.*
GARDARUEL, A. *Relation 1812.*
G.L.D.L. *Moscow ... le retraite de 1812.*
JOMINI, GEN. *Précis ... de 1812-14.*
LABAUME, E. *Relation complète de la Campagne de 1812.*
LEJEUNE, BARON. *Mémoires.*
LABEAUDORÈIRE, J.P. DE. *La Campagne de Russie de 1812.*
MARGUERON, COMMANDANT. *Campagne de Russie* (French Staff History, January, 1810-January, 1812).

Moniteur Universel, Le.
MARINGONÉ, L.J. VIONNET DE. *Fragments de Mémoires.*
NAPOLÉON. *Correspondance, Mémoires, etc.*
PICARD. *La Cavalerie dans les Guerres de la République et de l'Empire.*
PION DES LOCHES, COL. *Mes Campagnes.*
PAIXHANS, H.J. *Retraite de Moscow. Notes.*
PARTOUNEAUX, COMTE. *Explications.*
PRADT, M. DE. *Histoire de l'Ambassade* (to Warsaw).
ROGUET, COMTE. *Mémoires.*
ROOS, RITTER H.O.L. VON. *With the Grand Army of Napoleon.*
RAPP, COMTE. *Mémoires.*
SÉGUR, COMTE DE. *Histoire de ... 1812.*
SOLIGNAC, ARMAND DE. *La Berezina.*
SERUZIER, COL. BARON. *Mémoires Militaires.*
THIRION, A. *Souvenirs Militaires.*
VLIJMEN, GEN. VAN. *Vers la Berezina* (Documents).
VAUDONCOURT, G. DE. *Relation Impartiale de la Passage de la Berezina.*
ZIMMERMAN, G. *Autobiography* (Commissariat).

There are innumerable volumes of memoirs which deal in part with the campaign. Some need using with caution—e.g. Marbot's.

RUSSIAN, ETC.

Archives. (1) Published by P.J. Schukin.
(2) Published by Russian War Office.
BENNIGSEN, GEN. BARON. *Memoirs.*
BUTURLIN. *History of War of 1812* (French Translation).
BOGDANOVICH. *History of War of 1812* (German Translation).
CHICHAGOV, ADMIRAL. *Mémoires* (French).
CLAUSEWITZ, GEN. K. VON. *Der Feldzug von 1812* (English Translation).
DANILEVSKI. *History of War of 1812.*
EUGEN VON WÜRTTEMBERG. *Memoirs.*
JENSEN. *Napoleon's Campaign in Russia* (Danish).
LANGERON, GENERAL. *Mémoires* (French).
LÖWENSTERN, BARON. *Mémoires* (French).
OKUNEV, GENERAL. *Considerations, etc.* (French).
OSTEN-SACKEN, FREIHERR VON DER. *Der Feldzug von 1812.*
ROSTOPCHIN, COUNT. *La vérité sur l'incendie de Moscow* (French).
ZAPISKI. *Memoirs of Yermólov.*

ENGLISH

CATHCART, LT.-GEN. SIR GEORGE. *Commentaries.*
GEORGE, H.B. *Napoleon's Invasion of Russia.*
PORTER, SIR R. *A Narrative.*
WILSON, SIR R., GEN. *Narrative.*
WOLSELEY, VISCOUNT. *Decline and Fall of Napoleon.*

Note.—The number of works in the French language dealing with the campaign of 1812 is so enormous that no attempt has been made to give more than a selection.

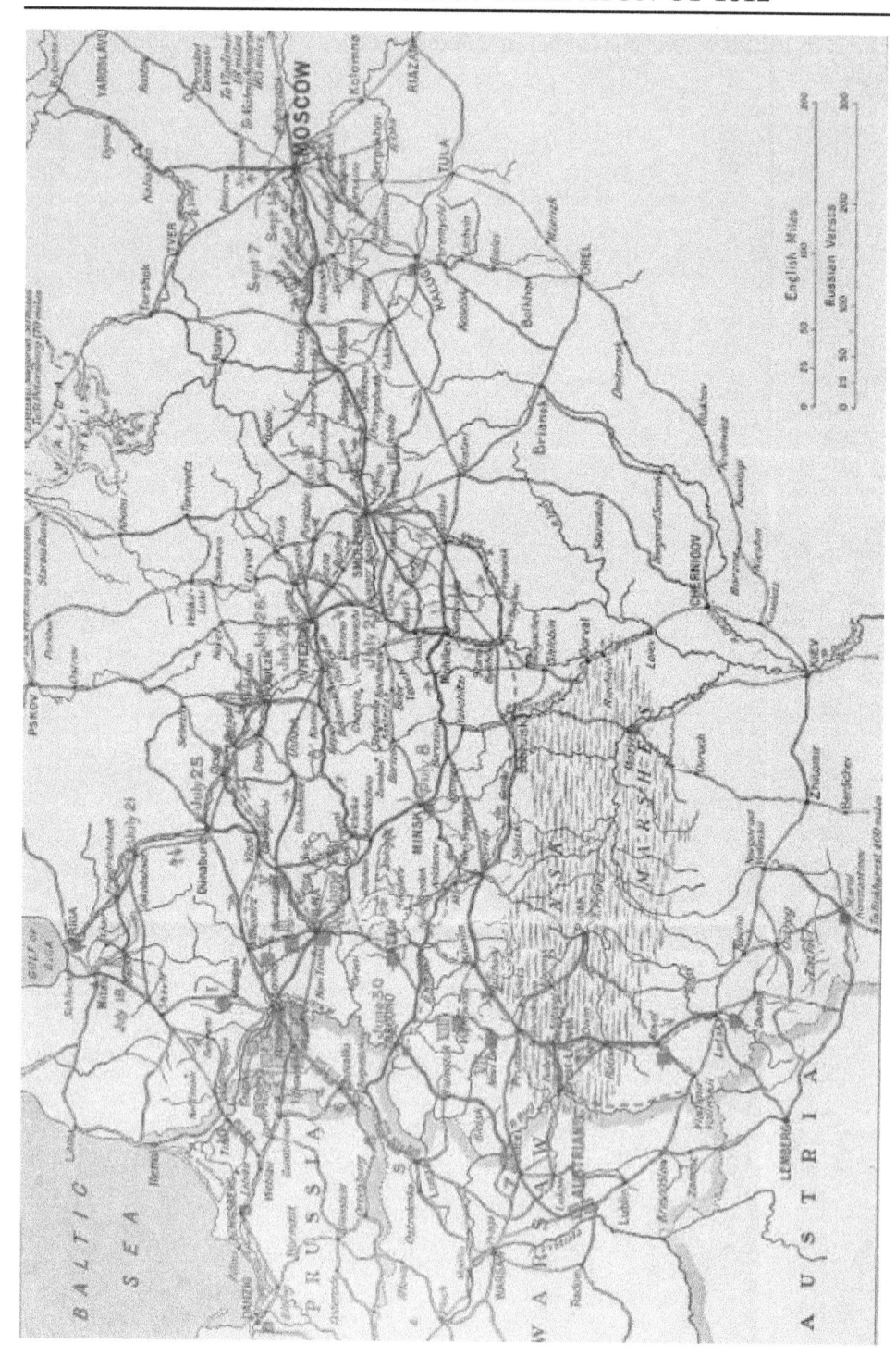

THE ADVANCE TO MOSCOW

BIBLIOGRAPHY

Napoleonic forces indicated by shaded blocks.
Russian " " solid "
Arabic numerals indicate Napoleonic Corps d'Armée.
Roman numerals indicate Russian Corps d'Armée.
Napoleonic lines of march indicated by solid lines.
Russian " " " broken lines.

The dates are those of the various stages of the French advance or on which they occupied important points. Each larger block, whether solid or shaded, indicates approximately 20,000 men.

NAPOLEON'S RUSSIAN CAMPAIGN OF 1812

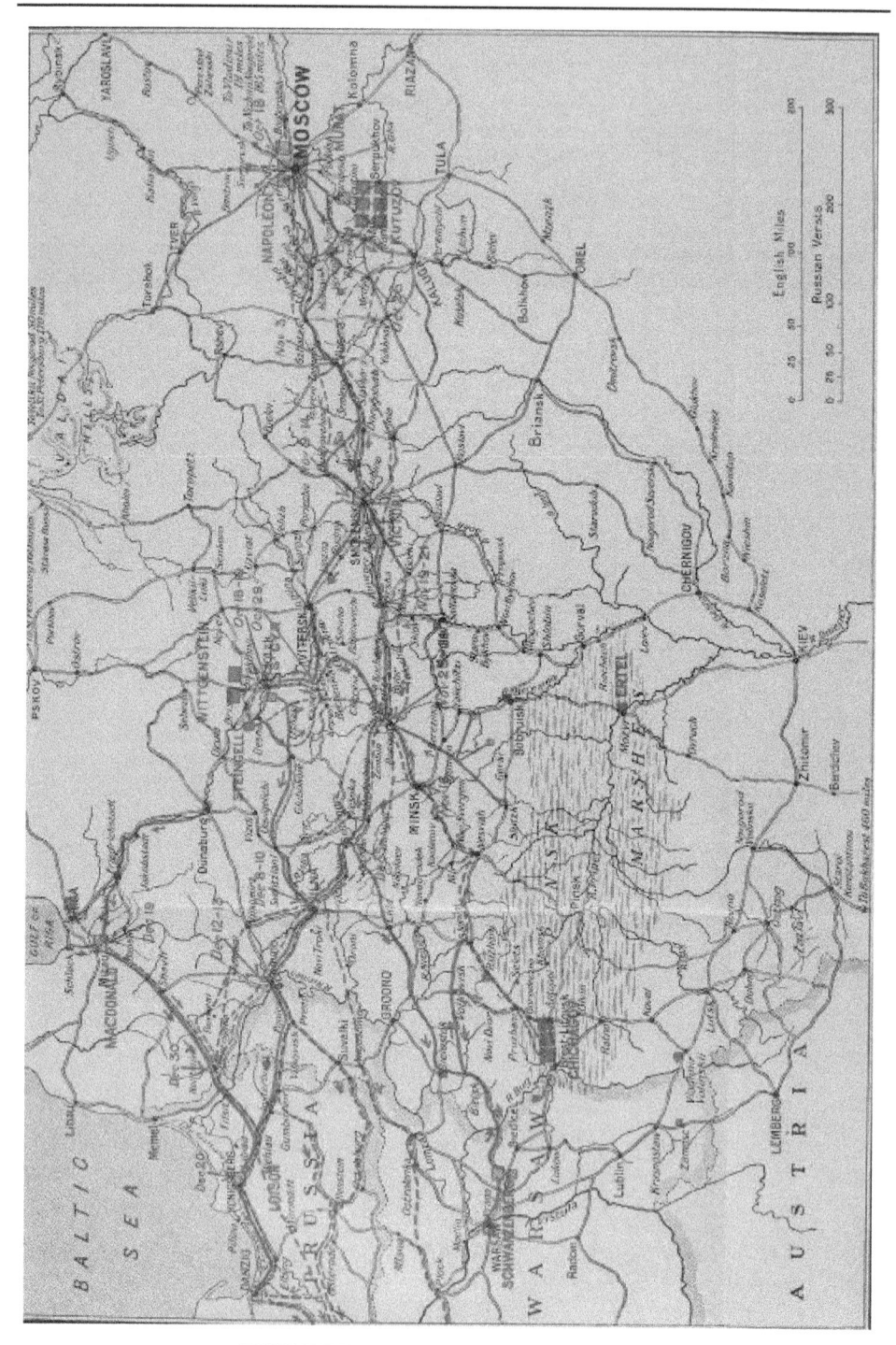

THE RETREAT FROM MOSCOW
Napoleonic forces indicated by shaded blocks.

Russian " " solid "
Napoleonic lines of march indicated by solid lines.
Russian " " " broken lines.

The dates are those of the various stages of the French retreat or on which they abandoned or lost important places. Each larger block, solid or shaded, indicates approximately 20,000 men.

INDEX

Symbols
1st Corps *10, 16, 23, 42, 46, 47, 52, 64, 72, 77, 84, 91, 107, 108, 111, 113, 121, 123, 131, 154, 157, 169, 171, 176, 185, 202, 203, 206, 208, 211, 212, 221, 224, 226, 260, 269, 270*
2nd Corps *8, 9, 38, 42, 47, 48, 66, 72, 111, 112, 113, 116, 129, 130, 144, 168, 169, 194, 200, 209, 211, 222, 228, 229, 235, 239, 240, 242, 243, 250, 269, 270*
3rd Corps *9, 10, 44, 47, 66, 72, 79, 81, 88, 94, 119, 123, 131, 134, 150, 156, 159, 168, 176, 206, 212, 217, 222, 223, 226, 227, 236, 249, 269, 270*
4th Corps *9, 47, 49, 51, 56, 65, 66, 72, 74, 76, 77, 83, 87, 88, 93, 95, 123, 130, 131, 132, 133, 137, 138, 156, 157, 168, 171, 176, 179, 180, 182, 183, 186, 202, 206, 216, 222, 223, 241, 256, 269, 270*
5th Corps *8, 9, 42, 44, 50, 58, 63, 88, 129, 130, 132, 138, 139, 156, 168, 169, 186, 211, 212, 216, 221, 236, 250, 269*
6th Corps *9, 11, 37, 41, 42, 44, 49, 50, 64, 65, 67, 74, 76, 87, 93, 112, 113, 116, 129, 131, 177, 180, 182, 194, 200, 201, 269*
7th Corps *8, 9, 24, 37, 54, 55, 58, 59, 60, 78, 79, 82, 88, 101, 102, 103, 107, 156, 182, 186, 222, 269*
8th Corps *8, 9, 11, 12, 41, 42, 51, 52, 53, 55, 73, 79, 83, 87, 88, 101, 102, 123, 126, 130, 131, 132, 133, 134, 155, 156, 159, 169, 174, 176, 182, 185, 221, 223, 233, 269*
9th Corps *25, 26, 145, 163, 164, 169, 201, 208, 217, 229, 240, 245, 246, 248, 251, 269*
10th Corps *11, 25, 41, 42, 44, 47, 57, 108, 169, 269*
11th Corps *8, 169, 170, 250, 269*

A
Aa river *109*
Achard *62*
Adamovskoë *202, 203*
Alexander I *3*
Alexander Petrovich Tormazov *34*
Alexei Petrovich Yermólov *36*
Alexiev *195*
Amey *199, 243*
Antopol *103*
Arakcheiev *2, 53, 78, 120*
Artillery *8, 14, 15, 16, 18, 20, 29, 30, 31, 38, 45, 47, 48, 49, 55, 59, 60, 62, 66, 69, 70, 71, 72, 74, 76, 81, 82, 83, 86, 89, 90, 91, 92, 93, 95, 97, 98, 104, 105, 107, 108, 109, 113, 115, 116, 123, 126, 129, 130, 132, 133, 134, 135, 137, 138, 140, 143,*

156, 157, 159, 162, 166, 168, 170, 173, 174, 175, 176, 177, 178, 179, 180, 182, 183, 184, 190, 193, 208, 209, 211, 215, 216, 217, 220, 221, 222, 223, 226, 227, 228, 229, 234, 236, 237, 238, 239, 241, 243, 250, 255, 256, 258, 260, 261, 263, 264, 265, 267, 269, 272, 274, 275

Augereau *170, 215, 269*
Augustowo *44, 45, 51*

B

Babinovichi *65, 67*
Badajoz *7*
Baron Guilleminot *179, 268*
Baron Löwenstern *166, 272, 274*
Baron Salza *97*
Bausk *109, 193*
Bechenkowiczi *40, 200, 201, 217*
Berezina *4, 15, 20, 21, 23, 36, 37, 40, 53, 55, 57, 58, 59, 63, 188, 191, 192, 201, 219, 228, 230, 232, 233, 235, 236, 237, 240, 242, 244, 245, 246, 247, 248, 249, 252, 255, 276*
Berezino *57, 59, 231*
Bezdizh *102*
Biala *192*
Bielostok *40, 41, 51, 53, 103, 169, 191, 254, 257, 268*
Bielovezhi *218, 219*
Bielsk *40, 51*
Billard *235, 242*
Bobr *40, 41, 57, 217, 235, 236, 237*
Bobruisk *4, 40, 41, 53, 54, 55, 57, 58, 59, 69, 77, 101, 170, 192, 236, 237, 256*
Bogdanovich *32, 89, 129, 141, 166, 191, 276*
Boghorodsk *159*
Bonami *134*
Borisov *4, 40, 41, 57, 58, 121, 169, 201, 228, 230, 231, 232, 233, 234, 235, 236, 237, 239, 240, 241, 242, 245, 247, 248*
Borodino *14, 21, 34, 38, 118, 121, 126, 127, 128, 129, 130, 131, 132, 134, 136, 137, 139, 141, 142, 143, 145, 157, 160, 161, 162, 174, 177, 183, 204*
Borovsk *175, 176, 177, 178, 180, 183, 185, 186, 202*
Brazhino *124*
Brest-Litovsk *12, 39, 40, 41, 53, 58, 101, 102, 191, 192, 201, 217, 218, 219*
Bridzievo *63*
Brilova *242*
Bug *39, 40, 58, 69, 102, 103, 191, 257*
Bukharest *7, 107, 189, 190*

C

Captain François *90, 134*
Captain Seslavin *163*
Captain Wasowicz *251*

Chabachevichi 237, 240
Chamberlain Mordvinov 201
Chasniki 200, 201, 217, 229
Chelkanovo 215, 221
Cherechev 104, 105
Chereia 217, 228, 230, 235
Chernishnia 156, 159, 166, 167, 168
Chilova 221, 222
Ciudad Rodrigo 7
Colonel Pion des Loches 256
Colonel von Wollzogen 63
Comte Baraguay d'Hilliers 163
Comte Daru 267
Comte de Rochechouart 233
Comte Durosnel 268
Comte Lobau 64, 268
Continental system 1, 3, 6
Cossack Colonel Lukovkin 231
Count Kotschubey 120
Count Lieven 63, 161
Count Ozharovski 163, 221
Czerikovo 156

D

Dahlenkirchen 192, 193
Danilevski 48, 276
Danzig 2, 9, 12, 26, 40, 43, 170, 250, 256, 257, 261
Dashkova 60, 62
Davigelishki 51
Desna 40, 64, 155, 195, 197, 199, 200
Dmitrov 159
Dnieper 4, 7, 40, 53, 58, 59, 60, 62, 63, 69, 72, 73, 74, 75, 76, 77, 78, 79, 80, 83, 84, 87, 88, 89, 91, 94, 95, 98, 99, 100, 119, 123, 124, 216, 223, 227
Dniester 190
Dorogobuzh 41, 98, 123, 124, 126, 159, 212, 215, 216
Doronimo 129
Drissa 4, 36, 40, 50, 51, 56, 63, 64, 65, 66, 69, 107, 110, 111, 112, 113, 193
Druia 51, 111, 195, 196
Dubno 190
Dubrovna 63, 222
Dukhovchina 215, 216
Düna 4, 7, 40, 50, 51, 53, 59, 63, 64, 65, 67, 69, 72, 78, 101, 108, 109, 110, 111, 113, 114, 115, 119, 187, 188, 192, 194, 195, 196, 197, 199, 200, 201, 230
Dünaburg 4, 40, 41, 51, 57, 64, 65, 69, 107, 108, 109, 110, 113, 193, 200

E

INDEX

Eckau *109, 192, 193*

F
Fatova *60, 62*
Federovskoië *208, 209, 211*
Feodor Vasilievich Rostopchin *146*
Fili *147*
Fominskoië *175, 176, 177, 183*
French Army Corps *12, 22, 110, 136, 164*

G
Gedeonovo *94, 97*
General Dorsenne *77*
General Okunev *43, 100*
General Sokolnicki *86*
Glogau *8, 9*
Glubokoië *200, 230, 249, 268*
Gonsherevo *202*
Gorbunovo *83, 93, 94*
Gorki *127, 128, 130, 138, 139*
Gorodeczna *34, 104, 105, 106, 107, 119, 190*
Gorodnia *182, 184, 185*
Graf von Preising *74*
Gridnevo *127, 129, 208*
Grodno *39, 40, 41, 42, 45, 49, 51, 52, 56, 268*
Gzhatsk *41, 124, 126, 127, 129, 164, 169, 176, 185, 208*

H
Horodetz *103*

I
Ielnia *83, 176, 178, 185, 212, 215*
Igumen *40, 57, 58, 231*
Illuxt *193*
Imperial Guard *8, 15, 26, 41, 42, 44, 47, 49, 73, 90, 107, 123, 130, 132, 169, 175, 177, 224, 260, 271*
Inkovo *76*
Insterburg *40*

J
Jakobstädt *40, 109, 111*
Jakubovo *111*
Jassy *190*
Jean Baptiste Eblé *237*
Joseph Anthony Poniatowski *23, 24*
Jurovo *221*

K

Kaisarov 163
Kalisch 9
Kaluga 74, 83, 148, 155, 156, 166, 175, 176, 179, 182, 185, 202
Kamenetz-Podolski 190
Katan 76, 78, 79, 84, 86, 87, 88, 100
Keidani 44, 47
Kiev 4, 40, 41, 43, 57, 59, 101, 107, 230
Kliastitzi 111
Kobrin 40, 101, 102, 103, 104, 105, 107
Koidanow 231
Kolomna 148, 150, 155
Kolopenichi 237
Kolotskoï 126, 127, 129, 143, 145, 205
Kolotza 127, 128, 132, 133, 134, 137, 139
Koltiniani 257
Königsberg 8, 9, 11, 12, 39, 43, 49, 103, 170, 255, 256, 257, 268
Kopis 248
Korythnia 80, 81, 82, 83, 84, 88, 222, 223
Kovel 107, 191
Kovno 39, 40, 41, 42, 43, 44, 45, 46, 47, 48, 51, 169, 251, 254, 255, 268
Krasnoï 79, 80, 81, 83, 86, 88, 89, 221, 222, 223, 224, 226, 227, 232
Kreminskoië 186
Krupki 234, 237
Krymniki 190
Krymskoië 145
Kubinskoi 145
Kurland 69, 108, 109, 169

L

Labiau 257
Larionovo 223
Lepel 40, 58, 200, 217, 240
Liadi 83, 221, 226
Liakhova 215
Lida 42, 44, 47, 50
Liozna 72, 77
Lochnitza 232, 233, 235
Lord Wellesley 7
Lossmina 80, 81, 222, 223, 224, 226
Lubino 83, 93, 94, 95, 96, 97, 98, 99, 118, 122, 123
Lublin 42, 44, 102, 191
Lukoml 229
Lutsk 9, 12, 40, 101, 107

M

INDEX

Major-General Golénischev-Kutuzov *216*
Maliavka *237*
Maloyaroslavetz *37, 175, 176, 177, 178, 179, 180, 181, 182, 183, 184, 186, 202, 203*
Marquis d'Alorna *73, 268*
Mathieu Dumas *73, 267*
Matvei Ivanovich Platov *36*
Maximovo *209*
M. de Villeblanche *164*
Medyn *176, 183, 185, 186, 202, 203*
Memel *257*
Merlino *222*
Michel Ney *23*
Michino *128, 130*
Mikalevka *iv, 212, 215, 229*
Mikhail Andreïevich Miloradovich *37*
Mikhail Hilarionovich Golénischev-Kutuzov *34*
Minsk *39, 40, 41, 42, 45, 47, 49, 50, 51, 52, 53, 57, 58, 73, 101, 121, 122, 169, 175, 188, 189, 192, 201, 217, 218, 228, 230, 231, 232, 233, 236, 239, 240, 251, 268*
Mir *51, 52, 53, 54, 55*
Mitau *40, 41, 57, 108, 109, 192, 193*
M. Lesseps *150*
Mohilev *40, 41, 53, 57, 58, 59, 60, 61, 62, 65, 66, 69, 72, 73, 77, 83, 169, 192, 236, 268*
Molodechno *236, 249, 250*
Momonovo *145*
Mozhaïsk *127, 139, 144, 145, 146, 155, 156, 163, 169, 171, 176, 183, 185, 202, 203, 205*
Mozyr *41, 59, 102, 170, 189, 192, 194, 217, 256*
Mstislavl *63, 83, 88, 89, 215, 216*

N

Nadva *78, 84, 87*
Nara *156, 159, 166, 167*
Nesvizh *40, 41, 51, 53, 54, 55, 103, 230*
Nevel *113, 195*
Nikolaev *52*
Nikolai Nikolaievich Raievski *37*
Nizhnii Novgorod *148*
Norway *8*
Novi Bykhov *62, 68*
Novi Dvor *42*
Novi Svergen *40*
Novi Troki *49, 51, 56, 254*

O

Oboiarzina *112*
Ochmiana *40, 50, 51, 52, 250, 252, 253*

Oldenburg 2
Orani 47, 49
Orsha 40, 41, 53, 58, 59, 60, 65, 67, 73, 77, 79, 99, 121, 122, 159, 169, 201, 202, 221, 223, 227, 228, 232, 233, 237
Ostrog 40, 188, 190
Ostrovno 65, 66, 67, 138

P
Panki 150
Paris iv, 6, 8, 10, 155, 215, 251, 252
Pavel Vasilievich Chichagov 36
Paymaster Duverger 154
Perebrod 64
Peter Wittgenstein 37
Pilwiski 43, 44
Pinsk 9, 12, 27, 39, 40, 41, 55, 58, 102, 103, 107, 188, 192
Plechenitzi 250
Plock 8, 9, 268
Poddubno 104, 105
Poland 1, 4, 5, 20, 23, 24, 39, 74, 82, 113, 122, 170
Polonka 103
Polotsk 23, 40, 41, 64, 65, 66, 107, 111, 112, 113, 114, 115, 116, 119, 166, 169, 170, 188, 189, 193, 194, 195, 196, 197, 198, 199, 200, 201, 230, 259
Poniemon 45, 46
Poriechie 67, 68, 69, 72, 74, 76, 78, 83, 87, 99, 100
Posen 9, 11
Praga 191, 243
Prenn 51
Prikaz Vidra 76, 78, 87
Prince Alexander of Württemberg 97
Prince Dolgoruki 222
Prince Eugen of Württemberg 38, 90, 271
Prince Karl of Mecklenburg 54, 272
Prince Khovanski 104
Prince Kudachev 163
Prince of Siberia 201
Prince Peter Ivanovich Bagration 33
Prince Radziwil 109
Prizmenitza 114, 115, 116
Propoïsk 68
Prudichevo 83, 94, 97
Prussia 3, 4, 5, 6, 10, 12, 15, 43, 170, 194, 195
Pruzhani 12, 58, 103, 104, 191, 217
Pskov 107

R

INDEX

Rasasna *77, 79, 84, 88*
Razitzi *111, 113*
Rear-Admiral von Müller *192*
Reserve Cavalry *4, 9, 11, 42, 44, 71, 91, 126, 144, 156, 183*
Riazan *148*
Riga *4, 30, 40, 41, 57, 69, 108, 109, 113, 169, 170, 189, 192, 193, 195, 230, 257, 258*
Rogachev *72, 77*
Romanovo *55*
Rossieni *42, 44, 47, 108*
Roussel *66*
Rudnia *67, 72, 76, 77, 78, 86, 87*
Rusa *145*
Russian Army *4, 27, 28, 31, 32, 38, 54, 56, 63, 65, 67, 72, 74, 76, 96, 98, 100, 103, 105, 106, 108, 114, 116, 118, 120, 129, 136, 139, 141, 142, 145, 150, 155, 156, 161, 162, 163, 165, 179, 180, 183, 184, 187, 189, 196, 203, 212, 219, 221, 223, 226, 229, 258, 273*
Russian roads *27, 160*

S

Saltanovka *59, 60, 61, 62, 69*
Schlock *110, 192, 193*
Sebezh *107, 111, 194*
Selets *60, 62*
Semenovskoï *127, 128, 129, 130, 132, 133, 134, 135, 138, 139*
Semlevo *124, 208, 212*
Semlino *145*
Shavli *9*
Sheïn Ostrog *88, 94*
Shevardino *128, 129, 132*
Siberia *88, 120, 160*
Sienno *217*
Sir Robert Wilson *19, 76, 89, 91, 142, 151, 156, 177, 205*
Sivokhino *111, 112, 116, 187, 193, 194, 195*
Sklov *73*
Slavkovo *124, 203*
Slonim *9, 40, 42, 52, 53, 58, 101, 103, 169, 192, 217, 218, 230, 257*
Slutsk *41, 55*
Smolensk *13, 21, 34, 37, 40, 41, 45, 57, 62, 63, 67, 68, 69, 74, 75, 76, 77, 78, 79, 80, 81, 82, 83, 84, 85, 86, 87, 88, 91, 92, 93, 94, 96, 97, 98, 99, 100, 102, 118, 120, 121, 122, 124, 145, 156, 159, 163, 164, 166, 169, 171, 175, 176, 178, 184, 185, 194, 201, 202, 203, 205, 208, 215, 216, 217, 219, 220, 221, 222, 223, 226, 227, 228, 232*
Smoliani *229, 230*
Smorgoni *41, 42, 47, 56, 251*
Sokal *39*
Solovievo *83, 87, 93, 98, 100, 123, 216*

Spanish envoy Zea Bermudez 7
Sparrow Hills *146, 149, 150*
Spas *113, 114, 115, 156, 167, 168, 197*
St. Alexander Nevski *161*
St. Andrew *123*
Staroi Bykhov *40, 59, 62, 63*
Staroï Konstantinov *101*
St. George *161*
St. Petersburg *vi, 4, 6, 9, 27, 40, 46, 64, 83, 88, 91, 93, 94, 107, 111, 113, 114, 150, 151, 160, 161, 163, 165, 166, 187*
Struria *197*
Studianka *233, 236, 237, 239, 240, 241, 242, 243, 245, 248*
St. Vladimir *161*
Surazh *67, 72, 74*
Surgeon-General Larrey *73*
Sventsiani *40, 42, 43, 44, 47, 48, 50*
Svislocz *55, 57*
Svislozh *218*
Svolna *113*
Sweden *1, 7, 8, 108, 187*

T
Tarutino *156, 159, 160, 161, 162, 163, 166, 168, 170, 175, 176, 177, 178, 180, 191, 258*
Tauroggen *257*
Teveli *105*
The Kremlin *148, 150, 151, 153, 155, 157, 158, 175, 176, 178*
the Pakhra *155, 156, 176*
Thorn *9, 12, 268*
Tilsit *3, 39, 40, 41, 42, 44, 47, 254, 257*
Tolochin *221, 233*
Torres Vedras *4*
treaty of Abo *187*
Treaty of Tilsit *7*
Tzarévo *124, 128, 130, 135, 138*

U
Uchach *66, 199, 200*
Uspenskoïe *127*
Usveia *229*
Utitza *128, 130, 131, 132, 133, 137, 138, 139*
Uvarova *222, 223*

V
Veliaminov *192*
Velikii Luki *166*
Velikii Novgorod *107*
Velizh *72, 77, 83*

INDEX

Vereia *159, 176, 177, 178, 179, 183, 185, 186, 202, 203, 204*
Verkalobovo *62*
Veselovo *231, 236*
Viasma *41, 124, 126, 159, 166, 169, 171, 186, 203, 208, 209, 210, 211, 212, 216*
Viazema *145*
Vileika *52, 56*
Vilia *43, 46, 47, 48*
Vilkomirz *42, 47, 48, 50*
Vilna *4, 6, 9, 11, 12, 39, 40, 41, 42, 43, 44, 45, 46, 47, 48, 49, 50, 51, 53, 56, 57, 64, 68, 71, 73, 77, 83, 93, 113, 118, 121, 122, 163, 175, 189, 194, 200, 219, 230, 236, 239, 240, 248, 249, 250, 251, 252, 253, 254, 255, 256, 275*
Vinkovo *156, 166, 167, 168, 171, 178*
Virgin of Smolensk *130*
Vistula *8, 9, 15, 26, 40, 50, 73, 77, 122, 127, 169, 170, 176, 219, 256, 257, 258, 261*
Vitebsk *39, 40, 41, 64, 65, 66, 67, 68, 69, 71, 72, 73, 74, 75, 77, 83, 99, 110, 113, 114, 118, 121, 122, 166, 169, 185, 201, 202, 203, 215, 217, 227, 232, 268*
Vladimir *148, 151, 159, 160*
Volkovisk *12, 41, 42, 43, 45, 49, 51, 56, 218*
Vologin *52*
Volokovaia *78, 79, 87*
Vop *216*
Voronovo *151, 156, 168, 175, 176, 177*

W

Warsaw *1, 2, 4, 5, 8, 9, 11, 20, 23, 38, 39, 40, 41, 42, 43, 44, 51, 56, 57, 58, 83, 101, 102, 103, 104, 122, 191, 192, 218, 250, 252, 261, 268, 276*
Wengrow *169, 191*

Y

Yukhnov *176, 185, 186, 203*
Yurí Dolgorúki *151*

Z

Zamosc *42, 104, 107*
Zaslavl *101, 190*
Zembin *231, 235, 236, 239, 240, 242, 248, 250*
Zvenigorod *145*

Lector House believes that a society develops through a two-fold approach of continuous learning and adaptation, which is derived from the study of classic literary works spread across the historic timeline of literature records. Therefore, we aim at reviving, repairing and redeveloping all those inaccessible or damaged but historically as well as culturally important literature across subjects so that the future generations may have an opportunity to study and learn from past works to embark upon a journey of creating a better future.

This book is a result of an effort made by Lector House towards making a contribution to the preservation and repair of original ancient works which might hold historical significance to the approach of continuous learning across subjects.

HAPPY READING & LEARNING!

LECTOR HOUSE LLP
E-MAIL: lectorpublishing@gmail.com

9 789353 361020